Center for Basque Studies
Basque Classics Series, No. 4

Koldo Mitxelena:
Selected Writings of
a Basque Scholar

Compiled and with an introduction
by Pello Salaburu

Translated by
Linda White and M. Dean Johnson

Center for Basque Studies
University of Nevada, Reno
Reno, Nevada

This book was published with generous financial support obtained by the Association of Friends of the Center for Basque Studies from the Provincial Government of Bizkaia.

Basque Classics Series, No. 4
Series Editors: William A. Douglass, Gregorio Monreal, and Pello Salaburu

Center for Basque Studies
University of Nevada, Reno
Reno, Nevada 89557
http://basque.unr.edu

Cover and series design © 2008 by Jose Luis Agote.
Cover illustration: Sketch of Koldo Mitxelena by Antonio Valverde, "Ayalde," courtesy the Mitxelena family.

Library of Congress Cataloging-in-Publication Data
Michelena, Luis.
[Selections. English. 2008]
 Koldo Mitxelena : selected writings of a Basque scholar / compiled and with an introduction by Pello Salaburu ; translated by Linda White and M. Dean Johnson.
   p. cm. -- (Basque classics series ; no. 4)
 Includes bibliographical references and index.
 Summary: "This work brings together a number of texts by Koldo Mitxelena concerning the Basque language--a non-Indo-European language of unknown origins--and its history and literature. Includes text of his unification proposal that made "unified Basque" possible"--Provided by publisher.
 ISBN 978-1-877802-80-5 (hardcover) -- ISBN 978-1-877802-81-2 (pbk.)
 1. Basque philology. 2. Basque language--History. 3. Basque literature--History and criticism. I. Salaburu Etxeberria, Pello. II. University of Nevada, Reno. Center for Basque Studies. III. Title. IV. Title: Selected writings of a Basque scholar. V. Series.

PH5024.M4913 2008
499'.92--dc22

2008044218

The Center for Basque Studies wishes to gratefully acknowledge the generous financial support of the Bizkaiko Foru Aldundia / Provincial Government of Bizkaia for the publication of this book.

Koldo Mitxelena:
Selected Writings of
a Basque Scholar

Table of Contents

Mitxelena's Life and Legacy

An Introduction by Pello Salaburu

Koldo Mitxelena[1] was and remains one of the most important and productive intellectuals in Basque history. Even today, twenty years after his death, his writings are still considered standard references for anyone concerned with the Basque language in the broadest sense that this term can have. Mitxelena's solid academic background, his erudition, his singular intellectual prowess, gained him many friends and admirers—and also, of course, a number of enemies. He never shrank from publicly expressing his opinion on a wide range of issues, particularly on matters internal to the Basque language, on which he was our most outstanding authority, but also on matters peripheral to Basque (practical usage proposals, for instance), and on much more general questions of a cultural or political nature. Thanks to Koldo Mitxelena, to his total dedication and vast intellectual contributions, Basque language studies eventually took a giant step forward and moved into their rightful place as a professional field of academic research. Mitxelena's proposals were also crucial for the development of *euskara batua*, or unified literary Basque, which was to become the much-needed standard for this ancient language. These two contributions—his rigorous analysis and intellectual authorship of the standardization of the language—were vital not only for our knowledge and understanding of Basque, but also for bringing it to the forefront in education and the mass media in the Basque Country today.

Life

Koldo Mitxelena was born in Rentería (province of Gipuzkoa, in the Spanish Basque Country) in 1915. He died in San Sebastián in 1987. As we shall see, his life was far from monotonous, for personal as well as political reasons.

Mitxelena was brought up in a Basque nationalist household, and the influence of nationalism colored the rest of his life. It should be remembered that unlike other countries, where classical European schools of thought (Libertarianism, Socialism, Communism, right-wing ideologies, etc.) dominated the political scene, twentieth-century Spain saw Catalan and Basque nationalist movements also playing decisive roles. Indeed, they were crucially important when it came to formulating the current Spanish state, and remain so for anyone trying to understand Spain today. In the Basque Country,[2] nationalism has always been present in public life, but ever since the death of General Franco (1975) and the subsequent end of the dictatorship, its role has been particularly apparent. Indeed, since the return to democracy in the early 1980s, the Basque Nationalist Party has uninterruptedly governed, alone or in coalition, the autonomous region of Euskadi. The Basque president, or *lehendakari*, has always been a nationalist.

In elections held during these years, over half the population of Euskadi has consistently voted for one of the three nationalist parties: the large Basque Nationalist Party (PNV), founded in 1895; the smaller Eusko Alkartasuna (EA), formed by a group that split from the PNV in 1986; and a party that has had several names (from Herri Batasuna to Batasuna) and traits, according to the needs of the moment. This self-defined "left-wing nationalist" party was formed after the death of Franco as a coalition of various small, radical parties and has carried a great deal of weight in Basque political life—much more than warranted by the percentage of votes obtained (approximately 10 to 18 percent in Euskadi). The main difference between these three nationalist options is that the first two are democratic, while the third is always considered the political arm of the terrorist group ETA. For this reason, it was outlawed several years ago, although its leaders still command a great deal of attention from the news media.

So as we were saying, Mitxelena was born to nationalist parents who lived in a small coastal town of some 5,000 inhabitants. His father, nicknamed Xexteroa (basket-weaver) by the villagers, was an artisan who made baskets in the basement of the family home in the upper part of town. It was in this house that Koldo was confined for three long years of his childhood, due to a tumor in his leg. Until he was eight years old, he had to content himself with watching life from the window and never went out to play. Consequently, he took refuge in reading. One of the few magazines available at the time in Basque (*Zeruko argia*, later entitled *Argia* and still published today) became his companion, as did the novels of Jules Verne and Emilio Salgari, which he read voraciously in Spanish.[3] Thanks to his illness, Mitxelena advanced far beyond his years and was put ahead of his class when he finally returned to school.

Until the age of twenty, his time was confined mostly to work at home and family life, which brought him into contact with ELA, the Basque nationalist labor union, and with the PNV political party. He eventually joined both and began attending their meetings. During those years he also became interested in various Basque literary movements, particularly the literary generation of the 1930s. The lyrical poet Lizardi, who wanted Basque to become *noranahikoa* (valid for all occasions), was one of the authors who had the greatest impact on him. But then General Franco rose against the Spanish Republic, and the Spanish Civil War broke out. The year was 1936.

When the PNV sided with the legitimate forces marshaled by the Republic against the uprising, Koldo Mitxelena signed up as a volunteer in one of the nationalist regiments. He was taken prisoner in Santoña, accused of military rebellion and sentenced to death by the Franco forces. The war was in its first year and was to last two years longer. The death sentence was finally commuted to a term of thirty years imprisonment. Mitxelena eventually spent six years in the prisons of El Dueso, Larrinaga, and Burgos, in two different periods. During his stretch in the Burgos prison, he met Spanish intellectuals, professors, and university students who had also opposed the Franco uprising. The friendship he forged with people like Francisco Jordá (who would later hold the Chair of Archeology at the University of Salamanca) opened up to him the work of Menéndez Pidal, one of Spain's foremost Romance language specialists, who had created a true school of Romance research and was instrumental in establishing modern degree courses in this specialty in Spanish universities. Menéndez Pidal had incorporated into these studies the comparative methods that would later have such influence on the work of Koldo Mitxelena.

According to our own beliefs, we Basques are famously sparse with words, but very loyal and true to them. It is not surprising, therefore, that upon his return from prison, history has it that Mitxelena's mother greeted him with a terse, almost literary *Etorri al zara?* "Are you back, then?" unknowingly using an expression not very different from the one supposedly spoken centuries earlier by Fray Luis de León, who, on his return to the University of Salamanca from years of imprisonment by the Spanish Inquisition, addressed his students with the famous words, "As we were saying yesterday . . ." Like Fray Luis de León, Mitxelena was eventually to find shelter in the peaceful life of Salamanca, far from worldly noises and following "the hidden path walked by the few wise men the world has known." But this would come later.

Mitxelena was twenty-seven when he returned in poor health to Rentería. A friend of the family, José Uranga, offered him a job as an accountant in a Madrid firm, and there, Mitxelena combined work with clandestine activities against the Franco dictatorship (in the vain hope that the European democracies and the U.S. would eventually evict the regime). These were the harsh post–civil war years, when repression was rife against anyone who dared to oppose the regime. Mitxelena was again arrested in 1946 and sentenced to another two years in jail. Finally, on a cold morning at the end of January 1948, he was released after stays in various prisons.

Now thirty-two, an age when many university graduates have already published significant research, Koldo Mitxelena enrolled as a part-time student of humanities at the University of Madrid (as the Universidad Complutense de Madrid was then known), where he combined work and study in order to pay his way. At about that time, he married Matilde, who would give him two children and share his life until his death in 1987. In those harsh, economically and socially depressed postwar years of the early (and most severe) dictatorship, the added problem of finding work with a penal record was almost insurmountable.[4] For ten long years, Koldo Mitxelena worked and studied, until in 1959 he defended his dissertation, impressing and astounding the committee with his knowledge and command of the field. This dissertation (*Fonética histórica vasca*[5]), whose influence has been decisive ever since, is one of the pillars underlying modern Basque studies programs.

It is amazing to see the work produced by Koldo Mitxelena during those years and in the following decade—scores of articles on Basque philology and linguistics, books that are still standard references in Basque linguistics, reviews of a wide range of works, translations, film criticism, and other types of writing. By way of example, in 1955 alone he published six articles, an interview, a translation, and eighteen reviews. The times were harsh, but the fame of his intellectual powers spread and in 1954 he was appointed technical director of the Basque

Philological Seminar "Julio de Urquijo," and member of the editorial board of *Egan*, a journal bearing timid witness to the presence of Basque in society. The rector (president) of the University of Salamanca, Antonio Tovar,[6] also recruited him to work on Basque studies at the University of Salamanca.

It was obvious that the natural place for Koldo Mitxelena to teach was at a university, particularly when specialists in his field could be counted on the fingers of one hand. There were, however, two important problems standing in the way of his university career. First, his prison record made it impossible for him to aspire to an official position anywhere, even at the high school level.[7] Second, except for independently organized lectures, seminars, workshops, and other such events, there were no university-level studies of any note in Basque linguistics and philology. Mitxelena would have to wait until 1967 when, with the help of many friends and academics, it became possible to create a chair of Indo-European Linguistics for him at the University of Salamanca, thus regularizing his service to that university begun many years before. Looking back later, both Koldo and Matilde felt that the years spent in Salamanca were the happiest of their lives. During that period, many other people who would eventually become leading researchers in Basque studies began to study at Salamanca—Altuna and Sarasola, to name but two.[8] From 1969 to 1971, Mitxelena found time to travel to Paris at the invitation of French linguist André Martinet to teach comparative linguistics at the Sorbonne as a *professeur associé*, and at the École Practique des Hautes Études as the *Chargé de cours*.[9]

However, the political changes that gradually began to take place following the death of Franco were to have a decisive influence on Mitxelena's life. In 1968 the University of Bilbao, forerunner to today's University of the Basque Country (UBC), was founded, and a few years later Basque language studies were introduced at Bilbao's century-old University of Deusto, run by the Jesuits, and subsequently at the UBC. These were years of transition, between a dying dictatorship and a new, fragile democracy that remained just over the horizon. They were years of upheaval at the universities, which were still under the influence of the 1968 students' revolt in France.[10] In 1978 Koldo Mitxelena was asked to come to the UBC to start up its Basque studies program. With his solid neogrammarian background, Mitxelena helped to design a syllabus based on language and linguistics, to which other subjects were eventually added.

Koldo Mitxelena was at his best in his role as a philologist and language historian, studying and comparing dialects, and comparing Basque as a whole with other neighboring languages. He delved deeply into other important fields as well, but he was above all a comparatist. He stressed the importance of both structuralism and generative grammar, but he was most comfortable using the techniques of reconstruction, evolution, comparison, etc. This was his field. As an expert neogrammarian, he handled data with ease and insight, always using clear, precise criteria in selecting data to build explanatory theories accounting for the causal relations between apparently unrelated facts. Without rejecting structuralism and its defense of closed theoretical systems, Mitxelena always sought further data, on which he based his ground-breaking analyses and proposals, some of which seemed adventurous when first presented but ended up being accepted by specialists as new information became available.

Once at the UBC, he continued teaching for a few more years until his retirement, receiving numerous awards and recognition both at home and abroad. His untimely death in 1987, at his home in San Sebastián, left all of us with a feeling of deep loss and bereavement. Koldo Mitxelena was a wise, prudent man, a great scholar and intellectual. He opened up and carefully charted many new pathways and never closed any doors. The debt that Basque linguistics owes him is unpayable. It is not just the fact that he was able to turn Basque philology into a science. That would have been merit enough. But on top of that, Koldo Mitxelena was graced with tremendous common sense, and this is what made it possible, following his death, for the Basque language to prosper. Thanks to him, it had the minimum resources necessary to survive and flourish in a modern, changing society. Koldo Mitxelena showed us all the road to knowledge, erudition, and critical thinking.

Legacy

Sometimes it seems as though there are not enough words in the language to give an adequate idea of the size and quality of certain contributions to knowledge. The research undertaken by Mitxelena was vast and his publications prolific. The full bibliography is contained in a volume published by the UBC on the occasion of a tribute paid to him in 1985, and occupies many pages of very fine print.[11] Almost all of it was published in Basque and Spanish, although there are a few articles in French and English.

First to be cited are his books: *Historia de la literatura vasca* (1960), his Ph.D. dissertation *Fonética histórica vasca* (1961), *Lenguas y protolenguas* (1963), *Textos arcaicos vascos* (1964), and *Sobre el pasado de la lengua vasca* (1964). All are original research and shed a great deal of light on different aspects of Basque, particularly on the history of the language, philological matters, borrowed terms, dialectology, and so forth. They are works that clearly illustrate Mitxelena's enormous erudition and assurance on a broad array of questions that had never before been dealt with. *Fonética histórica vasca* is still a basic, fundamental resource that goes beyond phonetics and addresses matters of phonology, morphology, the influence of Latin and other languages, history of the language, etc. The same can be said of his other books. In all of them Mitxelena traces and thoroughly analyzes the first records of Basque, making systematic theoretical and procedural observations, in particular when dealing with prehistoric stages of the language. One of these works, a sample of his uncommon rigor and elegance, is available as well in English and is therefore not included here.[12] Reading these works today, one is awed by the sheer magnitude of the problems that Mitxelena had to deal with.

One of Mitxelena's volumes is a magnificent history of Basque literature, understood in its broadest sense. That is, the history does not deal solely with literary works, but with works written in Basque, and includes discussions of Basque oral literature, ancient songs, and the like. It should be remembered that the first book published in Basque, a brief collection of poems contained in fifty-two pages including a prose prologue, was dated 1545.[13] So writing in the vernacular began late in the Basque Country, compared to other countries. This volume is still of great interest, even though several other histories of Basque literature have been published since then.[14] Mitxelena made a critical study of everything that had been written down through the centuries in Basque, selecting authors and works from a historical perspective with a view to discerning their points of interest for literature in particular, and for the Basque language in general. As Mitxelena's history was written many years ago, it naturally does not include the contributions of Basque authors in recent decades. But Basque literature has surged forward strongly in the past twenty years. Writers such as Atxaga, Saizarbitoria, Lertxundi, Txillardegi, and many others have produced powerful works of undeniable quality. Bernardo Atxaga, for example, received Spain's National Literary Award in 1988 for his novel *Obabakoak*, a work that has since received many other awards and been translated into nearly thirty languages. Mitxelena did not live long enough to see any of this and probably never suspected that a minority language such as Basque would come so far in such a short time. Clearly, nothing of the kind appears in his book.

In addition to these major works, Mitxelena's articles, dispersed in numerous sources that are occasionally hard to find, have been collected and made available by various publishers down through the years: *Lengua e historia* (1985), *Palabras y textos* (1987), *Sobre historia de la lengua vasca* (1988, two volumes). The articles written in Basque have also been collected specifically and published in nine volumes (linguistics, articles, literary criticism, general and critical works, literature) in 1988 under the title *Euskal idazlan guztiak* (Entire Basque Works). These writings address a broad range of topics: studies of the Indo-European and non-Indo-European languages existing in the Iberian Peninsula before Roman times; writings used in annotating them; onomatology; history of the Basque language; Basque and its relations to other neighboring and non-neighboring languages (with frequent references to languages of the Caucasus); dialectology and internal reconstruction of the history of the language; issues in comparative linguistics; reconstruction of protolanguages; bilingualism; contact between languages; contributions of other languages, such as Basque and Welsh, to the reconstruction of Romance languages and Vulgar Latin; influence of Latin and Romance languages on Basque (e.g., chronology of loan words); life and works of persons related to linguistics (W. Humboldt, Sánchez de las Brozas, etc.); conversations with renowned intellectuals; reviews of books on linguistics or literature, etc.

We summarize all this today in very few lines, but Mitxelena, often working alone, had to address linguistic problems whose resolution required not only solid knowledge of linguistic data, but also the vast perspective and insight that made it possible to draw general hypotheses from these data and fit together pieces of the puzzle. This is what he accomplished in analyzing the dialects of Basque, for example. Dialects of course retain information on previous stages of a language's development, meaning that one can use such data to posit general hypotheses about the historical development of the language. But such information never appears clearly and neatly. It is necessary to find the crucial fact or phenomenon, analyze it, rid it of secondary adherences, find how it may be linked to other apparently unrelated items or phenomena, and then formulate a proposal about the missing links that account for the linguistic changes that have taken place throughout time. This Mitxelena does prodigiously, arguing from facts, soaring in concentric circles for paragraphs before swooping in with a set of closely reasoned proposals.

Finally, special mention should be made of his *Diccionario general vasco*, one of the greatest works ever published on the Basque language. The dictionary appears under the name of Mitxelena, although he never lived to see its first volume, which was in press when he died. In subsequent years, fifteen more volumes were published, for a total of 16,000 pages of fine print. It is a gigantic historical dictionary based on a linguistic corpus of some five million words, containing hundreds of thousands of examples drawn from Basque literature and providing accurate information on Basque usage through time and with regard to the dialects. The team that worked on the dictionary was led for seventeen years by Dr. Ibon Sarasola, but Mitxelena figures as its author. This is as it should be, since Mitxelena was the one who designed the dictionary, chose the team, laid down the guidelines to be followed, and placed at the disposal of the team of experts a large portion of the data that he had accumulated throughout his life. The dictionary provides ample historical information, from the first traces of the language up to the 1970s, more or less. It was during those years when the dictionary was taking shape that the foundations were also being laid for the literary unification of Basque, a subject to which we will return in a moment. To end this section on Mitxelena's legacy, however, it should be noted that at the time of this writing, a team at the University of the Basque Country is compiling and editing our great linguist's entire oeuvre and will shortly begin publishing his *Opera omnia*, or complete works.

Unification of the Language

As noted earlier, written testimonies of Basque, or what is known as "educated writing" for want of a better term, appears relatively late. It is only in the sixteenth century that books began to be published in this language, and most of them were religious in nature. It goes without saying, of course, that for this same reason most of the authors were priests or monks. There were also numerous works of a didactic nature, including moral tales, fables, or studies of grammar. Mitxelena noted quite rightly that even this type of literature had a surprising readership. Over eighty editions of the volume *Exercicio spirituala* were printed before 1898, according to Vinson in his bibliography, and there were no doubt others that Vinson overlooked.[15] The situation has changed radically in the past forty years, with the appearance of numerous lay authors who write for aesthetic reasons, for the joy of literature, and not out of moral or religious convictions.

On the other hand, Basque oral literature, or folk literature, abounds and is comparable to that of any other nation. It consists of stories and legends handed down from generation to generation, and yet somewhat surprisingly, there is hardly a trace in them of ancient, vernacular forms. According to Mitxelena, Basque folklore scholars have been very disappointed to find not only that the collective memory is weak, but that "we have shown a real talent for covering with rust . . . novelties introduced late yesterday afternoon."[16] It was the great Basque anthropologist Barandiarán who finally identified and distinguished the true from the false, recovering for us the characters and places drawn from history that eventually populated our fields and forests with legendary beings, telling us the age-old tales of life between Christians and pagans, where the former were happily learning from the latter all the tricks of staying alive.[17]

For different reasons, we can safely say that Basque has never been the sole means of expression of the Basque people. Important in this regard are the facts that the Basque Country was always small, sparsely populated, and therefore subject to the influence of more powerful neighboring cultures. As Mitxelena pointed out on numerous occasions, bilingualism has always been present, in one form or another and to various degrees, in Basque life. This has had an important negative effect (along with several positive ones). Over the years, linguistic pressure has caused the Basque speech community to dwindle little by little. In the nineteenth and twentieth centuries, this erosion was particularly noticeable in the Spanish Basque Country. As recently as the 1960s we Basques have witnessed the final disappearance of some of our dialects. Thanks to the political restructuring of post–Franco Spain into a country made up of autonomous regions each endowed with many powers, it has finally been possible to slow the decline. Basque now enjoys official recognition and has a firm place in the news media and all levels of education, particularly in the Autonomous Community of Euskadi, where most Basque speakers reside. In Navarre, however, the measures needed to ensure survival of the language have still not been taken, and Basque continues to lose ground. On the French side of the border, where the number of Basque speakers is much smaller, the language is waning at an even faster pace due to the fact that in practice, it enjoys no legal recognition whatsoever.

Historically, Basque has been used in the home and with neighbors in small towns and villages. Many Basques, particularly those living far from major cities, have never spoken any other language. But apart from these cases and in town halls, it used to be difficult to find areas where Basque was used exclusively as the common language of communication. Accordingly, it is true to say that bilingualism has always been present, in one way or another, in Basque society. Clearly, whenever a public record was made of official acts, the use of Basque was historically more testimonial and exceptional than real. Documents were written up in Latin or in Romance languages. Furthermore, due to the fact that Basque was divided into various dialects with distinctly differentiated ways of speaking; that it lacked a literary culture; that it had few speakers, even fewer of whom had any influence in society; and the fact that culturally the Basque Country did not have any special importance (apart from specific individual contributions, of course) or a public university, it was enormously difficult for the Basque language to develop and increase its presence in other areas. Even when the Basque Country was belatedly Christianized, religious instruction was conducted in Latin (a language, by the way, that ensured the unity of the church) or else in Romance. This was true even in teaching the catechism, which certainly seems a bit absurd and can only be due to the "incomprehensible apathy that must have reigned for long periods," according to Mitxelena himself.[18] From a cultural standpoint, the historical snapshot of the country is most disappointing and contrasts with the importance of its industrial and economic development, led by persons who, with few exceptions, felt absolutely no links at all to any language apart from Spanish. To them, Basque simply did not exist. For such reasons, the publication of various significant works written in Basque in the eighteenth and nineteenth centuries had to be postponed for decades due to lack of funding.

In any event, this situation began generating controversy over the language as far back as the seventeenth century. The inhabitants of the Basque Country have always felt very attached to their language—a "tenacious adhesion" in the words of Mitxelena—and legitimate pride, because they considered Basque to be a fundamental sign of their identity as a distinct people. The controversies surrounding Basque gave rise to long arguments between defenders and detractors of the language. To the former, Basque was virtually perfect, a language whose internal logic was so great that it would be created naturally, *ex novo*, if a new language were needed in order to enable humans to understand each other. It could be traced all the way back to Paradise. For its detractors, Basque was nothing more than a dark well of obscure sounds, and of course incapable of meeting the communicative needs of a changing, nonagrarian society.[19]

Those who began to write in Basque starting in the sixteenth century suddenly found themselves facing an unexpected difficulty. Writing in Basque is not hard, and anyone educated in the language can do it. Indeed, the best example of this is Dechepare, who in his book proudly points to the achievement of writing in a language in which no one had previously written so many things one after the other. But writing is not what was difficult. The real challenge was to find a more or less common code of writing. To illustrate, let us take a simple example. A consonant sound such as the one at the beginning of the English word *chair* is found and transcribed in Spanish as *ch*, just as in English. In Basque, however, it is written *tx*, and is very common in words such as *etxea* "house." The problem is that to a French Basque speaker, this sound would be heard as *sh* (i.e., as in the French word *chic* or the English word *she*). Consequently, an author wishing to write in Basque but having at his disposal only the spelling conventions of French, or only those of Spanish, would (depending on place of origin) write the word for house as *echea* (if Spanish) or *etchea* (adding a *t*, if French). So we have three variants for the same word, which today is uniformly spelled *etxea*. And this is without counting other phonetic variations found in particular dialects, where the word may also be pronounced e.g., *etxia*. Clearly, without preestablished writing conventions, speech is written as it sounds to the writer with spelling variants popping up everywhere, like mushrooms in a forest.

This is a simple example affecting a minor point, but it is of great importance for the formal presentation of written works. All authors were aware of this, or at least the most important ones were, for in the prologues to their works, they wonder out loud time and again how, "if here a word is said like this, and over there like that, how can it be written so that everyone will understand it?" The written language, therefore, was divided, and authors—depending on their country, region, or school—tended toward widely different models, so that sometimes it was very hard work to understand a text written by someone from a different region. Of course, the differences were not limited only to spelling. Basque auxiliary verbs varied from one region to the next, and there were important differences in morphology. Witness, for example, the following three variants, all meaning "I will give them to you":

- *emongo deutsudaz* (Bizkaia)
- *emango dizkizut* (central region)
- *emanen derauzkizut* (Lapurdi)

And of course there were major lexical differences. Moreover, all such differences were felt within the space of just a few kilometers. All of us Basques have had the impression that, even within families, it is sufficient for a brother or sister to marry someone from a neighboring village, perhaps less than two miles away, for different forms to creep into a sibling's speech. This has happened down through history and is still happening today, although much less noticeably. In any case, prior to unification of the literary language, the differences that existed were so important that works were often published in different dialect versions.[20]

Before 1920, a new institution was founded in the Basque Country: Euskaltzaindia, or the Royal Academy of the Basque Language.[21] Its stated objectives were to safeguard Basque, foster studies about the language, and strive for a common unified literary language to be used by writers on both sides of the Pyrenees. The academy's founding members were the few persons who in those years devoted their time to studying the Basque language. As is natural, several of them belonged to the clergy.

The search for a unified standard of written Basque turned out to be a much more difficult undertaking than originally supposed. Various proposals put forward over the years finally had to be abandoned, and writers meanwhile continued using different writing conventions depending on their regional origins and personal preferences. Agreement was difficult because a decision in favor of one thing was tantamount to discrimination against many others. Worse still, it would seem like a decision against whole dialects that were in daily use. Returning to our earlier example, if it were decided that from now on people should write *emango dizkizut*, those who had always heard and said *emongo deutsudaz* or *emanen derauzkizut* would be very likely to feel slighted. In the case of authors wishing to write a grammar or textbook, the problem was crucial, as it was for radio announcers, for example. And what would happen if grandparents heard their grandchildren say *emango dizkizut*, when everyone at home had always pronounced it *emongo deutsudaz* (or more likely still, a contracted form like *emongotsutez*)? Clearly, it was a very thorny issue.

Koldo Mitxelena was appointed to a chair in Euskaltzaindia and was asked, while still working at the University of Salamanca, to draw up new guidelines for unification. The brief, concise proposal that he presented is included in this volume. Entitled "Ortografía," it was published in the official journal of the Academy.[22] Much more is included in its brief pages, however, than mere matters of spelling, since he also addressed issues of morphology, attempting to define what can be considered a "Basque word" and what cannot, as well as the problem of loan words and certain issues of syntax. At any rate, the visual impact of spelling obviously was of extreme importance at that time and carried much weight in the controversy that followed.

Mitxelena's proposal provides excellent evidence of his enormous common sense. He started from a general premise, that the survival of the Basque language depended on whether or not we would be able to accept a unified standard for writing. The best option, of course, would be for every one of us to be entirely familiar and comfortable with all the different dialects and ways of speaking—but that was out of the question. Accordingly, even though the language would lose its wealth of dialects if standardization were adopted, the wisest course would be to choose precisely that option.

Naturally, all efforts should be made to keep people from feeling affronted by one choice or another, but obviously a standard could not be devised without injuring someone's feelings. This was one of the prices that we would have to pay, according to Mitxelena in his opening premise.

From there on he presented an outline of what would have to be done, from the easiest to the most difficult tasks, stressing that basic initial agreements should first be reached on superficial matters such as spelling. He proposed a simple alphabet for writing Basque words, from which would be banished letters and combinations such as *c, ch* (at the time considered a letter in the Spanish alphabet), *qu, v, w,* and *y*. He also eliminated letters with a certain history such as the accented *r,* which would be replaced by the much more common *rr,* to denote the rolled *r* found in Basque and many other languages. This section is brief but very detailed, and covers the main problems with which writers had to contend on a daily basis.

Mitxelena proposed that Basque use the letter *h,* a proposal that would spark enormous controversy on the Spanish side of the border. He felt that the letter *h* was necessary to transcribe an aspirated consonant prevalent among French Basque-speakers, although unknown in the Spanish Basque Country. Common words such as *herri* and *harri* ("town/people" and "stone," respectively) are pronounced in very different ways on either side of the border. In the French Basque Country, they are aspirated, while on the Spanish side they are not. Therefore historically, writers have written them in two ways. Those who "heard" the *h* wrote it, and those who did not left it out. For this same reason, other words such as *nahi* "desire" are pronounced differently, and even their syllabic structure differs depending on which side of the Pyrenees the speaker lives.

Additionally, the presence of this ancient common consonant left its trace in many words in the peninsular dialects[23] whose speakers had, at some time in history, replaced the *h* with an occlusive, yielding *agoa, egun, kori*, etc., instead of *ahoa, ehun, hori*. Mitxelena made the risky decision of making an intermediate proposal between the different existing traditions. That is, everyone should use *h*. Peninsular writers should begin to use it habitually, while French writers should use it in fewer contexts than some of them were used to (e.g., many writers normally used the *h* in certain post-consonant positions, in words such as *ethorri*). The result, according to Mitxelena's proposal, was that a peninsular writer, for whom this letter was entirely new, would have to write *hitz* "word," just like his fellow writers on the other side of the Pyrenees. But the latter, on the contrary, would have to learn to write *ate* "door," like peninsular writers, rather than *athe*, as was usual among several French Basque writers.

Mitxelena's proposal was submitted for debate in 1968, at the Arantzazu Monastery in the province of Gipuzkoa, under difficult circumstances. The Franco dictatorship was still very much alive and any matter having to do with Basque, or that entailed a meeting of a dozen persons, was immediately suspect. The debates themselves were long and fierce. In fact, the chair of the Royal Academy of the Basque Language, Father Manuel Lekuona, who warmly welcomed Mitxelena's contribution on the opening day, ended up resigning. A division ensued in the academy, which transcended to Basque society and eventually degenerated into interminable discussions on the letter *h*. In the end, this poor little letter was seen as the culprit responsible for all possible problems afflicting the Basque language.

However, the standardization proposal, which was refined and developed in subsequent years, finally triumphed. One very important reason for its success was the decided support given to it by the younger generations, who had studied at universities and embraced the model without reservation, becoming its most enthusiastic standard-bearers. In later years, more events occurred favoring acceptance of the new standard. The Academy of the Basque Language firmly backed university researchers and specialists in the language and accepted them as full members when chairs became vacant, replacing their clerical or lay forerunners who had been much more self-taught. This trend was very clear during the terms of office of Luis Villasante and Jean Haritschelhar, the two persons who have consecutively presided over the academy for years, although in recent times relations between the academy and Basque universities have incomprehensibly cooled somewhat. The success of Basque unification was finally assured when, in the early post-Franco years, the first autonomous government of Euskadi, under the leadership of its president, Carlos Garaikoetxea, and the education and culture minister, Pedro Miguel Etxenike,[24] decided to firmly back the Arantzazu standard.

With the passing of years, standardization is now complete. It is used by writers, by government, by the media (press, radio, and television), and it is used at all levels of education, including a high percentage of university subjects which can now be studied either in Basque or in Spanish at the UBC.

This is an undeniable achievement of Mitxelena's. He designed the model that others accepted and willingly promoted. But it is also an achievement of distinctly historical dimensions that should be recognized as well. The course that other languages took decades to complete was a road that Basque has had to travel in just a few years. Mitxelena proved himself to be a painstaking researcher of matters concerned with the history of the language, but at the same time was a person with his feet very much on the ground, capable of making highly practical proposals. Due to his premature death, he never saw how successfully Basque has taken hold in so many different areas.

Anthology

Selecting works for an anthology is always undertaken with its future readers in mind. A selection intended for specialists in Basque, familiar as they are with many of Mitxelena's ideas and works, would be based on very different criteria from those used to compile an anthology intended for English-speaking readers who perhaps barely know Mitxelena and are only vaguely familiar with the Basque language and people. In the first case, the selection should include the entire content of *Fonética histórica vasca*, but probably not the work entitled *La lengua vasca*, to give one clear example. In the second case, the choice would be just the reverse.

Some works by Mitxelena have already been published in English, or are in the process of being published. As noted earlier, *Languages and Protolanguages*, a key work, has been available in English for several years now.[25] Two articles by Mitxelena have also been published in an anthology featuring a number of authors.[26] We also know that the same publisher is working on the final stages of a Mitxelena project that will include the book *Sobre el pasado de la lengua vasca*, a work that we had also originally selected for this anthology. In order to inform the reader of these different publications, here we have included only a few pages of such works so that interested readers will be able to read the complete text in English if so desired. An anthology must reflect all these considerations.

The magnitude of Mitxelena's work and the breadth of its subject matter make it necessary to consider other factors as well. His most technical works are not easy for non-Basque speakers to understand. The examples used are often not glossed or explained, meaning that they would not be fully comprehensible, even though the main argumentation can be followed perfectly. Naturally, a knowledge of the language or of its history would greatly help in this respect. However, even so, they are technical works with a certain degree of difficulty. Even a work like "Ortografía," which is actually quite simple and straightforward, requires a knowledge of Basque, because it was written for people who speak the language, and it also requires a certain familiarity with the problems arising from lack of a standard for the written language. Specialists will, of course, have no problems with this work.

Mitxelena's writings for more general audiences are magnificent, particularly *La lengua vasca*.[27] I believe that all readers will find it perfectly understandable, and for this reason we have given it first place in the selection.

Mitxelena published a vast number of articles on a wide variety of subjects. In many of them (some of which are included here) it is perhaps not necessary to have prior knowledge to understand what he is dealing with, although we should not forget that Mitxelena frequently used a very refined type of irony and numerous references to authors, works, situations, etc., that can only be grasped by those close to the topic. Such writing, requiring reading between the lines, is always disguised in the style characteristic of the author.

Let us turn now to the works chosen for this anthology. [28] As we have just noted, the selection opens with *La lengua vasca*, a work written for the general public. It is easy to read and provides an excellent overview of Basque, explaining most of the internal and external problems with which the language was faced. It is true that since the booklet was written, many things have changed, as is natural. A great deal of research has been undertaken in practically all the fields mentioned in the volume; Basque has been introduced into the media, government, and education; and Basque literature has been considerably revolutionized (for the better). But the book has not lost its currency. Whoever wishes to gain an idea of what the situation is like today regarding Basque can read these pages without hesitation, for they are still enormously useful.

The second work, "Los vascos y su nombre,"[29] was also written for a basically general audience, although Mitxelena's facility for relating data, theories, and historical references is strongly evident.

The third selection, "Romanización y lengua vasca,"[30] is another work for nonspecialists but one that deals more in depth with an issue touched on in the previous work—namely, what happened to the Basques and their language when the Romans reached the Basque Country following their invasion of the Iberian peninsula.

The next selection contains the first pages of Mitxelena's book entitled *Textos arcaicos vascos*.[31] The aim of this work, as Mitxelena says in his opening words to the reader, is "to offer a sample . . . of what historians of the language can learn from the data contained in ancient inscriptions and in medieval epigraphs and documents, [as well as from] a collection . . . of isolated sentences and longer fragments, in prose and in verse, that have come down to us in manuscripts in printed works from the 15th, 16th and 17th centuries." We have selected the parts concerning inscriptions from the Roman period that make reference to indigenous proper names, medieval testimonies of personal and place names, plus a number of glosses, words, and phrases. We have also included some later testimonies that refer to epic poems, wars, and other events. These excerpts all form part of a rather long book and require a certain amount of interest and perseverance on the part of the reader, since they are actually commentaries and annotations on ancient writings where non-standard Basque and Spanish spellings were used. The excerpts have been included to give an idea of some of the topics that Professor Mitxelena dealt with in detail.

This section is followed by two chapters from *Sobre el pasado de la lengua vasca*, a book that we mentioned earlier and which for years was the standard reference for all students of Basque philology.[32] Here Mitxelena addresses many of the topics touched on superficially in *La lengua vasca*, providing much more technical detail on Basque dialectology, differences between the dialects, prehistory of the language, the influence of pre-Latin Indo-European and traces of Romance in Basque, as well as its possible relations with other languages. These are the issues that recur most often in Mitxelena's bibliography, and in this book they are dealt with superbly. *Sobre el pasado de la lengua vasca* is perhaps the cornerstone of his work. Interestingly, the author himself notes that he wrote the book in haste under not very favorable circumstances during the 1962 Christmas vacation, and indeed, these words capture the essence of the work. Concise and precise, there is no room here for literary disquisitions. We have selected chapters 3 ("Historia y prehistoria de la lengua") and 6 ("Relaciones de parentesco de la lengua vasca").

Next in order are various portions of *Fonética histórica vasca*, Koldo Mitxelena's major work. Specifically, we have chosen chapter 19 ("El sistema consonántico antiguo") and chapter 11 ("La aspiración"), with the notes added in 1977. These sections are particularly interesting because here Mitxelena proposes for the first time the structure of what may be called the proto-Basque consonant system, and because he specifically addresses the problem of aspirated consonants, which years later was to be such a fundamental issue when he proposed his guidelines for a unified literary language. We are referring to the problem of the Basque *h*, alluded to earlier in this introduction.[33]

Also included in this section on historical phonetics, one of Mitxelena's specialties, is the brief paper entitled "De fonética vasca. La distribución de las oclusivas aspiradas y no aspiradas."[34] In this article, Mitxelena again takes up problems of historical phonetics dealt with in many of his other works. Readers interested in the controversy surrounding the standardization of Basque will find here much more information on the issue referred to in the previous paragraph.

To give readers a better idea of the many fields that Mitxelena studied, we have also included some works related to literature, specifically, two articles and two chapters from his book *Historia de la literatura vasca*. The first article, written in Basque, is entitled "Euskal literaturaren bereizgarri orokorrak."[35] The second, also forming part of the same lecture cycle, is entitled "Euskal literaturaren kondairarako oin-arriak."[36] These are followed by chapters 2 and 3 of his book on the history of Basque literature and deal respectively with the sixteenth and seventeenth centuries.[37] In the sixteenth century, Dechepare (Etxepare in Basque) wrote the first known printed book in Basque, and Leizarraga made his magnificent translation of the New Testament as a result of the conflict between Catholics and Protestants. The seventeenth century, for its part, was particularly important for Basque literature, with works by Axular (surely one of the best prose works ever published in Basque), Etcheberri from Sara, and others. Due to the size of the work, we have not included the entire book, but these two chapters are fully represen-tative both of Mitxelena's style in addressing such topics, and of the limitations of Basque, which as we have said has had a very short literary history.

Included next are four works of a very different kind. First is the report entitled "Ortografía,"[38] delivered to the assembly of the Academy of the Basque Language in 1968, which laid the groundwork for the debate on literary unification of the language. Second is a work in which Mitxelena analyzes, from the vantage point of time, the first steps taken toward this standardization.[39] The title, "De Arantzazu a Bergara," is indicative of the contents. The meeting where the guidelines were pre-sented for unifying written Basque was held in Arantzazu; the next major meeting took place ten years later in the town of Bergara, also located in the province of Gipuzkoa. At this new meeting, the main points were ratified, certain things were changed, and new proposals were presented. These are the ten years that Mitxelena analyzes. The next article, "La normalización de la forma escrita de una lengua: el caso vasco," again addresses the consequences of that initial proposal and the problems that arise when a process of these characteristics is undertaken.[40] It is written from a later standpoint, when several years have passed and the majority of writers have shown their clear inclination to use the new standard. The final work in this section is "Lengua común y dialectos vascos,"[41] where Mitxelena returns yet again to the problems generated by standardization processes. In this regard, it can truly be said that the effort to unify literary Basque has been very much like turning the entire country into an immense language laboratory.

To close the anthology, we have included a brief article, which might better be called a divertimento.[42] It happens quite systematically with Basque that now and then a supposed specialist will step forward after a cursory look at the language and proudly announce his/her conclusions and hypotheses. Some of them have pet theories about the paternal, maternal, or filial relations of Basque with other languages; others happily observe the influence that Basque has supposedly had on European river names and even on place names in Asia; while still others hazard laborious, all-encompassing explanations of the kind that explain everything and sweep away the many doubts that for years have bewildered us poor Basques. Such studies usually have two features (this is also systematic): their authors have hardly any knowledge of the language beyond what they might have gleaned from a pocket dictionary on a summer's afternoon, and they know absolutely nothing of what linguists or historians of the language have already published on the subject. Accordingly, this final article is devoted precisely to a book of this kind, which claims to explain Basque once and for all, but which in reality only manages to exhaust and exasperate the reader, amazed that so much stupidity has actually been published without anyone calling the author to account.

This, then, is what our anthology contains, although as we said at the outset, a different selection could have been made. Editors with other points of view and other interests would undoubtedly have focused on aspects of Mitxelena's work not touched on here. But we believe that this selection is appropriate and significant. What we would like is for speakers of other languages who have not yet read the work of this great intellectual to be able to do so, and therefore to have the opportunity of seeing that there once was someone who, defining himself as a "person," "Basque," and "nationalist" (in that order), deeply loved this corner of the world and devoted himself very seriously to studying what he considered to be the distinguishing feature of the Basque people—their language. The following pages are a small sample of his work.

Pello Salaburu

Professor of Basque Philology
University of the Basque Country
Member of Euskaltzaindia
salaburu@ehau.es

Editor's Note and Glossary

Editor's Note:

Occasionally, some of the original terms used by the author are respected, such as *euskara*, to denote the Basque language, or Vasconia, a synonym for the Basque Country. For the names of the Basque provinces (Guipúzcoa, Vizcaya, etc.) and their citizens (Guipuzcoans, Vizcayans, etc.) we have left the orthography as it appears in Mitxelena's original publications. Thus the earlier selections usually use Spanish spellings, changing to Basque orthography later on (although in other volumes of this series, modern Basque spelling (Gipuzkoa, Bizkaia, etc.) was used throughout).

In Mitxelena's work numerous references are made to authors, Basque terms, and place names that are more or less familiar to specialists in the field. In the first part (the translation of "The Basque Language"), editor's footnotes have been provided to succinctly clarify the meaning of some of these words or names as they arise in the text. Since this is a translation and not a critical edition of Mitxelena's work, a complete explanation of each such term would greatly exceed the limits of the volume and of the series itself. Moreover, on many occasions we would merely be dwelling on points that prove controversial even among the experts. We are aware that because of this decision, the text will be a little harder to read, but we feel that generally speaking, the author's original argumentation comes through with the same vigor nonetheless.

Agirre:

Juan Bautista Agirre (1742–1823). Called "Agirre de Asteasu" to distinguish him from other Basque authors with the same surname, he was a Catholic priest and the author of various religious works in Basque. In the opinion of some critics, he was the best Gipuzkoan author writing in Basque prior to 1880.

Añibarro:

Pedro Antonio Añibarro (1748–1830). The author of numerous books in Basque on subjects ranging from religion, the Basque language, a Spanish-Basque dictionary, etc. His style is very didactic.

Apraiz:

Odón Apraiz (1896–1984). A historian trained at various Spanish and European universities, he was an honorary member of the Royal Academy of the Basque Language. He worked particularly on the recovery of Basque in the province of Araba (Alava) and published various research papers on the Basque language.

Arana-Goiri:

Sabino Arana-Goiri (1865–1903). The prime promoter and ideologue of Basque nationalism, and founder of the Partido Nacionalista Vasco (PNV), the largest nationalist party in the Basque Country (1895). He wrote numerous books establishing the bases of his nationalist ideology, as well as various works on the Basque language.

Arrese-Beitia:

Felipe Arrese-Beitia (1841–1906). Basque poet and writer who participated on numerous occasions in festivals celebrating Basque.

Astarloa:

The Astarloa brothers were two Catholic priests and the authors of various works on Basque. Pablo Pedro (1752–1806) worked with German linguist Wilhelm von Humboldt and in 1803 wrote an essay in defense of Basque (for further information, see the second volume of this series of Basque Classics: *Anthology of Apologists and Detractors of the Basque Language*), in addition to many other works. His brother Pedro (1751–1821) wrote various religious works in Basque.

Axular:

Navarrese writer (1556–1644). He studied in Salamanca and was the author of the most important work in the history of Basque literature, *Gero*, a work of great erudition and inspired by certain Spanish Siglo de Oro authors. Axular shows a surprising mastery of written Basque, and the adaptations of other works that appear in his pages are remarkable for their linguistic beauty. He is the main exponent of the "Sara School" of writers, in reference to the village in the French Basque Country (although under the ecclesiastical demarcation of a Spanish province), where he was the parish priest.

Azkue:

Resurrección María Azkue (1864–1951). A Bizkaian priest, lexicographer, researcher of Basque folklore and author of numerous works on Basque grammar. His legacy is impressive and includes a range of genres: dictionaries, song books (he was a great musician), essays on Basque morphology, etc. Both his dictionary and his works on Basque grammar were essential references until a Basque studies program was established in Basque universities. He was the first chairman of Euskaltzaindia, the Royal Academy of the Basque Language.

Bähr:

Gerhard Bähr (1900–45). German linguist who published several studies on Basque.

Barandiarán:

Jose Miguel de Barandiarán (1889–1991). A Basque anthropologist with great influence on Basque scholars and to whom the third volume of this Basque Classics series is dedicated.

Bonaparte:

Louis Lucien Bonaparte (1813–91). Nephew of Napoleon I and trained in chemistry and mineralogy (fields in which he published several works), he is best known for his interest in languages. He undertook comparative studies of numerous varieties of European languages and is considered the father of Basque dialectology. During his five trips to the Basque Country, he acquired an excellent knowledge of Basque and drew up highly detailed classifications of its dialects and speech varieties. He published numerous translations into each of the dialects, made by his many collaborators following criteria laid down by Bonaparte himself. He was the most complete and important of all Basque dialectologists.

Campión:

Arturo Campión (1854–1937). A lawyer by training, he devoted himself to the study of the Basque *fueros*. Of changing ideology (liberal, *integrista*, nationalist, etc.), he always had a great love of the Basque Country and participated very actively in Basque cultural life. He was the author of numerous works, including a grammar of Basque.

Caro Baroja:

Julio Caro Baroja (1914–95). A historian and anthropologist, he was one of the initiators of the so-called historical-cultural approach. He was very attached to the Basque Country, where he lived for a large part of each year, and was known for his remarkable erudition. A professor at the University of the Basque Country, he published numerous works on an array of topics, many of which concern Basque history and customs—a subject on which he is considered one of our greatest experts—as well as matters having to do with the Basque language.

Corominas:

Joan Corominas (1905–97). Also known as Coromines, he was a Catalan philologist who published important lexicographical works, in particular etymological dictionaries of Catalan and Spanish. As an anti-Franco Republican, he spent several years in exile in different countries. He taught at the University of Chicago.

Cruz, Sor Juana Inés:

Sor Juana Inés de la Cruz (1651–95). A nun and well-known Mexican poet. Her father was Basque.

Eleizalde:

Luis Eleizalde (1873–1923). Gipuzkoan author, physicist and mathematician. He published various works on the Basque language and was a founding member of Euskaltzaindia, the Royal Academy of the Basque Language.

Etxeberri:

Joannes d'Etxeberri (or Etcheberry, 1668–1749), known as "from Sara," to distinguish him from another Joannes Etxeberri (from Ziburu). A physician by profession, he wrote various works includ-

ing a method in Basque for learning Latin and a quatrilingual dictionary, of which no copies remain.

Fita:

Fidel Fita (1835–1919). Catalan archeologist and historian. A Jesuit
priest who specialized in historical and archeological research and
the history of the Basque Country.

García de Salazar:

(Circa 1400–76.) Lope García de Salazar was a powerful leader in
the warlord battles that ravaged part of the Basque Country for centuries. His own eldest son imprisoned him in the castle of Muñatones
(Bizkaia) for years, where he finally died of poisoning. During his
imprisonment he chronicled the history of the country in numerous tomes: *Cronica de Vizcaya* (1454) and *Bienandanzas e Fortunas*
(1471–76).

Gómez-Moreno:

Manuel Gómez-Moreno (1870–1970). Spanish archeologist and
historian who deciphered the Levantine variety of Iberian script.
His work completely altered researchers' approach to Iberian and
showed that certain "Iberian" inscriptions used a variant of the Greek
alphabet and that the Southwest script masked what was actually
a non-Iberian language, whereas inscriptions in true Iberian script
reflected non-Indo-European Iberian and also Celtiberian, an Indo-
European Celtic language. His research put an end to the Basque-
Iberism hypothesis.

Gorostiaga:

Juan Gorostiaga (1905–91). A Bizkaian author.

Humboldt:

Wilhelm von Humboldt (1767–1835). Brother of Alexander, German intellectual, and one of the founders of the University of Berlin
(Humboldt Universität Berlin). Highly influential in the culture of his
country, he is remembered for his work in different fields, including
education, political theory, and literature. He was also interested in
a wide range of languages: European, Asian, indigenous American,
etc. On his trips to Spain, he met and worked with numerous linguists

specialized in Basque, a language he greatly admired ("It is one of the most perfectly formed languages, surprising for its vigor, word structure, and the brevity and daring of its expression").

Lafitte:

Pierres Lafitte (1901–85). Priest and writer. Member of the Academy of the Basque Language and author of numerous works on Basque. He is best remembered for his magnificent grammar of the Navarrese-Lapurdian dialect (1944).

Lafon:

Rene Lafon (1899–1974). Author of studies on Basque phonetics and of a doctoral thesis on the Basque verb system.

Larramendi:

Manuel Larramendi (1690–1766). A Gipuzkoan author who published numerous works on Basque. For more information, see volume 2 of this Basque Classics series: *Anthology of Apologists and Detractors of the Basque Language.*

Leizarraga:

Joannes Leizarraga (1506–1601). Sixteenth-century Basque writer, first prosist and author of a magnificent translation of the New Testament. When Queen Juana III d'Albert converted to Calvinism, she promoted the publication of the New Testament in Gascon and Basque as a way of spreading the new ideology, and Leizarraga was asked to undertake the Basque version.

Lekuona:

Manuel de Lekuona (1894–1987). Guipuzcoan priest and author of various studies on Basque literature. He served as chairman of Euskaltzaindia and was the editor of the fourth edition of *Gero,* by Pedro Axular, in 1954.

Marr:

Nikolai Jakovlevich Marr (1865–1934). Georgian (ex–Soviet Union) archeologist, ethnographer, and linguist. In an attempt to unify linguistics and Marxism, he developed a linguistic theory which for years was official Soviet policy.

Mirande:

Jon Mirande (1925–72). Basque poet and writer. Born in Paris, he also published stories, translations, and nonconformist articles.

Mogel:

Juan Antonio Mogel (or Moguel, 1745–1804). The best-known of a family of writers. A Gipuzkoan priest, he published numerous works on religion and on Basque grammar, but his most famous work is *El doctor Peru Abarca, catedrático de la lengua vascongada en la universidad de Basarte o diálogo entre un rústico solitario bascongado y un barbero callejero llamado Maisu Juan.* He was the uncle of writers Bizenta Antonia Mogel (1782–1854) and Juan José Mogel (1781–1849).

Ochoa de Arin:

José Ochoa de Arín was the author of a Basque catechism published in 1713.

Oihenart:

Arnaud Oihenart (1592–1667). A Basque historian, he was the first writer to publish nonreligious works in Basque. He wrote a highly praised Latin history of the Basque Country containing the earliest known description of Basque grammar. He also published a collection of proverbs and original poems in Basque.

Orixe:

Nicolas Ormaetxea "Orixe" (1888–1961). A Basque writer and translator, he was noted for his defense of a "pure" Basque uncontaminated by words from other languages.

Peñaflorida:

Xabier María de Munibe e Idiaquez, Conde de Peñaflorida (1723–85). A liberal, he created what was known as the Seminary of Vergara and contributed decisively to spreading the influence of the Enlightenment. He was one of the founders of the Real Sociedad Vascongada de Amigos del País, to which belonged the brothers Elhuyar, who managed to obtain tungsten or wolframite. He wrote and composed two operas, one in Basque and Spanish. He held various political posts.

Sancho Garcés I:

(865–925). King of Pamplona from 905 to 925. He occupied parts of Aragón and conquered land as far as La Rioja. He fought against the Moors.

Schuchardt:

Hugo Schuchardt (1842–1927). German linguist who undertook various studies of Basque. He also published research on many other languages. To him we owe the second edition of the work of Leizarraga in Strasbourg.

Schulten:

Adolf Schulten (1870–1960). German historian, archeologist, and linguist, and an expert in Ancient Iberia. He discovered the ruins of Numantia, the city conquered by the Romans, and conducted many excavations seeking the ruins of Tartessos, the Greek name for the earliest city in Western civilization. Author of a monumental work.

Stempf:

Victor Stempf (1841–1909). German linguist who published several works on Basque and defended the passive nature of the Basque verb.

Tovar:

Antonio Tovar (1911–84). Spanish philologist, historian, and linguist, professor at the University of Madrid (Universidad Complutense), he was appointed rector or president of the University of Salamanca during the dictatorship, although later he became quite critical of the regime. A man of great integrity, he published numerous works, taught in various countries, and received many awards. He had relatives in the Basque Country, which facilitated his study of the Basque language and relations with the Mitxelena family. He conducted important research on Basque and sat on many academic committees at the University of the Basque Country.

Uhlenbeck:

Christianus Cornelius Uhlenbeck (1866–1950). Dutch linguist and professor of Sanskrit and Indo-European linguistics at the University of Amsterdam. He published a number of comparative studies on Basque phonetics and grammar, and, in particular, on the passive nature of the Basque verb.

Unamuno:

Miguel de Unamuno (1864–1936). Basque by birth, professor, and later rector (president) of the University of Salamanca. Writer of literary and philosophical works, he is one of the foremost representatives of the "Generation of 98" (in 1898 Spain lost its colonies in the Philippines, as well as Puerto Rico and Cuba, to the United States, events that had tremendous repercussions in intellectual circles). Because of his opposition to the military dictatorship of Primo de Rivera in 1925, he was forced into temporary exile in France. Once back in Spain, he again became an outspoken critic of dictatorship when Franco took over the country. He wrote his Ph.D. dissertation on Basque, a language about which he knew a great deal but which he publicly criticized as inadequate for modern life.

Untermann:

Jürgen Untermann (1928–). German linguist. One of the world's foremost experts on the ancient languages of Iberia, especially Iberian.

Villasante:

Luis Villasante (1920–2000). Bizkaian priest and author of various works concerned with Basque grammar and literature. During his term as chairman of Euskaltzaindia, the academy adopted resolutions standardizing written Basque.

Zamarripa:

Pablo Zamarripa (1877–1950). Basque writer and author of various works on Basque grammar.

Zumarraga:

Fray Juan de Zumarraga (1475/1476–1548). Franciscan priest, first bishop of Mexico, and a native speaker of Basque, as shown by the long letter he wrote in Basque to his sister. He is best remembered for his defense of the indigenous Mexicans before the representatives of the Spanish Crown.

Basque Terms

Erdaldun:

In Basque, all non-Basque languages are "half languages." Accordingly, a person who speaks only a language other than Basque is an *erdaldun (erdara+dun)*, just as one who speaks Basque (and possibly some other language as well) is an *euskaldun (euskara+dun)*. There are numerous references to all these terms in the article entitled "Basques and Their Name" in this volume.

Erdara:

According to some authors, the term *erdera* actually means *erdi-era* "half-language" (*erdi* "half" + -*era*, a suffix used in some language names: *Indoeuropera* "Indo-European," *bulgariera* "Bulgarian"). From this standpoint, for a Basque speaker, other languages are not whole languages, but merely half tongues.

Euskaldun:

A speaker of Basque. See *erdaldun*.

Euskaldun Berri:

Name applied to people who have learned Basque as a second language. See *euskaldun zahar*.

Euskaldun Zahar

In contrast to *euskaldun berri*, the term applied to persons whose mother tongue is Basque and who grew up using the language. Both terms are relatively recent (used mostly after 1975) and were coined to distinguish native speakers of Basque from those who learn the language outside the home. The term *euskaldun zaharra* is usually understood as referring to native Basque speakers born in rural areas. It is not pejorative. Over time, its meaning has become more ambiguous because the situation is more complex: there are thousands of persons who have spoken Basque since childhood, but learned it in school, not at home. Such people are not referred to as *euskaldun berriak*, a term which occasionally can have pejorative connotations, although the opposite happens as well.

Latinado:

Term originally used to refer to persons who spoke or wrote in Romance, during the centuries of the Moorish occupation of Spain. There were actually two contrasting terms: *vascongado* "a Basque speaker" (*euskaldun* in Basque), and *latinado* "non-Basque speaker" (*erdaldun* in Basque).

Ultrapuertos:

Literally "beyond the mountains." The term used to refer to Basques living on the other (French) side of the Pyrenees, in what today is known as Basse-Navarre.

Vasco:

Euskaldun and *vasco* are not equivalent terms. *Euskaldun* is a Basque word used to designate persons able to express themselves in Basque, regardless of origin and place of residence. *Vasco* is a Spanish word used to designate persons who live in the Basque Country, regardless of the language they speak. There is no specific word in Basque to designate those who live in the Basque Country, although a number of neologisms have been proposed without success. Moreover, the Romance languages lack a specific word to refer to people who are able to speak Basque, regardless of where they live. In Spanish, the generic term *vasco-hablante* "Basque speaker" is used instead.

Vascones:

In principle, the Vascones would be the inhabitants of "Vasconia," although historically speaking, they were a pre-Roman people originally from present-day Navarre and lands extending south and east from there. They had a great deal of contact with the Romans.

Vascongado:

Historically, Spanish has used the terms *vascongado* and *vasco*, as well as others, to refer to the inhabitants of the Basque Country (whatever its geographical borders at the time; as explained in the introduction, *vascos* referred specifically to the inhabitants of the area of the Basque Country located on the other side of the Pyrenees, when seen from present-day Spain). Today, the term *vascongado* is rarely used and, in the mind of people who are unfamiliar with the history of our country, it seems to have pejorative overtones.

Vasconia:

> Throughout history, the Basque Country has been known by a number of different names (see note 2 in the introduction to this volume). In this volume we have respected Mitxelena's use of the term "Vasconia" in the original Spanish. It is a Latin-based word with historical connotations that has been in use since the end of the fourth century A.D., but which is almost never used by speakers when expressing themselves in Basque. Today it enjoys very limited use. Generally speaking, it refers to the territory where the Basque cultural and anthropological community lives. As such, it is the equivalent of Euskal Herria (Basque Country), the term used historically by Basque speakers and which today has replaced "Vasconia."

Vascuence:

> Spanish term used to refer to the Basque language. It used to be the common way of referring to Basque, but today has largely been replaced by *euskera*, the term imported directly from Basque.

Vizcaino:

> Spanish term for people who live in Vizcaya (Bizkaia), one of the provinces of the Spanish Basque Country. Historically, however, *vizcaino* was also used in Spanish to designate Basques in general.

CHAPTER I

The Basque Language

La lengua vasca. Durango: Leopoldo Zugaza, 1977.

I have been asked to write something by way of introduction to the Basque language as a prologue to this volume. While I feel very honored, it is an invitation that I would be quite happy to turn down. There is such an inevitable risk of repeating what has been said many times before, of boringly reiterating things that everyone knows, that if, for example, it were a speaker that I had been asked to introduce, I could be excused for resorting to the pat formula of declaring that he is so well known that he needs no introduction.

But since I am not allowed that way out, I will simply have to begin *ab ouo*, against the advice of Horace, and follow, although very incompletely, the general precepts of the law. A description as good as any other of the subject in question, and which at least has brevity in its favor, might be this: Basque is a small language that still survives—i.e., that is still used for the purposes of human expression and communication—in a similarly small community mostly found straddling the French-Spanish border at the western end of the Pyrenees, where the shores of the Bay of Biscay form a right angle.

This description is confined to today, without reference to the past. As for the question of when the language was born, we could answer, as everyone knows, that we Basques and our affairs have no dates and that our ancestry fades back—alas, all too quickly—into the darkness of time. However, the question was poorly formulated and objections must

---

All the notes in this chapter are editor's notes.

be raised. Therefore, my answer was merely intended as a momentary omission, and we shall have to return to the question later.

That introduction, despite its brevity, nevertheless requires a clarification. To say that a language is small—or for that matter, to say that it is big—is a figure of speech. No allusion is made to size in any material sense of the word because, although much has been and is still being said about the nature of languages, everyone seems to agree that they cannot be measured in terms of dimension: otherwise greatness or smallness would be much less concrete and too subjective. A small language is simply a language that has few speakers, comparatively speaking, just as a large language is merely one that is used by many. To take as our standard of measure the space occupied by such populations would be more confusing. Remember the apparent enormity of certain Hyperborean languages, which on world language maps are stretched way beyond reality due to the distortion of cylindrical projection. It takes an effort to realize that those immensities are occupied only by a handful of nomads.

Basques and Their Language

We should perhaps invert these terms, Basques and their language, and say instead the Basque language and those that possess or speak it, since the language has in itself its own denomination, by which I mean that it possesses and is entitled to its name, whereas the Basque people must make do with a derived, reflected one. The fact is that the people who spoke Basque down through the ages called it *heuskara*. I am using the earliest recorded form, since its *h*, due to one of the whims of fashion, has regained its lost distinction[1]: in Guipúzcoa today, but not in centuries past, the majority say *euskera*. A Basque, a native of the country, is simply an *euskaldun*—one who "has" Basque, i.e. a Basque speaker. This creates, and for many years now has continually created, a serious problem: what do we call the descendents of Basques, the children born in Vasconia, all those who wish to be Basques but who don't speak the language? To include them it would be necessary to extend the real, current meaning of the word *euskaldun* far beyond its etymology—either that or create a neologism, which some consider unnecessary. But this only means that it would be unnecessary in an ideal situation in which *euskaldun* and *vasco* were coextensive, a situation which, however desirable, is not a reality today.

And it is not only a question of name. Indeed, it is fair to say that if we Basques exist today as such, as a community or people, it is above all thanks to the survival of our language—to its presence or, at least, its proximity. It is a legacy that we received at birth, without seeking it or working for it, and it is not sufficient for us to tacitly fail to accept it if what we want is to reject it; instead, we must actively shed it, something that can't be done without a sense of pain, if the person is at all sensitive—witness the case of Unamuno. This is not at all to underrate the value of other (political, governmental, socioeconomic, cultural) factors that have had great, and sometimes decisive, influence on the shape and survival of this people. But a people cannot exist without self-awareness, whether direct or reflected, and a core or secondary part of this awareness has always been the factor of language.

This is not, however, to affirm that our language has molded our awareness or, as is sometimes said, that it has shaped our mentality, for better or worse—on the contrary. That is at best a dubious hypothesis, certainly much more dubious than the one that sees in our language innumerable reflections of our past as a people, of our history. Actually it is much simpler and much more immediate. A language, besides being a means of expression and communication—the entire or partial vehicle of a people's culture, not merely an element of that culture—is also something much more external and equally significant. It is a sign of identity. All languages are, or can be, depending on the circumstances, both a nexus—a bond of union for those who speak it—and a barrier for those who do not. To overvalue it as a banner, to exhibit it with ostentation, can be dangerous and reprehensible, but to overlook that real, though accessory, function would be to disregard the evidence. My opinion therefore is not very different from that of people who, in a current controversy, maintain that it is not by chance that the "borders" (however imprecise and variable depending on the person) of what today and in recent times is known as Vasconia or the Basque Country, encompass the Basque-speaking region, leaving outside it those areas that at one time spoke and used Basque, but lost it several centuries ago.

On the Question of Names

Without going so far as agreeing with the common Basque dogma (noted by Barandiarán) that everything that has a name exists, it does seem natural to think that this distinguishing feature, which both unites and separates and about which everyone is aware, must have a name—and one that is equivalent to an emblem or flag. As we know, this is a universal phenomenon and there is no proof that there has ever been anything similar to the state of linguistic promiscuity that is sometimes imagined. Although switching languages is more like a change of register than a change of mentality—a different way of thinking and feeling—a bilingual or even plurilingual person can modulate his melody going from one instrument to another, mixing words and even phrases in one language or the other, but not without having to wonder, if at some point he stops to think, whether it is the flute or violin that he is playing or is going to play next.

We have mentioned the name that the Basques give to their language; but we should add that, just as Vascuence or Romance (which in Latin would be *vasconice* and *romanice*) is quite realistically what Coseriu has called a "nominalized adverb"—"(to speak) in the Basque manner," or something of that sort—the same thing is true of its opposite, *erdara*, which comprises all other languages, although the term is commonly used, depending on the period and place, to designate the neighboring language whose presence is most manifest. This does not (and I stress this for sensitive souls) necessarily mean that we Basques have been or are so short on intelligence that we can't distinguish between languages whose differences are readily apparent. In fact, to show the total pointlessness of this kind of reasoning, we could take advantage of this fact to turn against Unamuno his famous argument (which was quite unoriginal, by the way, apart from being based on ignorance of facts, which by that time were public knowledge, and on the distortion of others that he knew perfectly well) about the words for "tree" in general and for the different species of trees. With *erdara* we would have elevated Basques to the supreme level of abstraction represented by the concept of "outlandish language" in general![2] Worldwide, however, it is not at all rare for human groups to capture in one term all or many of the languages around them and even the peoples who use them (e.g., German *welsch* ["foreign"], etc.). And although people are right in believing that *erdara* (related to *erdi* "half") originally meant "(to) half (speak)," this should not sound more discourteous to our neighbors than the fact that in Russian, for example, *némec* "German" is related to *nemój* "mute."

What has never been explained satisfactorily is how *euskara*, on the one hand, and *vascos* (Latin Vascones, accented on the first syllable) on the other, might be related. There is a superficial resemblance (i.e., the presence in both of the consonant group *sk*), but it would be necessary to justify in detail the remaining correspondences. Thus, it would appear that the most prudent course today is to think, along with Tovar, that they are actually different names with different origins. The one, in Basque, is the name we gave ourselves, related perhaps to that of the Aquitaine tribe Ausci,[3] while the other would be the Indo-European name given to us by some of our neighbors. This is also a frequent occurrence in the world. The second name could be attested to in its most ancient form in the *ba(r)scunes* legend on coins possibly minted in the present-day territory of Navarra.

This is more interesting because closer to us is the problem of the duality of *vascongado*, a word current among us in the past, and *vasco*, which in written records clearly designated an Ultrapuertos [over the mountains]—i.e., a French Basque. Some say that *vasco* is recent and came from France, but J. Garate noted that, in clear opposition to *latinado* "Romance speaker," it appears as early as Lope García de Salazar. At any rate, it would be worth doing a historical study to ascertain its exact origin and also its different meanings. Other names, particularly *vizcaino*, should be studied as well.

Now then, the present situation is clear, even though the details leading up to it are not—except for the most recent past, with which we are familiar because we have lived through it, unhappy though the memory may be for some. Today *vasco* is the neutral term that everyone uses normally; on the other hand, it may occasionally be loaded with emotional meanings, but it does not connote them necessarily. The term that is definitely marked, and not always favorably, is *vascongado*, a word that has become archaic, except possibly in a small number of pat expressions.

These processes are almost complete and should be lamented, because the lost duality would have allowed more subtle distinctions, but the tide can hardly be turned at this point. A similar phenomenon is happening with *vascuence*, the ordinary Spanish name for Basque, which despite its historical neutrality now sounds pejorative to many people. Unless I am quite mistaken, today even in Castile *vasco* is replacing *vascuence*: *hablar (en) vasco*, *saber vasco* ("to speak (in) Basque,") etc. Here I merely take note and will leave for later my considerations on the original meaning of *vascongado*.

Scientific Interest of Basque

Even though it will mean a further delay before addressing the core issue, I feel I must give a preliminary explanation of the (not always well-understood) reasons why, in the past and present, major linguists and other researchers have always felt such interest in the Basque language and, secondarily, in other aspects of our cultural heritage. I say secondarily because as far back as the early nineteenth century, Wilhelm von Humboldt plainly saw, somewhat to his surprise, that the Basque language was by far the most faithful, if not the most easily interpreted, witness to our past. Other aspects which were noticed less because they were mixed up with apocryphal traditions, have turned out to be more productive, thanks especially to the work of Barandiarán, but I do not think that the situation has changed essentially.

First of all, we must do away with a number of myths. The great majority of linguists agree, I believe, that we do not have any measure whatsoever for determining how developed or backward a language is. The richness and regularity of the morphological apparatus is not a sign of perfection, as previously thought by linguists such as our own Astarloa, nor does simplicity (always offset by other complications) constitute a sign of progress, as maintained for example by Unamuno, following Jespersen. There are no primitive languages in the world; at most, there are languages spoken by primitive peoples. It is true that at certain moments in history and due to extralinguistic circumstances, some languages are less well suited than others to meet the needs of a particular type of civilization. But such momentary deficiencies, which normally lie in the lexicon (a component of the language that is far from central), can be rapidly overcome by resorting to neologisms or loan words, if the speech community feels the need.

A very widespread myth is that there are languages that are more "difficult" than others (Basque being one of them)—a myth as absurd as the one that says there are languages that are more "philosophical" or more "progressive" than others. Because with these issues, everything depends on standpoint. For whom is one language more difficult than another? Speakers of a Romance language always find it easier to learn another language from their same group; they might even find it easier to learn a non-Romance Indo-European language than a non-Indo-European one, provided at least that it is within the same area of Western culture. What has yet to be demonstrated is that a person from China or Japan would find it easier to learn Portuguese or Rumanian than to learn Basque. The one would probably be just as hard as the other.

Turning now to the age of languages, I will try to explain, hopefully more successfully than before, something which is elementary and therefore evident to all linguists. It is rational, because chronologically true, to affirm that Hittite or Mycenaean Greek are older than Latin or the Slavic languages, since they can be documented back to the second millennium before our era; or that, by definition, Plato's Greek is older than modern Greek. From this point of view, by the way, our language is not very ancient, as we shall see later. A different matter, but one that is also at least somewhat rational, is the question of archaic languages. For example, it is usually said, because there are elements for comparison, that Lithuanian, spoken approximately since 1500, is an archaic language, because it retains well-preserved features of ancient Indo-European languages—recorded in very remote centuries—although it has also innovated profoundly in other respects.

Now then, with regard to ultimate origin, any language is in itself as old as any other. The dawn of human language is infinitely remote, and it is only as of the first appearance of writing—yesterday morning, as it were—that we can try to learn something about particular languages. But in this recent period, however immense when measured by the scale of our lives, we can parody Virchow and say that all languages come from some other language; better yet, that all states of a language come from some previous state.

Names should not be allowed to lead us astray, as has happened so many times. Since there are several Romance languages and each has its own name, we firmly believe that Spanish and French are different languages from Latin. Besides, experience has shown us, often to our chagrin, that we cannot understand a Latin text without long instruction, despite our familiarity with one or more Romance languages. On the other hand, since now there is practically (discounting our ever-present friend "diglossia") only one Greek language and it is still called Greek, we tend to think that ancient and modern Greek are merely variants of the same language. However, a high school student studying Greek will probably stumble just as much in translating Thucydides as an Italian student will in translating Livy. Similarly, we Basques, and even the linguists among us, would no doubt be very hard pressed to translate a "Basque" text from 2,000 years ago, if we had the good fortune of coming across one. What would have happened with many of our well-known *Refrains and Proverbs* from 1596, if they had not been accompanied by a Romance version? Take number 233, for example: *Yquedac ta diqueada.* Just as Lorca said of a line by Ruben Darío (*púberes caneforas que portan el acanto*, where *que* is the outstanding word due to its clarity), here the only thing we can understand is *ta*.

So where does this interest that we were talking about come from? From the fact that Basque, while neither more ancient nor more modern than its neighboring languages in absolute terms, is indeed older in a relative sense. It is more ancient in situ—it is a resident that settled much earlier in this part of Europe—because the western and southern reaches of this area experienced two decisive events. First, in a long, largely obscure process, the area was almost completely Indo-Europeanized, and later, closer to our time, there occurred the Romanization of the south, with the spread of Latin that accompanied the Roman conquest.

In the path of these two floods, the only point not inundated was Basque, a lone island which, together with the fragmentary, poorly understood testimony of a few groups of inscriptions, enables us to gain an idea of what the linguistic landscape of these European regions might have been like not only prior to their Romanization, but prior even to their Indo-Europeanization. For this reason, and ever since the Romantics discovered that relationships between languages can help to fill in the prehistorical outline of countries and peoples, scholars have attempted again and again, as we shall see below, to find the genetic relationships that might link our language to other languages or language groups.

It is not that Basque, typologically speaking, has anything particularly surprising, marvelous, or freakish about it. It does, however, have its own, sufficiently peculiar physiognomy to merit study in its own right. And above all, for those interested in contact between languages, it affords an opportunity to see in detail how a small language, subjected for at least two millennia to the constant pressure of neighboring languages that had all external advantages in their favor, could remain faithful to its ancient type, despite the many and profound changes it has undergone. And finally, discovering the nature and scope of these changes is not the least of the fuels firing enthusiastic research into the language.

Borders

As noted by Lafon and repeated here above, the Basque speech community is in the heart of Vasconia, but its borders do not coincide (nor have they ever done so in the centuries whose history is best known to us) in any precise way with any political or administrative frontiers. The area of the speech community is, as we said, quite small: Lafon allows it 170 kilometers from east to west, and 60 kilometers from north to south. Nor is it easy, given the lack of even approximate statistics, to calculate the number of Basque speakers. Roughly speaking, the number could be guessed to stand at more or less half a million.

Undoubtedly there are Basque speakers dispersed throughout the world, particularly in America, but the native soil, which is what interests us most, comprises the *Pays Basque Nord* in the French department of the Pyrénées-Atlantiques (excluding, as far as Basque is concerned, Bayonne, Biarritz, and Anglet), a good part (center and east) of Vizcaya, small smatterings in Alava, the north of Navarra and, if we discount some enclaves, all of Guipúzcoa. Accordingly, one can see that Guipúzcoa lies, without any merit whatsoever, in the very heart of the speech community and for many centuries has had no border zones. This does not mean that no other languages are spoken within its territory. The use of other written and official languages is public knowledge, in particular the existence of a Gascon colony of obvious social and economic influence in San Sebastián and environs. Given the small size of the Basque speech community, it is necessary to believe that, throughout the country, many people were at least bilingual. We may wonder how well many people in the sixteenth century were able to understand the plays put on in Spanish in Rentería and Lesaca, for example, but we cannot doubt that such plays took place. Furthermore, it appears evident that bilingualism created among the population an arguably gentle, but vertical class or cultural barrier, although not a horizontal or geographical one. But bilingualism must be seen as working both ways, and therefore no documentary proof substantiates the idea that St. Ignatius Loyola, to cite a controversial case, could have not known or forgotten his mother tongue. The cultural aristocrats of Guipúzcoa (and Peñaflorida is an eminent example) were distinguished because they spoke one or various other languages apart from their own, not because they knew and used only such languages.

Parts of western Vizcaya, broad areas of Navarra, and some parts of Alava were undoubtedly Romance speakers from very early times— definitely ever since writing became sufficiently available. In compensation, so to speak, we know that in the Middle Ages, Basque was found throughout La Rioja, in the valleys of the Tirón and the Oja (conclusive evidence for Ojacastro, dating as late as the thirteenth century, has been discovered by Merino Urrutia), and throughout the modern province of Burgos. As for the Pyrenees, there appears to be no direct evidence, but Corominas's systematic study of place names clearly supports the hypothesis that Basque-type speech forms were found well into the Middle Ages in the high Pyrenean valleys, far to the east of present-day

Vasconia. To the west, it cannot be said that Basque place names disappeared entirely beyond the historical Basque-speaking area, but it is true that the cut-off here is much more pronounced, so that what predominates are poorly determined place names of a vaguely Indo-European nature, featuring a more recent Latin layer. The most natural explanation is that the difference in density from one end to the other must be due to differences in the date of language change.

The history of the decline of Basque is too well known to describe it again in detail here. By around 1500, and possibly much earlier, there must have been no Basque-speaking areas left south of the Ebro River. In Alava, bearing in mind that Romance predominated in its capital as early as the sixteenth century, it is logical to think that by the eighteenth century, Basque must have lost much ground, as Odón de Apraiz claims. In Navarra, such losses started mostly in the nineteenth century. In clear contrast to this shrinkage in the south, the northern borders have remained stable for hundreds of years. It should be noted that there, until relatively recent times, the competing language was, in different forms, Gascon, a sharply differentiated dialect of Occitan.

The Antiquity of Basque

The oldest vestiges that we have of Basque are proper names: place names and, especially, names of persons and divinities that appear in Aquitaine inscriptions from the Roman period. They have been found from the Valley of Arán to the Basque Country of today, represented by a votive inscription near Tardets whose testimony seems irrefutable. To repeat once again oft-cited examples, women's names such as *Andere* or *Nescato*, and men's names such as *Cison* or derivatives of *Sembe-*, are inseparable from modern Basque *andere*, "woman"; *neskato*, "girl"; *gizon*, "man"; and *seme*, "son." In addition to nouns such as these, there are also adjectives and suffixes with exact correspondences to modern Basque. Until recently, it was not certain that proper names of this type could be claimed south of the frontier, but a few years ago the Lerga epigraph in Navarra added a few names to the list. *Ummesahar*[4] is the clearest example.

This is the first indisputable proof that in the territory of the Vascones an ancient form of Basque was spoken in the first centuries of our era. Of course, indirectly, through inference, no one doubted this before, although it is very possible that as early as the beginnings of Roman rule the territory was no more monolingual than medieval or modern

Navarra. Its southern region was subjected to heavy Celtiberian influence—that is, to influence from an Indo-European language—before the Roman Conquest.

This is actually one of the few things that no one has doubted, and curiously enough, it was probably a name—that of the Vascones—that exorcised all skepticism, for everything else has been the subject of debate. For example, Schulten, that excellent scholar and fierce interpreter of classical writings, postulated, followed by Bähr, a movement of Basque-speaking Vascones westward and then to the north, meaning that the Basque spoken beyond the Pyrenees would have been, in contrast to all ancient testimony, a consequence of medieval invasions. Moreover, the historical state of affairs in the territory of the Vardulii and Caristii would be the result of the change in language brought about by the Vascon expansion.

The arguments used to support this theory are not very strong. If we leave aside the written records, which say nothing of what such authors try to make them say, there are, first of all, proper names of Indo-European origin, as noted by Gómez-Moreno. The proof, however, is incomplete, because it tells us nothing of Guipúzcoa and very little about Vizcaya, and besides is excessive, since in part of Navarra the same names are found as on the plains of Alava. Nor should we forget that personal names are highly subject to fashion.

Finally, there is the word *vascongado*: the so-called Provincias Vascongadas or Basque Provinces would thus, by virtue of their etymology, be "Vasconized" rather than Vascas or Basque. I do not know, and am sure that nobody knows, the exact reasons for this denomination, but there is no need whatsoever to deny that its formation might have run parallel, though with a morphological particularity that no one has taken the trouble to explain, to that of the Romanzado dialect in Navarra and, let me add on my own, to that of Navarzato in Roncal and that of Sarracinatu in a document found at San Juan de la Peña listing the boundaries of the monastery of San Martín de Cercito. To what extent can this show Saracen influence in the one case and Navarrese influence within Navarra, in the other? The toponymy of Romanzado is, moreover, in large part Basque, despite the name of the dialect.

Everything will remain doubtful until and unless much more direct evidence is found, if that ever happens. What there is, however, does clearly emphasize certain fundamental facts, which should be stressed. In contrast to what happened with the Cantabrians, the Romans do not seem to have encountered great resistance on their drive into what we can suppose were Basque-speaking areas. The Romanization of the region, which had as nearby centers the two major urban nuclei (the two Iruñas: Pompaelo among the Vascones and Veleia among the Caristii), managed to drive deep into some areas, but must have been very slight in others to judge by the lack or extreme scarcity of archeological remains in part of Vizcaya, in Guipúzcoa, in the north of Navarra, and in the French Basque Country.

For all its weaknesses however, the Romanization process would undoubtedly have led, had it continued without interruption, to an inexorable end: to Latin replacing the language of the country and the disappearance of Basque. But early on—perhaps as early as the middle of the third century—the efficiency of the imperial apparatus began to wane in this region, and its inhabitants, once peaceful and submissive, gradually began to actively oppose the economic organization imposed by Roman rule. That this resistance finally became open, victorious rebellion against the Visigoths (and Franks) is well known: see the article by M. Vigil and A. Barbero, *Boletín de la Real Academia de Historia*, 156 (1965), 271–339. And so the Basque language, by that time undoubtedly reduced to its last few stalwarts, was given the possibility first to survive and then to expand widely during the dark centuries of the Middle Ages.

Basque Structure

After this historical digression and before discussing prehistory per se (which, in the case of language, can only be based on comparison studies), we must provide a true internal picture of our object, having concluded the nominal, external description that has occupied us thus far. This way, we will at least have something that we can compare to other things.

The task, however, is a thorny one. If all attempts at portraying Basque inevitably seem superfluous and irritating to those who speak the language, it will certainly not be easy to give to non-Basque speakers a picture that is at least clear, though naturally incomplete, of something as complex as a language always is, without going into technicalities with which such readers are obviously unfamiliar. Using technical jargon may sometimes be an extravagance, a deceptive veil cast in order to keep the layman from looking into seemingly unfathomable mysteries; but jargon is also, in large measure, a strict necessity if we wish to describe succinctly and accurately what would otherwise have to be expressed in roundabout ways that are tiresome and ambiguous.

As we know, even restricting ourselves to the present day, at bottom there is not just one Basque language, but a number of dialects and varieties. Remember that ancient Greek is also known by the single name of Greek, despite its profound internal differences. For the moment, to simplify we will look basically at the central forms of Basque—those close to the Guipuzcoan dialect.

It is worth repeating once again that language is a system of signs and that every sign has two facets: the signifier and the signified. That is, a sequence of units that can be perceived by the ear as different or identical to each other and that are differential because they have a function: serving as the support for distinguishing something that is not perceived by any of the senses—i.e., meanings.

The set of these differential units (or put more solemnly, the phonological system of the language) is, in the central dialects, of a relatively simple type which we could say is almost Spanish: five vowels, a set of unvoiced occlusives (p, t, k) plus lax-voiced occlusives (b, d, g), two rolled r's, one soft and the other hard (r, rr), etc. Where Basque displays greater extravagance is in the sibilants, because there is a Spanish-like apical s, which is written as s, and another predorsal s, pronounced holding the tip of the tongue low, written z and very similar to the French voiceless s in *sens, poisson*, etc. And together with these fricatives there are the corresponding affricates, represented by tz (which is pronounced like the z in German: *ziehen, Zeit*, etc.), and ts, plus two ch sounds, today written as x (roughly similar to ch in the French *cheval*, or to sh in the English *shy*), and tx, pronounced like the Spanish ch in *chaval, chico*, or the ch in church. There is an aspiration, represented by h, known today only in the northern dialects, but which once must have been absolutely general: Aquitaine *Aherbelste deo, Hautense, Harbelex, Harsi, Herauscorritsehe; Narhunges, Abisunhar*, in Lerga; *Bahaheztu*, mod. *Maeztu, Uhulla*, mod. *Ula, Hurizahar, Harriolha*, etc., in Alava in 1025.

Although, in theory, one can never hold too many cards in linguistic reconstruction, there is always the risk—an inevitable risk for reasons of principle—of holding too few. In any case, one is inclined to think that, with a slight margin for error, proto-Basque, the theoretically single ancestor of the historical Basque dialects, must also have had a simple phonological system made up of under thirty units. This means that the complexities of the modern Souletin dialect,[5] with its *ü* and its nasal vowels, its voiced sibilants and aspirated occlusives (*ph, th, kh*, like English *pit, time, cat*), can be explained, and indeed are explained, on the basis of a simpler system. Moreover, the phonemes of the reconstructed system, in addition to being relatively small in number, were subject to severe restrictions on their distribution within words. There was no initial *r* (thus the preceding vowel in *errota* "mill," perhaps due to its origin from Spanish *rueda*, and similarly with *arrazoi* "reason" (Spanish *razón*), *Erroma* "Rome" (Spanish *Roma*, etc.), and consonant groups such as *br, kl*, etc. were probably lacking. There are reasons for thinking that the configuration of the ancient syllables is well represented by words such as *a(h)o* "mouth," *(h)andi* "big/ large," *begi* "eye," *bi(h)otz* "heart," *esker* "thank/grace," *gordin* "raw," *oin* "foot," *sabel* "abdomen," *urde* "pig," etc.

Things become complicated, as always in linguistics, when we turn from phonology to grammar. It is a true but painful fact that the phonological typology of languages—speaking now of a classification not based on community of origin, of the same type as the botanical taxonomy of Linnaeus—is much more advanced, due to its simplicity or one-sided units, than the general typological classification founded on grammatical structure and secondarily on the lexicon, which still today is, like a toddler, just taking its first steps.

Therefore I shall have to cling, for want of a better option, to a rather blurry, inadequate notion handed down from the Schlegels, and say that generally speaking Basque is, like Turkish for example, one of those languages that are still called agglutinative. Remember that agglutinative languages, like isolating, inflective, and fusional languages in the same repudiated but oft-used classification, constitute a kind of ideal model and are never actually found.

Whereas in a language such as Latin, one of the so-called "inflective" tongues, we find in the nominative plural *porta-e* "doors," *domin-i* "masters, lords," *templ-a* "temples," *host-es* "enemies," *arcu-s* (long *u*) "bows, arches," etc.—different endings expressing identical grammatical categories (here, number and case simultaneously). In an agglutinative language that behaves as it is supposed to, there should be only one unvarying form as the expression of a category, and only one category as the content of each. From among the many Basque examples of this, we could choose *bizar-dun-a-ren-a-re-ki-n* with "the one belonging to the bearded man," literally "beard-having-one's one-with," a string of uniform, univocal signifiers, each determining the previous one and, in turn, modified or determined by the following signifier.

This means that Basque is a language with declensions, but nevertheless that it practically has only a single one, which is always formed with the same suffixed items, unlike Latin and Russian, for example, which have various and very different declensions, depending on the class of nominal or pronominal stem. Verb conjugations or inflections are also regularized, although not so much as the nominal declension or inflection.

We should note in passing that word formation devices are abundant in Basque. When speakers resort to loan words, it is often out of convenience or laziness rather than due to a lack of possibilities in Basque. On the one hand, there are abundant, highly particular, nominal and verbal derivational suffices (meaning "inclined to," "full of," "-'s," "abstract quality," etc.), and word composition continues to be quite productive, as in Greek and the Germanic and Slavic languages, as opposed to the Romance languages which, like Latin before them, only keep alive the procedure in certain, comparatively few types. For example, *oilasko-izterra* "chicken thigh" is the way we normally express what in Spanish would be *muslo de pollo* lit. "thigh of chicken." Or, to repeat an example that I find very suggestive of the difference between matter and form, the term *mano de almirez* "pestle," literally "hand of mortar," was translated in 1562 as *almeriz-mano* "pestle hand."

Ergative Constructions

Ergative constructions are a core grammatical feature that Basque shares with many other languages, present and past, but none of which are very close at hand geographically. Indeed, I believe that we would have to go as far as the Caucasus to find our nearest neighbors. Accordingly, if we want to relieve the expression "ergative" of its pompous impenetrability, we had better use examples.

Gizona etorri da is "the man has come" (Lat. *Homo uenit*), but the exactly parallel expression *gizona ikusi du* is not "the man has seen it/her/him" (Lat. *Homo uidit*, expressed in Basque as *gizona-k ikusi du*), but rather "(someone) has seen the man" (Lat. *Hominem uidit*). In other words, what in translation is the subject of an intransitive verb (*gizon-a* lit. "man-the") is not expressed in the same way as the subject of a transitive verb, since the latter needs an additional suffix -*k* marking the active or "ergative" case (both meaning the same in pseudo-Greek). Instead, the subject of an intransitive verb is expressed in the same way as a direct object. If we are intent on finding parallel versions for transitives, we could look at the passive transformation: "the man has come" which is similar to "the man was seen," but "it was seen by the man." This gave rise to the myth (widespread among linguists a few years back and always frowned upon by Basques, who, due to deep psychological mysteries, find it offensive) that the Basque verb is passive in nature. This is a myth because, as has been known at least since Saussure, there must be a minimum of two terms in order to have an opposition. That is, there can be no passive if there is no active, nor a masculine if there is no feminine. Both of these—the lack of grammatical gender contrast in nouns and the absence of a voice distinction in verbs—occur together in Basque. And I can safely assure those who worry from lack of personal experience that neither the one nor the other is sufficient to cause the sky to fall for lack of support.

Simplifying things somewhat, there are three cases of what can be called real grammatical declension, in contrast to others, since these three are related to the auxiliary verb in a way that can truly be called concordance in person and number. First there are the two that have already been mentioned: the nominative, or inert case, which has no formal marker, or which, if you will, has a zero marker, and expresses (I mean always in terms of translation) the subject of an intransitive verb or a nominal predicate (*etxe-a berri-a da* "the house is new," *mendi-a zabal-a da* "the mountain is wide," with an article; or without one: *iru mendi dira* "(they) are three mountains"), and the direct object of a transitive verb (*etxea/ mendia ikusi du* "(s/he) saw the house/mountain"). Next there is the active or ergative case, characterized by the suffix *-k*, denoting the subject of a transitive verb (*gizon-a-k ikusi du* "the man saw it," *iru seme-k erosi dute* "three sons bought it"). Finally there is a dative case, marked by *-ri* or *-i*, depending on whether it follows a vowel or a consonant, denoting the indirect object of verbs of both kinds (*gizon-a-ri* "to/for the man," *iru gizon-i* "to/for three men").

The Basque Verb

What I have just said leads us almost by the hand to a discussion of the Basque verb—a phenomenon which to the minds of some is so perfect a product of the collective spirit that only its intangible nature has kept it from taking its place among the seven wonders of the world, while to others it is an unwieldy, clumsy instrument because it is so complicated.

Let us look at the facts, leaving aside value judgments which can only have, at most, subjective value within the realm of personal tastes and preferences.

The Basque verb is, to say it in a single word, pluripersonal. If we have not lost all memory of our boring grammar classes, perhaps we will remember that famous rule, valid for Indo-European languages in general and also for others, according to which the verb must agree with its subject in number and person. If in "The man comes" we change the subject from "the man" to "two men," then we will have to change the verb as well ("come," not "comes"), a change that does not occur if we change the direct object ("He bought two houses" has the same verb form as "He bought a house").

Now then, the Basque verb agrees in number and person not only with the subject, but also with the direct object, and (obligatorily in the Spanish Basque Country) with the indirect object. Thus the auxiliary verb constitutes a kind of cipher or compendium of the sentence, indicating its general direction and the number and grammatical nature of the nominal or pronominal items making up its fundamental structure. Put the other way around, in a nominal phrase such as the proverb[6] noted by Lafon in another variant, *zozo-a-k bele-a-ri ipurbeltz* "'Black ass' (said) the magpie to the crow," there is an implicit tripersonal verb such as *dio* or *zion* lit. "s/he it says (to her/him)," or "s/he it said (to her/him)."

Looked at another way, "(the) father has spoken" is *aita mintzatu da*, but when we introduce an indirect object such as *seme-a-ri* "to the son," we have to transform *aita mintzatu da + semeari* into *aita semeari minzatu zaio*. In other words, we have to replace the unipersonal *da* "is" with *zaio* "is-to/for-her/him." If, to the sentence *aita-k txapela galdu du* "father has lost the beret," a dative of interest is added such as *seme-a-ri* lit. "son-the-to/for," the sentence becomes *aitak txapela galdu dio semeari* lit. "father-the beret-the lost has-it-to him son-the-to/for" "the father lost his son's beret." That is, the tripersonal auxiliary *dio* "it-to her/him" is used instead of the bipersonal *du*.

If anyone thinks that this might introduce unfathomable complications, we had better say at once that there are circumstances that impose severe restrictions on such a possibility. First of all, the auxiliary forms of the verb are the result of juxtaposition in a fixed order of a small number of simple elements: *di-gu-zu* lit. "it$_{acc}$-us$_{dat}$-you$_{erg}$ (V)" is to *di-zki-gu-zu* "them$_{acc}$-us$_{dat}$-you$_{erg}$ (V)" as *di-zu-gu* "it$_{acc}$-you$_{dat}$-we$_{erg}$ (V)" is to *di-zki-zu-gu* "them$_{acc}$-you$_{dat}$-we$_{erg}$ (V)," etc. Moreover, the formation of certain tenses is, in the precise sense of the word, almost isomorphic with others, so that once some quite unabstruse rules have been learned, a speaker can go univocally from one form to another: from *di-gu-zu* to *zen-i-gu-n* "you$_{erg}$-it$_{acc}$-us$_{dat}$-past (V)," and from *di-zki-gu-zu* to *zen-i-zki-gu-n* "you$_{erg}$-them$_{acc}$-us$_{dat}$-past (V)," etc. And furthermore, in practice it all boils down to knowing two verbs, the intransitive and transitive auxiliaries. Beyond these, there are only a very small number of "irregular" verbs, whose pattern is in any case very similar to that of the auxiliaries. That is, they have certain simple tenses (*d-akar-t* "it-bring-I" like *d-u-t* "it-have-I," *n-ekarr-en* "past-it-bring-I" as *n-u-en* "past-it-have-I," etc.), while in others they follow the general pattern of nominal form of the verb plus auxiliary.

This, by the way, is the greatest difference found between what we might call old (sixteenth century) Basque, and that of our days: the simple verb forms were much more numerous and complex then than now; the tenses and moods were better differentiated and, in general, the structure of the system was further removed from the patterns of neighboring languages. Speaking of the latter, we should say that the difference between Spanish *se lo he dado* and *eman di-o-t* "I gave it to him" is not as astronomical as might seem at first glance. At bottom, it is all a question of the obligatory incorporation of pronominal indices into the verb, an incorporation that supposes that the order of these indices is fixed and that they cannot be separated by anything else—negation, for example. We should also note that Spanish, which like Gascon not only can but must employ a construction like *se lo he dado al hijo* "I have given it to my/the son," where *se* refers to and anticipates the indirect object noun phrase *al hijo* "to my/the son," is so to speak halfway between Basque (*seme-a-ri eman di-o-t*, lit. "son-the-to give have-it$_{acc}$-him$_{dat}$-I$_{erg}$") and normal French, where *je le lui ai donné au fils* would be completely ungrammatical. Quite another matter are the changes wreaked by colloquial language, such as *je l'ai vue à l'oeuvre, la police*, etc.

Basque Dialects

Languages, like everything else in the universe, are subject to the general law of change, although not everyone appears to understand this. Let me make it clear, though, that I am talking about unqualified change, with no evaluations attached to it such as negative connotations of decline and decay, or positive ones of progressive evolution. If the immutable landscape that we see around us is constant only in appearance, if even the mountains change (the Andes, the Alps, and the Himalayas are, according to the experts, relatively recent), then no one should be surprised by the fact that languages, like customs, institutions, and moral values, also undergo modification. Everything is a question of *tempo*, of rhythms that are more or less slow. In the case of languages, the tempo is such that the course of a human lifetime is more than enough for changes to become clearly perceptible. In my childhood and youth, the defenders of the purity of Spanish argued themselves hoarse warning people against the dangers of Gallicisms. But for many years now, English has been having the most direct effect on Spanish. Today, people say *romance* in Spanish (a loan word with an even more drastic effect since the word itself already existed in the language) when they mean *idilio*, and the word *emergencia* is considered proper and normal when before, at most, it would have been said of scuba divers. Corominas calls this a "recent, useless and vulgar Anglicism."

F. de Saussure used to say that in a community there is constant tension between the contrary forces of the bell-tower spirit, that tenacious preserver of differential peculiarities, and the spirit of exchange or interaction, which leads to convergence and leveling. Since languages change both in time and in space and there is no reason why they should undergo the same changes at different points; the outcome is inevitably the rise of different varieties, which may differ more or less, but which are nonetheless distinct. Take pronunciation, for example, and the notable differences detectable in the Spanish spoken in Spain—differences that become all the more pronounced if we include the Spanish spoken in Latin America. These differences are not only phonetic, but also phonological. There are still some backwards folks (myself included, perhaps because of my mother tongue) who insist on making a distinction between *pollo* and *poyo*, but unless some miracle happens, they will soon go the way of the dinosaurs and Tasmanians; many people now make no distinction between *casa* and *caza*, *siervo* and *ciervo*.

Next to linguistic fragmentation (e.g., the Romance languages, unidentical siblings descended from an essentially unitary Latin), we can also find the opposite phenomenon, for example, in Koine Greek, which (except in a few residual cases) replaced the ancient dialects. One would say, however, that the former process is the natural, spontaneous tendency of languages when no decisive outside factors intervene. In our case, the disintegrating factors have generally had free rein, while cohesive forces have been few and far between. What is surprising in this context is the fact that so many innovations, including some relatively recent ones (not only phonetic, but also morphologic, syntactic, and lexical), have affected the entire Basque-speaking region.

Since we lack a quantification method, we are not yet able to measure the extent of the divergences in Basque. Mutual intelligibility, which is often put forward, is an unreliable criterion due to its relativity. It is often the case that when two Basques from different regions and no knowledge of dialectology meet, they each feel that the other's speech is an incomprehensible hullabaloo; but after a short while they begin to discover to their surprise, even without the help of good old Peru who guided Maisu Juan,[7] that "all that noise" makes some sense after all and that it begins to sound surprisingly like one's own tongue.

The differences affect pronunciation both because of the number and nature of the phonemes used and because of their frequency in the stream of speech. Throughout the Spanish Basque Country there is a phoneme like the one which in Castilian is represented by *j*, but in some areas (Guipúzcoa, for example) it is very common, while in other areas it appears only in recent loan words or in a few terms such as *jaun* "lord, master," or *Jaungoiko* "God." Other differences affect morphology (Basques in Vizcaya express with the suffix *-gaz* "with" what others denote with *-ki*, *-kin*, etc.), particularly verbal morphology. Some differences are syntactic, while the greatest number (and the ones most noticeable to the layman) are lexical.

For different reasons, some of which are excusable and some not, Basque dialectology has not progressed much. Our Linnaeus was Louis-Lucien Bonaparte, who (unfortunately for us) remained merely one of the precursors, albeit a very important one, of modern dialectology. He was unable to free himself, as Menéndez Pidal says, of the "unitary concept of dialect" and from the prestige of the necessarily standardized literary varieties of the written language, which he always confused more or less with the local forms of the spoken language. What today we would call his error lay in not having seen that a dialect, in a country such as ours where variation is the result of secular sedimentation, is a macroscopic concept which, seen up close, dissolves in a gradual accumulation of individual, differentiated phenomena.

If one visits the country village by village, house by house, one does not find uniform dialects with clear lines of continuity, but only isoglosses, or the boundaries of atomized linguistic phenomena, each of which delimits its own area. Sometimes, as happens with Guipuzcoan and Vizcayan, there are many which, while not exactly superimposed, do overlap within a small space. When the contour lines on a map tend to come together, the slope is steep; similarly, where there are many isoglosses, there is a brusque change in speech. But it is more frequently the case that isoglosses—our contour lines—are more or less separate and that an observer must therefore sharpen his ears and attention to perceive the differences.

Whether good or bad, Bonaparte's classification is the only one we have and the one which, with a few small corrections, has been used by Azkue and all the rest of us. Whatever its defects, it cannot be wholly bad, since it offers a valid reference framework that no one has been able to replace with another. He was not an original or deep thinker (and therefore could not go beyond the science of his time), but Prince Louis-Lucien was nonetheless a wise, meticulous observer who recorded everything large and small. His beautiful map retains all its value, as long as we remember that reality is much more complex than the way it looks in the colored picture. To progress further, we must make the old dream come true of drawing up a linguistic atlas of Basque. The fact that we still lack such an instrument in this small, size-limited, apparently progressive country does not do us much honor.

Bonaparte's Classification

Although during the course of his life, Prince Louis-Lucien expressed different opinions, they are simply different versions of a single, fundamental idea. Given his view of dialects, it was inevitable that academic questions should arise, such as whether the Baztan dialect is a variety of High Navarrese or Lapurdian. What I mean is that these are problems that cannot be resolved satisfactorily in favor of one hypothesis or the other. Everything depends on the weight one gives to some criteria over others, since Baztanese is in a certain sense High Navarrese and Lapurdian, and in another sense it is neither. We could say that it represents, as an intermediate area, a certain intersection of traits from both dialects.

From west to east, the dialects are: Vizcayan, Guipuzcoan, Northern and Southern High Navarrese (names that only correspond to geographical coordinates, because the latter reaches further south than the former), Lapurdian (with or without Baztanese), Western and Eastern Low Navarrese, and Souletin. The last three have well-differentiated varieties in Spain: Aezcoan, Salacen, and Roncalese, respectively.

It should be noted, first, that such divisions coincide only partially with actual regions of the country. Western Guipúzcoa speaks Vizcayan, and we must discount the far northeast corner of Guipúzcoa towards Pasajes as well, which is classified as speaking Northern High Navarrese. Bonaparte, however, considered the speech of La Barranca and Ergoyena[8] as Navarrese Guipuzcoan. It is also interesting to note that the isoglosses that the prince chose as fundamental generally run from north to south or, to be more precise, from northeast to southeast. This clearly means that in ancient times the Pyrenees were not a differentiating barrier, but that, as happens further east in the Romance zone, there was direct communication between valleys running into each other on either side of the range. However, the loss of the *h* in High Navarrese is undoubtedly an old phenomenon, prior for example to the change from *au* to *ai* in many contexts at the eastern end of the country, which gave rise to *gai* "night" in Roncalese and Souletin (vs. the common *gau*), although Roncalese *aintz*, Souletin *ahüntz* "goat" (vs. the common *a(h)untz*).

There has been much speculation on the external causes of dialect boundaries, yielding at least two theories that merit consideration. The tribal divisions of antiquity can perhaps account for the High Navarrese enclave in Guipúzcoa, since according to the old geographers Oeasso was located in Vascon territory; it is less certain, but also possible, that the boundary between Guipuzcoan and Vizcayan coincided more or less with the line between the Vardulii and Caristii. The ecclesiastical divisions of the Middle Ages could also have maintained and accentuated at least the differences: until the days of Felipe II, the Baztan region formed part of the diocese of Bayonne and the Vizcayan-speaking area of Guipúzcoa belonged to the diocese of Calahorra.

Toponyms are almost the only thing that can shed light on the nature of the language that was spoken in La Rioja, and written records are sufficient to indicate that it was a western variety of Basque, closer to Vizcayan than to any other dialect. The same can be said of the language spoken on the plains of Alava. Here there is further proof, in particular a vocabulary dating from the sixteenth century, probably composed in Vitoria, which gives a sufficient picture of an autonomous, well-differentiated, but clearly Western dialect.

Unfortunately and irremediably, there are woefully few studies or documents about the Basque spoken in the Americas from the sixteenth century onward, among other reasons because it appears to be the case that the co-existence there of Basques from different regions gave rise to common or unified varieties based predominantly on one dialect or another. But there are only a very few studies of Basque in the United States, all quite recent.

In response to Bonaparte's classification, some researchers (Uhlenbeck, Gorostiaga) have suggested a two-part division, with Vizcayan on the one hand and all the other dialects on the other. This is probably an exaggeration arising from the strong individuality of Vizcayan and the rapid accumulation of isoglosses (between Legazpia and Oñate, for example) to which we referred above. But there are many "Vizcayan-like" phenomena found in larger or smaller areas of the Goyerri in Guipúzcoa and even Navarra, meaning that at most there is a difference of degree. Moreover, it can be shown that Vizcayan has gradually accentuated its particularities over the past five centuries, often due to different selections drawn from a common heritage: from *erra (erre) dezagun* or *daigun* "let's burn it," to cite one case, Vizcayan has retained only the latter possibility.

As for Guipuzcoan, it seems that it clearly ranked behind Vizcayan—not to mention Lapurdian—in its use as a written language during the sixteenth and seventeenth centuries. Only in the next century, thanks above all to Fr. Manuel de Larramendi, did it really gain literary status, which thereafter it never relinquished. Nevertheless, Larramendi, due to the great influence of his *Trilingual Dictionary* (1745), actually confused things regarding knowledge of what was really the speech of Guipúzcoa in his time. Fortunately, there are quite a few earlier fragments, and above all Ochoa de Arin's *Catechism* (1713) which, while far from being a model of style or even a lively version, is a linguistic document of incalculable value, thanks to Ochoa's faithfulness to the original and his lack of literary pretensions.

Kinship with Other Languages

I think almost everyone has the idea that the singularity of Basque lies, apart from other virtues, in its privileged-because-exceptional status as a "language island." It should be noted however that this status might be exceptional here, in this part of the world, but if we look at all the known languages, present or past, it is very far from being a unique case. One of the most serious defects of the genetic classification of languages is that it is not at all complete. As happens with people, a family relationship can be shown provided that it is close enough, but it would be very difficult for us to prove that we are *not* related, say, to William the Conqueror.

Before embarking on a discussion of (necessarily remote) genetic relationships, there are two prior tasks to be taken care of for reasons of method and because they will help us to recover at least some of the fundamental traits of ancient Basque, or the language spoken some 2,000 years ago.

First we need to distinguish what is most recent and due simply to what we could call affinity—i.e. to the influence or interference of neighboring languages. It is a well-established fact that languages of the same or different origin that occupy neighboring areas gradually take on numerous common features over the centuries. In our case, one immediately thinks of the uninterrupted effect of Latin and its successors, the Romance languages, over the past two millennia.

From them we have taken, above all, innumerable words. Many were incorporated quite long ago, and we are still borrowing them. But concerning a pre-Latin Indo-European influence, there is surprisingly little strong proof in the Basque lexicon. Latin-Romance interference is also apparent in less tangible aspects of the language. We have a definite article which bears the plural in nouns, but rather than preceding the noun, it is attached behind as a suffix (as in Rumanian or the Scandinavian languages), clearly because of the suffixing (as opposed to prefixing) nature of the language; we have compound tenses formed by a participle plus auxiliary (*etorri da* like *il est venu, er ist gekommen; ikusi du* like *ha visto, s/he has seen*), and periphrasis for the future such as *ikusiko (ikusiren) du*, similar to *ha de ver* "will see/is to see"; interrogatives and indefinite pronouns employed, more or less successfully, as subordinating particles, etc. This influence cannot be weighed or measured, even in the lexicon, which is one of the most quantifiable parts of the language. Suffice it to say that the effects have been immense, but that even so, what remains from antiquity is also immense and indeed of greater importance, in both matter and form.

We must also try to reconstruct the form and, where possible, the value of the units of the ancient system at all levels. Although still far from our goal, much progress has been made in this area through what are called internal reconstruction and comparison studies, which, in our case, are based on the divergences found between Basque dialects— divergences that are considered extremely small by comparatists. Here loan words, particularly the oldest ones (*bake* "peace," *bike* "pitch," *goru* "distaff," etc.) whose original form is well known (the accusatives *pacem, picem*, with a short *i, colum*), provide a solid basis for reconstruction.

In order to avoid getting side-tracked, I feel our examination of attempts to prove Basque's relationship to other languages should be limited to the three hypotheses that have been given the most credit by experts in the field and have even occasionally been considered as definitively proved: i.e., Iberian, Hamito-Semitic, and languages of the Caucasus.

In the case of Iberian, it is necessary to distinguish language from writing. If we are speaking about written Iberian, we are referring to an autonomous, semi-alphabetic and semi-syllabic script used in inscriptions in ancient Hispania, from Narbonne on the Levantine coast, to the Ebro Valley and part of the *meseta* (plateau). Following a lamentable history, Iberian pronunciation was deciphered a little over fifty years ago (with the exception of one sign which remains doubtful) by Manuel Gómez-Moreno. I would like to stress that today we can read [i.e., pronounce] written Iberian, but we cannot understand it. Further south, there is another system of writing (a variant of the former), but this script is even less well understood.

When it became possible to read these Iberian inscriptions, it was found, to the uncomfortable surprise of Schuchardt and others, that the uniformity of script masked a duality of language: part of the inscriptions (generally speaking, those of the interior) were written in a language that is now called Celtiberian, which was undoubtedly Indo-European. Therefore, when we say "Iberian" meaning Iberian language, we are referring to the other inscriptions found closer to the coast (probably including a good part of Andalusia) and which are harder to read, as noted above.

Basque-Iberism, or the hypothesis that historical Basque is nothing more than a recent form of Iberian, cannot be substantiated. If the claim were true, one would have to admit that Basque holds the key—however fragmentary and imperfect—to at least a partial understanding of the meaning of some Iberian texts. Unfortunately no one has been able to achieve this.

On the other hand, there are numerous coincidences that keep us from abandoning the idea that there may be some kind of relationship. True, these are formal, external coincidences, since the inscriptions cannot be read for meaning. The phonological system of Iberian (with double *r* and double *s*) could not have been very different from what we can reconstruct for proto-Basque; its syllabic structure and therefore the form of the signifiers (words or morphemes) are very similar; noun composition, to judge by proper names, was of the same type, etc. Some signifiers are shared by both languages (but we cannot be sure that they are the same signs, since we do not know their Iberian meanings), and Antonio Tovar has presented as very likely the idea that there are also coincidences in certain grammatical indices.

The hypothesis of a relationship with Hamito-Semitic languages (Acadian, Hebrew, and Arabic on the one hand; ancient Egyptian and Coptic, Lybic, and Berber dialects, etc.), defended above all by Hugo Schuchardt, today has few supporters—for good reasons, I feel. The lexical coincidences found are few and not very convincing, and it would not be easy to find, in all the languages of the world, two terms of comparison that could be structurally more different. Let us just take the example of "internal flexion," which is much more developed in Hamito-Semitic than in Indo-European languages such as Greek and Balto-Slav: the meaning *to write* is manifested in Arabic, for example, by the three consonants *ktb* (perfect *kataba*, imperfect *yaktubu*, *kitâb* "book," plural form *kutub*, etc.), with a movable vowel system that follows certain patterns or schemes depending on the noun or verb categories to be expressed. None of this is found in Basque, nor, we should stress, is it found in the Iberian inscriptions—as we can tell simply from reading their sounds, without understanding them. The African origin of this language, which so often is taken for granted, is therefore a completely gratuitous supposition. Nevertheless, it may of course be true, but in such cases it is not the doubter who bears the burden of proof, but the believer.

When we speak of languages of the Caucasus, we are referring to languages that do not belong to well-established families (like Iranian Osetic, etc.) and that are or were spoken (prior to 1864) in the Caucasus. Father Fita was perhaps the first to study the possibility of a relationship between Basque and Georgian, which has writings dating from the fifth century. More recently, A. Trombetti proposed multiple Basque-Caucasian comparisons, albeit as part of his general theory of the monogenesis of languages. In specific form, the claim of such a relationship has been defended and developed above all by C. C. Uhlenbeck, G. Dumézil, K. Bouda, and R. Lafon.

The hypothesis has in its favor a general verisimilitude. If somewhere there are to be found remains of an ancient, large language family whose western representation has been reduced to Basque, the most likely thing would be to think of the Caucasus, which is crawling with languages and is a typical zone of refuge. Typological considerations, valid simply as indications, not as proof, are also not contrary to the hypothesis. Some of the Caucasian languages (those of the northeast, above all, but also some in the south, such as Georgian and its group) immediately call to mind Basque phenomena. If we wish to be modest, we can also state this the other way around, and it will be equally true.

But from here to claiming that there is a proven genetic relationship between one language and another lies a huge gap. First of all, we should clarify the internal family relationships. The fact that some Caucasian languages are clearly related to others, such as the southern or Kartvelian languages, is beyond all doubt; that among the different groups of northern languages there are relationships, however distant, is perfectly possible and even probable. What is not clear is the nature of the connection between the languages of the north and those of the south.

Comparing lexical and grammatical items taken from one of the Basque dialects with others chosen from among any of the (approximately thirty) Caucasian languages, as has occasionally been done, might prove highly convenient, but it removes all strength from intended proof, which can only be based on probabilistic criteria—i.e., on bringing to light a sufficient number of homologies that can be accounted for only by postulating a common origin. This, however, has not been done, and indeed cannot be done. Now that, as of 1950, there has been a decline in the disastrous influence of N. J. Marr on Soviet linguistics, comparative as well as descriptive work on the Caucasian languages is moving ahead there with greater progress, especially in closely related groups, and always with good results, which in some instances have been extraordinarily brilliant, as in the case of the Kartvelian languages.

Although long, this is the only road that is viable. There is still the possibility that the linguistic complexity of the Mediterranean basin in the broadest sense will one day prove to be much greater than imagined now. If so, it will become immensely more difficult to relate Basque genetically to any other language that has survived to the present day. The ability of current methods to penetrate into the past—an ability that does not seem likely to increase a great deal—is unfortunately very limited. But there is also the possibility that luck will one day be on our side. Meanwhile, we should not forget that the truly marvelous thing in our case is not the fact that this language has no known relatives, but the tenaciousness with which a small community (that of our forefathers) has managed to keep Basque alive and in full currency despite unfavorable circumstances.

By Way of Epilogue

The fact that these pages were originally destined to appear in a collective volume entitled *Guipúzcoa* (which came out, I believe, in 1968 but was not widely sold) gave them a certain character. The idea, whether fulfilled or not, was to reach a wide readership, and this is why no bibliographical references were included. The article was also very dry and notably Guipuzcoan, as can be seen even in the Basque examples that were used. This latter feature seemed obligatory under the circumstances, although it did not correspond to my deepest convictions at the time, much less now. To me, the important thing is our country (with a capital *c*, despite the small letter with which it is written), and our country is not Guipúzcoa, or Vizcaya, etc., but something much wider and higher. And if this is clear at all, it is clear about Basque, which has given its name to Euskal Herria. In "Basques and Their Language," I mention and discuss, perhaps more allusively than directly, the uncomfortable fact that in Basque, *euskaldun* is now a highly ambiguous term, since there are Basques (too many, in fact) who are not *euskaldun*, just as there are *euskaldunak* (I myself know many) who are not, and do not wish to become, Basques. As far as language is concerned, the only advantage that a native-born Basque has over a nonnative is the greater probability of not being an *erdaldun* or, to be more precise, an *erdaldun huts*; not being *arrotz, atzerritar,*[9] or however it is said, does not give one any other privilege. And since *euskaldun* corresponds to and contrasts with *erdaldun*, I would like to know what, in the judgment of many respectable and respected experts, the fourth proportion is in *erdaldun*: *euskaldun*:: *arrotz*: X.[10]

I am not unaware that someone has written *basko* in place of the X, in an attempt at humor, although it seems to me more macabre than humorous to conjure, with forced ingenuity, a situation that is so painful to many. Nor does the invention have anything good to say about the erudition of its author, since his model can only be Dechepare, the author of the first book printed in Basque, who used *basko* in a very different way: Stempf himself stresses in his lexicon that Dechepare "favors *euskaldun*." And Stempf could stress this since the four examples that occur in the volume coincide in meaning, as can be seen from this one example: "*bascoec* bercec beçala duten *bere lengoagian* scribuz cerbait . . . material" [not translated by author]. From my own experience, I can only add to the testimony of Dechepare that back in the years of my youth (and even then it was archaic), I sometimes heard the term *baxkoak*, not without a certain pejorative note, applied to "nationalists," who were naturally Basques.

Naturally as well, it is also known that a solution was once proposed, and even accepted by many: $X = euskotar$. But this solution is now rejected or avoided, although I'm not sure exactly why. Of course it is a neologism, but not all neologisms, particularly those that are youngsters of some eighty years of age, are *eo ipso* condemnable, especially if they possess, as this one does, the excellent virtue of filling a highly uncomfortable void. I should add, to continue building up this still very incomplete dossier, that the term was prohibited from public use in 1936–37 due to the Glorious Uprising, for reasons which I imagine are probably not the same as those now raised against it. Let this be a guide in a preliminary attempt to reach the point where we can discuss the many taboos and prohibitions that exist among us without self- or otherwise-imposed restrictions.

The reference to a "recent controversy" is proof (though none was needed) of the evanescence of words, even when chiseled in writing. Suffice it to say that the controversy took place in the San Sebastián press and that it had to do with the role of Basque in the survival of the Basque phenomenon. The discussion continues, and undoubtedly will continue, even when the polemicists and their points of view are no longer the same.

In "On the Question of Names" there is a fairly unkind allusion to Unamuno that I would like to explain so as not to seem guilty without attenuation of putting into practice the maxim, "If you see a dead Moor, run him through," in imitation of one of my seniors in age, dignity, and government. It is not just that there are a number of indigenous terms for "tree," starting with *zuhamu*, which appears as far back as Dechepare, our first author; more precisely, it is the fact that Unamuno defended, with his head held high, the absurd thesis that *arbola* "tree" is not Basque but Latin, Romance, or whatever. I would like to know how a term that was used by Arrese-Beitia (*Arbola bat zan Paradisuan . . .*) and is the key word of what, ever since it was first sung, is to my mind the Basque anthem (i.e., "*Gernikako arbola*"), can be "not Basque." If we subscribe to the opinion of Unamuno, we would have to reach the patently absurd conclusion (since in this case we are talking about a language "of culture") that in the title of the well-known journal *Language, Journal of the Linguistic Society of America*, there is not—except for one proper name (America), which is common property—a single term, other than the two words *of* and *the*, that can be called "English," unless we prefer to call them "American," in line with the norms of Gallimard's *Série Noire*. The point is, *language* is no less English to the people who publish and read the journal than the word *lengoajea*, in contemporary spelling, was Basque to Dechepare.

As for the name of the *Vascones* (with a short penultimate vowel or, in other words, with the accent on the first syllable), J. Untermann has added an argument for those skeptics who doubted the equation of Tovar: its main difficulty lay in the fact that Celtiberian *b-* could hardly have corresponded at that time to Latin prevocalic *u-*; that is, to a kind of English *w*. Since the coin legend *bars-*, with an *r*, appears not to be older, but indeed more recent than *bas-*, this would suggest, with good parallels in support thereof, that the real reading underlying the inscription might be /bras-/, in which case its similarity with /was-/ would disappear completely. It is a well-known fact that Iberian script had no direct means of representing the groups of consonants that are technically known as *muta cum liquida*—i.e., *br, bl, kr, kl*, etc.—which seem to have been unknown both to the Iberian and the Basque of that period.

Concerning *latinado*, or *ladino*, the earliest record that I know of in our country was found in a document in Leire, probably from the eleventh century, which lists as among the miserly *Blasco Latinato* and *Xemeno Latinato* of Izal, in the valley of Salazar. Since there we can hardly be speaking of people whose mother tongue was Arabic, we would have to interpret these instances as the equivalents of *Erdara* and *Erdalduna*, "foreign language speaker," in records from Irache and from Artajona.

Regarding the section "Scientific Interest of Basque," I would insist on an obvious fact which nevertheless needs to be repeated, perhaps because of its very obviousness. That is, there are no languages that are more difficult or, for that matter, easier, than others, unless such terms strictly refer to definite persons or groups. And it amounts to the same thing to say "difficult" or "complicated," the latter being a very unfortunate term spotted recently in a news item that certainly could have been written more clearly and with greater exactitude.

Even so, it should be said that the search for genetic relationships (a clearly theoretical question if ever there was one) has great practical consequences. Thus, if only for this reason alone, I am not entirely in agreement with the opinion expressed among us by a certain expert researcher, according to whom interest in such minutia has disappeared from the forefront of the linguistic movement. As if curiosity about the past of languages and peoples, and above all about the past of one's own language and people, were a question of fashion!

Today there is much more information available than when I wrote those lines. There would be many titles to quote, but I shall drastically reduce my references. For reasons of (not only temporal) priority, I will mention first the book by José María Sánchez Carrión, *El estado actual del vascuence en la provincia de Navarra (1970), factores de regresión, relaciones de bilingüismo* (Pamplona, 1972); cf. also by the same author "Bilingüismo, diglosia, contacto de lenguas," *Anuario del Seminario Julio de Urquijo* (= *ASJU*) 7 (1974): 7–79. This was followed by the (so far) fundamental paper by Pedro de Yrizar entitled "Los dialectos y variedades de la lengua vasca: estudio lingüístico-demográfico," *Bol. De la R. Soc. Vasc. de Amigos del País* 29 (1973): 3–78; see as well his "Los dialectos y variedades de la lengua vasca," *ASJU* 7 (1973) 3–36. And finally, I will make reference to a very recent book that brings together in a few pages a variety of data from widely different sources: Luis C. Núñez, *Opresión y defensa del euskera* (San Sebastián, 1977). Whether a good decision or not, I have deliberately omitted works in Basque and those which, in Basque or any other language, deal with literature.

From these and other studies, one can deduce the curious fact that the number of Basque speakers has not declined, but indeed has increased: we can say with reasonable confidence that they now number over 600,000. Of course, what has increased is the total number, not the proportion, which naturally is lower.

The medieval presence of Basque in the areas of Upper Rioja and Burgos is, in my opinion and, I believe, that of many others, the result of an expansion. While this seems to me to be the most likely reason, it is nothing more than an opinion and cannot yet be demonstrated. I believe, however, that between the idea that the Basque of that area was a survivor of the first Romanization, and the theory that it was imported in the tenth century, a third possibility exists. One is entitled to think that the surplus population of Alava and neighboring areas (what has since come to be known as the Basque Country has always been a land of emigration) would seek an outlet in the basins of the Oja and Tirón, the Oca and the Arlanzón rivers, and in the district of Los Obarenes. Such movement, whether spontaneous or forced, might have begun as early as the Late Empire and continued throughout the period of the Visigoths, without interruption, in the eighth and ninth centuries. I have recently been told that this hypothesis is not at all original, and I am pleased that this is so.

This brings us to "The Antiquity of Basque," and for once I am going to refer the reader to a work of my own, "Lenguas indígenas y lengua clásica en Hispania," first published in the *Proceedings of the 6th International Congress of Classical Studies* (Madrid, September 1974) and reproduced in *Gaiak* 3 (1977): 341–352, where it can easily be found by readers in our country. Though lacking other virtues, its aim is to provide a sort of compendium of the facts on the subject that seemed to me most important, together with a reasonably complete bibliography of the works published until that date, with updated reference to the works of Barbero and Vigil.

We now know, at last, that the urban nucleus of Oeasso, which is important to us due to its position, was actually located in Irún and not near Oyarzun, where it had often been sought. This provides real support to the old hypothesis that the name *Irun* coincides with that of *Iruiñea*, the Basque name for Pamplona and probably that of the *Iruña* in Alava, which was usually thought to be derived from *(h)iri* "town," plus some other not-well-specified element. The differences lie in the fact that the second name [*Iruiñea*] has an *-e* and a (perhaps expressive) palatalization that the first [*Irún*] does not have. Moreover, the former has, as is all too often overlooked, a suffixed definite article, as has Bizkaia, for example, so that the declension is *Iruiñe-a, Iruiñe-a-n*, like *Bizkai-a, Bizkai-a-n*, or *Iruiñe-ko, Iruiñe-ra, Iruiñe-tik*, like *Bizkai-ko, Bizkai-ra, Bizkai-tik*. Consequently, it is very likely that back in the Middle Ages, the name was synonymous with a common town name, in the style of *Elburgo, Lapoblación*.

It seems natural to think that these towns would be given the name "la ciudad" [the city] *par excellence*, not only due to their importance but also, as I said before, due to their location. Santacara, to cite another case, the probable *Municipium Carense*, lay too far to the south.

Olite, whose occupation is usually attributed to Suintila and which effectively is said to have undergone expansion during the Visigoth period, was called in Basque, according to authors of the sixteenth and seventeenth centuries, *Erriberri*. Oihenart, followed by many modern scholars, does not appear to have been right in interpreting this name as *urbs noua*: it is not *urbs*, but *terra noua*, according to practically all nonrecent translations (*tierra, patria, pays, contrée*, etc.). Thus, it could be something like the Basque Extremadura, one of the furthest outposts reached by Basque-speaking people along the Cidacos, on the road from Pamplona to Tudela, although this does not mean that they did not also penetrate further to the east and west of this basin. This opinion, whether right or wrong, is not meant to be taken as original.

I am not going to add to or remove anything from "Basque structure," and it must therefore remain as unsatisfactory as it was when first published. I hope, however, to be allowed to clarify a point which at the time, more out of prudence than ignorance, I failed to explain. I said that "word formation devices are abundant in Basque . . .: there are abundant . . . nominal and verbal derivational suffices . . . and word composition continues to be quite productive."

What I failed to explain was the extreme scarcity or lack of what technically are known as preverbs, those that in Latin, for example, make it possible to derive from *capio* "take/get," a diverse range of words composed with the ending *-cipio*, such as *ac-cipio, con-cipio, de-cipio, ex-cipio, in-cipio, per-cipio, prae-cipio, re-cipio, sus-cipio*. These verbs are the ones which, as loan words, posed that picturesque problem that American structuralists struggled with for so many years in their work on English. A one-to-one analysis of "conceive," "deceive," "perceive," "receive," seems unmistakable: on the one hand, there are the initial segments *con-, de-, per-, re-*, which recur in many other words and whose meaning can even be guessed in some of the most favorable cases, and on the other, the item *-ceive*, which has no independent existence. This situation, by the way, occurred as well in the lender language, French, which has *concevoir, décevoir, percevoir, recevoir*, but nothing that corresponds, that I can recall, to Spanish *caber* or to Basque *kabitu*.

These preverbs are not included in any list of linguistic universals nor has it even been proven that having them increases or improves the expressive possibilities of a language. But the fact is that the Indo-European languages, exemplified sufficiently in this case by the European ones, have them through inheritance or reacquisition, and that they constitute an easy instrument for deriving five, ten, or fifteen new verbs from each verb, while our *ekarri* remains a sterile root that yields no other fruit than the causative *erakarri*.

Such preverbs are also available in the Kartvelian languages, beginning as far back as the oldest Georgian, and so far as I know, they also appear in Hungarian, for example. Indeed we could say, exaggerating a little, that preverbs are one of the constituent elements of our civilization, since that is what they are in almost all the languages, large or small, that serve as its vehicle. And this civilization is ours only because we, at least at the highest levels, have been and are receivers, not creators. Therefore, as receivers, we are condemned to receive, together with ideas and products, the linguistic forms to which they are united.

Ever since the earliest Basque writings, the preverb *des-*, sometimes replaced (or dissimulated) by *ez-*, has been in general use: *des-egin* "undo," etc. It was accepted without hesitation by Larramendi, his contemporaries and successors, who greatly broadened its scope of use: *des-agertu* "dis-appear," *des-lotu* "unleash," etc. But the tide changed around 1900 and all this, including what was oldest and best established, was condemned without recourse. Other preverbs such as *mez-* (corresponding in form and meaning to French *mé-*), whose use was always dialectal, did not improve their status.

For some years now there has been an increasingly evident trend towards more or less systematically filling this gap with new compositions. Today it is usual to find, in writing and even at certain levels of speech, items such as *aurreiritzi* "pre-judgment/pre-judice," *azpimarkatu (-marratu)* "underline," *kontraesan* "contradict" (cf. *maisu*: *kontramaisu* "master" / lit. counter-master "boatswain," etc. in the older lexicon), *meta-hizkuntza* "meta-language," *telegidatu* lit. tele-directed "remote control," etc., etc.

There is nothing really new, to my mind at least, in the section "Kinship with Other Languages," since we can't count as such the flash in the pan (which appeared here in the summer of 1976) reported by respectable (for one reason or another) newspapers such as *Pravda, The Times, Le Monde,* and the *Journal de Genève,* among many others. Its supposed Georgian discoverer read to his own satisfaction an inscription composed in a perfectly legible script known as Iberian, and in a language that has nothing to do with Georgian (and therefore, with Basque)—that is, it is undoubtedly Celtiberian, an Indo-European and, to be more precise, Celtic language. This identification is accurate, but unfortunately that does not mean that the inscription can be understood entirely. We are still in the trial-and-error phase regarding Celtiberian in general, and this bronze, discovered in Botorrita near Zaragoza, in particular. One of the details that appears to have been recognized is a word related to the Basque word for "silver": *zil(h)ar, zirar*. This is the name used most widely, but it is felt that *urre zuri*, used in some Vizcayan speeches, is older.

Regarding Bonaparte's classification of Basque dialects, I would like to return again to a certain point, owing to the following words of mine published in 1960:

> Although he was primarily concerned with speech, due to a happily fortuitous inconsistency (from the literary point of view, at least), most of the versions that he had drawn up are in fixed varieties that had been standardized by writing—that is, they are written in what his follower, Campión, called in 1894 "the four literary dialects of the euskara language: Vizcayan, Guipuzcoan, Lapurdian, Zuberoan."

In this, by the way, Bonaparte, a forerunner of modern dialectology, also proves himself to be a forerunner of Soviet linguistics, which faithfully reflects legislation by always distinguishing between written and nonwritten varieties, apparently condemning the latter never to gain the status of the former.

No matter how enamored of Basque, Bonaparte was after all a foreigner in the country and had to choose, or get his collaborators to choose, from among different variants of each of those standards. Accordingly, in the cases I am most familiar with, it is clear that he generally preferred the Vizcayan that we could call "Moguelian" (which is also that of the two Astarloas: the theoretical and the practical one), as opposed to that of Añibarro, for example. As is always the case, each has a geographical basis which, to simplify, could be seen as Marquina-Durango as opposed to Arratia. The former was subsequently followed by Arana-Goiri, whereas the followers of Añibarro, Zavala, etc. included Azkue and Zamarripa.

Guipuzcoan deserves a few lines of explanation because the example is more complicated than would appear at first glance. Bonaparte, as the guide of his collaborator (who on this occasion was, significantly—for more reasons than one—the Vizcayan, Fr. Uriarte), accepted Larramendi's standard, the speech of Beterri in Guipúzcoa, as was the case with Lardizabal, although the latter was from Zaldibia. That is, even then we can see that the principle of territoriality was far from being decisive. One of the differences that most catches the eye, due to the frequency of the items concerned, lies in conjugations. While in Beterri, the auxiliary *duen* "has" contrasts with *duten* "have," or in the past tense *zuen* with *zuten*, writers from Goyerri (Aguirre de Asteasu, etc.) used *duan/duen*, *zuan/zuen*. What this and other details show is the lack of autonomy of the Guipuzcoan standard, which inevitably tends either toward the west (Vizcayan), or toward the east (Lapurdian and Navarrese, particularly Mendiburu).

It is therefore not the case that literary cultivation of the language has taken place at the caprice of writers, who scarcely had guides to follow or models to conform to. On the contrary, one would say that, in view of their multiplicity, there has been an excess rather than a lack of standards. The bad thing is that their possibilities of being exported have always been small, although their influence, while mostly diffuse, managed to make itself felt far from the original nucleus.

If territorial divisions, the scarcity or lack of cultural institutions, and the absence of towns or cities with power to spread their influence (when such power has existed, it has been used to spread Romance), etc. do not sufficiently account for the dialectal fragmentation of Basque, it would suffice to note the almost total absence of a cultural policy among us, particularly as concerns the Basque language.

Throughout this century, the breakdown of the old standards has become increasingly evident, although not everywhere at the same time. The Academy of the Basque Language, which today is the only institution officially recognized throughout the Basque Country, was founded as a result of the Basque Studies Congress held in Oñate in 1918, first and foremost to establish a unified, literary standard for Basque, as forthrightly expressed by Luis de Eleizalde. Unfortunately, the academy, which has contributed so much to the study of Basque, has not done anything at all on this score—though it is not difficult to guess the reason for such an omission, which is not at all due to laziness or oversight. Hoping for impossible unanimity, it has put off taking any practical decisions that cannot be taken without thereby provoking friction and conflict.

With the gradual lifting of the "tombstone" laid on our people and language following the Spanish Civil War and World War II, major changes took place. Some of the essential points where these can be seen, as has become particularly evident in the ten years transpired since the first version of this work was written, are, in addition to an extraordinary and reasonably well-coordinated publishing output, the introduction of Basque as a vehicle of education through our *ikastolas*[11] (as a supplement to the transmitting of Basque in the home, like a wild plant or weed), and the ever more frequent teaching of "adults" in Basque. A fairly significant example of this change can be seen in the increasing presence of *euskaldun berri,* or speakers of Basque as a second language, among whom are found some of our best-known authors in recent years.

All of this would never have happened without profound changes in the type of language proposed and used. Following a movement that was traditionalist as far as Basque was concerned, although manifested in educated and populist tendencies otherwise more opposite than coincident with each other, and which is perhaps best exemplified by the classical Lapurdian[12] advocated by Fr. Villasante (with express mention of Axular as his model and of the ideas of its first prophet, Etcheberri from Sara), and practiced also by Jon Mirande from Soule, the Academy found itself forced, by pressure from the environment and not out of suicidal recklessness, to pronounce its policy on core issues whose resolution could no longer be delayed. The best known—though by no means only, or even the first—manifestation of all this was the meeting at Aránzazu in 1968, fifty years after the academy was founded.

There, a form of the language called *batua,* or unified Basque—unified, naturally, in intent—received a degree of confirmation, at least in some of its general lines, which I am not going to explain here, much less defend, since I can be considered an interested party in a more precise sense than the natural one, according to which all Basques should be interested in the matter.

No one has created this *batua;* or better expressed, it has been created by many. It can be said to combine complementary features of the language used by a range of authors—and not the least notable ones— over the fifteen or twenty years prior to 1968. This means that it existed before what we could call its specification and is still being formed. Moreover, it has a well-defined, central-eastern dialect base. That is, in line with what we noted earlier, it is based on the Guipuzcoan of Beterri with a heavy Lapurdian and Navarrese influence, unless we wish to invert those terms and speak of a Navarrese Lapurdian plus a not negligible portion of Guipuzcoan. And it is not that the Vizcayans or Souletins have been shunted aside: the case is that the form of language chosen, which must be only one by definition, leaves them in the marginal situation assigned to them by geography itself.

Incidentally, except for details, it is very much like Azkue's *gipuzkera osotua,*[13] with one essential difference: the latter has been as much praised as ignored in practice, whereas *batua* is as reviled as widely used, or, to be more exact, people revile it precisely because so many use it. For my part, I am not in the least reluctant to admit its defects whenever they are demonstrated, but the fact that we need, if the language is to survive, a single *unified* language seems to me to be beyond all reasonable debate. A *single* unified language for certain uses, as has been stressed so often, and curiously enough, *not* for literature. No one wants to see the demise of the dialects, which here above all have a natural place, in literature understood as poetry or one of the fine arts. What we need more than anything is a supradialectal prose, however colorless, aromaless and insipid, and this is *batua's* raison d'etre.

As far as I know, in order to fill the void, this form of the language has only one alternative that can give it any competition. I refer to what I will call, with all due respect and because I believe I am not mistaken about its sources, "liturgical" Basque. To this written form of the language (which, by the way, is not so different from *batua*), I find two drawbacks, both of which are quite serious. In the first place, its somewhat surreptitious emergence, since it was born, in its Guipuzcoan form, to fill needs which, while no doubt important, coincide only in small measure with those noted here. The second drawback, which has just been alluded to, is its Guipuzcoanism: it is not known whether there are hopes that it will become, for whatever purpose, the language of people who don't speak Guipuzcoan, although its unexpected because unexplained presence in a recent pan-Basque political document would seem to indicate higher ambitions.

And now, to remain faithful to my constant penchant for anticlimax, I will end with two bibliographical references. Worth reading today, as a remarkably compact synthesis, is the booklet by Jacques Allières, "Les Basques," *Que sais-je?* no. 1668 (1977). And since what is truly exceptional in the case of our language is its survival, I recommend reading J.M. de Azaola's "Vasconia y su destino," Madrid, *Rev. de Occidente*, in particular II, 1 (1976) p. 86ff.

But the case is, even leaving behind the past and concerning ourselves strictly with the present and future, that a genetically isolated language like ours has, in times of difficulty, nowhere to turn for models that are nearly ready for use, models that are easily found when there are languages belonging to the same family. Furthermore, no one would deny that while the written forms of Catalan and Galician are easily understood by people whose first and everyday language is Spanish, the same is not true of Basque. This very summer, a professionally well-known colleague and friend thought he saw a political message in a sign that said *Liburu eta diska azoka* ["Book and Record Fair"], because of the one word that he thought he recognized and which is the only one that he should not have.[14] This happened in Fuenterrabía, and the sign presided over an array of book and record stalls generously exhibiting their wares.

The difference is even more notorious in the area of spoken language. Our same friend, the Spanish-speaker, may be upset and might even consider it discourteous towards himself and other Spanish-speakers, to find Catalan used in a course delivered at the University of Barcelona. Despite this fact, if he is interested in the subject being taught, he will surely need no more than a couple of weeks to be able to follow the course satisfactorily. But this same person, provided with grammars, dictionaries, and, if possible, a good teacher, will need something like a year to be able to understand anything at all in a class conducted in Basque at the kindergarten level.

This comprehension difficulty strictly conditions our language's growth possibilities, for example in the crucial area of education. I would be the last person to recommend passive resignation, which is the accusation usually made against people who express criticism of persistent maximalist positions. Much has been, is being, and will be done, and whatever seeds are sown will yield good fruit provided that we dream with our feet firmly on the ground, without levitating like our friend from the hovel in Arteche, who suspended the law of gravity whenever he closed his eyes.

Regarding "Borders," I confess myself guilty of having repeated commonplaces that were at most generally valid for historical circumstances when our new situation had already been described by Julio Caro Baroja back in 1955. This new situation is characterized by the fact that we can no longer apply to Basque the concept of territoriality that was maintained up to the Basque Economic Agreement passed in 1936. Even so, the linguistic tradition or history of the different Basque regions still carries a lot of weight even today, although what really distinguishes them is whether they have a smaller or greater density of Basque-speakers in their population. Another correspondence to something very real is found in the idea of a border zone, although facing outward, not inward, as I had the chance to see a short while ago, without much pleasure, in Villarreal de Alava.

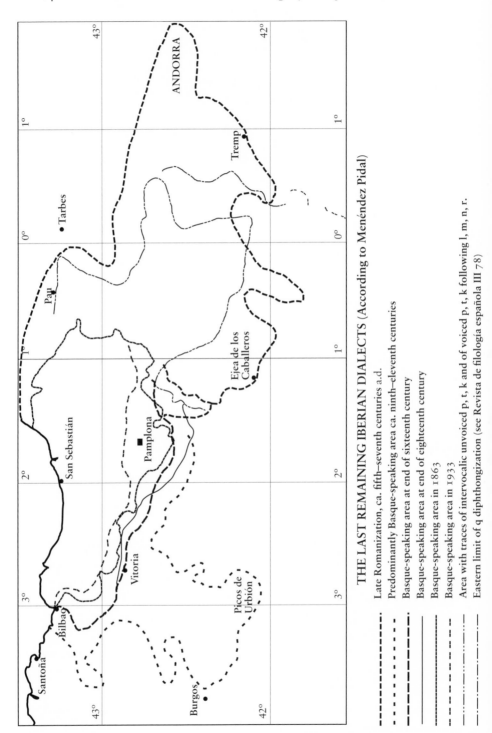

THE LAST REMAINING IBERIAN DIALECTS (According to Menéndez Pidal)

Late Romanization, ca. fifth–seventh centuries a.d.

Predominantly Basque-speaking area ca. ninth–eleventh centuries

Basque-speaking area at end of sixteenth century

Basque-speaking area at end of eighteenth century

Basque-speaking area in 1863

Basque-speaking area in 1933

Area with traces of intervocalic unvoiced p, t, k and of voiced p, t, k following l, m, n, r.

Eastern limit of q diphthongization (see Revista de filología española III 78)

CHAPTER 2

Basques and Their Name

"Los Vascos y su nombre," *Revista internacional de estudios vascos (RIEV)* 29, no. 1 (1984): 9–29. (Also in Luis Michelena, *Sobre historia de la lengua vasca* 2, San Sebastián: Anales del Anuario del Seminario de Filologia Vasca "Julio de Urquijo" / Diputacion Foral de Gipuzkoa, 1988, pp. 538–54.)

1. Here I will discuss a subject that has interested me for years—but alas, not enough to get me to work on it assiduously, or at least as assiduously as I should. I have tried several times to shift the responsibility onto other shoulders, but my powers of persuasion have not been sufficient to generate the necessary enthusiasm. I find myself, therefore, having to trust my own initiative, with the help of documentation that boils down, more or less, to the good or bad fortune of chance findings. And finally, since this article was originally written as a talk, the portraits that I wanted to make have had to be reduced to mere sketches.

Apart from this *captatio*, which is no less true for sounding so trite, let me stress the humbleness of my objectives, contained in the title of these notes. I will not be dealing with elevated and supposedly permanent aspects of our collective nature—aspects such as our matriarchalism or our millennarism, graceless substitutes for our old Cantabrism and our respectable pre-Christian Christianity; the perfection of our megalithic art, like that of our auxiliary verb, pertains, after all, to other fields that are better defined.

I am concerned above all with names, with denominations recorded over the past two millennia, more or less. It is true, however, that one cannot discuss names without somehow examining the extralinguistic circumstances accounting for their existence. Because, as some might justifiably say, names do not merely express and signify that earlier world, but also configure and delimit it, and even create it to a certain extent.

I will not deny that there is a little, and even a lot, of ongoing professional distortion if I try to go, as we Basques say, *izenetik izanera* or from names to things, but the value of language data can hardly be exaggerated, at least in circumstances such as ours. If there is no general two-way univocal correspondence between peoples and languages (and there is not), we do usually concede at least a close correlation leading from the one to the other, and from the latter to the former. Leaving aside generalities but not repetitions, the preservation of a language is necessary if we are to understand the existence of a people, no matter what the latter is like.

Indeed on the question of the most remote past, even Arana Goiri, who tended to be concerned mostly with what he called "race," occasionally found it difficult to separate it from language, as we can see from an extract that I've taken from a critique of a work by Lewy d'Abartiague on the origin of the Basques (*Obras completas*, Buenos Aires, 1340ff.), a mystery that has yet to be solved: "Language is the only instrument we have left that will allow us to investigate that long protohistoric period of the race." That he was speaking of race is clear, for it is no simple matter to couple genes with phonemes and syntactic constructions.

Such leaps and bounds from one category to another are always dangerous. They include, at the very top of the list, the well-known attempts to jump from weapons or pottery to languages. To say that a people are Celtic if they speak a language that is Celtic, to the limited extent (limited particularly, although only very vaguely, by time) that a language, such as modern Irish or ancient Celtiberian, can be taken as such, seems to me more natural than ascribing Celt-hood or Celtic-ness to the use of certain goods or to the knowledge of a set of techniques. But it does not, in any case, ensure a stamp of authenticity: if we look at language, we also find arguments for and against. The Celtism of the Irish is a commonplace, despite the fact that the Irish language is not much used. It used to be, however, in recent times throughout the country, or at least in most of it. Perhaps we could also allow the Celtism of the Cornish, which insofar as language is concerned would (through salvaged memories) take us back to the eighteenth century, but it would be very hard for us to admit that because the Pictaui were Celts, the present-day inhabitants of Poitou are still Celtic.

2. The most ancient name that we all, consciously or unthinkingly, use in relation to our people is that of Vascones. I refer readers to the well-known article by A. Schulten, "Las referencias sobre los Vascones hasta el año 810 después de J. C.," *RIEV* 18 (1927): 225–40, which is valid even for the many who do not accept the historical conclusions that he tried to draw from the texts. This can be justified or accounted for at least by how magically the words *uasco, uasconicus* lead us by the hand to *vasco, vascongado,* etc., although you can be sure—and this is a precedent destined to entail historic consequences—that neither all the *uascones* spoke Basque, nor were all Basque speakers *uascones.* Clearly, and without entering terrain even more shrouded in doubt, the Aquitaine proper names of the beginnings of our era come from an *éuskara*-speaking people. With this word, which sounds like a breath from the past, I am attempting to avoid the quicksands of confusion that could lead us to say with Iztueta (*Guipuzcoaco dantza . . .* 1824, p. 5): "*Euscaldun garbi garbia zan, bada, Tubal; baita beraren aita Jafet, asaba Noe, eta are lenagoacoac ere.*" The name of the *Ausci* might be, as has often been claimed, the first record of names in *eusk-.*

As it happens, curiously and irritatingly enough (although external parallels do exist), the form of the Basque root *eusk-* (*heusk-* in two sixteenth-century authors) does not sit well with the Latin and Romance *uasc-, vasc-,* or *basc-.* More clearly, apart from having analogous referents, both forms share the presence of an internal consonant group *-sk-*, which we could even imagine to be an infix, but this is as far as the similarity goes. It is true that experts have posited more than one common protoform, from which, by two different paths (regular phonological processes that are different in Basque and Romance), we could arrive at the documented situation. Thus, I recall the note by Wilhelm Giese, *E.-J.* 3 (1949): 139ff, where he comments without approval on the idea of Juan Alvarez Delgado: *eusk-* yielded *eusk-* in our language, as was to be expected, and from there other subsequent forms followed. But, in a language of the Celtic type, postulated as a mediator, more exactly in a variety where the diphthongs had evolved as they did in Irish, we would have *ua* from *eu,* *ou* (cf. *túath* from *teuta, touta* 'tribe, people'), but this is a process which, in addition to being exclusively Goidelic, not Celtic in general, only happened late in the Middle Ages. For this and other reasons, Giese concludes as follows:

We may have to relate *Vascones* with ancient Basque *ausk-*, but this hypothesis does not seem to me at all necessary, even with the support of *Ausci*, modern Basque *eusk-*, and it may be that they are different words. Even taking into consideration the recent studies of Alvarez Delgado, the matter remains as problematic as it was before.

In any case, for now it is enough to stress the difficulty of linking Basque forms with Romance forms within the time frame that is most accessible to us. The question of origins, which is highly interesting in itself, does not concern us for the moment.

3. Records abound of the term "Vasco," also in Greek transcription, and its derivative *uasconicus*, the former prior to the beginning of our era. Perhaps we should add for those (increasingly numerous) persons who are unfamiliar with Latin and tend to let themselves be led by the habits of today, that "Vasco" is an *n*-stem noun, oblique case *Vascon-*, plural *Vascones*. Therefore, when dealing with examples like those of Silius Italicus (*Vasco insuetus galeae, Vasco leuis o galeae contempto tegmine Vasco*), we must not forget that the text is not in Romance, so that Latin *uasco* is different even in form from Spanish, etc., *vasco*; in Latin it is simply the straight [nominative/vocative] case, deprived as frequently happens in that language of the nasal that appears in other cases, among which are all the plurals, including the nominative-vocative plural. And, in case the reader has ever heard of the *uasca tibia* taken from Latin texts, he must not think of the *txistu* [Basque recorder], for even if the reference were true, the adjective would have nothing to do with the Basques.

Dating from around the year 800 is the first mention of the *Nauarri*, in clear relation to the Vascones. J. M. Lacarra, *Historia política del reino de Navarra* I (1972), p. 30, gives the following explanation:

> After being the head of a district, Pamplona fell under the power of the indigenous chief who ruled over the territory, to which the city eventually gave its name—*Arba Pampilonense*—and whose people came to be known as *pamploneses*. Frankish chroniclers gave them another name—*navarros*—which thus appeared for the first time in history and was the name they applied to the Basques living on the southern side of the Pyrenees. The human group settled in Pamplona did not hold authority over a district; on the contrary, the city was subject to the indigenous authority that ruled over the countryside. This is why Frankish authors tell us that in the 8th century Pamplona was the fortress of the Navarrese.

The length of this quote is justified by the existence of familiar discussions related in various ways to the Navarrese and their similarities to, or differences from, their neighbors to the north and west. Another quote that merits our attention is the famous text by Aimery Picaud that has been handed down to us from the twelfth century. The clear distinction established therein between *Nauarri* and *Bascli* undoubtedly refers to what would be, or already were, cis- and trans-Pyrenean peoples, a distinction preserved in the nomenclature, however altered in form, many centuries later. What in any case is clear is that, although the Pilgrim's *Nauarri et Bascli* differed in that the latter had lighter skin than the others (*Bascli facie candidiores Nauarris approbantur*), they were not dissimilar in other respects (*Nauarri et Bascli unius similitudinis et qualitatis in cibis scilicet et uestibus et lingua habentur*), and today it is their language that we are most interested in.

4. The name of the Vascones was modified in two ways during the High Middle Ages [ninth–eleventh centuries]. In line with a widespread phonological tendency, "Vasconia" became "Wasconia" in France: in Frankish texts there is a general W-, as opposed to V-, found almost exclusively in Visigothic sources. "Wasconia" was followed by "Guasconia" (the following step in the phonological change alluded to above), and finally by the familiar Romance forms, among which "Gascuña" is surely the best-known example here. However, in a good part of that "Wasconia," despite the denomination, there existed a highly characteristic variety of Occitan known as Gascon, which was still very much alive and in the twelfth century extended as far as San Sebastián and environs. This is so despite the fact that Gascon shows undeniable signs of a Basque substrate, just as Basque shows clear, and apparently more recent, signs of Gascon influence.

To this must be added the fact that in the south, at least partially as a consequence of the betacism taking place in the Romance spoken next to the Basque-speaking region (*b* and *v* are universally indistinguishable in Basque, as is known even in aphorisms), we find frequently, if not predominantly, forms with *b*-, such as *Bascones* or *Villabáscones* on the banks of the Arlanzón, whose mid-tenth century onomastics has often been discussed due to its singular nature. I recommend, as an example, R. Menéndez Pidal, *Enciclopedia lingüística hispánica* I (Madrid 1960) p. xivff. Finally, we should note that later *b*- became generalized in France and from there extended throughout Europe, although in 1821 W. von Humboldt still preferred to write *die Vaskische Sprache*.

5. But *váscones* or *vascones* fell into disuse centuries ago, since it is used almost exclusively to lend temporal color or to underscore Greek and Latin denominations. Let us recall that, among other things, the accent on the first syllable both in the singular and in the plural makes it phonically uncomfortable—not unviable, since the position of the accent could be varied, which is what has happened to the *vascón* that we usually hear. *Váscones* is possible, but who would dare to say *váscon*? There was still the matter of altering the *-c'n* cluster that remained following syncope [loss of the unstressed vowel], as may have occurred earlier with the *Bascli* mentioned above.

Toponyms, however, bear witness to the past vitality of *Báscones* and its family. But what later appeared in its stead is the derived term *bascongado* or *vascongado*, which is accompanied by the name of the language, written either as *basquenz* or as *vascuence*. Even today, the term *vascuenz* can still be heard in parts of the mountains of Navarra.

This is the language to which Navarrese documents in Latin usually refer, as *in basconea lingua* (Leire, 1060) or, alluding to its speakers, *quem bascones uocant* (Leire, 1085). Reference to this language also occurs (although always with a margin of doubt unless other reasons can be invoked) in circumlocutions such as *quod nominatur, uocatur, dicitur* (occasionally with the addition of *a rrusticis,* etc.) or *quod nominatur rustico uocabulo, ab antiques uulgalibus,* etc. See Lacarra, *Vasconia medieval* (San Sebastián, 1957).

As has been suggested, not everything "rustic" or "vulgar" necessarily points to Basque, since together with the Latin of the documents a Romance language was also being spoken. Each case must be examined separately. In any event, it seems obvious to me that the language designated in the twelfth century as *lingua Nauarrorum,* in a document always quoted as dealing with the history of the Basque language, is not the same language that in 1390 and as far back as 1344 was referred to as *in ydiomate Nauarre (terre)*. In this we must follow the opinion of F. González-Ollé, "El romance Navarro," *RFE* 53 (1972): 45–93; see as well his *Textos lingüísticos navarros* (Pamplona, 1970). When dealing with the languages of a country, and particularly so in our case when discussing Navarra, one must always bear in mind dates as well as place.

6. Mention of *vascongado* and *vascuence* always brings with it, if not serious problems, at least some bothersome discomfort. There are those who cling to these terms, despite their manifest decadence, and there

are others who raise their voices against them with repugnance. There have also been those who have decided, for the sake of truthfulness, to destroy what are now called myths (individual or collective ways of thinking, always motivated and not always lacking in extrasubjective justification), but the part of the essay that I have managed to read does not seem to me to be totally satisfactory.

For some time now, at least since the turn of the last century to judge by the writings of Arana Goiri, there have been members of our community to whom the words *vascuence* and *vascongado* sound not only bad, but almost injurious. Justification is not lacking for this, especially if—as increasingly happens among us—history is reduced to the memories of each individual or, at most, to the (not always bias-free) memories of each individual and his small group of friends or companions.

Restricting ourselves to the present century and little more, the fact is that (not entirely justifiably, as I will explain later) both *vascuence* and *vascongado*, but particularly *vascongado*, have gradually fallen into disuse, and that there have been efforts to compensate for this, shall we say, "natural" loss by artificial means—in other words, through coercion and imposition. Despite this, the trend has continued to such an extent that today (after a buildup of many years) the only such word left in practice is *vasco*, both inside and outside the Basque Country; *vascongado* is little more than archaic, except perhaps in very limited areas where it is maintained as a traditional term. Indeed, things have reached the point where *vascuence* is now replaced—again both inside and outside the Basque Country—by *(el) vasco*, unless the speaker prefers, as happens more and more often, to switch languages when the propriety of names is at stake.

This rejection of *vascuence* and *vascongado* is doubtless due to the insistence of certain groups (whose focal point is probably not far from Bilbao) to systematically go against the general trend and rub people the wrong way with their noisily ostentatious "vascongadism," where *vascongado*, once the simple key has been decoded, no longer meant *vasco* but the opposite or enemy of *vasco*. But this (generally) recent group policy should not make us forget a long and constant history. For it is beyond all possible doubt that *vascongado* and *vascuence* were not invented or diffused by others to denigrate us, but are words that have been used, by others and also by ourselves, without any pejorative intent whatsoever. Thus, *vascuence* has been, and even still is for those who are not horrified by the possibility of being considered quaint, the traditional denomination in Spanish, and therefore the neutral term for the language of the Basque Country. Indeed, all languages usually have a domestic name for every foreign tongue known to their speakers. What the Germans call "Deutsch" is known as *allemand* in French, "German" in English or, closer to the original, *tedesco* in Italian. In speaking this way, no one is appropriating someone else's belongings or meddling in his affairs.

On the subject now of mutual offenses, I am not going to try to minimize the derision conveyed by our use of the term *maqueto*; *jebo* and similar words were not highly laudatory either. I can, however, affirm that for one thing, the frequency of use of *maqueto* is fast approaching zero here; and secondly, I can also affirm that there is nothing Basque about the origin of the term, as far as anyone knows. Echave Sustaeta and even the great diffuser of the term himself, Arana Goiri, both knew this. At least the latter recognized as much in 1897 when he acknowledged that *maqueto* was a word of recent creation and restricted diffusion. In the footnote on p. 1168 of his *Complete Works*, he clearly agrees that at the beginning of that century Vizcayans used unfriendly names (I believe that among them *motz* is the one that dates back the furthest in writing) to refer to certain people from outside the domain of Vizcaya, but "today, in the western part of Bizkaya, the nickname most used is *maketo*, which was already being used before the last Carlist war, and whose etymology no-one can be sure of," an observation which suggests that the author was not convinced of its Basque origin, but rather thought the opposite. The restriction to "the western part of Bizkaya" is confirmed by the limits that he sets on p. 1213 on its current use "from Galdakano to Portugalete and from Mungia to Valmaseda."

Although many people here and there try to ignore the fact, it is notorious that Sabino Arana seriously understated the western limits of *maketo*, or rather *maqueto*, just as he did with *comparsa*. At the end of the century it was in use in Portugalete and in Valmaseda (towns which did not speak Basque), but also much further west in Romance-speaking territory. Because the curious thing is that the term is still current among mountain people and the Cantabrians—at least it was in Torrelavega around 1967 to designate people from *Ultrapuertos* or beyond the mountains (i.e., from Castile) and not, unless I'm badly mistaken, people from Asturias or Vizcaya. We can scarcely conclude otherwise than that the word came to us from the west, a fact that I repeat here, even though once again it is like writing it in sand.

7. As noted above, the word *vascongado* was not at all disparaging, no matter how much more is left to be revealed about the open secret of its exact meaning. Thus the inanity of those who like or liked to wield the term *Gobierno vascongado*, for it amounts to nothing: their *animus iniuriandi* is readily apparent, but the injurious weapon fails to materialize. Their mistake is due to ignorance—that kind of ignorance usually called crass, perhaps because of the slime it trails in everything having to do with our people's past. The autonomous government of 1936, which was *vascongado de jure*, became *vizcaíno de facto* only through adhesions, and then at the best of times.

The truth is that *vascongado* originally alluded first and foremost to one who is "Basque in speech"—i.e., to that which, in the first place (unless we do violence to the language) means *euskaldun*. A person who does not speak *euskara* is called an *erdaldun* (there are Medieval records in Navarra of *Erdalduna* and *Erdara*, the monikers for non-Basque languages in general), and in Romance *latinado* and, I suppose, other names as well.

I shall simply draw on a few references from among countless others. For our oldest reference, which in the case of Basque is medieval, take [the ancient Charter known as] the *Fuero General de Navarra*, where, together with "una pecha que es clamada açaguerrico *en bascuenz*," "otra pecha que es clamada alfonsadera, *en basquenz ozterate*," we find at the same time "esta zena es clamada *en los bascongados* on bazendu avaria" or "la cayll que dize *el bascongado* erret bide." By contrast, where it says "port al ferme dize *el Navarro* gayces berme" or "don dize *el Navarro* ones berme," it may be alluding to an unrestricted use of the original language of these expressions.

Our modern reference, meaning yesterday and perhaps also today, is the highly expressive testimony of Andrés de Mañaricua, *Alava, Vizcaya y Guipúzcoa a la luz de su historia* (Durango, 1977) p. 25:

And even today this meaning survives among Basque speakers. Several years ago, I went to take up my post in a village in Alava located on what was then the frontier between the Basque- and Spanish-speaking zones. The villagers asked me: "Are you a *vascongado*?" They knew that I was from Vizcaya; what they wanted to know was whether I spoke Basque.

I am no expert, but I cannot accept the firmly held conviction predomi-
nant among many of us that the term "Provincias Vascongadas" is a
kind of infernal artifact created to nourish separatist aspirations. I don't
know when the term originated (it existed at least as far back as the
early eighteenth century), but it seems natural that our provinces, which
once were even called the "exempt provinces," should be given, if only
for reasons of economy, a common name pointing more towards union
than division. A case in point is the speed with which the "Vascongada"
diocese of Vitoria was dismantled not so many years ago.

Someone may raise the objection that Vizcaya was (or still is, in the
blurry land of legitimacy) a seigniory rather than a province, but this
difference, now erased among us, was already merely decorative back in
1800. I refer the reader to the *Diccionario geográfico-histórico de España*
II, published by the Academy of History. Under *Vizcaya* it says: "seigniory also called a county: one of the three provinces known as *vascongadas*, and which gives the general name of *vizcaynos* to the inhabitants
of all of them." It should not be necessary to add that, administratively
speaking, Navarra was clearly distinguished here due to its status as a
kingdom, its parliament incorporating the three estates, etc.

Besides, largely due to internal impetus, we have been separating
ourselves from the Navarrese, and they from us, since at least 1200.
The law of 1841 with its permanent consequences, plus the distancing
of 1932—consummated in 1936 but actually primed in 1931—by the
supposed Unionists, did not reduce the distance that recent absurdi-
ties (which we shall charitably imagine as being divinely inspired from
above) have only aggravated to an extent that is difficult to calculate and
even more difficult to repair.

8. As mentioned earlier, the meaning attributed to *vascongado* referred
above all to the Basque language and not to Basque origin. Still, it was
inevitable that one meaning should blend into the other, first driven by
the (rather difficult-to-prove) assumption that people of Basque origin,
whether by birth or by ancestry, were, mostly at least, also speakers of
Basque.

Let us listen again to Mañaricua, 1977, p. 22ff:

There are words which, with the passage of the centuries, have had their
original meaning obscured and even lost. And so it is with the word
vascongado, which today is applied to the natives of Alava, Guipúzcoa

and Vizcaya, as distinguished from all other Basques. Originally the word had no ethnic or political content, but only linguistic meaning.

And he adds, touching on a polemical matter that we are not concerned with for the moment:

> *Vascongado* was not a person who, not being Basque, became *vasconizado,* as many people thought basing this belief on an etymology that derived the word from Latin *vasconicatus,* and which is repeated even today. *Vascongados* were Basque speakers: thus a Basque-speaking Navarrese was a *Vascongado.*

I cannot silence, however, my opinion that the Latin word on which this etymology is based is not on any known written record.

As it has already been presented, we can draw examples from Father Larramendi's *Sobre los fueros de Guipúzcoa,* published by J. I. Tellechea Idígoras in 1983 and a work, written in 1756–58 according to the editor, that is very representative of an author who, in linguistic matters, *ezker-eskuin,* was one of the best.

When he says (p. 57) ". . . *y que si quieren ponernos obispo aparte, sea vascongado guipuzcoano"* (". . . and that if they want to give us our own bishop, he should be a Vascongado from Guipúzcoa"), it seems natural to think that he means a Basque speaker—a condition which, to Larramendi, was surely indispensable—and that besides he should be a Guipuzcoan and not a Basque from just anywhere, whether or not he spoke the language of the country, on the condition that he was from that region.

In other cases, however, it is less feasible to reduce these meanings to language. "And if by happy or sorry chance I had not already honestly boasted of being a Bascongado in order to stand up to them and scare them off . . ." This can hardly be taken as referring to language, although he has just spoken of "our language": in any case as we know, his defense of the language was made in Romance. *Bascongado* appears again on the following page with connotations that are impossible to pin down.

It means what now would be called *vascos* on p. 5: "The incredible indolence of the Guipuzcoans and other Bascongados leaves me even more upset." The same thing is generally true, I believe, for "the Bascongada nation, the earliest populators of Spain and even its environs" (p. 58). And even if we allowed that everyone was monolingual in that remote period, this would not be entirely acceptable for the (less remote) future (p. 59): "And we shall build a Republic entirely of Bascongados, originally the earliest Spaniards."

It is obvious that Larramendi needed a name like *vascos* and that none existed at the time with that meaning. And since he didn't want to speak of *vizcaínos*, a name he hated to see extended to other Basques, as is well known, he had to broaden the weakened sphere of application of *bascongado*.

On the other hand, there was still the possibility of resorting to the somewhat archaic device of invoking supposed, and unsubstantiated, ancestors. Thus, on p. 60ff.: "This way, if we elect a king, he shall reign as and be called the King of Cantabria, and he shall be given the Kingdom." Or again: "We shall have to fight wars. So be it. But they will be Cantabrian wars, a name that should give us courage. We are descendants of those valiant Cantabrians . . . and their blood and courage still course through our veins." However, such ancestry had already been denied us, even though some people may still have been calling the Basque language *cantabrismus* in Latin.

9. Let us now, finally, turn our attention to the Basque Country, to the *Vasconia* whose history was written by Oihenart, and to its inhabitants, leaving aside the language that has attracted our interest so far. I have just mentioned in passing that Larramendi did not like to hear *vizcaíno* applied to persons not born in Vizcaya, no matter how Basque they were in origin and language. He did, however, recognize the fact of its application, as could not have been otherwise, and said so for example in the work just cited: "And as Your Excellencies know, Bizcaya has the honor of being known everywhere by that name, which is used throughout the *Bascongada* Provinces, including those of France, where people both say and write 'French Biscaya.'" And in a note to this passage on p. 296, Tellechea rightly adds: "This nomenclature survives today in the geographical name '*Golfo de Vizcaya*' [Bay of Biscay]."

On these broader connotations of Vizcaya, see e.g., Mañaricua, 1977, p. 25ff, and above all Fr. Anselmo de Legarda, *Lo 'vizcaíno' en la literature castellana* (San Sebastián, 1953), p. 9ff. There is one testimony in particular that I cannot resist transcribing because of its far-off setting, although I realize it is quite well known. I am speaking of the passage by Bernal Díaz del Castillo, *Historia verdadera de la conquista de Nueva España*, ch. cxv, where Cortez explains to Montezuma, not without resorting to half-truths, the reason for the differences between his men and those led by his enemy Pánfilo de Narváez:

> And our emperor has many kingdoms and counties, and within them there are many different peoples . . ., and we are from within Castile, which is called Old Castile, and we are called Castilians, and the captain who is now at Cempoal and the people under him are from another province, which is called Vizcaya, and they are called *Vizcaínos* and they speak like the Otomíes, land of Mexico . . . .

Otomí, as can be seen in any reference work, is a different Mexican language not related to Nahuatl or Aztec, belonging to a family widely extended through North and Central America.

Since it is a question that I have not studied in detail, I shall merely summarize my impressions concerning the use of *vizcaíno* and very particularly the restrictions that I am aware of:

1. Its application displeased the Guipuzcoans, for example, even before Larramendi. It was a name employed by others, not by themselves, along the lines of what happens with *giputz*, a label given to Guipuzcoans by people who are not Guipuzcoans or, more precisely perhaps, by people who do not speak Guipuzcoan. This is a fortiori the case with *provinciano/probintziano*, used by Navarrese and Vizcayans.

2. As for *vizcaíno* when used with reference to the language, something which plainly had also begun to happen with *vascongado*, it could not have been univocal. People from Portugalete or Valmaseda, to mention the already mentioned, would have been considered *vizcaínos* in the sixteenth and seventeenth centuries, and *vascongados*—even if they only spoke Romance.

3. *Vizcaíno* was employed in Castile: I mean in what is called Castile when speaking of the Catholic Queen Isabella, but without implying that it was also in use in the kingdom of Aragón. I know little about the connotations of *navarro*. There were undoubtedly Navarrese who were called Vizcayans, but weren't there also non-Navarrese Basques who were, however, called *navarros* around Zaragoza?

4. *Vizcaíno* was Spanish, not French or, to use Oihenart's terms, it was Iberian, not Aquitaine. It is true that we have the lyrics of a well-known French song from around 1500, whose first verse I transcribe here from J.-F. Bladé, *Etudes sur l'origine des Basques* (1869), p. 263.

> *Une mousse de Biscaye,*
> *L'autre jour près ung moulin,*
> *Vint à moi sans dire gaire,*
> *Moy hurtant sur son chemin*
> *Blanche comme ung parchemin :*
> *Je la baisè à mon aise,*
> *Et me dist sans faire noise :*
> *Soaz soaz ordonarequi(n).*

It is impossible, rather than difficult, to determine whether the person being talked about in the song is from one side of the Pyrenees or the other: the refrain in Basque, which is repeated in each verse, is not very characteristic, except for the vague detail that *-arequin* is more central and eastern than western. More significant, but not conclusive either, is the name given to the language of *la mousse*, according once again to Bladé:

> *Par mon serment, vecy rage !*
> *Ce n'est francoys ni latin ;*
> *Parlez un autre languaige,*
> *Laissez votre bisquayn.*

10. In centuries past, however, Vasco was common, although with a meaning which, today at least, seems a little strange. Back then, Vasco only meant "Basque from Ultrapuertos," as can be seen from sixteenth- and seventeenth-century expressions such as *tierra de Vascos* or *navarro de Vascos*—that is, from the sixth merindad [division of the Kingdom of Navarre, now known as the French province of Basse Navarre]. The term seems, therefore, to have come from the north, as attested to by its French and perhaps even Occitan use. I will merely add that Simin Palay's *Dictionnaire du Béarnais et du gascon modernes* speaks of *Bàscou*, fem. *Basquéte*, and also, but only in feminine, *Basque*, equivalent of *Basquéte"Basquaise, fille du Pays Basque,"* which, he adds irreverently, may also mean*"nom de vache."* I abstain from any considerations about origins regarding *Bàscou*: I would simply be interested in knowing its earliest documented use.

I only know of one exception to this universal use of *vasco*, the interest in which, as far as I know, was first pointed out by Justo Gárate. It is quoted in J. Caro Baroja, *Materiales para una historia de la lengua vasca en su relación con la Latina* (Universidad de Salamanca, 1945) p. 17ff., and occurs in a passage from *Las bienandanças e fortunas* by Lope

García de Salazar, vol. XXf., VII V, dealing with the valley of Ayala: "... that land being populated by *Vascos* and *Latinados*. ..."

The strangeness of this is greater when we remember that *vasco* is contrasted here with *latinado* for reasons of language, at least primarily. All of which is more surprising still if we bear in mind that Lope García de Salazar has modified his source, which in all probability was *Árbol verdadero de la Casa de Ayala*, written by Fernán Pérez de Ayala a hundred years earlier and continued by his successor, the chancellor Pero López. The text in question can be seen in Caro Baroja, *Materials para una historia* ..., 1945, with notes 27 and 28, and in A. de Mañaricua, *Historiografía de Vizcaya* (Bilbao, 1973) 32ff:

> *E los que vinieron a poblar la tierra de Ayala, dellos eran vascongados e dellos latinados. E los vascongados llamaban a éste don Vela, Jaun Velasco; e los latinados, don Belaco.*

> (And of those who came to inhabit the land of Ayala, some were *vascongados* and some *latinados*. And the *vascongados* called the latter don Vela "Jaun Velasco"; and the *latinados* [called him] "don Belaco.")

11. Together with the Romance *vasco* which, except in the above-quoted example (and surely in others that people with more knowledge could add), was much narrower in scope than at present, there are (a very few) instances in Basque of the word *basko*, appearing as far back as our first printed book. Indeed, there are several examples in Dechepare, of which I will quote the second to last:

> *Bascoac oroc preciatzen*
> *Heuscara ez iaquin harren*
> *Oroc icassiren dute*
> *Oray cerden heuscara*

The version of René Lafon, *BAP* 8 (1952) 19, is as follows: *Les Basques sont appréciés de tout le monde, bien qu'on ne connaisse pas l'heuscara.* Stempf, s.u. *basco*, simply noted: *steht für euskaldun.* And Altuna, the latest editor and commentator of *Linguae Vasconum Primitiae,* says more or less the same thing.

I have referred on several occasions to this term and have always at least taken for granted that Dechepare was the first and last to use it. In any case, my opinion is expressed very forcefully in a work that has recently been published, although the original dates from much earlier:

I am speaking of *Etre Basque* (Toulouse: (Privat), 1983), edited by Jean Haritschelhar. I refer the reader to p. 23 where, on the subject of Dechepare, it says:

> Cela ne laisse pas donc d'être une coïncidence digne de retenir l'attention que ce dernier, auteur du premier livre imprimé en langue basque, soit aussi le seul à employer *basco* en basque, et qu'il le fasse à quatre reprises, comme synonyme, au moins à première vue, de *euskaldun*, qu'il écrit *heuscaldun*. Il l'emploie, en d'autre termes, pour désigner quelqu'un qui entre autres attributs, possède celui de connaître la langue basque.

By the way, there is also an error in the Isasti quote cited above, on the previous page.

The copyediting error appears also in other areas, and in particular when one reads, and interprets what one reads. Moguel's little masterpiece is well known, or perhaps I should say that for some it is too well known, since until I proofread Angel Zelaieta's "*Peru Abarca-*ren hiztegia," *ASJU* XI–XIII (1978–79): 89–198, I hadn't realized the exact meaning of a passage on p. 187, where the priest says "*Erosico ditut, topau aldaidazan, basco ta guiputzeco liburubac bere, eusquera guzti guztietacua aituteco.*"

This serves as a conclusion to the part of the work which, starting on p. 153, introduces into the dialogue a Guipuzcoan and a "volunteer" from Baigorri, a turncoat or deserter from the conventional army. From their conversation with the Vizcayans—at first difficult, but afterwards easy—one has to conclude that they all speak the same language, which also implies some sort of community between them.

It is not a short or insignificant fragment. It was most aptly cited by Arturo Campión in his *Conferencia que pronunció con motivo de la inauguración del Nuevo batzoki en Rentería, 25 Septiembre* 1920, printed by Tipografía Baroja, although I don't know if it has been included in some volume of miscellaneous works. "Of this mentality," he says, "full of mutual suspicions, mistrust and misunderstandings, a curious example has been preserved in the *Peru Abarka* of our good Moguel," and he goes on to present the scene. So it is not as though no one had seen or heard the text.

Now then, this *basco* of Moguel is not exactly "*Nafartarra,*" as thought by Zelaieta; or perhaps I should say, it is and it isn't. It is true that it is from Navarra, or rather Basse-Navarre, since here the distinc-

tion between "lower" and "upper" is pertinent. This Navarrese is, therefore, *Nafarroa behereko, baxenabarreko,* or however you want to say
it; what it cannot be is *Nafarroa garaiko* or from Upper Navarra, since
on several occasions it is called *prances, prancesa,* or *prances euscalduna,* begging the pardon of possible readers. So it is nothing other than
an "Ultrapuertos" Basque, represented circumstantially by a Lower- or
Basse-Navarrese.

I refer the reader to what I wrote next to Zelaieta's piece in that
edition of *ASJU,* p. 216ff, from which I quote this note: "It is readily
obvious that underlying *basco ta quiputzeco (liburubac)* is *basco ta qui-
putzean,* referring primarily and directly to the territory and only indi-
rectly to the language spoken within it."

12. I arrive now at what I consider the crucial point of this article—the
fact that, to refer to the people of this country, we have had a univocal
name in French (and I believe, as noted above, in Occitan) for many
centuries, just as, barring a name or two that are troublesome for some
Basques, we now have one in Spanish, but we do not have one in the
language today that is exclusive to Vasconia.

I used the phrase "the people of this country" to refer to the people
who can somehow be considered to be from here, and not precisely due
to their surnames, which are only valued by certain persons who are irremediably anchored in the past, about which, by the way, they have very
little good information. And in case there are people who still haven't
heard, I would like to point out that there is no correlation between
a Basque surname and the Basque language. Historically, "Carrera,"
"Portugal," "Toledo" (plus "Toledochipi"), and "Zamora" are as much
from here as "Aguirre" and "Zabala," to mention only Guipúzcoa.

Besides being from here, I feel it necessary to add that, whether they
are from here or there or are in one place or the other, they have to *feel
like* they are from here. I realize that, in saying this, I am distancing
myself from the opinion of professor Savater, well known for his discovery of R. L. Stevenson, in a long, recent article in *El País.* It is not that I
disagree with his conclusions, or with his premises, which I merely find a
bit incomplete. Indeed, many Basques *know* that they (by which I mean
we know that we) are Spanish, just as many others *know* that they are
French, something that is hard for anyone to forget.

It is also hard to misplace the obvious fact that we do not *know*
that we are Basque, at least not to a comparable extent, and I trust that

no one will demand formal proof of this—which, in any case, would be simple enough to give, starting with our National Identity Card. In our sad circumstances, the only thing we can do, since we don't know ourselves to be Basque, is to *feel*, or *not feel* that we are.

I need to reiterate the fact that there is no name in Basque that covers those, and only those, that are (feel themselves to be, etc.) Basque. In all sincerity, to me it seems evident that *euskaldun* is inadequate for this purpose, however much I would like the truth to be otherwise. It is possible that authors such as Hiribarren, Elissamburu, Adéma, etc., like some on our side, worked on the premise that *euskaldun* = Basque, but that is because they were concerned with only one part of the country (which does not include Bayonne, Anglet, etc.), where at the time the one meant the other, unless they were referring to a past in which things were still as they should be. Even so, "Zalduby" himself, to cite just one example, saw that this equivalence was in danger of being lost. See *RIEV* 2 (1908): 758:

> *Euskaldunek arrotzekin*
> *Ahanztea Eskuara,*
> *Odolari hori berdin*
> *Ukho egitea da.*
> *Gauden erne sar ez dadin*
> *Ahalke hoi gutara.*

13. I do not care at all, here and now, about the obvious fact that *euskaldun* comes from *euskara*; etymologies only interest me when I am concerned with historical linguistics. On the other hand, I do care about the form in which words are used in whatever language, and very especially the meaning attributed to them. This is particularly so when the language concerned is *euskara*: it was my first language and I have never stopped using it, although I have never employed it in a way both *opportune et importune*, as is now the custom in certain media, without afterwards repenting of it and thinking of ways to make amends. I have, moreover, a not inconsiderable knowledge of the language spoken in different areas of the country both today and in the past, and I am not too unfamiliar, even for professional reasons, with whatever has been written in this language, throughout the land.

Therefore it is natural that, when I read or hear something in Basque, I sometimes find it good, sometimes average, and many times (in contrast, thank goodness, to our indisputable Malherbes and Vaugelas) hanging in the balance between acceptable and rejectable. But occasionally, and above all recently, there have been too many things that I find bad, including some that sound downright abominable. However, I don't know how much this is worth next to the "linguistic intuition" of people who cite book, chapter, verse, page, and line of some work chosen from an *Autores buenos (y malos)* that has yet to be written for lack of a Father Ladrón de Guevara or Garmendia de Otaola. But in any case, one would have to admit that when those two were writing, they were able to base their work on a much firmer and broader consensus.

Anyway, whatever my thoughts or feelings may be worth, there are sentences that would drive me mad if I heard them frequently. For example: *euskaldun honek ez daki euskaraz, euskaldun hau erdalduna da, erdaldun hori euskalduna da,* etc. However, there is nothing surprising in their supposed translation into Romance: *ese vasco no sabe vascuence* "that Basque doesn't speak Basque," or perhaps at an earlier time *ese vizcaíno no es vascongado,* etc. If this is the case, and it will continue to be so as long as those of us who have learned the language in a certain way are still around (and, what is worse for those who oppose this view, as long as there are people who continue learning that way), no one will be able to remove *euskaldun* from its venerable hinges. As it says on a "Korrika" sign defying the wind in a street in my peaceful home town: *Ez al dakizu euskara dela euskaldun egiten gaituena?*

In any case, *euskaldun* will continue to be a constant temptation as long as *vasco* doesn't have an acceptable and accepted equivalent—and not because we now seem never to take a step without basing it on some semantic paradigm in Spanish which we try to match slot by slot: people for whom feeling Basque means "acting Basque" find it impossible not to have an appropriate means to refer to themselves, and this in their own language (whether they know it or not). Iparraguirre succumbed to this temptation when he affirmed that the sacred oak tree of Guernica was beloved *euskaldunen artean,* as did, more surprisingly still, Arana Goiri himself when in his *Itxarkundia,* published in 1879 (*Obras completas,* p. 2405), he included a couplet whose wording was altered almost ad libitum in the 1930s:

> *Itxartu zaiz, bizkattarrak,*
> *Aupa, euzkeldun gustijak*

In my opinion, such temptation should not be allowed to persist, because it will constantly give rise to irksome misunderstandings. From time to time one reads and even occasionally writes somewhat inadequate alternatives such as *euskal-herritar, euskal-herriko,* and similar possibilities. As I said in *La lengua vasca* (1977), p. 67, I personally would vote for *euskotar,* a term which at least has the honor of having been prohibited by the Franco dictatorship. But it seems that, for reasons which perhaps someday will be made clear, the immanent censors of today coincide on this point (and others) with the transcendent censorship of not so long ago.

I will naturally not try to hide the fact that the term is the creation of Sabino Arana, as was the almost universally accepted *Euskadi*—and there is no need to add that in all these names I replace his *z*'s, which in some cases appear rather late, with *s*'s. In any event, among us, a neologism (from 1897?) that has reached the ripe old age of eighty is old enough to be venerated. And I should add, to avoid confusion, that although Bidebarrieta Street existed centuries before *euskotar,* the latter was coined earlier than Juventud Vasca de Bilbao and is some twenty years older than *Aberri.*

14. In what I have said and am going to say, I am trying to distinguish facts from proposals, meanings from use, etc., and I apologize for any errors made in failing to demarcate fields that should be kept sharply distinct. My inclinations in favor of the prefix *eusko-* in composition rather than *euskal-* are, however, much stronger than those that incline me toward *euskotar.*

This prefixed item was introduced by Sabino Arana in an article in the March 1901 edition of *Euzkadi,* and by the way has, right at the beginning, a note of interest: "People say *euskera,* with an *s*; but now I write [*sic,* because until then he did not do so] *euzkera,* because I feel that this is the pure form, based on the etymology that I attribute to it . . . As is well known, the *z* sound . . . is similar to that of the *s* in French." See *Obras completas,* p. 1783ff, and the first part of *Artículos publicados en la 1ª época de 'Euzkadi',* 1901 (Bilbao, 1908).

The linguistic bases for his considerations on "Obtención de *euzko*" [title of the first section of Arana's article], etc. are clearly very weak, but there are others based on equally tenuous grounds that have survived, having to do with language (I refer the reader simply to *Euskadi*) and other fields. Its artificiality is in any case reduced to *-o,* the final vowel, and I have been assured that not always fully authorized "roots" have abounded, for example in Hungarian, since the eighteenth century.

Once again we find ourselves caught in the distinction or confusion of *vasco* and *lengua vasca*, with an inevitable area of overlap, whereas I was in favor of separation and even of divorce years ago. Since I know that people have been going around whispering as much, I am happy to take this occasion to declare that I personally had rather a lot to do with the conversion of *Euskal Kontseilu Nagusia* into *Eusko Kontseilu Nagusia*, which has had a more recent and better-known prolongation.

There is also an article entitled "Euskal-zalekerija" by Arana Goiri in *La Patria* 1902, *Obras completas*, pp. 2086–88, which ends with these words: "Eta ezpa-da gura neugaz etxi *euzkel* eta *euzkera euzko-ele* tik datozala eta *euzko* euzkeldunen errijaren antziñeko ixena dala, esan bediz *euzkelerri-jai, euzkelerri-dantza* . . .; *ez iñoz be euzkel-jai, euzkel-dantza* . . ." Because curiously enough, although the fact is not inexplicable, *euskara* is as united to *euskaldun* as it is to *Euskal herria* for those who consider word formation, but perhaps because the name of the Basque Country is a second-degree descendent, the latter is much freer of linguistic associations for speakers. Anyway, it is not necessary to accept the protasis of Arana Goiri (*ex falso, quodlibet*) to arrive at a conclusion that is quite similar to his.

Whatever the origin of *eusko* and whatever its historical basis, as long as there are no substitutes available, using it will, in my opinion, have a prophylactic value, since what we are dealing with is a problem of hygiene, of collective mental health, rather than a question of language. Think of our Basque writers in the Basque press, Basque literature, Basque research, recently in Basque television, etc. Introduce the term *euskal*, first with the meaning of *vasco* in current Spanish usage, and we immediately find that there is a tendency to impose its strong, linguistic meaning. And from this muddle (as they say in a well-known Latin aphorism), only more muddles can come.

To my mind, Jean de Sponde or Blas de Otero (not to mention S. Manteli or Oscar Rochelt) are Basque writers because they are writers, a quality that no one would dare to dispute, and because they are Basque. Obviously, however, they do not represent literature *en lengua vasca, d'expresión Basque, éuskara* or, as they used to say before the Glorious Uprising and long after, *euskérica*, an adjective that was used recently by L. M. Mújica. Nor do they represent what I suggested in the mistitled *Historia de la literature vasca* (1960), refusing to follow my own advice: "The traditional, precise Spanish term for designating literature in Basque is '*literatura vascongada*.'" But if we can not, as well as should not, use this term, we certainly can easily reserve *euskal* for those cases where it is apt.

In other words, *suum cuique*—without this getting anyone's dander up in Oyarzun. *Gu gara euskal prentsa* or *Euskal prentsa gu gara*, as some said quite rightly—quite rightly as long as this is not translated as "We are the (entire) Basque press," something which is obviously false and which, as such, is inimical to public tranquility. Therefore, I repeat, if *eusko* were not available, we would have to invent it.

Thankfully, however, it is available, because neither Franco nor his post-Franco followers have been able to do away with it. I can't resist the temptation, on this score, to recount what happened to me during the discussion period that followed the talk I referred to at the beginning. A young opponent rejected *eusko* with pronounced disdain, alleging that it was a term that had "only been used by a political party"—a party which, though not said, supposedly merited no consideration in our community, despite the fact that it usually obtained a fairly considerable number of votes.

I am not quite sure what is happening to some of our younger generations. Perhaps they are so preoccupied by the need to remember all the surnames burdening their memory that they have forgotten the history of their own country, not to mention that of elsewhere. It is not a question of what happened in 1900, 1920, 1931, 1936, etc.; now we can't even remember what was going on in 1960 or 1970. So I took the liberty of giving, as a kind of reminder, an array of examples: *Eusko Abertzale Ekintza* was "*Acción Nacionalista Vasca*" [not to be confused with *Partido Nacionalista Vasco* (PNV), the largest Basque nationalist party], one of whose battalions was called during the war *Eusko Indarra*; the entity for which this journal is the mouthpiece (and no one can claim that it was composed only by nationalists) was and still is called *Eusko Ikaskuntaza*; the Basque government of 1936, which was a coalition government, was called *Eusko Jaurlaritza* even back then; the book by Jon Bilbao is called *Eusko Bibliographia* because it doesn't deal only with linguistic matters, while that of Vinson, which includes works in and on Basque, is entitled *Essai d'une bibliographie de la langue basque*; José Miguel de Barandiarán popularized in several publications the still current name of *Eusko-Folklore*, and so on and so forth.

I listed some of these examples on that occasion, and perhaps others, thus giving, I felt, a fairly full response to the objection. But, silly me, I didn't realize until it was pointed out to me later that I had failed to mention the song (not hymn) that my young opponent had surely sung many times—a song invented for people who, although they fought in a real war, never felt on the whole very bellicose:

> *Eusko gudariak gara,*
> *Euskadi askatzeko*

No one has yet dared—despite, I am sure, the ready advice of interested parties—to amend this to *Euskal gudariak*.

In my opinion, therefore—and just to step outside these four walls for a moment—James Joyce was an *Irish* author, even though he wrote (and he was fully and sadly aware of it) in "the language of the oppressor," as some good folk would say in the language of the oppressor.

15. I shall just say a few words, because more would be too much, on the subject of *Euskadi*, which is a neologism that comes from a nonexistent *euzko-/eusko-* that undermines our grammar, etc., etc., but which today is accepted both inside and outside of Vasconia.

The founder of Basque nationalism, and I suppose there are no doubts about his name, is a person who, both in word and deed, exhibited various and even contradictory features which have rarely been duly considered—that is, examined from a certain distance. When a cold, detached, work has appeared, and to me this would be the case of the work by Larronde, it is shunned in favor of products by the partisan militants.

Accordingly, I hesitate to express my opinion that it is not unfair to attribute to him estimable good taste as far as his ear was concerned and regarding a good part of the material that he produced. I remember, as token examples, girls' names such as *Edurne* or *Igone*, etc., although one has to admit that with boys' names, due to the *-a* imposed in many cases because of the well-known bias of Astarloa, he was not so fortunate. Consequently, *Euskadi* is a name that sounds, to me and surely to many others, not bad at all.

People have written that it is "an ill-formed neologism" or something of the kind, and I cannot entirely agree with that opinion. I now tend to agree with the view expressed by Justo Gárate, and would say in my own words that it is "a not so (well- or ill-*re*formed) neologism," because in this case there are very clear models for the creation in the work of the reformer himself prior to the reform.

Let us take a few lines from *Obras completas*. From 1887, written in 1885, "Etimologías euskéricas," p. 39: from the words *euskera* and *euskeldun* "have been formed the names *Euskera-uria* or *Euskeria* and *Euskera-erria* or *Euskelerria* . . ." to denote the nation or race. Similar suggestions are found in "Los partidos fueristas de Euskeria" (1987, p. 1375); "Un partido y dos procedimientos" (1899, p. 1780); and see especially the note on *Euzko*, 1901, on p. 1827:

> Todos los demás nombres que emplean en español los escritores vaskos, a saber: *Vaskonia, Euskaria y Euskeria* son españoles, sin haberme valido el pretender en el citado Pliego de mis *Etimologías Euskéricas* [el trabajo de 1885] prohijara el euzkera estos dos últimos.

> "All the other names used in Spanish by Basque writers, namely *Vasko-nia, Euskaria* and *Euskeria* are Spanish, despite my failed attempts in the aforementioned Defense of my *Etimologías Euskéricas* [his 1885 work] to argue that the latter two are derived from Basque."

In other words, *Euskaria, Euskeria*, where the suffix was the alien part, were Basquified by introducing the suffix -*di*, yielding a "collection of *euzko/euskos*," whose -*o* was regularly changed to -*a*. Except that, in actual fact, -*a* was already present in *Euskaria*: what is not documented is the "primitive" vowel -*o*, from which -*a* "was derived."

16. I will conclude with *vasco*, which is almost where I began. We have already mentioned certain curious aspects of its history: the fact that its meaning only covered part of what today are called the Basques, the fact that it came into (limited) use late in Spanish Romance, details that seem to point to a northern origin, etc.

While its use in past centuries, and also in French Romances, has not been well delineated, I tend to agree with an idea of Antonio Tovar's that I have heard several times, although he has not discussed it in writing as far as I know.[1]

The discussion must be based on the well-known fact that nouns in Romance come, although in very small proportion, from the nominative or subject case in Latin, even in Spanish: cf. *sastre* from *sartor*, like *Sartre* in France. This is much clearer in French and in Occitan, where the contrast *subject case/accusative case* or *straight/oblique* case was manifest until quite late: fr. *le roi/le roi*, occit. *lo reis/lo rei*.

The difference is greater when it is not only a question of the presence or absence of an ending, but of differences brought about depending on where the accent is placed, something that happens with the so-called imparisyllables: fr. *chanter/chantor, peintre/peintor*. And here we have stems ending in *-n*, to which *Vasco/Vascone* belong, although in Latin there is no change in the accented syllable.

Our present-day *Vasco* would come, therefore, from the Latin nominative case, through a Gallic language, or Occitan, to be more precise. The model would be the one which, in Old French, appears in examples such as *ber/baron, falc/falcon, gars/garcon*. A detailed study, however, remains to be done.

CHAPTER 3

Romanization and the Basque Language

"Romanización y lengua vasca," in *Fontes Linguae Vasconum* 16 (1984): 189–98. (Also in *Sobre historia de la lengua vasca* 1, San Sebastián: Anales del Anuario del Seminario de Filología Vasca "Julio de Urquijo," 1988, pp. 156–65.)

1. I have the impression that the rotund title I have used here may be no more than a way of dressing up a very limited subject, already over-worked here and elsewhere. In the final analysis, this will end by drawing attention to a lone language within a comparative context of some breadth, a language that was alive two millennia ago and still lives today. For in a generally accepted sense, now that it has authentic meaning, it can be said that we are dealing with *one* language, although it may not sound today as it did then.

I will say, by way of introduction, that when we speak of this language, Euskara or Basque, there are three peculiarities that awaken the interest of the people, both the layman and the initiated, more than any others. With the intention of limiting myself to the basics, I shall dispose of them in the following order:

a) We have not yet found, nor do we expect to find in the near future, a place in the genetic classification that belongs to Euskara. This is another way of saying that its origin is unknown.

b) Even lacking sufficient outlines of typological classification, at least we can say that this language differs a great deal in structure from its neighboring European languages and equally as much from the African languages of the Mediterranean.

c) Lastly, it is the only European language that has been preserved from the previous centuries to the beginning of our era on this part of the continent without having been erased by the advance of the Indo-European languages, and especially by Latin and the Romance languages.

No one disputes that there is a close relationship between a) and b): in spite of the overwhelming number of coincidences owing to contact, the distinct point of departure and disparity of origin continues to be reflected, after millenia, in structural differences. It has also been long thought that the first aspect (or the first two together) has a great deal to do with the third. However, we will treat this later on.

2. The following discussion originates with the idea that, in addition to being the most obvious and ostentatious, language change is possibly the most important alteration in the acculturation process in addition to being, obviously, the most manifest and attention-getting. Clearly it is not required that an ethnic group, a nation if you will, have a single language nor that their language be unique to them as opposed to being shared with other communities. Neither is it certain that the loss of the language brings with it the disappearance of the national personality, and there are many examples that prove this. On the other hand, there seem to be enormous variations in the group's adhesion to its own language, both now and in times past.

Moreover, one must add that a language can be ascribed to a people or country in many different ways. Thus we can maintain, without depreciating the exceptional achievements of the "Israeli miracle," that Hebrew has never exactly been a dead language, although for many centuries it was not the normal, unrestricted language of any Jewish community. On the other hand, as Diehl says, "Latin continued being the official language, as strange as it seems," in administrative territory of the first level throughout the Byzantine Empire during and after Justinian's time. In summary, it would not be difficult to find correspondences of the most varied types between languages and peoples, as well as between usages and spheres of usage within each of those groups.

One may ask what problem is posed by the survival of a language when so many known languages from antiquity have been preserved without showing any signs of imminent extinction. It is true that one might answer in turn that there is no lack or scarcity of languages that have disappeared either long ago or recently, without taking into consideration the legion of unknowns that we can certify defunct on good grounds, although we cannot certify their numbers. For that reason we must now clarify a very precise aspect of this question of death and survival.

This has to do with local character that customarily presents these phenomena in time and space. We are speaking of this part of Europe and the last 2,000 to 2,500 years. And in this part, the west, a process—or better, two distinct phases of the same process—has been almost completed, different from that which occurred in the eastern part of the Mediterranean basin and surrounding areas.

The two phases, the effects of which were not limited to the linguistic arena, are the Indo-Europeanization of this zone, followed by Romanization in a less extensive area, a phenomenon that might be called Latinization if we restrict ourselves to language.

If we take as a given the idea, shared by many who study the question, that the Indo-European *Urheimat* or the focal point of the diffusion of those Indo-European languages was not western but rather from central Europe beyond the Rhine and the Danube, there is very little to the west that does not display this character today: everything is Romantic, Celtic, or Germanic. Etruscan, the origins of which are still veiled in uncertainty, disappeared quickly and completely, so much so that it didn't leave any clear indications about its nature, in spite of the efforts of the now popular Claudius. Iberian, which was of another class, also disappeared, as did Ligurian, if we may unite indices of very different character and value beneath that name. Even the language of the Picts in the extreme north of Great Britain was extinguished without leaving a trace of its ancestry.

3. The extension of Latin that more recently prolonged and closed the cycle of Indo-Europeanization, has been less widespread: the preservation of what came before is clearly marginal. Gaul and Celtiberian, apart from Lusitanian, disappeared. They were imported Celtic languages (that is, Indo-European) and they disappeared just as Venetian and Mesapian, Italic languages in the strictest sense, did before them. At the edge of the Romance-speaking regions, however, there remains a border of nondisplaced languages: British, Germanic dialects, Libyan-Berber. All of them border languages generally in contact with similar languages spoken outside Roman territory.

In other words, this only happened where the Roman Empire did not have time to arrive or establish itself. The defeat of Varo put the definitive brakes on advances into German Territory. Conquest in the

British Isles was recent and incomplete, given that Hibernia and the territory north of the walls of Hadrian and Antoninus were outside the sphere dominated by Rome. There is no need to emphasize that in North Africa, where Punic (the language of colonization) is also still known, the Libyan-Berber substratum has persisted, in contact with a very broad, though lightly populated, southern territory far from Latin influence. Not even Arabic has eliminated it completely.

Having pointed that out, one can underline the fact that, from the Atlantic and the Rhine to the Mediterranean, nothing is left from previous times that is not Latin-based in origin. Latin or Germanic, but the latter does not interest us at present, even if we keep in mind the recent consequences of the *Völkerwanderungen* in the area considered here. Thus, the rule is stronger because of the exception: there exists a non-Romanized stronghold in a corner of the Gulf of Bizkaia, north and south of the Pyrenees, where Euskara—the Basque language—is still used. For we must emphasize here that Romanization is being taken in the sense of supplanting the ancient language, without taking into account any influences it might have received from Latin and Romance languages. Those influences have been important to us, although their intensity has varied with location and time period.

4. If we focus more on geographic considerations, we must point out two areas within the broad sphere of Roman domination with imprecise boundaries: the western area, which we were just concerned with, and the eastern one. The latter has shown itself, in effect, much more benign than the western with respect to inferior languages in one way or another. I am not going to consider the cause of the divergence, a task greater than my abilities, because it's enough for the moment to examine the results, the only aspect that interests us here. These being different, the historical situation also had to be different.

We know, then, that in the Near East Sumerian, Acadian, Elamite, Hurrian, etc., and Urartian disappeared. The languages of Anatolia also disappeared, although perhaps some lasted longer that we think for the substitutions are in large part recent, coming after the expansion of Helenism with Alexander and his princely heirs, which we take as terminus post quem. And Rome came to be the ultimate and greatest promoter of this type of acculturation, as has been frequently indicated.

As that which was hidden begins to be revealed, in the East we establish that Aramaic, one of the languages of the New Testament, is still living and how it continues to live, although diminished in modern times. Egyptian, transformed into Greek in writing and in vocabulary, survives as Coptic, still spoken around 1500 in spite of the Arab tombstone, and is still used today as a sacred language. In the first centuries of our era, Armenian and Georgian arose out of the previous nothingness; there are translations into Gothic, the first Germanic language known through abundant texts. Languages like Ilirian and Dacian, which were erased, fell within the area of Latin linguistic influence. At any rate, Albanian is still preserved.

This does not mean to suggest that indigenous languages were lost only in these lands, but it does seem admissible to me that in the extensive zone of the empire in which Greek was the first language, at least in what we could call higher usages, discounting the officiality of Latin in a limited use, other languages were given a lot more room. In that area at that time and for a long time to follow, the coexistence of diverse languages in the same locations was occurring, as was the maintenance of the same language communities over nonconnected territories.

5. What happened in pagan antiquity happened later more clearly in Christian antiquity, undoubtedly because we know the facts of that time better. At least in principle, everyone was preached to in their language: from this came the religious texts, whether mere translations or not, in Armenian, Georgian, Syrian, and Gothic, without going farther east. This tendency continued with the Slavic languages, from Cyril and Methodius, to the extent that they are eastern or received their inspiration from Byzantium. Traces can even be found in Komi in the fourteenth century.

This is not what happened in the western part of the empire, or even among the ruins of the empire. In agreement with the rule that demanded *in necessariis unitas*, it was thought at first glance, and not without basis, that unity was never so imperative as in the official language of the church. From there, Christianity gave the coup de grace to indigenous languages, already threatened and in close proximity, in countries such as Gaul.

Marginal languages, Celtic and Germanic in our case, were fragmented and late to arrive, conceived rather as shortcuts to accessing the single canonical language, which explains the abundance of glosses and annotations. This factor has also surely influenced the late appearance of Romance languages in writing, although they had to be taken into

account in the spoken form for a long time before, to judge by what was
put forth at the Council of Tours (813), and so on.

6. In a discussion about the reason why the Basque language has arrived
alive in modern times—a discussion that would be little more than a
critical summary of interminable previous debates—it is necessary to
determine certain aspects which, accepted as axioms (although they be
far from accepted in an historical sense), they do not have to be defended
again and again later on. Those who do not accept them can reject them
or modify them without going into the examination of what follows.

First of all, it is evident that when we speak of how the language has
been preserved we do not speak of factors that made the current outcome necessary, but of factors that made it possible. In order to forestall
questions, I gather from this a consideration that is repeated in lively
debates about the causes, in particular the historical ones.

Within the material consideration, as the basis of this examination,
and according to what history tells us, I would hazard to affirm that the
Basque language has never found itself more swept along by a current
racing to oblivion than during the Roman period. We know that Latin
displaced Basque dialects from east to west along general lines, and that
it could well have wiped out the ones that remained. It could have caused
them to disappear, and here we enter a very thorny field of conjecture,
wondering what would have happened if certain conditions had lasted
longer.

For how long has the opinon held sway that the language is headed
for total ruin if some radical change does not occur? This opinion is of
rather recent vintage. Cardaberaz and Landazuri lamented in the eighteenth century that Basque was losing territory in Alava and they did not
suggest in any way that the regression would be a passing thing. Iztueta,
however, felt safe in the following century—or at least that's what he
said—in the heart of the Gipuzkoan block, surrounded by Basque walls.
Those like Iturriaga who saw the danger, albeit not imminent, insep-
arably tied to the changes that were happening ever faster, were few.
Humboldt was, as far as I can tell, the first to make a precise prediction
around 1800: by 1900 there would be no more than a written memory
of this language.

7. There remains to explain the reasons why the empire that erased so
much of what had come before it in the social and cultural realms did

not do away with our little language in these places. I call it little because few people used it, none of them educated, in a poor area whose conquest suggested we did not know bloody battles. The territory, in addition to being small, was passable. Indeed, people traveled through its very center.

It has been alleged that smallness, poverty, weakness, and barbarity were advantages instead of inconveniences since they kept the country, hardly sensitive at all to the influences from outside, from becoming the sought-after prey of foreigners. This country, the old Euskal Herria, was represented in Hispania by the *saltus Vasconum*, to borrow Caro Baroja's phrase, to which without qualms I would add the Atlantic territories toward an uncertain west. Not the *ager*, which undoubtedly did a poor job of guarding the old idiomatic heritage—which does not mean that it lost it completely right away; we must remember Lerga, for one. Nor was urban life flourishing here; when speaking of the zone next door to *saltus* one is always speaking of Navarrese Iruña and of the Alavese one, which did not carry that name by mere chance. Lapurdum, to add another example, was only documented much later. This allows us to understand that the Roman influence, Latin with regard to the language, was of light intensity in these zones in which the archeological remnants are still so scarce. In another area, the conclusions to which Gerhard Rohlfs and Jean Séguy arrived independently with regard to place names demonstrate specifically that Latin (and Gallo-Latin) formations are becoming more and more rare as we get closer to the modern department of the Atlantic Pyrenees. At the same time, we find an identicalness more than a similarity between Gascuña and part of Aragon plus Navarra: I speak of the suffix -*òs*, -*ués*, Basque -*otz*, -*oze*.

But the intensity, even if low, had to be effective by its very constant repetition, as it was always working away—unless, clearly, it didn't last. And according to what is generally admitted, it did not go on: the Roman administration, framework of the Roman order, soon began to function poorly and eventually arrived at the point where it did not function in areas that were ever bigger and more important.

That this must have happened in the third century, in the next century, or even later is not too important. The tempo of the mutations was not the same then as it is now.

In any case, the result was that with the weakening of the foreign power our own strength increased, a strength that was translating into opposition, in such a way that up until Leovigildo (and again we name well-known persons) and his Merovingian contemporaries, the Basques had a period of two centuries <u>in round numbers</u> in which to move as they wished without having to pay great attention to foreign pretensions.

8. One feels obligated to think that things were very different in these *saltus* and in the space that surrounded them, much more different in contrast with the truly Roman world: Pompaelo could not have been the same as Caesaraugusta or Burdigala. This alternative, more than a disparity, undoubtedly occurred in the economic and social organization of both dominions, an aspect to which we must return. One must admit, then that the coexistence of two communities—neighbors in space but distant in treatment—in which a certain balance had been reached, was unstable by necessity but not too much so (remember, for example, the way in which the militia had to interfere), and that balance was able to last a long time. All things considered, it would have reached an inevitable end if the contact had been maintained without some radical variations.

After Tovar, people spoke of linguistic change, and the language, which is one of the constitutive factors of a community, had to be a firm factor of separation at the same time as it was immediate and patent evidence of the separation itself.

Any language can disappear in order to make way for another, whether it is similar or not. All things considered, it seems reasonable to suppose that the process is easier and even simpler when the occupying language is close to the language of the occupied territory. Thus, we do not know for certain, or at least I do not know, how Navarrese Romance disappeared, save for a few remnants (plus the Aragonese non-Pyreneean branch) in the face of Castilian pressure. Basque dialects have also been lost by Romanization, even in Navarra itself, but not without an echo—at least after 1872–76. No one has written anything similar to *El último tamborilero de Erraondo* about the death of a variety of Navarrese Romance by slow consumption, a language whose existence has been ignored, as it seems, by a few historians.

By taking this path we could arrive at the explanation, ceteris paribus, for the disappearance of the language of the Cantabrians, who also manifested their rebellion over time, as opposed to the preservation of our own. Or within what would shortly be called Vasconia, the disappearance of Celtiberian, which was surely spoken in Cascante, for example, as well as in the heart of Celtiberia.

Even though we reject Walde's hypothesis, there is no doubt that Latin and ancient Celtic, especially if we're dealing with "q-Celtic," were much more like each other than, for example, modern Portuguese and Irish or Gaelic. However, since the Cantabrians spoke something that was at the very least late western Indo-European, whether or not it was precisely Celtic, they had fewer obstacles to render it into Latin, a closely related language, than the Basques who were speaking something genetically distinct.

This reasoning would offer, if correct, an easy solution to a difficult problem. In spite of this advantage, it would have to face down serious inconveniences. In the first place, for the ingenuous observer (and even for the initiated) the first practical criteria of interlinguistic proximity lies in the possibility, short term or long term, of the mutual understanding between speakers of diverse languages. Seen in this light, it is difficult to believe that the proximity proposed by the comparisonist was as clear cut for the speaker. Even phonologically, where the difference must have been much clearer in the beginning, it does not seem that Latin-speaking peoples found themselves very close to the Canatabrians.

In fact, there is some embarrassingly clear and even trite evidence. Mela III, 15, speaks to us of the Cantabrian peoples and rivers *quorum nomina nostro ore concipi nequeant*. And it had to be more work to understand current phrases of the language than to repeat or transcribe proper names.

9. It is not feasible to determine how much weight this structural divergence factor carried in the conservation of the native language, but all in all, it is difficult to believe that the essential factor was not another class of diversity, that it could be extralinguistic or, even better, a diversity that encompassed the linguistic factor as one of its aspects.

It can be unwaveringly affirmed that, as is customary in these cases, the spoken language itself was perfectly capable of serving the vital needs of the community before the arrival of the Romans. It was undoubtedly a fine instrument of communication for the socioeconomic organization of the members of that community. What the Romans brought to the dominated people, with variations demanded by circumstance, was indisputably superior and carried with it great benefits. I will limit myself to mentioning, without referring to classic texts, the dialog of the Jewish zealots in *The Life of Brian,* faced with question, "What have the

Romans brought us?" Even the most intransigent found it difficult to respond in the pure and simple negative.

The common way of life of the indigenous people was perceived as a poor one in the minds of the conquerors and colonizers since it had been classified as barbarous, even in the modern sense of the word: Strabo would have called it *thēriôdes*. But just as happened with so many peoples, such as the Indians of the North American prairies or of the Argentine pampas, a radical rejection of the foreign element, which is not going to be favorable for the home folks during the lengthy preliminary period, commonly manifests on such occasions. Moreover, in general, it is difficult to accept impositions.

To say that we know very little of the Basque organization is almost an exaggeration. It has been classified as tribal, a term I have used myself more than once and which provokes reservations if not used in a very strict sense—that is, almost empty of meaning. It would not be rash to assure ourselves that our organization, if we can include ourselves with our ethnic ancestors, had fewer inequalities of class or group, by a defect of hierarchization, than the one the Romans were trying to impose upon us and which was passing into our tradition by means of domination and contact.

The language itself does not add a great deal to our enlightenment. As I suggested once before, the western *ugazaba*, from *ugatz* (*ugaz-*) plus *asaba*, could very well have been in another time something more than the boss of some workers or the master of some servants. In Bizkaia *ibar jaun* was documented in 1596, translated as "merino" without knowing for certain if the approximated correspondence was at least correct in origin. At least in Navarra and in Sola, and the latter during the high Middle Ages, *ibar* was the name that designated the valley more as an administrative term than a geographic one before *haran*.

10. In the European west, Christianization often finished off what pagan Romanization had already broken. In our country, specifically, one could say that Christianity did not offer support for our language until the modern age, above all because of the confrontation between the Reformation and the Countereformation.

As we know, there has been a long debate between those who advocate the early or late introduction of Christianity among us. The evidence employed is varied, although generally it serves only as an indicator. Naturally, everyone recognized that Christianization began through rather important nuclei before expanding throughout the population of the *saltus*. Everyone probably also accepts that the new religion was introduced quickly in the cities, in Pompaelo for example, without thinking about the apostolic age.

The language has repeatedly been thought of as a possible source of information, and it has been used in this sense, without having served to arrive at unanimous conclusions. We must keep in mind, among other considerations, that the religious and even ecclesiastical lexicon also changed a great deal, as is normal for the cultural lexicon. For example, we have for "paradise" *baradizu*, the first and most archaic form in evidence, more firmly rooted than *paradizu, paradisu,* or *paraiso.* It all depends on the area our evidence manages to cover. Some of us have become aware late in the game that *dekuma* (not registered in the DRA) and *tekuma* "tithe" were documented in Roncal and Salazar, along with *detxema* and *amarren,* the latter from *hamar* "ten."

At any rate, the fact that the language has endured constitutes an argument in favor of the hypothesis that Christianity spread at a later date, given the demonstrated lethal power of evangelization with regard to indigenous languages. On the other hand, and assuming that Christianity would have spread in a general manner among the population groups that had constituted its primary support for centuries, it is difficult to believe that the current situation is what it is. Because, as we know, diffusion in this area signifies exclusion and even proscription of all—including language—that is converted from being "our own" to being "foreign" and "hostile." Especially with regard to what happened in the Visigothic era, here could be another key to the different comportment of the Cantabrians and Asturians, Christianized and as a result Romanized at an earlier date.

At any rate, a more thorough investigation would be of great interest, one that pays less attention to the usual roles of what religion was among us, including the linguistic field, during the dark centuries when we believe it was established without opposition. To me at least it seems strange that the *Confiteor* has the aspect of the oldest prayer preserved amongst us.

11. In closing, I shall comment on something that I have mentioned more than once, although never on this type of occasion. As I believe that apparent digression can be instructive or at least graphic, I shall move from the historical to the novel that would like to be historical.

I know only too well that our historical-legendary narrations, no less ours because they are written in Romance, do not enjoy good standing, although in recent times the historical novel has lifted its head by the grace and the labor of Humberto Eco. I would not reject that unfavorable judgment although I would have to stress that studying literature is not studying masterpieces and leaving the rubbish disdainfully aside. On the other hand, I would not reject it out of hand as if there were no well-marked classes within it.

As an example, it is enough to compare the famous *Tradiciones vasco-cántabras* by Juan Vicente Araquistain (1866) with *Amaya o los vascos en el siglo VIII* (1879) by Navarro Villoslada. Personally, to state it clearly, I think that the latter is better than the former as a book: at least, anyone who has read them both (I don't know if there are many today who find themselves in that situation) will have to recognize that the novel reads better than the traditions. But this is not the aspect upon which I wish to touch.

I wish to underline that the historical base is not the same even from a distance, and this is not something that depends on the fifteen years that separates their publications. Araquistain swallows everything down to the stem, and we find in him once again—but now very late—the Cantabrians who are us with all *their* paraphernalia (let us respect the classic languages, at least in questions of number), *gau-illas*, etc. Navarro Villoslada of Viana, in contrast, gives a version of what occurred here around the year 700 that can be considered the novelized version born of reading Barbero y Vigil, if the anachronism were not so dreadful.

He provides a version, undoubtedly severely retouched, from a firm traditionalist foundation. With regard to another aspect, I do not believe that an illustrous Navarrese politician is at all correct in his recent public commentary, although he reveals a lack of knowledge of the pertinent literature. There is nothing distinctive in Navarro Villoslada's use of "Spain" or "Spanish." He is merely conforming to everyone else's usage—Carlists and Liberals alike, including Iparraguirre or Campión—who reviewed his novel. What *is* distinctive and what distinguishes him from the commentator is his use of "Basque" *vasco* underlined in the title of the work.

To begin with, the Christianization of the above-mentioned Basques was far from being complete, although it was well underway. Paganism persisted in the *saltus* that continued to be free of the Visigoth power, although it may have been subject to incursions. The *ager* was Christian, the knower of Latin, pro-Visigoth, although the mountain people charged with menial occupations were abundant there, and not at all submissive. At that moment, as a result of the Arab victory, Pamplona was the hand that the rebel players wanted to win, the hand being a continuation of Roman order.

And that hand was won, although not at the time and in the manner indicated by the novelist. Lacarra, never much of a novelist, says in his *Historia política del reino de Navarra I*, p. 47: "We saw that Pamplona, with an ethnically and culturally differentiated population, had lost its position as an urban-center director that it held in previous centuries. The urban aspect had been dissolved into the Basque rural and tribal aspects that predominated everywhere . . . When the foreign-director element disappeared, in order to settle in Pamplona one had to count on the acquiescence of the rural population of La Cuenca and those who dominated the passes and access, both in the north—Roncesvalles—and in the south or the west. *This population, according to what we have seen was Basque-speaking, and with a social structure clearly different from that of the surrounding countries.*" The italics are mine, but the reader can find other analogous references in the work, that is, those mentioned in this very passage.

12. While drawing this picture that offers a frame acceptable for consideration (if we suppress literary flourishes, traditionalists, etc.), Navarro Villoslada had an immediate model that inspired him. Certainly even his Roman-Visigothic Fuenterrabía, which now would be better called Irún, had good reason to exist, although it referred to an undoubtedly previous epoch.

Like us, he had in mind the image of a mountainous Basque Country, neighbor to a broad, rich, Romanized zone—within a common Vasconia—which in its day was expanding toward the north. Only in those days the south was more "ours" than in the time of don Rodrigo.

He also had in mind the two Carlist wars and in particular the first one, the real one, the one that was not originated by the pressure to occupy an empty space. Also, Zumalacárregui had his power in the region of Teodosio and García, and he was opposed to the urban, garrisoned world, directed by people who looked with aversion on the spirit that animated the Carlist followers by adhesion or by necessity. He could move almost anywhere he wanted, but should not have penetrated the private preserves that were the sole secure residences of his enemies. When he tried that, though against his will, he failed and died as well.

All this is no more than an attempt to comprehend, or rather a sketch of an attempt to understand, what was a little-known and much-argued situation. It has all the inconveniences of a diagram based on meager, uncertain data. We hope that one of the great outlines of what could have been will correspond in some way to that which was. Be that as it may, we need a global image of this decisive period of our continuity, since something that has marked and continues to mark our collectivity in a striking way comes from that time.

I am not fond of moralizing, but now I am tempted to do so. It seems to me that the history of the Basque language, at that time and beyond, shows that modest factors, as opposed to brilliant prestigious ones, demonstrated their value and effectiveness all along. And it is not certain that arrogant spirits prevailed where humble methods conquered.

The choice of methods will have to be made according to place and situation, but as the old saying goes, *asmuz ta jakitez* (with will and intelligence).

CHAPTER 4

History and Prehistory of the Language

"Historia y prehistoria de la lengua," in *Sobre historia de la lengua vasca*
1. San Sebastián: Seminario de Filología Vasca "Julio de Urquijo," 1988,
pp. 23–30.

3.1. When the term "history" appears to be related in one way or another
with a language, it is important to keep one essential distinction in mind:
the one that separates the internal history of the language, comprised
of data from linguistic documents, from its external history, that of the
people for whom it has served as a principal or unique vehicle of communication and that of the territory where it has been in use.

This distinction has strong foundations not only in the order of
knowledge, but also in the order of reality. On one hand, it is possible to
construct the history of a language without paying more than marginal
attention to external historical events, just as we may also know a great
deal about the history of a country during a specific period without possessing more than fragmentary information about its linguistic situation.
This separation, which does not have to be a divorce, finds its justification in the fact that a language consists of an autonomous system—
isolated in a way, although not completely closed off to the outside like a
monad—a system only superficially affected by the most transcendental
historical events, which are especially reflected in the language's most
artificial and least structured part: its vocabulary.

History's impact on a language can be profound, but only through
mediation of another language. Languages that enjoy an easy life can
disappear without leaving more than a few traces of their existence, as
occurred with Romanization in Spain, or they may survive but carry the
mark of the contact deeply imbedded within, as could be seen in Eng-
land after the Norman invasion, or closer to home with Basque after the
Roman conquest.

3.2. Another essential distinction, an even more radical one, must be established between the history and the prehistory of languages. Everything that we can know, which is quite a bit, about the prehistory of languages when we use reconstruction techniques to enter into a past undocumented beyond the first accessible evidence must be separated in an emphatic manner from the historical, and in fact it is customary to do so by using asterisks to separate merely reconstructed forms from those for which we possess documented proof.

The history of a language is a strictly historical discipline and is constructed, therefore, in agreement with common historical methods, making use of all available evidence in the best way possible. In our case, this evidence, since we can form an abstraction of its content, offers us the advantage of not having to worry too much about its veracity, since this is a given except in the relatively rare case where the falsifier has tried to deliberately alter the tenor of the langauge in order to give his product the air of antiquity.

Having clearly distinguished between history and prehistory, one must immediately concede to the former its indisputable priority which by rights belongs to it. In the area of theory, no one will deny that a handful of well-verified facts is worth as much as any hypothetical structure, no matter how ingeniously it has been built. However, in practice this priority is not always in fact recognized.

In our case, the difference in the procedures can be observed by comparing two outstanding figures: Achille Luchaire and Hugo Schuchardt. Luchaire was a historian and only secondarily a linguist: his undoubtedly sufficient knowledge of Basque does not appear to have been too deep or extensive. Schuchardt was a brilliant linguist who added an unequalled knowledge of ancient and modern Basque to his vast linguistic experience. And given all that, it is not Schuchardt, but Luchaire—perhaps because he was a historian before anything else—who appears to us today as a model when we want to work on the history of language. He pointed out the sources for the study of medieval Basque and began to use them systematically, a work that has not been duly continued, and beyond that, he pointed out the importance of Aquitanian proper names for getting to know the most ancient accessible phase of the language.

3.3. In addition to the greater value that must be attributed to proven facts in contrast with reconstructive hypotheses, one must keep in mind the inexhaustible wealth of the historical, a reflection of multiform reality, which cannot be compared to the brutally simplified outlines of reconstruction.

All reconstruction, although dealing with recovering aspects of a disappeared reality—and succeeding, at least in the most favorable cases—always possesses characteristics born of and deduced from the method that we have used in order to arrive at it. And as this method contains—implictly or explicitly—a postulate of simplicity, the results will emerge deformed as a consequence of the schematic contortion to which the data have been submitted: between two states of language, the more ancient and the more recent, reconstruction always seeks, by definition, the shortest possible path, without taking into account the twists and turns of the road that is not at hand to be restored.[1] If we are charged with following this road in full or in part along its vacillating course, thanks to historical data, it would be silly to insist on marching along the line traced with ruler and drawing pen on the maps of reconstruction.

If, for example, we were only to make use of the Latin point of departure and the modern point of arrival, the evolution of the Spanish imperfect indicative for verbs ending in -er and -ir could be represented as a simple straight line: from the Latin -ēba-, ība-, by the hiatus of e, after the loss of the intervocalic labial, one arrives naturally at the modern -ía. But texts show us that in old Spanish, from the thirteenth century for example, the forms -ies, -ie, -iemos, etc., predominated (normally stressed on the more open vowel: -iés, etc.), although -ía was normal in the first person singular.[2]

Naturally, such simplifications are more frequent in languages whose histories are more poorly studied. To cite only one of the current superstitions we hold, among those who today prefer to write *nire* "my, mine" instead of *nere*, many think that *nire* is not only "more correct" but also "more ancient" than *nere*, given that its vowel has the support of the personal pronoun *ni* "I." This can seem reasonable, but it is no more than a supposition that documents radically reject.

Without going back to the past too much, we see through the texts that all varieties of Basque appear to have known a possessive *ene* "my, mine," that stood in contrast with an intensive or emphatic whose more generalized form is *neure* "my own, of mine," one variation of which is *nere*. Where *nere* is in use today we have, therefore, an ancient form, although being used outside of its ancient context: *nire*, on the other hand, is merely an analogical modern form built on *ni* according to the model *i: ire:: gu: gure*, etc.[3]

3.4. As we know, the extensive Basque texts began in 1545 with the publication of the book of poems by Dechepare.[4] The sixteenth century offers us already abundant documentation (there is no need to discuss its literary interest here) with works of such notable antiquity in certain aspects as Leizarraga's translations or the Bizkaian *Refranes y Sentencias*.

For some zones, documentation came later. Thus, one must wait until the seventeenth century for the first extensive high-Navarrese texts, while the *Doctrina* of Sancho de Elso does not reappear. Also from the seventeenth century are the abundant writings in Laburdin from Sara and Saint-Jean-de-Luz in one of the best epochs of Basque literature, and the first works in more or less pure Souletin (Zuberoan) came even later. We do not find sufficient information about Gipuzkoan until the beginnings of the following century, with Ochoa de Arin's catechism (1713).

The eighteenth century brought us, above all, the highs and lows of the great work by Father Larramendi. We mentioned the favorable aspects of the work already above (1.5) [not included in this anthology]; it remains only to speak of its insufficiencies. These consist of the inextricable labyrinth into which he plunged regarding so many questions about later Basque lexicography through his all-encompassing genius and his carelessness in distinguishing between data gathered orally or in writings—which are more abundant than usually thought—and about the products of his imagination that found acceptance in more authors than is generally believed.

With the research by Prince Bonaparte, the nineteenth century brings a fitting knowledge of Basque dialectology. But we addressed that topic earlier and need not return to it.

3.5. What must be clearly understood, although it is known only too well, is that the progress in recognizing the materials has been accompanied by an uninterrupted, and in large part irreparable, diminution of the materials themselves as the area in which the language is spoken has been shrinking. The last century saw a great retreat of the language in Navarra, undoubtedly influenced by the two Carlist wars, a retreat that occurred earlier in Alava because it took place in the eighteenth century, although we lack definite information about the details of the process, just as we do for part of the Basque-speaking zone to the west of the Nervión. We do know that in Vitoria they basically spoke Romance during the sixteenth century, although not in the surrounding towns, and perhaps we have preserved a sample of this Alavese variety in vocabulary collected by Landucci in 1562. In contrast, the northern limits of the language appear to have remained constant from 1500 down to the present day, and perhaps for several centuries before that.[5]

More ancient and also more imprecise was the extinction of the Basque language in the Rioja and in Burgos, whose medieval extension has been studied with so much precision by Merino Urrutia.[6]

One chapter of the external history of the language that is about to be written and that I will merely mention here is the one that should deal with the exterior expansion of the language in the Modern Age, which is no less interesting for being modest. In it the Basque of America will be studied, a topic about which we find more incidental allusions than concrete descriptions,[7] traces of Basque language of the sixteenth and seventeenth centuries in Newfoundland and especially in Iceland, where we even have samples of the picturesque *pidgin* used by the Icelanders and Basques in order to understand each other after a fashion.[8] The jargons of occupations, such as the "barallete," whose lexicon—their unique characteristic—often displays more or less deformed Basque words.[9]

The medieval boundaries of the language could be traced with precision by means of a detailed study, location by location, of the lesser place names, a study that would have a more solid foundation when it could be based on documented forms of the modern names. Thus could we uproot the idea, one that we are all inclined to hold, that the boundaries of the Basque language, even assuming them to be stable, coincided with those of historical Vasconia, the definition of which, on the other hand, is not the same for everyone. In reality, everything indicates that its borders were very sketchy and that they delineated a scattered territory.

3.6. History can never be incisively separated from prehistory. We cannot say, therefore, that the history of the Basque language began with Dechepare in 1545, nor in the previous year, nor in the following year, nor even with the first brief texts and short lists of words that began to appear with the spread of printing. In fact, it is clear that a good part of the material, in printed or manuscript form, that the authors of the sixteenth century have transmitted to us dates from a previous epoch, although its language had been modernized at certain points.

Refrains, anecdotes, and songs are contained in this chapter, as well as the emblematic slogans of some families, as rightly pointed out by Father Villasante[10] (such as that of the Martiartu family or the Bengoechea de Aulestia family), the first evidence of which would have to be dated with greater precision than has been done to date.

Fragments of ballads from the last centuries of the Middle Ages deserve special attention for their historical-cultural interest. Events related to the wars between factions are narrated in these ballads, wars that present the most visible face of the revolutionary process that succeeded in configuring the modern aspect of Gipuzkoa and Bizkaya, at least in their fundamental characteristics, by destroying archaic structures. These fragments are rare, incomplete, and poorly preserved, but even in this state they can shed light not only on our knowledge of the language but also on our understanding of events that penetrates more deeply than the superficial motives of "being better."

3.7. With regard to assigning a date, we could point out the end of the tenth century as the point of departure after which information about the Basque language began to be abundant, although deficient by its very nature.

Direct information consists of glosses, beginning with the two Basque phrases included in the *Glosas Emilianenses*, lists of words such as that contained in the *Guía del peregrino a Santiago de Compostela* from the twelfth century, occasional explanations of proper names, and brief following texts such as the one in the manuscript of the cathedral of Pamplona, dated around 1400.

In addition to this scant material that allows us access to the two faces of linguistic signs, we can also make use of other much more abundant material consisting of proper names, especially place names but also the names of people, material that has been studied only in the slightest way until now.[11] Navarra is undoubtedly a privileged region in this respect, but when it comes to pointing out some document of an especially archaic nature, first place would probably belong to the so-called "Reja" of San Millán, dated 1025, a list of names of Alavese villages that can be compared with variations in different later medieval documents.[12]

3.8. The first centuries of the Middle Ages constitute an almost total lacuna in our documentation. We must move forward, almost to the

Roman epoch, which has left us with a certain number of place names transmitted by classical authors or by inscriptions, only one small part of which has an indisputably Basque appearance.

As compensation, the Latin inscriptions of Aquitania, with maximum density in an area that extends from Saint-Girons to Bagnères de Bigorre and also—on the plains—in the country of Ausci, give proof of the existence of Euskara through the names of people and a divinity that they contain, since some (*Andere, Cison, Nescato,* etc.) hardly differ at all from Basque words we all know.

Only one of these inscriptions, the one containing the name of the divinity *Herauscorritsehe* (in the dative, as usual), has appeared in the modern zone of Basque speech, near Tardets. In Spanish territory, excluding the valley of Arán, until recently we did not have more than a doubtful example in the epigraph of Andrearriaga (Oyarzun), but now we can add with more certainty the names of people from the inscription of Lerga (Navarra) in an intensely Romanized area.[13]

3.9. It is unlikely that one day we will find ourselves in the position of establishing with some precision the fluctuating borders of the language during the Roman era with evidence that is not merely indirect. The reason for this can be stated briefly as: the use of writing among our ancestors went hand in hand with Romanization, and Romanization not only excluded the written use of the indigenous language but also tended to prohibit the use of their own place names. Only under especially favorable conditions and undoubtedly during a brief span of time could Latin have cohabitated with the Basque place names that we find in one part of Aquitania. Later we will deal with the non-Basque, indigenous, Indo-European place names that appear in certain points of Alava and especially Navarra.

One glance at a map of the country on which material signs of Roman influence are gathered, such as the excellent map by J. Caro Baroja,[14] is enough to convince oneself that the intensity of that influence varied greatly from region to region. It is logical to think that the indigenous language found refuge in the extensive zone that remains blank, on the margin of Latin culture, although it would not have disappeared completely from the more acculturated territory. The rural zones could maintain their traditional existence without great variations, without having the imperial administration or the cities worry too much about them, unless special interests intervened.[15]

In our case space played in favor of the language. Like a wave, Romanization advanced from the east to the west, parallel to the Pyrenees, toward the same point in opposite directions: from the north and northeast in Galia, from the southeast and south in Hispania. The only space with certainty that they did not manage to flood completely was the territory situated on the corner of the Gulf of Bizkaia, equally distant from the centers that radiated the Romanizing impulse on both sides of the Pyrenees.

Pompaelo, the Navarrese Iruña, and Ouéleia, the Alavese Iruña, were certainly not comparable to Osca in their influence, not even in their greatest era, and Lapurdum to the north was even less influential.

The principal defense of the language certainly did not lie in strength, but rather in the very military and economic weakness and insignificance of the country and its peoples. In contrast to what happened in more progressive zones, their cultural backwardness made Latin much less attractive to them. And the rustic, primitive way of life known there was not enough to promote the immigration of Latin-speaking peoples accustomed to other modes of existence. Finally, one must not forget that the Atlantic did not have the importance at that time that it would acquire later on and, besides, there is no proof that our ancestors had any skill or vocation as mariners or fishermen.

3.10. In any case, time effectively acted in favor of the language, the survival of which at certain moments had to appear extremely doubtful. With the long period of anarchy that followed the death of Alejandro Severo (235 BCE), the always-shaky balance between the city and the countryside was being replaced by the ever-increasing predominance of the latter. The cities were weakening and the empire was becoming more rural, and with ruralization the language of the countryside began reclaiming the territory lost to the language of the city.

But what decided the future of the language, as pointed out so astutely by Caro Baroja,[16] was not the Roman epoch but rather the period that followed it. The linguistic Romanization of Galia and Hispania was not interrupted by the invasions but instead continued and definitively consolidated at that time. The Basques, who accepted Roman rule without major resistance and thus gained for themselves a comfortable place to live within the new political order, in contrast, radically refused to admit, "even theoretically," says Caro Baroja, the rule of the Franks and Visigoths. The reasons behind this rebellion, stubbornly maintained for centuries, will remain hidden from us but not so its consequences, which are still evident today.

In any case, everything indicates that during the dark centuries of the Middle Ages the Basques abandoned their previous passivity and entered into a period of expansion, dedicating themselves to the penetration of neighboring regions, a period that is still comparable mutatis mutandis with that which occurred at the end of the fifteenth century. Also at that time, we have the impression of being in the presence of a poor but vital country that, barely able to feed its population, poured it out like a wave over the surrounding areas, as we know happened at the end of the Middle Ages.

Onomastics or place names (*Villabáscones*, etc.) were not the only indications of Basque colonization, studied many times by Menéndez Pidal. Anthroponyms, or people-related words, of immediate Basque origin reached an extension during those centuries that Basque has rarely or never achieved in a linguistic sense: cf. *Annaya, Eita* (*Aita, Echa*), etc. It doesn't matter that the etymologies of these nouns or components of names are more or less obscure or even perhaps of Latin origin (*Orti*, etc). The important part, the only thing that matters here, is that the center of this radiation is found in several cases to be from among ourselves, as can be proven in documentation.

3.11. We will not touch here upon the thorny problem of the contacts by the ancient Basques with other peoples who spoke the Indo-European language.[17] We will merely observe that, along with the inferences that can be obtained from an examination of cultural materials, one must pay attention as well to linguistic proofs, and we shall concern ourselves with those in chapter five [not included in this anthology].

We will do no more than mention the question of the Basque dialects, already treated in previous chapters. Can some correlation be established between these and the ancient tribal divisions? Could they rather be connected to more recent events such as the ecclesiastical divisions? There is no reason to exclude these explanations. Regarding the first, the most notable coincidence observed thus far is in Gipuzkoa, the territory of which is not dialectically unitarian nor does it correspond entirely to the extension assigned by the ancient geographers to one of those peoples, in such a way that the High Navarrese–speaking zone would coincide with Basque territory and the Bizkaian-speaking zone to the west would correspond to the Caristio territory, with which the

Vardula part of Gipuzkoa would be the home of the modern Gipuzkoan dialect.

Toponymy could do a lot to clarify—or at least to raise the question of—certain historical problems, but it would have to be a toponymy studied more with geographic criteria than etymological criteria. Population names ending in -*oz*, in a zone that is or has been until relatively recently Basque speaking, constitute a small part of the extensive surface extending through Aragón and Gascuña: population names ending in -*ués* and in -*ós*. According to G. Rohlfs,[18] these names constitute a trace of an ancient Aquitanian substratum and have their center in Spain in the region of Jaca. But they are not spread to the west except in a well-delineated part of traditional Vasconia, in Navarra, and in the French Basque country. In contrast, in the western zone we have abundant population names ending in -*ika* extending through Bizkaia and Alava, correlates of which are lacking or extremely scarce in Gipuzkoa and Navarra.[19]

Also, the frequent population names ending in -*ain* appear with maximum density in Navarra, but they penetrate more to the west than the names ending in -*oz*; to the north they are rather numerous in Soule and we could say that they extend into Gascon territory with names ending in -*ein*. Also, in toponymy, as we have seen happen already with dialectal isoglosses, each area has its own contour. The expansion of names ending in -*oz* and names ending in -*ain* have very different dates, much more ancient probably in the first case than in the second, which appears to fall well within the Middle Ages, even though that would be previous to the first documents.

The study of toponymy also sheds some light on the ancient boundaries of Basque speech: the boundary appears to be much more clearly delineated to the west than to the east, as Tovar so rightly observes. If Basque dialects were spoken beyond the historical western frontier of Basque in Bizkaia, they were replaced at a very remote date by Indo-European dialects.[20] To the east, on the other hand, the transition was gradual and the place names of Basque type continued to extend to the east with variable density all along the Pyrenees. We can expect much from the exhaustive analysis being carried out on this material by the eminent specialist J. Corominas in the Catalan domain.[21]

CHAPTER 5

Relatives of the Basque Language

"Relaciones de parentesco de la lengua vasca," in *Sobre historia de la lengua vasca* 1. San Sebastián: Seminario de Filología Vasca "Julio de Urquijo," 1988, pp. 56–73.

6.1 As proven by what we have seen thus far, Basque is not by any means an isolated language or a language islolate as it has often been called. This is an idea that has been expressed repeatedly with particular force by Antonio Tovar, and it is undoubtedly basically correct. But the relationships with neighboring languages that we have been discussing here are not those one usually thinks about when asked about a language's relatives or, as is often said, about its origins.

There are two ways of classifying languages, neither of which is entirely satisfactory: typological classification, which pays attention to similarities of structure; and genealogical classification, which groups languages into families that originated from a common language.[1]

Typological classification has produced certain denominations (such as agglutinative languages, flexive languages, etc.), which have become popular, but it has not produced a taxonomy comparable to the botanical and zoological classification systems of Linnaeus. This is not the time to study the reasons behind the failure of linguistic typology, reasons that have not been well studied. Neither will we do more than mention the latest developments. Sapir distinguished the different coordinated axes that can serve to fix the typological position of languages and furthermore increased their number. And ultimately, given that generally there are no animals that are more fishlike than others but there are languages that are more or less agglutinative than others, J. H. Greenberg has introduced quantity as the basis of a new system.[2] With that system, in reality, classification is replaced by measurement, just as was done with modern physics when it broke decisively with Aristotelian diagrams, and may God grant the same happy outcome in our case.[3]

The disadvantage of genealogical classification, to dispense for now with confusing theoretical problems, is that it is in the early stage of its possibilities. As Benveniste says, "By the very nature of things, it only has value between two dates," although these limits in time are rather imprecise. From the beginning we must keep in mind that however much we know or might come to know about the living or dead languages of the world, this knowledge only represents an infinitesimal fraction of the whole of human language. But even within this limitation—and in part because of it, because of the irreparable loss of links that are indispensable to the reconstruction of the chain—genealogical or genetic classification has had no more than partial success, since we do not know what to do with many of the known languages: especially in the upper stages, genetic relationships between constituted families escape our knowledge and it is feared that they will continue to escape it unless some unforeseen revolution of methods amplifies the power of our current means.

To conclude with this preamble, let us state precisely the reciprocal position of both types of classification. We do not know to what point researchers can structurally differentiate languages that have a common origin, in the first place because no process for measuring their divergences has been found: we only know that they can differentiate a great deal. Neither can we say how far we can allow ourselves to be guided by similarities of structure when we are looking for genetic relationships. The most prudent path is to believe, with G. Deeters,[4] that such similarities only constitute an indicator, positive or negative, of a common origin.

6.2 The genealogical relationship of two or more languages can only be proven by means of material coincidences, not by formal similarities, in structural order. And the coincidences sought for this purpose are equivalents, not simple analogies. Elements recognized as equal are those with a common origin, and in order to identify those magnitudes of equality we have to find regular correspondences, independent of the fact that the equalled terms might or might not be similar in substance.

According to Pisani's proposal,[5] material coincidences observed between languages can be divided into two large groups, by reason of their origin: on the one hand, the group of fortuitous or casual coincidences, and on the other, the group of historical coincidences.

The first group contains two subgroups. In the first are included coincidences of pure chance: to those cited in 5.5 [not included in this book] you may add, as a further example, the agreement between Old Irish *cen* "sin" and ancient and modern Sardinian *chene, chena*, with the same meaning.[6] The second group is comprised of what we call expressive formations—for lack of a better name, onomatopoeic or similar formations—in which the phonetic form is motivated by the meaningful content, and which tend to be similar in the most disparate languages. Schuchardt, for example, thought that Basque *lilluratu, llilluratu, luluratu* "dazzled, fascinated" came from the Latin *delirare*, but the same configuration of the Basque word has external parallels—although with a different meaning—such as Sardinian *duddurare* "ballonzare, ballonzolare" and *allilliradu* "rigid."[7] This invites us to suspend our judgment on the matter. It was Schuchardt himself who coined the concept of "elemental kinship" in order to bring together these coincidences that suggest a common origin.

In the second group we find the equivalents owed to a common heritage and those from loan words. Both, as Pisani says, suggest a historical motive: unity originated from similar or dissimilar terms, among which is established an equation based on regular correspondences of sound.

6.3 Therefore, within the historical coincidences, the only ones that interest us at the moment, one must distinguish between those due to heritage and those that originated as loan words, a feasible task within the well-known limits of time. In other words, it's one thing when two languages possess related morphemes, and another when the languages themselves are related to each other, that is to say, when we are dealing with diverse forms of what once was the same language.

This is the reason why pronouncements like Deeters'[8] are insufficient. According to Deeters, the proof of genetic kinship of two or more languages is the existence of etymological equations according to regular phonetic correspondences. Good correspondences between several related Basque and Albanese morphemes can be established, and yet no one would maintain on that basis that these languages are related to each other, since the correspondences are established between adventitious elements whose common source is none other than Latin. Consequently, it is essential to the demonstration that the correspondences be based on components of basic vocabulary and on grammatical indices.

Beyond material coincidences, more complex factors play a part in the demonstration, one such being similitude in the distribution of morphemes. An example taken from the noun and pronoun declensions from the Hittite[9] will serve to clarify this better than any explanation, if we relate it to what is observed in an Indo-European language such as Latin.

In Hittite, certain nouns form the nominative singular, the case of the subject of transitive and intransitive verbs, by adding a sibilant to the stem. In the accusative singular, the case of the direct object, there is a nasal instead of a sibilant: nominative *aruna-s* "sea," accusative *aruna-n*, like Latin *lupu-s*, accusative *lupu-m*. In the same declension, however, other nouns, those called neutrals, have the same form for nominative and accusative: nominative-accusative *pedan* "place," exactly like Latin *iugum*, nominative and accusative.

In another type of declension—that is, in the declension of other stems—while the nouns of "common" gender form the nominative and accusative singulars by adding -*s* and -*n* respectively, it is the pure stem, without any type of addition, that serves as the nominative-accusative in the neutrals: on the one hand, nominative *heus* "rain," accusative *heun* and, on the other, nominative-accusative *genu* "knee," the same as in Latin there is nominative *fructus*, accusative *fructum*, but nominative-accusative *genu*. In the plural the same difference between both genders is observed and the same coincidence between both languages: nominative plural *hewes*, but *genuwa*, like Latin *fructus, genua*.

In the pronouns, Hittite continues marking the nominative/accusative singular opposition in the common gender with -*s* / -*n*, but in the neutral -*t* is the characteristic of the nominative-accusative: common nominative *kuis*, accusative *kuin*, relative and interrogative, neutral nominative-accusative *kuit*, cf. Latin masculine-feminine nominative *quis*, accusative *quem*, but neutral nominative-accusative *quid*.

Neutral stems in -*r* in the nominative-accusative alternate in Hittite with stems in -*n* in oblique cases: nominative-accusative singular *pahhuwar* "fire," *mehur* "time," genitive *pahhuenas, mehunas*, etc., which can be compared to Latin nominative-accusative *femur, iter*, genitive *feminis, itineris*. The personal pronoun of the first-person singular also presents a stem in the nominative that is distinct from the stem of other cases, in Hittite as well as in Latin: nominative *uk* / accusative *ammuk*, Latin nominative *ego* / accusative *me*. This would be even more obvious in the pronoun of the first-person plural if we were allowed to introduce an Indo-European language other than Latin into the comparison: Hittite nominative *wēs* / accusative *anzās*, like German *wir* / *uns* or English *we* / *us*.

Anyone would hesitate to attribute to chance such notable analogies in languages so distant from each other in time and space, and a comparatist would not need more in order to firmly believe in their genetic kinship.

6.4 The kinship of two languages can be proven, as we have just seen, on the condition that they are sufficiently proximate. There are also cases in which material coincidences, though not sufficient for a complete demonstration, make the hypothesis of a distant kinship likely. But what does not exist, and cannot exist by the very nature of things, is a demonstration that two languages *do not* have a genetic kinship between them.

To say that two languages are not related is simply a graphic way of expressing the opinion that no proximate demonstrable genealogical link unites them. And given that this is a general principal, it is as applicable to the genetic relationships of the Basque language as it is to those of any other language, living or dead.

By beginning with languages that are proximate in space, we saw in the previous chapter that no one has been able to discover any special affinity between Basque and Indo-European and that even traces of contact with Roman expansion through western Europe in the previous era are scarce. Neither has anyone seriously defended the hypothesis of a kinship between Basque and the Finno-Ugric languages, or in a more general manner, the Uralic languages.[10] Between Indo-European and Uralic, in contrast, very striking coincidences have been observed since ancient times, although too scant in number to allow us to arrive at definite conclusions.

Basque has been compared with a growing number of languages from all parts of the world, by the work of aficionados who have limited themselves to gathering a fistful of curiosities, with neither seriousness nor rules. But linguists of great authority have attempted to demonstrate a kinship with Basque for two groups of languages. These are the Hamitic-Semitic (Acadian, Hebrew, Arabic, ancient Egyptian and Coptic, ancient Libyan and modern Berber dialects) and the Caucasian languages.

6.5 Nevertheless, before continuing it is necessary to touch briefly on the question of Basque-Iberianism, which is far from finding a satisfactory solution.

In the linguistic sense, as far as we can ascertain today, Iberian is the ancient Hispanic non-Indo-European language that we know through inscriptions on the Mediterranean coast from Ensérune in France and in the valley of the Ebro, created in an indigenous writing system also called Iberian. The language in some epigraphs in Andalucia seems to be the same, although noted in another writing system that has not been deciphered at every point.[11]

The difficulty of the problem as posed consists of having at our disposal two groups of data which do not reconcile well with each other. On the one hand, we observe a series of coincidences with Basque in these texts. These coincidences or similarities affect the phonological systems, since Iberian, as far as we can tell through the writing system, appears to have not been very different from ancient Basque both in the number and nature of its units as well as in the possibilities for their combinations. From this arises the curious Basque sound when an Iberian text is read out loud according to our knowledge and understanding.

The agreement is not limited to distinctive units but extends also to the meanings. Repetition allows us to isolate certain Iberian morphemes in the texts that coincide with Basque morphemes, not only in their general configuration—in the so-called canonic form—but also in the number, order, and nature of the phonemes that compose them. Thus, Basque words like *argi* "light, clear," *beltz* "black," *lagun* "companion," *osaba* "uncle," etc., appear to have their correlates in Iberian inscriptions. Furthermore, as Tovar so convincingly proposed, grammatical indices such as the Iberian *-en* appear to coincide with the corresponding Basque both in form and in meaning: Basque *-en* "of."

In the face of all of this there arises a single incontrovertibly powerful fact. The Iberian inscriptions can be read, thanks to Manuel Gómez-Moreno, except at one doubtful point, but they are not as yet understood. And this, regardless of what the nonspecialists say,[12] would hardly occur if Iberian was an ancient form of Basque or at least a language that was closely related to it. Not that Basque sounds have not changed in the course of the last two millennia, nor that Basque has not lost a good part of its ancient lexicon, but phonetic changes are recoverable for the most part—that is, they can be recognized, which allows us to reconstruct more ancient forms than the ones evidenced in historical language—and the losses suffered in the lexicon are not so great as to keep us from recognizing Basque words in a small number of Aquitaine place names evidenced in the first centuries of the modern era. One would hope then that if luck were to deliver to us some ancient Basque text, we would be able to understand its general meaning, even if many details escaped us, and recognize the grammatical structure of its sentences. Nothing of the sort has occurred, however, with the Iberian texts.

Be that as it may, the fact is that Iberian, for all its difficulties and contradictions, constitutes today the most promising field for those who wish to penetrate the prehistory of the Basque language. It is not possible to predict what those texts will reveal to us on the day when the research, supported by the appearance of new materials, is far more advanced.

6.6 The hypothesis of a genetic relationship between Basque and Hamitic-Semitic languages has an objective foundation, but is—or was, when it was in favor—more than anything an uncertain conclusion, the premise of which was born of error and confusion.

H. Schuchardt, putting the cart before the oxen as the old Basque saying goes, tried to show in *Die iberische Deklination* (1908) that Basque and Iberian coincided substantially in something as central to a language as declension. As Iberian had its roots in the north of Africa, according to the traditional idea, it was obvious to look there for ancient and modern relatives of Basque. This led him to the Hamitic-Semitic languages, giving this family a greater extension than is generally attributed to it, at least today.[13]

Schuchardt's Basque-Iberian hypothesis collapsed because it was built on sand. He had based it totally on the texts in Iberian writing, which was read, furthermore, in a very deficient manner, as was then in fashion. When they were able to read it, it was seen that the same writing had been used to transcribe two very different languages, one of which— the one we call today Celtiberian—was indisputably Indo-European. Thus, a good part of the Iberian endings compared with the Basque endings turned out not to be Iberian, and other ones that were Iberian turned out to have a reading very different from that which Schuchardt attributed to them.

In spite of everything, some of Schuchardt's now-expired concepts continue to hang over the current research, namely the idea that Iberian, as we now know it, is related to the north of Africa. Well then, linguistic kinship can only be demonstrated by linguistic arguments, and there is nothing in Iberian, to our understanding, that relates it to North African languages, at least if by North African we do not mean a pre-Berber or pre-Libic language or languages. But we know practically nothing about those and it would be absurd to inquire into the kinship of mental creations.

You will recall that the Hamitic-Semitic group[14] unites two components that are very distinct with regard to their internal coherence. The Semitic languages (Acadian, Aramaic, Hebrew, etc.) form a well-linked group: in reality, for a comparatist, they are more like slightly differentiated dialects whose divergence is not much greater than what we find within the Romance, Celtic, or Slavic languages. Hamitic, on the other hand, constitutes a very heterogeneous group whose internal and external relations with Semitic are far from being clarified.

But even so and even with our almost total lack of knowledge about the grammatical mechanisms of Iberian, there is one characteristic of Iberian that sets it completely apart from the Hamitic-Semitic languages. Its morphemes, like those of Basque, demonstrate a constant form, without the internal flexion—variation of vowels within a fixed consonantal framework—so characteristic of both Berber and Arabic.

With regard to the comparisons of vocabulary presented by Schuchardt, they received the coup de grace by means of a critical article by E. Zyhlarz, popularized among us by G. Bähr,[15] where it was proven, with the same lack of respect for phonetic correspondences that distinguishes the cited works of Schuchardt, that it is perfectly possible to present an equivalent number of "good"—that is, tempting—etymological equations between German and Coptic words. It is not necessary that we discuss them now, since even a summary examination is sufficient to realize their extreme superficiality. There is one, however, that continues to be cited (Basque *umerri* "lamb": Acadian *immeru*, etc.), and that's enough to judge the worth of many approximations. There is no need at all to go clear to Mesopotamia in order to explain this Basque word, which is a transparent compound: *umerri* in addition to "lamb" (in Oyarzun "sacrificed lamb," as opposed to *bildots*) is in Bizkaian "sheep more than two years old, unlike *giberri*, which is younger" (Azkue), and in Basse-Navarre "new offspring of an animal," according to Salaberry. In other words, *umerri* is none other than the compound *uma-berri*, literally "new young."

6.7. After this preamble, we can now enter into an examination of the hypothesis of a genetic kinship between Basque and the Caucasian languages, the only hypothesis that has been the object of serious and laborious testing. We are not going to summarize the history of the idea, presented to us by Father Fidel Fita, with respect to the Georgian. The suspicion that the two small, conservative islands situated at both extremes of the Mediterranean were the only evidence that has come down to us from a formerly very extensive linguistic family was a perfectly natural one and it found support in the name of Caucasian Iberia mentioned by the classic authors, an eastern parallel to our western Iberia.[16]

Basque-Caucasian approximations are found in abundance in the works of N. Marr and especially in those of A. Trombetti, but the stadialism of the first and the defense of monogenesis of the language by the second have deservedly fallen into disrepute, and this means that today they are not kept in mind except to the extent they have been repeated by later authors. The hypothesis, summarized by C. C. Uhlenbeck, has been developed by those quite familiar with the Caucasian languages: by G. Dumézil in the last chapter of his *Introduction à la grammaire comparée des langues caucasiennes du Nord* (Paris, 1933), by K. Bouda,[17] and by R. Lafon.[18]

Since speaking of Basque-Caucasian linguistic kinship implicitly suggests that we will find before us two comparable terms, it should be remembered that only one, Basque, does not present internal obstacles to the comparison. But the other side of the relationship is extremely complex and it is important, above all, to enumerate its components and try to determine its respective position.

6.8 The phrase "Caucasian languages" alludes to something more than a purely geographic grouping and to something less than a linguistic family in the genetic sense. In the first place, in the West when one speaks of Caucasian languages alone, one thinks of that which the Georgian linguists call "Iberian-Caucasian" languages: only languages spoken in the Caucasus or near there, languages that do not form part of well-established linguistic families, are included under this name. For example, Oseta, an Iranian and therefore Indo-European language, is not included, even though one of its characteristics, undoubtedly due to the vicinity, places it in proximity to the Caucasian languages in the strictest sense. Upon grouping them together we must refer moreover to the situation of the languages before 1864, the date of the emigration of the Ubykhs to Asia Minor to escape Russian domination.[19]

We will only mention in passing certain languages of ancient Asia, languages of unknown affiliation (Hatti or pre-Hittite, Hurrita, Haldean, or Urartean, and even Elamite and Sumerian), whose genetic relationships with the Caucasian languages are bitterly disputed.[20] That alone is sufficient evidence that they are far from being proven. Furthermore, if we wish to arrive at clarity in our conclusions, it is not recommended that we complicate the problem with an accumulation of data, some of which are poorly determined and of doubtful pertinence.[21]

The same can be said of Burushaski, an isolated language that still lives in the mountains of Karakorum, which H. Berger has tried to relate genetically with Basque,[22] after other attempts to tie it to the Caucasian languages. It is preferable not to add new difficulties to an already-thorny task.

6.9 In the precise sense in which we have just defined them, the Caucasian languages can be classified into two large groups: the languages of the northern variation, which we will indicate from this point on as CN, or Caucasian of the North, and those of the south (CS), also called Kartvelian. Fortunately, the geographic distribution of the languages coincides in this case with their linguistic similarities, according to the opinion of all the experts.

There are no doubts concerning the genetic unity of CS, formed by Georgian, Mingrelian, Lazic, and Svanic. Even Svanic, the most divergent member of the group and unfortunately also the least studied, is unmistakably characterized as a Kartvelian language because of its morphology, in spite of the fact that its vocabulary has moved far away from that of its related languages.[23] Deeters has presented the kinship relationships of these languages by means of the following tree:[24]

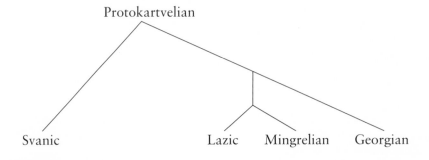

Protokartvelian

Svanic   Lazic   Mingrelian   Georgian

This group is the best known and the most accessible, thanks especially to the fact that Georgian, as evidenced from the end of the fifth century, has been and continues to be an important cultural vehicle. Even so, it is not easy for someone who is not a specialist to move within this group with security and comfort. When we are not happy with the description of languages and we want to interpret them diachronically in their historical and prehistorical evolution, we must be warned that we will find known countries whose configuration is delineated on good maps, and also terrae incognitae where we can only trust our instinct for orientation, for lack of a better guide. In this respect, the landscape of the Kartvelian languages constitutes a type of middle ground. Georgian, as we have said, has a long history, but the phonetic changes that this history documents are relatively small, and for the most important phonological problems, we have to refer to prehistory. For that exploration there are no resources save those provided by internal reconstruction and above all comparison.

The bald fact is that today, until they publish a work that may soon be announced,[25] we have at our disposal an outline of comparative morphology for CS, principally for the verb thanks to Deeters, but not a phonetic comparison, and the latter is the first and most essential step of any comparison. This is due in part to the fact that Soviet linguists, through work by Marr especially, have not approached these questions until recently with the same methods as Westerners, as we shall see later on.

The nonspecialist would like to pose questions that the specialists refuse to answer, no doubt because of the real difficulties that they know better than anyone. Georgian, for example, has a relatively simple phonological system, but there are very few languages with consonant groups as abundant and complicated as Georgian.[26] These groups may proceed in part from the segmentation of ancient consonants of complex articulation, such as labialized occlusives. But often we have the correspondence of Georgian CC: Mingrelian-Lazic CVC. It is natural to think that in Georgian a vowel has dropped through one of those frequent cases of vowel syncope that internal reconstruction allows us to establish, but it can also happen, at least on occasion, that sister languages have alleviated consonant groups by inserting epenthetic vowels: Georgian *tma*, Mingrelian-Lazic *toma* "hair," etc.

6.10 Or let's take the vowel system. Within the group formed by Georgian, Mingrelian, and Lazic, excluding Svanic, two groups of seemingly contradictory facts are discovered at first glance. We have, on the one hand, the type of abundantly evidenced correspondence that usually gives the comparatist the secure feeling that he is standing on solid ground, by the dissimilarity of the terms that link: Georgian *e*: Mingrelian-Lazic *a*; Georgian *a*: Mingrelian-Lazic *o (u)*.[27] But besides these there are also copious other correpondences whose terms are phonetically analogous: *e : e, a : a*, etc. Faced with this situation V. Polák[28] follows the fundamental principle of comparative reconstruction according to which each one of the correpsondences postulates and defines a phoneme of the proto-language, arriving at a common stage of a system of ten vowels, separated by a correlation of quantity. This can be very orthodox, but not necessarily correct because there is also the possibility, toward which H. Vogt is inclined, that loan words from Georgian have entered en masse, with little alteration of form, into the sister languages.[29] Perhaps the solution is not elegant, but it has large elements of verisimilitude.

In any case, Polák wants to obtain too high a yield from the comparison, since in no place does it appear that one has been able to reconstruct, by means of crossed correspondences, ten unities in the protolanguage, outside of systems that do not contain more than five unities. Notice that this would continue to be correct for the prehistoric form of the subgroup even when it was true that the vocalic quantity, as in Svanic dialects, was to represent the continuation of something ancient.[30]

6.11 In the northern group, everyone recognizes the existence of three subgroups: the languages of the northwest (CNO), those of the center (CC), and those of the northeast (CNE), or the languages of Dagestan.

The CNO group, formed by Abkhaz, Ubykh, and Circassian (a classification that does not coincide with the list of literary languages that have been developed in the USSR for practical reasons), constitutes a rather homogenous group, although phonetic correspondences do not appear to be well established yet perhaps because of the exuberant wealth of the phonological systems of these languages. We also have at our disposal for these languages a comparative morphological outline in Dumézil's book, *Etudes comparatives sur les langues caucasiennes du Nord-Ouest* (Paris, 1932).

The whole of the CC and the CNE is much more motley and not all the languages that make them up are well known. Central Caucasian comprises three very similar languages (Chechen, Ingush, and Bats), whose comparative phonetic system has been established with few difficulties by A. Sommerfelt.[31] For the confusion of languages of Dagestan in northeast Caucasian, diverse classifications that do not coincide on all points have been proposed. We follow Dumézil's classification here: (1) the Avar-Andi-Dido group in northern Dagestan; (2) Lak; (3) Dargwa; (4) Archi; (5) the Samuric languages (Küri, Tabassarian, Agul, etc.), and (6) Udi, spoken in two villages, which should hardly be connected to the previous group.

The specialists seem to be in agreement that the northern Caucasian languages constitute a family in the genetic sense. The kinship is naturally much closer in the CNE and in the whole of the CNE and CC. It is now accepted that the works of Prince N. Trubetzkoy[32] firmly established the unity of the CN: a rather complete system of phonetic correspondences relates terms or roots of languages from all the subgroups, and the etymological equations cover components of the basic lexicon, including pronominal and numeral themes. With this, the first steps were taken toward the restitution of the phonological system of the common language.

6.12 The comparative morphology of the CN group is, nevertheless, a more difficult task especially because of the very different structures of the CNO on the one hand, and of the combined CC-CNE group on the other.

It seems natural to think that the most appropriate road to reconstructing large characteristics of the common language would be comparative work spread through the minor groups formed by clearly related languages, in order to arrive step-by-step at the confrontation of the two major groups of the family. This has not been done, or rather only in the last few years has it been attempted, especially through the work of Soviet linguists. It has even been suggested by V. Polák[33] that it is not feasible because the continuity of linguistic facts that unites each language with its neighbors is radically opposed to the establishment of that hierarchy.

Everything considered, this very well may not be as decisive as it seems at first glance. The continuity of linguistic phenomena is something that can be proven in any area on the condition that the closeness is not very recent. We do know, in fact, that these phenomena extend like oil spots blotting out the borders between languages and even between language families. It would moreover be very risky to jump to such distant conclusions without more than a summary knowledge of some of the pertinent materials. Where the comparative method has achieved brilliant results, it has done so thanks only to the meticulous, tenacious, and continuous labors of a legion of specialists.

The immense distance that separates the CNO from the CC-CNE, with regard to structure, leaps to mind. To begin with, the declension so abundant in CNE hardly exists in the other group: it's completely lacking in Abkhaz and is no more than rudimentary in Ubykh and in Circassian. But the difference of greatest importance, since it directly affects the economy of phrase, consists of the existence of or the lack of nominal classes.

Except in some languages where fossilized classifiers or class indices have been discovered, the system of classes whose distant western parallel would be grammatical gender is the basic element of the grammatical mechanism of the CC-CNE group. In these languages the verb, at least in its most typical variety, is strictly speaking impersonal. Normally it does not contain any reference to the person, but rather to the grammatical class of the subject in intransitive verbs and to the object in transitives. Thus in Avar *v-ugo* "am, are, is" is the lone prefix and indicates that the subject is a rational being of masculine sex, as opposed to *j-ugo* whose subject is feminine rational, although its Spanish translation would be the same, and *b-ugo* whose *b-* alludes to an irrational entity. In the same manner, we have *v-ačana* "carried (to a masculine rational being)," *j-ačana* "carried (to a feminine rational)," *b- ačana* "carried (to an irrational)."[34] The class indices also mark the agreement of the adjective with the noun whenever possible.

The systems of classes are rather distinct in the different languages, especially because through diverse combinations of singular indices with plural ones we can, with a lesser number of indices, arrive at the complicated state of eight known classes in Bats. Nevertheless, the dominant opinion (Deeters, Dumézil, and in part Čikobava) is that historic multiplicity can be explained by means of a system of four classes that can be indicated approximately as follows:

Classes	Singular	Plural
I	w	} b
II	j	
III	b	} d
IV	d	

The content of the classes in the protolanguage can even be determined to a certain point. The first two were limited to rational beings with a sexual distinction. The irrationals were distributed, according to criteria that are more difficult to specify, among the last two classes, without sex having anything to do with that distribution in the names of animals, which seemingly entered the third class for the most part.

In the CNO group, only in Abkhaz are there indices of a system of classes, in the verb, in possessive prefixes, in nominal pluralizers, and in the numerals. However, it approximates only distantly the system of classes in the CNE and CC groups in their typical forms and is much more reminiscent of what is called gender in the western languages. On the other hand, it is very doubtful, as can be seen through Deeters' considerations,[35] that the facts we observed in Abkhaz represent an archaism, a remnant of the class system of the protolanguage, and not an innovation.

In any case, it is evident that between the pluriperson verb of the CNO, which can contain several personal indices, and the much simpler verb of CC and CNE, which is dominated by the category of class, there exists what we could call a typological chasm. Certainly this is not enough to exclude genetic kinship between these groups, but it does not facilitate the establishment of a comparative grammar.

6.13 When the comparison is made between northern Caucasian and southern Caucasian—that is, the Kartvelian languages—the situation is even more complicated. We can summarize the problem in very few words: there is a great typological divergence between the two principal groups of the CN, but there are also notable material coincidences within a system of phonetic correspondences that affect the basic lexicon. Between CN and CS there are notable differences of structure and, what's more, material coincidences are lacking or very rare. I shall mention one such as that observed between the names of the "heart" and between CN "fire" and CS "to burn," a relation that has been extended to Basque *gogo* "mind, etc." and *su* "fire." But material coincidences in short number can be noticed between any two languages or groups of languages and more if they are united, as in this case, by vicinity.

Faced with such a situation, the only prudent attitude is the one that maintains, as do many Western and Soviet linguists, that the genetic kinship of CN with CS is not proven, and moreover if it does exist, it is a very distant one. So distant is it in reality that there is no great probability that it can be demonstrated with the methods available to us today, as their power to penetrate time is very limited.

6.14 It is only natural that this skepticism has not managed to modify the convictions of the believers in the original unity of all the Caucasian languages. This belief, which is a primary fact in all probability, can find secondary justification, as always happens, in a rational superstructure built as support.

We have already seen that the class system of one part of the CN is lacking as an active category in the Kartvelian languages. But since it is a fact that languages can preserve for a long time inoperative remnants of what were once living elements of their structure, supporters of the unity of the Caucasian languages have sought out and think they have found, beginning with historian I. Džavaxišvili,[36] fossilized class indices in Kartvelian morphemes that have a very different function in the history of these languages (personal indices in the verb, for example) or that have no function—that is, they are not significant units for the synchronic analysis of the language even in the most ancient accessible stage of Georgian.

Before discussing this, it is necessary to insert a brief parenthetical statement about the general linguistic ideas of the "Titlis school." Although its leader, the academician A. Čikobava, played a very visible role in the official condemnation of the Marr doctrines, the Western linguist finds much in his ideas and processes that contradicts his own concepts and methods in the field of diachronic linguistics.[37] In a more explored field, on the other hand, there are only nuances of difference between the works of a Soviet linguist like Abaev on Oseta and those of Benveniste, for example, on that same Iranian language spoken in the Caucasus.

Čikobava holds the importance of diachronic linguistics in high esteem. To say, as he does, that "the system of a language cannot be understood without taking its history into account" is certainly not exact, unless we interpret it as a platitude in the sense that a language cannot be understood *historically* without taking its history into account. For it is clear that this system can be understood and described without paying the least attention to the origin of its components or to its previous phases, to the evolution of which we owe the outcome at any given moment.

We also find in Čikobava a manifest confusion between the history and the prehistory of a language. When he affirms "the more we delve into the history of the evolution of Ibero-Caucasian languages, the more manifest becomes that which they have in common," what he suggests is not exact, literally speaking, for the only Caucasian language that has a history worth mentioning—in the strictest sense of the word—is Georgian. For that matter, the inadequate term *history* should be replaced by *prehistory* if we want to speak precisely.

And here in the research on prehistory is where there is a radical divergence in the proceedings. For us, the first step and at the same time the essential step in this inquiry consists of comparative reconstruction: the phonetic correspondences that are established between the compared languages permit us to identify and define the distinctive units, the phonemes, of a prehistoric stage of the language with which in a determined order we reconstruct the forms of this protolanguage, using the phonic configuration of the meaningful units. Thus, from the comparison of Latin *piscis*, Irish *íasc*, and English *fish*, we obtain a phoneme *$*p$, defined by the equation Latin p- = Irish zero = English f-, and a protoform *$*peisk$-/*pisk*- "fish."

On the other hand, the problems put forth by Čikobava and solved by him in his own way include those much more complicated ones that were customarily called glottogonic. In reality, using a previous supposition (in this case the unity of origin of all Caucasian languages), everything is reduced to imagining some credible lines of evolution that have resulted in the stages of language that are accessible to us. The stage of a common prehistoric language, the protolanguage, could have possessed a system of classes. The system could have known in the beginning a bipartite division ("persons"/"things") that became tripartite by a subdivision of the second class. This new system, in turn, could have given way to another with four classes, two for people and two for things, in order to arrive at a new tripartite outline in some of the languages ("man"/ "woman"/ "thing"). Finally, it is possible that languages, such as the Kartvelian group, unfamiliar with the nominal classes throughout their history might nevertheless preserve traces of morphemes that have ceased to be active elements of their grammatical structure. Therefore, we can say that Topuria is right to think that *d*- or *t*- in some Kartvelian verbal roots is nothing more than an ancient indicator of class.

All of this is undoubtedly possible, and even credible, and it would be rash to reject the possibility. But in order for evolutionary outlines of this sort to have demonstrative value, it is necessary to show that such a line is, if not the only possible one, at least more probable than any other. In other words, we must show that there is sufficient reason to prefer it to any possible alternative. And to our understanding, that is what the Georgian linguists have not done. Preoccupied by undoubtedly more important questions, they have not taken care to lay the most humble yet indispensible foundations of all reconstruction.[38]

6.15 If the kinship of CN with CS is a credible and reasonable hypothesis but not a demonstrated fact, as I have tried to explain in this long digression, this means that the kinship is, in the best of cases, distant enough that its proof would offer enormous, perhaps insurmountable, difficulties. Under these conditions, it seems rash to introduce the Basque language into the comparison with the hope that it could serve as a bridge between CN and CS at the same time as its kinship is established with the Caucasian languages.

If one breaks from the common origin of all Caucasian languages, as occurs in the essays of K. Bouda and R. Lafon, for example, then the Basque forms cannot be compared at will with forms from CN or from CS, but only with forms that are common to these last two groups. In effect, only the pan-Caucasian forms offer a guarantee, as K. Vogt[39] has indicated, that they form a part of the estate of morphemes of proto-Caucasian.

On the contrary, one must limit the comparison to one of the two possible alternatives: either Basque-CN or Basque-CS. Typological considerations could serve as an incentive for guiding the investigation in one sense or another. On different occasions structural analogies between Basque and CNO have been indicated, especially in the typical pluripersonal verb, but neither is there any lack of curious analogies between Basque and CS. For the whole of CN, however, one would have to decide ahead of time whether the more archaic characteristics are those of CNO similar to Basque or those of CC+CNE which are so distant in many aspects from our language. And this question today does not appear easy to solve.

One characteristic that is common to Basque, to the Caucasian languages—except for Udi, although with considerable divergences—and to some ancient languages of old Asia, but not exclusive to them, is the so-called "ergative construction" whose contrast with the nominative/accusative opposition of Indo-European languages can be seen in the following examples: Latin *homo uenit,* Basque *gizona etorri da*; Latin *hominem uidit,* Basque *gizona ikusi du*; Latin *homo uidit,* Basque *gizonak ikusi du.* With regard to the supposed "passivity" of the verb by which we continue to explain the peculiarity of this construction, Čikobava is quite right to maintain that where there is no opposition of voice that confronts passive and active forms—as in Georgian, for example—the verb can only be considered as neutral or indifferent in this respect.[40]

6.16 What balance can we find today in the results of the most interesting exploration of the Basque-Caucasian linguistic relationships, thanks especially to Bouda and Lafon?

We possess an impressive number of approximations, some of which are extremely tempting, between Caucasian and Basque words and a certain quantity—smaller, but still impressive—of equations between grammatical morphemes from one side or the other. With regard to phonetic correspondences, it seems to be tacitly accepted in general that what is similar must be considered identical with regard to origin, but in one concrete point, that of the sibilants, Lafon has proposed a partial system according to which the Basque apical sibilants (*s, ts*) would correlate to the Caucasian recursives or glottalized sibilants, and the Basque predorsals (*z, tz*) would correspond to the Caucasian aspirated sibilants.

What should we think about this enormous mass of comparisons? In this material, the opinion of the specialist who knows the tricks of the trade—generally because he has used them himself—is usually very different from that of the layman, since the specialist knows that one must wait upon the quality and not the quantity of the approximations. He knows, for example, that the similarity between grammatical indices that are usually considered to be proof of kinship is not as demonstrable as it seems because such indices, generally of little importance, can coincide by chance in the most diverse languages: thus -*kh* in the nominative plural of Armenian nouns does not have any certain shared origin with -*k* in the plural of Basque nouns. Another thing is when the similarity of affixes adds concomitant phenomena such as, for example, alternations. Comparing Latin *genus,* genitive *generis,* with Greek *génos,* genitive *géneos,* and Old Slavic *nebo,* genitive *nebese* "sky," we see that the coincidence is not limited to the ending -*s,* lost in Slavic, but rather extends to the variation of the timbre of the vowel of the final syllable of the stem.

With regard to vocabulary comparisons, the old adage "all that glitters is not gold" almost always proves true. In our case there are numerous examples that have been rejected with good reason because at least one of the terms was a loan word (Armenian in Georgian, Latin in Basque, etc.), because the compared forms were of doubtful antiquity or of a proven recent character, or because the comparison was based on erroneous analysis of the component morphemes, etc.[41]

One illustration will suffice. According to Bouda,[42] Basque *ezkutu* "hidden" along with Roncalese *ozkume* "hiding place" are related etymologically with a Circassian verb that means "to hide." Basque *azku* "tejón/badger" would proceed from the same root (analyzed *a-zku*, like *e-zku-tu* and *o-zku-me*), with a correlation in southern Caucasian: Mingrelian *mu(n)čkv-i*, Georgian *ma-čv-i*. Now, the fact is that we do not really know where the Roncalese *ozkume* comes from nor how it should be analyzed nor what its relationship is, if it has one, with the other two Basque terms, but we do know something more about the latter, such as: (1) that *ezkutu, izkutu* (and *ezkutatu, izkutatu*) have a closer relative in Romance *escudo, escudar*, etc., and; (2) that the ending of *azku*, a Souletin variation with an accented nasal -*u*, suggests with certainty *-*one* (cf. Souletin *arrazu* "reason," *arrathu* "rat," with accented nasal *u*). Whether this *azkone* is linked in turn—as has been suggested—to Latin *taxo, taxonem* "tejón/badger"—a late word and seemingly of Germanic origin—is another question that we do not need to answer in order to reject the Basque-Caucasian approximation.

Nevertheless, among this crowd of approximations there are some that continue to be attractive, even after having been submitted to a severe examination: some like that of Georgian *k'ordzi* and Basque *ikorzirin* "callo/callus" are even more attractive because any comparatist will instinctively mistrust such a notable similarity in forms separated from the period of the common protolanguage by an abyss of five or six millenia at least. But even assuming the best, we must keep in mind that the comparisons are not established between two languages, but rather between forms taken from any Basque dialect, as we have just seen, and from any epoch, one of which is given priority according to the needs of the moment, and forms taken from any Caucasian language. With that, if we recall that there are no less than thirty of these languages we will not be surprised at the growing number of apparently good equations.[43]

6.17 But the decisive argument that leads us to believe that the Basque-Caucasian linguistic kinship is not proven is something else. The comparative reconstruction that tries to penetrate the prehistory of languages, in a past that is not directly witnessed, has no right to be more than a function of the history and is justified to the extent that it serves to clarify genetically the documented stages of language. And it is indisputable that, from this point of view, the hypothesis of Basque-Caucasian linguistic kinship has been shown to be, up to now, singularly unfruitful. The enigmas of Basque and Caucasian prehistory, both large and numerous, have not been explained at all by the comparative essays realized thus far. And while this situation continues, that is while the hypothesis continues to be ineffectual and sterile, it cannot pass from the state of belief or personal opinion, no matter how respectable.

Furthermore, it is evident that such a hypothesis cannot serve any great purpose while the work of reconstruction within each group, Basque or Caucasian, is no more advanced than it is at present. Years ago Meillet, with his sober sense of reality, categorically pointed out: "In the research of language relationships, there are two moments: the first consists of researching possible similarities at first glance . . . The second moment consists of building a precise history of the languages under consideration by constructing a comparative grammar; there is no proof until this work is rather advanced. The process that consists of bringing together a Basque fact with such and such a fact of one of the Caucasian languages—quite diverse, as we know—or with one of the Hamito-Semitic languages—also very diverse—permits one to propose a lot of similarities, but it excludes a veritable demonstration on account of the overly large number of possibilities it contains."[44]

6.18 We conclude, sadly, with another pessimistic note. Neither should we place great hope in the relatively new glottochronology, a method that A. Tovar[45] has applied in a very interesting way to Basque. Now that the criticism has extended to the very mathematical roots of the method,[46] we cannot expect, with M. Swadesh, that it will permit us to salvage lapses of time before which the classic comparison had to confess its impotence. It might be helpful to obtain a first impression when there is no time to delve into a detailed investigation, but it can never substitute for such research and certainly not surpass it.

In summary, the affiliation of the Basque language continues to be a mystery, as is the case with many other languages, living or dead. It is possible that we will always lack certain lost links that would be indispensable in order to reveal the mystery. It is also possible, but not very probable, that such links exist although we have not been able to recognize them, or that some fortunate trace might bring to light data thus far hidden. Also it is possible that an improvement in current methods or the discovery of new techniques might put more powerful instruments in our hands.

Be that as it may, since we do not possess powers of prophecy, it is certain that the search will continue untiringly in the future without becoming discouraged by the meager harvest of the past. We hope that Fortune, always the friend of the bold and persevering, will see fit to smile upon us.

CHAPTER 6

The Ancient Consonant System

"El sistema consonántico antiguo," in *Fonética histórica vasca*. 2nd ed.
San Sebastián: Seminario de Filología Vasca "Julio de Urquijo," 1990
(reprint of 1977 ed.), pp. 371–77.

19.1 Ancient Basque seems to have had a simple vowel system, with
three levels of openness. Except for certain cases of the permutation *i* /
u in initial position, which are not clearly understood, the modern facts
are well explained by assuming five ancient phonemes and in practice,
implicitly or explicitly, all authors have operated with these units in their
reconstruction.

Ancient Basque, in all probability, did not know a correlation of
length in vowels. For that reason, in the most ancient loan words from
Latin, Basque vowels *a, e, i, o, u* reproduce the Latin vowels of analogous tone, without paying attention to their length, long or short.

The number of ancient diphthongs is rather more difficult to determine. In more recent times, medieval and modern *au, eu, ai, ei, oi* (and
ui, which seems to be a variation of *oi*) have been documented. In
Aquitanian (and also in Iberian) the graphic group *ou* appears, possibly
a diphthong.

Many modern diphthongs appear secondary. Even in the dialects
that have /h/, the very frequent examples of *ai, ei, oi* in the final syllable
of words with two or more syllables very probably are diphthongs: *ibai*
"river," *izei* "fir tree," *idoi* "marsh," etc. Of the diphthongs, *oi* appears
least frequently and *eu* alternates often with the bisyllable *e-u*: *neurri* /
negurri "measure," etc. If Corominas (see *leme,* Adiciones) is right in
thinking that Basque *leun* (> sul. *leñ*) "smooth" comes from Occitan
teun(e), as is likely, then the bisyllabic variation *legun,* already seen in
Laburdin of the seventeenth century, would be secondary.

The most important result of the comparison has to do with the number of syllables of the reconstructed bases. Anyone who pays attention to all the evidence will necessarily arrive at the conclusion that Basque, undoubtedly like most languages whose history is somewhat familiar, has been reducing the number of its signifiers and not increasing them by splitting vowels and interjecting consonants. In order to determine the ancient number of syllables in a base, evidence from Basque-French dialects is fundamental, where aspiration has prevented contractions that have occurred in other dialects, but because of the restrictions to which *h* is subject in the frame of the word, this evidence is valuable principally for the first two syllables. For the end of the word, when the syllables were long, we take into account some Bizkaian variations, such as that from Marquina or Oñate. See examples in 5.1, to which we can add among others the Bizkaian of Izpaster and Marquina *belaar* "back or side of a mattress or pillow," "any flat surface on a barrel," Low Navarrese Salazar dialect (and Souletin according to Gèze) *belar* "front," Meridional *belar*, dialect of Aezcoa High Navarrese *bepelar* (<bet- "eye") "eyelash, eyebrow."

19.2 With respect to consonants, it is difficult to determine even the approximate number of units in the ancient system. You cannot reconstruct contrasts that have been confused in the stages of language in evidence. On the other hand, the processes of internal reconstruction that have been used here can very well be too drastic and perhaps have tended to underappreciate evidence of differences that have been considered secondary and invalid in a sufficiently ancient stage of the language.

The first simplification, and a far-reaching one, has been that certain soft or palatalized phonemes, whatever their number in ancient Basque, constituted a group apart, a secondary system subordinate to the principal one of hard, nonpalatalized phonemes. This was done in chapter 10 [of *Fonética histórica* . . .], not without precedent. This manner of thinking is based on the state of affairs demonstrated by the modern dialects but, upon projecting it on the distant past, the modern conditions have become purified and sublimated. This process has internal justification, given that the Basque facts can be easily explained by proposing a separation and strict correlation in proto-Basque between both systems and by adding certain demonstrated phonetic changes plus the Romance influence. It is much more doubtful that this construction will have unconditional validity if one day we are in a position to compare Basque with a related and sufficiently divergent language.

In the case of /j/, although we have not stated it clearly, one must distinguish the cases in which it begins the word from those in which it appears in an interior position. In the first case it can be proven that often it is secondary and the result of an ancient vowel, *e*, before a vowel, which is not to say that this is always the case. In the interior position, where it occasionally alternates with *ih*, it poses problems that for now cannot be resolved (see 4.11 and 9.7) [Note: these 2 sections are not included in this book.]

19.3 In a separate work,[1] based principally on the similarities of the behavior of phonemes, especially on the coincidence of the neutralization of oppositions in analogous contexts, with all the reservations imposed by such a hypothetical restitution, we arrive at the following reconstruction of the principal phonological system of ancient Basque:[1]

Strong:	–	t	c	ć	k	N	L	R
Weak:	b	d	s	ś	g	n	l	r

In other words, leaving /h/ aside, the system did not know more than one single correlation that contrasted strong phonemes—that is, those having tense articulation—with weak phonemes—those having more lax or shorter articulation—unless voicing or aspiration were pertinent characteristics. There was a lack of a hard labial occlusive and also a labial nasal (see chapter 13) [of *Fonética histórica* . . .], although they would soon enter into the system.

Voiced double consonants (occlusives) and voiced groups in Romance appear to be represented by unvoiced Basque equivalents (12.5) and the reproduction of the unvoiced fricative *f* by Basque *b*, as well as the permutation *b/f* (13.4), seem to indicate that labio-dental or bilabial *f* was at one time a stylistic variation of /b/ in some signifiers. This can be offered as proof that until well into the Middle Ages it was not voicing or its absence that forced occlusives of both series into opposition, but rather their more or less lax or tense articulation.

One difficulty that becomes immediately apparent is the lack of similarity of the differential characteristic between the two series of occlusives on the one hand and the two series of sibilants on the other. In the first case, the tenuous ones are occlusive in some contexts and it seems necessary to admit that in the interior of the word, between vowels, they were fully voiced even in ancient times. On the contrary, the sibilants /s/ and /ś/ are always aspirant and furthermore unvoiced between vowels.

Martinet believes[2] that one valid explanation could stem from an older system that opposed in each order voiced or unvoiced affricate sibilants and occlusives, with neutralization in final position. The tendency toward aspiration of unvoiced ones and muffling of the voiced ones would come later, both in the occlusives as well as in the sibilants, but in the latter, as its articulation weakens in initial position, [ch-] blurs into a voiceless fricative [s-] with the representative of the ancient voiced affricate phoneme in that position, while [th-] became *h-* and zero. You could say that the loss of sibilants between vowels and the possible cases of rotacism (conversion of intervocalic s into r) mentioned in 14.8 would be better explained by attributing phonological voicing to some phonemes of this class.[3]

It would also be necessary to determine if the units included in our hypothetical system are strictly contemporary, a question that concerns the antiquity of /L/ and /N/ above all, for which we refer to 18.11 [not included in this book.]

19.4 Even discounting the many doubtful aspects, it becomes clear that ancient Basque had a relatively simple consonant system. The phonemes were not numerous and their possibilities for combination were very few. The groups of consonants, which appeared in the interior of the word and possibly at the end but were lacking at the beginning, were always of decreasing aperture: sibilant plus occlusive, voicing plus sibilant or occlusive, voicing plus sibilant plus occlusive.

In addition to the fact that there were few phonemes and few variations of consonant groups, there was no lack of positions in which oppositions that were distinctive in other positions were neutralized. The type of language that ancient Basque tended to be, and that in many aspects represented historical Basque, was adjusted to the Spanish model so graphically described by Amado Alonso, in which "oppositions that function as signifiers and differentials in syllabic tension, cease in relaxation, where they either do not exist materially or if they exist they cease to be intentional and lose validity for that reason." But the neutralization was not limited in Basque to implosion. It clearly tended to suspend postconsonantal oppositions and even those occurring at the beginning of a word, as surprising as this might seem. The result for comparative reconstruction is that certain contrasts (unvoiced / voiced in occlusives, affricate / fricative in sibilants, etc.) are only fully recognizable between vowels and to a much lesser degree after *r*.

19.5 From the diachronic point of view, the question lies in knowing if we had been moving toward neutralization during the period covered by this attempt at reconstruction, that is, during approximately the last two millennia, or if it came from an older period. It does not seem too daring to suppose that the indifferentiation in the implosive part of the syllable represents something very old, nor to think that the opposition of hard and soft voicing perhaps never existed except in the interior of a word and specifically between vowels.

Historical Basque does not offer ways of distinguishing two ancient series of sibilants occurring after *n* and *l*, which does not mean that in a more ancient stage of the language they could not have been contrasted. With respect to the distinction of two series of occlusives after both consonants, we have already suggested (18.10) that perhaps the neutralization was very ancient. In this way, Roncalese and Souletin, the dialects that best distinguish *lt* from *ld*, etc., may not represent an archaic stage, but rather may be innovators, having abandoned the ancient practice of uniformly producing soft occlusives in that position in loan words and new formations before the other dialects did so.

Aquitanian nouns seem to indicate that there were already only fricative sibilants in initial position, given that *x*- does not occur more than once, in *Xuban deo* (cf. *Sembe-, Seni-, Silex*, etc.). For this to be so, there was a time when, of all the consonants, only the occlusives maintained the hard-soft opposition, common intervocalically for all the others, in initial position.

Aspiration

"La aspiración," *Fonética histórica vasca*. 2nd ed. San Sebastián: Seminario de Filología Vasca "Julio de Urquijo," 1990, pp. 203–24.

11.1 According to Larrasquet, /h/ is articulated with the mouth open, as much in the Souletin dialect as in Low Navarrese and Laburdin. The tongue takes the position of the following vowel and a brusque contraction of the diaphragm produces a rapid and intense puff of air. The aspiration is voiceless in intial position, but only exceptionally between vowels, especially when these are of the same timbre. Between nasal vowels it is nasal.[4]

It can appear in the following contexts.[5]

a) At the beginning of a word, before a vowel or diphthong: Souletin *hárri* "stone," *haur* "child," Leiçarraga *harri, haour*

b) Intervocalically: Souletin *ãhã'lke* "shame," *lehũ'* "lion," Leiçarraga *ahalque, lehoin*

c) Between diphthong and vowel: Souletin *áuher* "lazy," *óihan* "forest," Leiçarraga *auhen* "lamentation," *oihan*

d) Before a vowel, after *n (n'), l (l') r (R)*: Souletin *sénhar* "husband," *sínhets* "believe," Leiçarraga *senhar, sinhets*; Souletin *añhá(r)a* "swallow," *üñhü'rri* "ant"; Souletin *élhe* "word," *ü'lhün* "dark," Leiçarraga *elhe, ilhun*; Souletin *büllhür* "a lien made with young branches twisted and interlaced"; Leiçarraga *orhe* "dough," *erhi* "finger" (modern Souletin *óhe, éhi*); Leiçarraga *vrrhe* "gold," *vrrhets* "pass" (modern Souletin *ü'rhe ürháts*) As Lafon observes, we are dealing with "groupes disjoints," that is to say that the syllabic division passes between *h* and the preceding consonant.

e) The three northern dialects also know aspirated occlusives: *ph, th, kh*. They are voiceless, although in one Souletin variety at least, according to the description of Larrasquet, they tend to be voiced in rapid, careless pronunciation. They appear at the beginning and in the interior of the word, interior after a vowel, diphthong, *n, l*, and *r*[6]: Souletin *phárka* "pardon," *thü* "spit," *khéñü* "sign," *ápho* "frog," *ítho* "to drown," *ákher* "male goat," *ü'rpho* "pile of manure," *gáltho* "request, question," *ínkhatz* "charcoal," etc.

There is never an *h* after *m* or a sibilant. After a sibilant, the occlusives are never aspirated, as in the well-known English case.

11.2 The French-Spanish border coincides along general lines with the division of the dialects that have /h/ and those that do not. Consistent with Bonaparte's data, *Verbe* xv, note 3, published in 1869, aspiration was not heard south of the border except in Zugarramurdi and some in Alquerdi, where Laburdin is spoken, but not in Urdax. Neither was *h* used in the popular language of the Laburdin coast (Saint-Jean-de-Luz, Ciboure, Urrugne, with Béhobie, Hendaya, and Biriatou), but it was used in Ascain, Guéthary, and Bidart. All in all, its frequency was much less in the Laburdin dialect (except in the subdialect of Arcangues) than in Low Navarrese and especially in Souletin. In addition /h/ is also maintained to the south of the border in the Low Navarrese of Valcarlos and Quinto Real.

The disappearance of *h* on the Labourdin coast must be recent. In the works of J. de Etcheberri of Ciboure, published around 1627, *h* is a frequent letter and its usage was absolutely regular, as regular as in the works of Leiçarraga. For Saint-Jean-de-Luz we have the express evidence of P. d'Urte, *Grammaire*, 9, at the beginning of the eighteenth century: "L'H on le met deuant et apres les voyelles, et on le prononce toujours avec aspiration. *hartça*, ours. *herioa*, la mort. *hiria*, ville. *sukhaldéa*, foyer. *olha*, forge. *ognh[a]çéa*, douleur qui regarde le corps . . ." (The H is placed before and after vowels, and it is always pronounced with aspiration. *hartça*, bear. *herioa*, death. *hiria*, town. *sukhaldéa*, fireplace. *olha*, oven. *ognh[a]çéa*, mourner who watches the body . . ."

11.3 With regard to its antiquity, Luchaire demonstrates that the Gascons of Bayonne and Lower Adour used to transcribe Basque aspiration during the Middle Ages by means of an *f*, as well as *h*; *Ferriaga (Harriaga), Fondarraga (Hondarraga), Sufarasu (Zuharrazu), Olfegi (Olhegui)*, etc.[7]

Furthermore one can state with near certainty that in Spanish territory extensive Basque-speaking areas, especially Alava and La Rioja, were also familiar with aspiration up until and including the thirteenth century, at least. This is evidenced by the frequency and regularity with which the letter *h* appears in the list of Alavese towns known as La Reja (Grid) of San Millán, *CSMill.* 91, from the year 1025, and in many other documents.[8] In Navarrese documents, on the other hand, *h* appears especially between vowels (*Erret Ihera, Ihiza*, and *Iiza, Lehet*, and *Lehet(e), Uharte, Uart(e)*, and *Huarte*, etc.) and its use at the beginning of a word is rare and inconsistent.

In summary, one could say that /h/, once common to all the varieties of the language, has been preserved until rather late in the western part of the country (Alava, Rioja, Bizkaia); nevertheless, in spite of certain spellings in *RS* and also other old Bizkaian texts such as that of Landucci, it must not have existed any more by the sixteenth century. It is highly probable that the loss began through High Navarra, in contact with Aragonese Romance that had no *h*, and in the greater part of that region it was an out-and-out fact in the eleventh century.

11.4 In the Aquitanian inscriptions *h* is a very frequent letter. It is especially abundant in initial position (*Halsco, Harbelex, Harsus*, which has been compared with Basque-French *hartz* "bear," *Hotarris* gen., etc.)

and between vowels (*Aherbelste*, dative; *Bihoxus*, cf. Basque-French *bihotz* "heart"; *Lohitton*, cf. Basque-French *lohi* "mud, dirty" and old usage "body," etc.), but also occurred after *l* (*Belheiorix*, *Lelhunno* dat.) and *r* (*Erhexoni* dat., *Bar(h)osis*, *Berhaxsis*) and sometimes after *t* (*Baisothar* . . . , *Hontharris* gen.). As the last example shows, and others like *Hahanni*, *Hahanten(n)*, it can appear twice in the same word.

If we compare medieval Spanish documents with the use of Basque dialects that knew aspiration, the coincidences are generally notable.

For *h-*, cf., among others, *Haizcoeta*, *Haizpilleta*, *Hazpurua*, *Hazteguieta*[9]: *haitz* "rocky crag" (*Manual* I, 111, Oihenart, *Prov.* 134, etc.); *Farana* (*DL* 55, Oña, year 1236), *Harana* (*DL* 142, Vitoria, year 1291): *haran* "valley" (Leiçarraga, etc.); *Harizavalleta*: Souletin *há(r)itx* "oak"; *Harrieta*, *Harriolha*, *Harrizavallaga* (but *Arbelgoihen*, *Arriaga*, *Arzubiaga*): Leiçarraga *harri*, Souletin *hárri*; *Heguilior*, *Heg(u)iraz* (*CSMill.* 229, year 1076, *Heguilaz*; *DL* 88, year 1229, *Heguilaz*, but in Navarra *Eguirior(r)*, twelfth–thirteenth centuries): *hegi* "riverbank, edge" (*Manual* II, 124), Souletin *hégi* "edge, angle"; *Huriarte*, *Huribarri*, *Hurigurenna* (*CSMill.* 48, year 952, *Ulibarrilior*; *DL* 88, year 1229, *Vriart*): *hiri* "town" (Leiçarraga, etc.), Souletin *hí(r)i*.

Without initial aspiration, *Arzanhegi*, *Arçamendi*: common *artzai(n)* "shepherd," in compounds *artzan-* from *ardi* "sheep"; *Essavarri*: common *etse*, *etxe* "house"; *Ibarguren* (and *Borinivar*): Souletin *íbar* "broad flat prairie"; person's name *Ochoa*, *Oggoa*: Aquitainian *Oxson (Osson)*: Leiçarraga *otso* "wolf," Souletin *ótso*. La Reja has *h-* in some cases in which it should not be etymological: *Haberasturi*, Basque *aberats* "rich," *Hamezaga*, Basque *ametz* "oak," *Hobecori*, cf. person's name *Ov(i)eco*.

After *l*, *Elhorriaga*, *Elhorzahea*, *Elhossu*: Leiçarraga *elhorri* "hawthorn," Souletin *elhórri* "thorn"; *Olhabarri*, *Olhaerrea*, and as the last part of the word, *Harriolha*, *Mendiolha*, *Zuazulha*[10]: Souletin *óha* "shepherd's hut," cf. place name *Olfegi* (modern *Ohlegui*), in a document from Sordes, at the beginning of the eleventh century.

In short, the coincidences are far from negligible, especially if we keep in mind the changeable quality of aspiration in the modern Basque dialects and the frequent omissions that are observed in Spanish documents.[11]

11.5 As a demonstration of the distinctive value of aspiration, one can cite pairs such as the following:

Leiçarraga Souletin *har* "worm" and "take": *ar* "male."

Souletin *hardít* "who enjoys good health" (Leiçarraga *hardit* "daring," 2 Cor. 11, 21): *ardít* "ardite (coinage)."

Leiçarraga *hari* "to that," Souletin *há(r)i* "to that" and "thread": Leiçarraga *ari (da,* etc.) "to be in action," Souletin *á(r)i.*

Souletin *ézi* "well, because": *hézi* "tame."

Souletin *ütz* "leave": *hütz* "silent fart."

Leiçarraga *auhen* "lamentation": *auen* "qui te habet."

Leiçarraga *hala* "thus, in that manner": *alha (da,* etc.) "to eat, to graze": *ala* interrogative particle; Souletin *hála, álha, ála.*

Leiçarraga *haran* "valley," cf. Sauguis 112 *arhan* "plum," modern Souletin *áhan.*

Leiçarraga *belhar* "grass": *belar* "forehead" (both in Ap. 9, 4).

Leiçarraga *eri* "sick" (Souletin *ei*): *erhi* "finger" (Souletin *éhi*).

Oihenart *zorhi* "ripe" (*Prov.* 18): *zori* "luck" (*Prov.* 54).

In his study on aspiration, Lafon was inclined to see phonetic variations of the same phoneme in *p, ph,* etc., instead of distinct phonemes. This seems doubtful in historical Basque. In fact, except for a word here or there, a particular occlusive in a particular signifier is always either aspirated or not aspirated within the same dialectal variety: we are not dealing with changeable stylistic variations within it. On the other hand, today it is not always foreseeable how a particular occlusive will be pronounced, based on considerations of the phonological order. Thus, in initial position, Souletin has *phéna* "pain, sorrow," but *péa* "pear." In any case, it is certain that the yield of this opposition is always extremely low and on certain occasions nonexistent. Lafon points out in Leiçarraga the pair *bati* "to one" / *bathi* "resolution, resignation," which perhaps were also differentiated by some prosodic characteristic. In the Souletin variety described by Larrasquet, *óker* "burp" and *ókher* "twisted" (cf. *úrthe* "year" / *húrte* "period of rains")[12] seem to be distinguished from each other.

11.6 Repeated doubts have been expressed about the etymological value of *h*: thus Gavel, on different occasions, and Schuchardt, *Die iberische Deklination,* 6. Aspiration would be etymological (see 11.13) when it is a continuation of: (1) an ancient proto-Basque *h*; (2) Latin *f-*, with or without Romanic mediation; (3) an ancient intervocalic *-n-*; and (4) ancient strong or voiceless occlusives in initial position. The reasons that have been presented, plus others that could have been added, evidently do not allow us to conclude that aspiration is always secondary, but it does allow that in a particular case, when the etymology of the Basque word is unknown, one cannot go beyond a simple opinion about the primary or adventitious character of aspiration in that term.

With regard to initial position, the most important in this respect, the following reasons can be used:

1. *h-* appears in loan words with no justification whatsoever. Thus, among others, in Laburdin *harea* (from the seventeenth century), Souletin *háiña, hariña* "sand," Dechepare, Leiçarraga, etc., *harma* "weapon" (*harmatu, harmadura*), Leiçarraga, etc., *harrapatu* "to capture" (from the Romance *arrapar*, see Corominas, s.v.), Souletin (Gèze) *harroka* "rock" (Leiçarraga *arroca*), Dechepare, etc., *hautatu*, Souletin *haitátü* "chosen, elected" (see Corominas, s.v. *alto*, note 5), Leiçarraga, etc., *hauzu, haizu* "permitted" (see above 4.3), Souletin *(arima) herrátü* "soul in pain," Souletin (Gèze) *hezkabia* "ringworm" (Latin *scabies*), Leiçarraga, Souletin, etc., *hira* "ire, rancor," Leiçarraga, etc., *hiraka* "discord" (Latin *ebriaca*, Pyrenaic Aragonese *biraca*), etc.[13]

2. A lack of aspiration where you would expect to encounter it: Leiçarraga, etc., *ume* "offspring," from **kume*, to judge by the compounds, but Souletin *hü´me*, Sauguis 111 and 114 *humia(c)*.

3. It is not unusual to have disagreement between different dialects with respect to initial aspiration.

   In monosyllabic Souletin words, *h-* seems to have been generalized: *ho(r)* "dog," Leiçarraga, etc., *or*; *hun* "good," Leiçarraga, etc., *on* (Dechepare *hon*); *huñ* "foot," Leiçarraga, etc., *oin*; *hur* "water," Leiçarraga, etc., *ur*.

   In longer words, Souletin *áizo*, Leiçarraga *auzo* "neighbor," Laburdin *hauzo* (*Manual* I, 12, etc.); Souletin *háitzür* "large hoe, mattock," Leiçarraga participle *aitzurtu* (and *aitzurrerik*, Leiçarraga 16, 3); Souletin (and Dechepare) *áize* "wind," Leiçarraga, etc., *haize*; Souletin *a(r)ági* "meat," Leiçarraga *haragi*; Souletin *he(r)áki* "to boil," Leiçarraga *erakin*; Souletin *ézür* "bone," Leiçarraga *hezur*; Souletin *odéi* "cloud," Leiçarraga *hodei*; Souletin *ógen* "injury, offense," Leiçarraga *hogen* (Dechepare normally *ogen*, once *hogen*; Axular *hoben*, see 13.4, note 8); Souletin *órdi* "drunk" (Dechepare verbal stem *ordi* "to get drunk"), Leiçarraga *hordi*; Souletin *ostádar* "rainbow," Leiçarraga *orzadar*, Laburdin *holtzadar* (*Manual* I, 83, II, 142, Voltoire, etc.); Souletin *hü´rrün* "far," Leiçarraga *urrun*.[14]

4. Within the same variation there are discrepancies in related forms: Leiçarraga *hire* "yours (fam.)" / *eure* "of yourself (fam.)," old Souletin *hire* / *ore*; Leiçarraga *hi* "you (fam.)" / *euror* "you (fam.) yourself"[15] Leiçarraga (and Axular 267) *amorz* "fifteen," along with the noncontraction form *hamaborz*, cf. *hamar* "ten"; Leiçarraga *erts* "to close, etc.,"participle *ertsi*, but adjective *hersi* "narrow, closed in" (Axular *hertsi* "closed" and "narrow"); Souletin *hats* "breath," (Gèze) *atsegin* "pleasure."

11.7 In initial position or not, we must naturally attribute to Basque itself the aspiration of voiceless occlusives in Latin-Romance loan words.

It is also evident, as demonstrated by compound words and loan words, that aspiration has developed within Basque itself between vowels in hiatus as well as after *n, ñ, l, ll, r*, and *rr*: Souletin *Johane, Johañe* "John" (Leiçarraga *Ioannes*), Leiçarraga *lehoin* "lion," Souletin *lehü´*; Souletin *anhúa* "provisions for the trip" (Latin *annona*), *mánha* "to order," *uñhü´* "onion"; Souletin *gelhá(r)i* "servant" (Latin *cellarius*), *golhare* "spoon" (According to Gèze; Roncalese *gollare*), Laburdin *solharu* "granary" (d'Urte, *Grammaire* 25, etc.; Leiçarraga *solleru*, Act. 20, 9); Laburdin *sorho*, Souletin *sóho* "meadow" (with old *-l-*), Souletin *áha* < old *arha* "to rake" (from *arare?*),[16] *marhünka* "wrinkle" (Gèze). In compounds, Leiçarraga *onherran* "to bless," *onherizte* "love," cf. *erran, eritzi*[17]; Leiçarraga *ilhargi* "moon," Souletin *larhárgi* "of clear skin," cf. common *argi* "light, clear."

In compounds, there is an *h* after diphthongs at the end of the first part of the word when there is only one syllable: Leiçarraga *gauherdi*, Souletin *gaihérdi* "midnight" (common *erdi* "middle, half"), Souletin *gaiháldi* "night" (common *aldi* "time, occasion"), Laburdin *de(i)hadar* "shout, clamor" (common *adar* "horn"). However, this does not seem to occur outside of compound words: common *maiatz* "May," Souletin *maiastü´(r)ü* "carpenter."[18]

It is also extremely rare for a Romance diphthong to be destroyed by epenthesis of *h* between its two elements: French-Basque *beira* "glass, vessel made of glass," *gauza* "thing" (Souletin *gáiza*), *laido* "affront," *laudorio* "praise" (Souletin *láida* "to praise"), *lausengu* "flattery," *mairu* "Moor," etc.[19]

11.8 Unlike what happened in the spelling of Medieval documents, the modern dialects do not allow two aspirations in the same word.[20] In compounds, when the coincidence of two aspirations will result from it, normally the first is eliminated by a regressive dissimilation comparable to that observed in Old Greek (present *ékho·*, future *hékso·*, etc.)[21]: Souletin *ilhérri* "cemetery" (Dechepare), *ílhort* "to abort," Oihenart *ilhots* "sad song, elegy" (*Poes.Voc.*), cf. *hil* "death"; Souletin *aurhide* "brother of the same father and mother," cf. *haur* "child" (Leiçarraga *haourride* and *haour*).

It is possible that this limitation did not exist in the oldest period (see 20.13). Keep in mind that dissimilation has been produced even when the second aspiration was secondary and born by virtue of 11.7; Dechepare, Leiçarraga, etc., *ilhargi* "moon," formed from *argi* and the old name for the moon and for month, probably **(h)ile* (cf. old Indian *candrámas-* "moon"), that appears in the compound *hilebethe* (Leiçarraga *hilabete* in *Onsa* 114) "month," literally "complete month" (see 21.5, 1st).

The few exceptions are explained in two ways, either because the components have not lost their autonomy to the point of constituting a true compound (which is perhaps what happened with *hilebethe*) or more frequently by analogy: Souletin *hílhotz* "stiffly dead," etc.

On the contrary, when the first two syllables of a word begin with an aspiratable occlusive, the initial syllable has priority, so either only the first occlusive is aspirated or neither of the two is aspirated: Souletin *phárka* "to pardon," *phíka* "magpie," *phíper* "pepper," *théka* "legume pod," *thípil* "naked," *thipíña* "cooking pot," *kháko* "hook," *khólte* "stake, post," *khórpitz* "body"; *pipíta* "pip," *pikarrái* "naked," *ténta* "to tempt," *tínta* "ink," *kükü´so* "flea," *künkü´ño* "tree overloaded with fruit." In other words, the two types **kheke* and **keke* exist, but **kekhe* does not.[22] However, a word can begin with a nonaspirated voiceless occlusive and later carry *h* between vowels: Souletin *kehélla* "rustic song," *tahárna* "inn," *tahálla* "tablecloth, napkin," etc.

11.9 Paying attention to the whole of the spoken chain, aspiration is subject to various restrictions, which R. Lafon has specified:

1. *h* plays a very small role in morphology. It does not appear in any casual suffix. There is no postposition such as *baithan* among them. In reality we are dealing with a noun provided with casual suffixes that is an autonomous element in the chain.[23]

2. The *h* is never placed between the final consonant of the stem and the suffix that begins with a vowel: *bat-en* "of one," *bat-i* "to one," etc.

3. In the same case, neither does *h* appear after the final vowel of a stem: *semearen* "of the son, the son's," *semeari* "to the son," as opposed to *seme haren* "of that son, that son's," *seme hari* "to that son," although by any reckoning the article and the demonstrative of the third person were originally identical.[24]

4. It is rarely found in the finite verb, except in the imperative: Dechepare, Leiçarraga *ikhusi* "seen" / *(ba)dakusat* "I see it"; *ekharri* "brought" / Dechepare *dakartela* "that they bring it," Leiçarraga *dekarke* "he brings it (with him)," etc. [25]

5. It is almost always lacking in the nominal forms of the causative verbs: Leiçarraga *erakutsi* "shown," *irakatsi* "taught," Souletin *i(r)akútsi, e(r)akátsi,* cf. Leiçarraga *irakur* "to read," Souletin *i(r)ákur.*[26]

6. It is lacking in many particles: interrogative *ala* and disjunctive *edo* "or," *eta* "and." In *alba-* and *albait- (albeit-)* the first element is undoubtedly *ahal* "to be able."[27]

11.10 Within the frame of the word, as a result of the dissimilation pointed out in 11.8, aspiration is subjected to very severe limitations. Whatever its ancient state, it has been seriously altered in order to arrive at its modern regularity.

Thus, the type *epher* "hare," *athe* "door" (Souletin "pile"), *akher* "male goat," that is, the type with an initial vowel and an aspirated occlusive at the beginning of the second syllable, is so general that we can assume the disappearance of a great number of ancient initial aspirations. This can be the case, for example, for *urkhatu* (Souletin *ürkhátü*) "hung," from Latin *furca.*

The exceptions are few and due to particular causes, which cannot always be specified. Included among the exceptions are expressive words (*húpa* an interjection, *hapataka* "at a gallop"), loan words (Souletin *hátu* "natural effects," cf. Spanish *hato*)[28] and analogous formations: Souletin *húntü* "improved, fertilized" (Leiçarraga *onthu*), *húrte* "rainy season," *húrtü* "smelted," formed on *hun* "good," *hur* "water." There are some participles such as Souletin *húrtü* "taken," *héltü* "arrived," that depart from the norm and perhaps have been formed in a relatively recent era by extension of the new participle suffix added to the old roots *har, hel.*[29] Moreover, there remain some examples that are difficult to classify, such as Souletin *hóki* "three-legged stool" ("normal state" according to Azkue) that seem to be a variation of the common *toki* "place," Leiçarraga *hunki*, Souletin *húnki*, Laburdin *ukitu* "to touch, touched" (see above 2.5), etc.[30]

Also very frequent is the following type: *aski* "enough," *aste* "week," *azpi* "thigh," *azkar* "strong, vigorous," *aztal* "talon," etc. The word *ospe* "fame," written with *h-* by Oihenart would test the loss of initial aspiration if it is, as it seems, a compound of *hots* "noise, sound." The aspiration of Dechepare and Leiçarraga *heuskara* "Basque language," later *euskara*, etc. (see 4.7), could consequently be the origin.

One can also suspect generalization in the type represented by Souletin *áiher* "who arises easily," *aihen* "stump, stock," *aihotz* "pruning shears" (both in Gèze; Axular has *haiotz)*, *éihar* "dry," *óihal* "cloth," *óihan* "forest," *óihü* "shout."

11.11 Another important restriction must be added. In a three-syllable word, aspiration can appear, in addition to initial position, between the first and second syllable, but not beyond.

For *h* arising from intervocalic *n* (see 7.5), Souletin *báhe* "sieve," *xẽ'hẽ* "often," *ãhã'te* "duck," *ãhã'be* "blueberry," *ũhũ'(r)e* "honor," but *ardũ'* "wine," *orgã'* "cart," *sasũ'* (voiced *s*) "season," etc.

In participles with the suffix *-ki*: Leiçarraga *ilkhi*, Souletin *élkhi*, but Dechepare *eduki*, Leiçarraga *ebaki, iguriki, iduki*, Souletin *ebáki, etxéki, idéki, e(r)adóki*, etc.

In the more common type of participle, the one formed with the suffix *-tu*: Dechepare *bathu*, Leiçarraga *deithu, gurthu, onthu, sarthu, sorthu, zaurthu*, Souletin *déithü, góithü, górthü, gréüthü, lánthü, léinthü, lóthü, mínthü, sárthü, sórthü*, but Dechepare *lotsatu, samurtu*, Leiçarraga *agertu, gazitu, gezatu*, Souletin *agértü, aizátü, ausártü, bardíntü, edértü, ezagü'tü*, etc.[31]

In a similar way, aspiration also appears in compound words between two members of the word when the first has no more than one syllable: *gau* "night," *lur* "earth," *on* "good," *su* "fire," *(h)ur* "water," *zur* "wood." From there, contrasts follow such as Leiçarraga *gauherdi* "midnight" / *eguerdi* "midday" (Souletin *gaihérdi / egüérdi*), *janhari* "food, meal" / *edari* "drink" < *edaari*, evidenced in Bizkaian, and others collected in 21.8.

Souletin seems to distance itself from the ancient practice of the other northern dialects. It has trisyllabic oxytone nouns [nouns with the stress on the last syllable] derivatives with stressed suffixes, compounds,

loan words) that carry aspiration immediately before the stress: *a(r)*
akhói "fond of meat," *arrathũ'* "rat," etc. Even in nouns of more than
three syllables, generally loan words, aspiration can go not only between
the first and second members (*enthelegátü* "understood," *lükháinka*
"blood sausage," etc.) but also later on: *ba(r)anthálla* "February" (which
J. Gorostiaga suggests comes from the Latin *parentalia*), *bo(r)ontháte*
"will" < Latin *uoluntatem*. In contrast, Leiçarraga has the pariciples
debetatu "prohibited," *ixukatu* "dried," without aspiration.

11.12 Independent of its current phonological position, already discussed in 11.5, there is no doubt that at one time *t* / *th*, etc., were no
more than phonetic variations of the same phoneme. Its aspiration or
lack thereof seems to have depended on its position in the word, and
perhaps in the end on its position with respect to the stress.

a. It seems undeniable also that, among words which today begin with
   an occlusive, the type represented by *begi, bide, bekhatu, daratulu,*
   dekuma, gathea, gerezi, gizon, that is, by words with initial voiced
   occlusives, is the oldest and most characteristic type as a whole, both
   in the traditional lexicon and in old loan words.

   All in all, there are words whose Latin-Romance origin is far from
   having been proven and which begin with an unvoiced consonant
   that is normally aspirated in dialects with *h*: Souletin *phitz* "to light,
   to revive," *thü* "saliva," *khe* "smoke," *khent* "to take away" (Dechepare *khen*) and more. To these one must add a good number of loan
   words: Leiçarraga *pherde* "green," *phorogatu* "proven, tested," *thallu*
   "class, genre," *thatxa* "defect" (Soueltin *thatxatü* "[animal] illness
   of the stomach"), *kheinu* "gesture, sign" (Souletin *khéñü*), *kharrika*
   "street" (Souletin *kharríka*).

   Finally, the third type is basically made up of loan words that begin
   with an unaspirated unvoiced occlusive: Leiçarraga *pelat* "thing or
   coin of little value" (Souletin *pelát* "slap"), *populu* "town" (Souletin
   popü'lü), *tenda* "castrates," *testamentu* "testament" (Souletin *testa-
   méntü*), *kamelu* "camel" (Souletin *kamélü*), *kanabera* "cane" (Souletin *kanabé(r)a), kantoin* "corner" (Souletin *kantũ').*[32] It generally
   deals with the most recent layer or the least assimilated layer. For this
   reason nonaspiration has been considered the mark of high culture:
   cf. Souletin *khi(r)istĩ'* "Christian," but *katolíko.* Also on occasion we
   are dealing with the secondary loss of voicing of an initial voiced con-

sonant: Leiçarraga *putzu* "pit" (Souletin *pü´tzü*), but High Navarrese *butzu*.

Loss of voicing is more than a mere hypothesis in examples like *pikain* "first fruits, etc." < **bit-gain* < *bihi-gain* "upper part of the grain,"[33] Leiçarraga etc., *kalte* "damage, harm" from *galdu* "lost": as in Giupzkoan Bizkaian *kurpil* "cart wheel" < **gurdi-bil, pekorotz* "cow pat, horse dung" < **betgorotz* < *behi-gorotz,* the loss of voicing of the initial consonant of the second member has had as a consequence, through dilation, the loss of voicing of the initial occlusive.

Notice also that aspiration is lacking in certain words that owe their form to being used as the last member of compounds, from which they have been introduced into autonomous use: Leiçarraga *kide* "contemporary," as opposed to Bizkiaian *ide* (see Lafon, *EJ* 3(1949), 146 onward and section 21.7 in this work), Laburdin *toki* "place" (Axular, etc.).

b. Within the interior of the word an aspiratable occlusive normally appears as aspirated in accord with the conditions indicated. Consequently, it is interesting to examine the most important exceptions.

   1. It is lacking in some expressive words that have or used to have a palatalized consonant: Souletin *gü´ti* "little," *ttípi, txípi* "small."[34]

   2. One could say that in loan words the position of the Latin stress continues to influence pronunciation. Although I will return to this in section 21.3, I can tell you now that, limiting ourselves to the consideration of bisyllabic and trisyllabic words, aspiration is often lacking when the occlusive falls after the syllable of original stress while in the nominal forms of the type exemplified by Leiçarraga *berthute* the occlusive situated before the stressed syllable in the original language is normally aspirated. Thus in Leiçarraga *bake* "peace" (Souletin *báke*), *dorpe* "clumsy" (Souletin *thórpe*), *gorputz* "body" (Souletin *khórpitz*), *lako* "wine or oil press" (Souletin *láko,* but *lakhu* "lake" *Manual* I, 107, Axular, etc.), *lekoa* "league (distance)," *lukuru* "interest," *mukurru* "extreme, limit" (< Latin *cumulus*), *mutu* "mute" (Souletin *mü´tü*), *neke* "work, fatigue" (Souletin *néke*), *zeta* "silk" (Souletin *zéta*), Souletin *jókü* "game," *méta* "pile," *sóka* "thick rope," etc. Although, as I said before, at times we are also dealing with aspiration (Laburdin *bikhe* "fish" < Latin *picem,* etc.), the fact that aspiration appears in participles and other derivatives of

base forms in which it is lacking corroborates the relationship we have suggested between Latin stress and Basque aspiration: Leiçarraga *nekhatu* "tired" from *neke* (cf. *muthatu* "changed, mutated"), Souletin *zethátxü* "thick sieve," cf. *zéta.*

3. Aspiration is also lacking in some old participles that were bisyllabic in historical Basque: Leiçarraga *iaiki* "to get up" (Souletin *jáiki, jéiki), iauki* "to commit" (Souletin *jáuki*).

11.13 In spite of the fact that the processes studied here must have often cause the disappearance of *h* in initial position, there still remain examples in which *h*- can very well be the continuance of a previous sound. Nevertheless, the cases of the prosthetic addition of *h*- examined in 11.6 must certainly lessen any confidence we have that *h*- might be etymological in a specific signifier, but they do not destroy it totally, at least when the word has a certain phonic configuration.

It would be risky to make a pronouncement about the old initial sound of Souletin *ilharre* "heather," *CSMill.* 91 *Hillardui, Hillarrazaha* (cf. Souletin *aurhíde*, see above, 11.8, from *haur*), Souletin *ü´kho* "negation" "stuttering" (cf. *ürkhatü*, above, 11.10) or *áste* "week" (cf. *azken* "last," perhaps superlative of eastern *hatz* "trace, track," western *atze* "posterior part"). But we are inclined to think, for example, that the initial aspirations that follow are not prosthetic: *hartz* "bear," Aquitanian *Harsus, hobi* "grave, sepulcher" (cf. Souletin *héida* "fair," *hólla* "leaf," from Bearnese), *hegi* "edge," etc., cf. *-tegi, habia* "nest," Latin *cauea, harri* "stone" from **karr-*, well represented in Romance, etc. I must add that, given the confusion of the modern situation, it is difficult to specify which of the consonants that have vanished from initial position have left a trace of themselves behind as aspiration, nor under which conditions this aspiration might be lost.[35]

To cite one possibility, in complex words, when the beginning is farther from the stress than in the simple word from which its first element came, the aspiration that was preserved in the first element has disappeared. Souletin *ardai* "tinder," undoubtedly oxytone, cf. Gipuzkoan *ardagai*, Laburdin *hardo* (see below 12.16).

11.14 Inside the word, between vowels, *h* does not lend itself to conjecture about its antiquity because of the very ease with which it can appear and disappear. Anyway, it seems that it continues to mark the ancient syllabic boundaries, the same in *bihotz* "heart," Aquitainian *Bihoxus*, as in *lehoin* "lion" (Gipuzkoan *le(g)oi*). It has already been pointed out (11.7) that *h* does not usually dissociate the elements of a Latin or Romance diphthong: this allows us to conclude with some verisimilitude that the syllabic division is very old in cases such as *ahuntz* "female goat" (as opposed to *hauts* "ash, dust"), *lohi* "mud" "body" (cf. *goi* "upper part," *oihan* "forest").

Of course, this is only valid within certain limits, since aspiration has regularly been lost in the prehistoric period in the French-Basque dialects in some positions, as will be seen in section 20.13.

Before a vowel and after a diphthong, we have seen that the following type is very generalized: *aihen, aiher, leiho*, etc. In *goihen*, superlative of *goi*, the aspiration must be secondary. But beside that, although scantly represented, there are signifiers such as *lehia* "haste" and *gehi-*. Also, it is possible here that the aspiration has not changed the ancient syllabic divisions.

We are led to believe that it could have been a common type by examples such as French-Basque *eihar* "dry," High Navarrese / Gipuzkoan / Bizkaian *igar*. The old form would be, consequently, *ei-ar*, not *e-jar*, which assumes High Navarrese / Elcano / Salazar dialect *ear*, Roncalese *éxar* (see 9.7). The same occurs with Low Navarrese *auhari*, Souletin *aihá(r)i*, Roncalese *aigári* "dinner" (see 4.4), but western *abari, afari*: the division [au-ari], not [a-wari], is understood by accepting a derivative with the suffix *-(k)ari* (cf. *barazkari* "midday meal"). In loan words, the following faithfully preserve the primitive divisions: Souletin *áuher*, Low Navarrese *auher*, Salazar dialect *auger, aguer*, Roncalese *aurér* "lazy" (see Schuchardt, *ZRPh* 23 (1899), 179), and Low Navarrese / Laburdin *ahul*, Souletin *áhül* "weak" < Romance *ávol*.

11.15 In the speech of Spaniards, zero often corresponds to the intervocalic *h* or the *h* between diphthong and vowel of the northern dialects. Nevertheless, quite frequently the correspondence is *h*: *g* or *r*, which by dissimilation can become *l*: French-Basque *beharri* "ear, hearing," High Navarrese / Baztán / Salazar dialect *begarri*, High Navarrese / Salazar dialect *bearri*, Roncalese *biárri*, High Navarrese / Gipuzkoan / Bizkaian *belarri* < **berarri*, cf. French-Basque *beha*, Roncalese *béa*, Salazar dialect *bea* "listen, pay attention"; with *h* from **n*, Bizkaian *arabi* "blueberry," *agate, arata* "duck," Meridional *segi* "child."[36]

From here arise the correspondences *-g-*: *-g-* and *-h-*: *-(g)-* in common Basque *begi* "eye," *egun* "day," *nagi* "lazy," *ago* "you [fam.] are," *agur* "goodbye," but French-Basque *behi* "cow," *ehun* "hundred," *nahi* "will, desire," *aho* "mouth," *ahur* "hollow of the hand," Spanish-Basque *bei, e(g)un, nai, a(g)o, a(g)ur*.[37]

The fact that aspiration, or the ancient substratum of modern aspiration, must be kept in mind as a real entity in reconstruction is inferred from the fact that it hardens into *-t* in all the varieties when left in final position as the first member of a compound (see 12.10): *bet-* from *behi* "cow" (and from *begi* "eye"), *bit-* from *bihi, bigi* "grain," *zot-* from *zohi, zo(g)i* "field." It has thus been confused with *g*, before the final vowel was dropped, in all the dialects. As counter proof, it must be noted that no case seems to have been proven in which *-t* emerges from *h* originating from an intervocalic *n*. In this last hypothesis *-n* does exist in compound words: High Navarrese / Gipuzkoan *mingain* "tongue" (literally "upper part of the tongue"), Low Navarrese / Bizkaian *minondo* "base of the tongue," etc., from **bini, mihi*.

11.16 It has been proven (11.7) that *h* was born in Basque itself after a nasal, lateral, and vibrant in numerous loan words and compounds. Also aside from these: Souletin *bé(r)a* "the self," *bé(r)e* "the self's," but *be(r)héz* "separately" (in reality the instrumental of *bé(r)e*, from which comes *bé(r)hez* "to distinguish, to separate," participle *bé(r)hézi* (Oihenart *Poes.* 46): Souletin (Gèze) *berhañ* "meanwhile" (Oihenart *Poes. Voc.* "Berainic, S. De son mouuement"), cf. Laburdin *beregainki* "especially," from *bere* and *gain* "upper part, surface."

The frequency of these groups *nh, lh*, etc., is not the same. It is current that *n* (infrequently) and *ñ* are followed by aspiration: Souletin *géñha* "to save," *éñha* "to get tired" (from *aun-, *eun-*), *iñházi* "lightning," *mánha* "to order" (Leiçarraga *mana*), *sénhar* "husband," in compounds *enhü'de* "wet nurse," etc. The word "brother"—Leiçarraga *anaie*, Souletin *anáie*—does not have *h* anywhere and, in agreement with what has been pointed out for occlusives in 11.12 b, 2, it is lacking in loan words such as Leiçarraga *leinu* "tribe" (with *h* the trisyllable Souletin word *leñhü'(r)ü* "dawn, ray"), Souletin *máñü* "bath" (but *mañhátü* "bathed"), *zéñü* "signal, bell" (but Gèze *zeñhare* "mark, sign").

Quite frequent is *lh*: Leiçarraga *alhargun, belhar* "grass" (but *belar* "forehead"), *elhur, ilhun*, etc. Moreso in Souletin: *bílho* "hair" (Leiçarraga *bilo*), *ílhe* "wool" (Leiçarraga *ille*), *alhába* "daughter" (Leiçarraga *alaba*). A certain number of words do not carry aspiration in any dialect: Souletin *béle* "crow," *belátz* "sparrowhawk," *elíza* "church," *olío* "oil," *zélü* "sky," *zóla* "base," Leiçarraga *zelata* "ambush," the same as Souletin *óllo* "hen," *ollár* "rooster."

More rare is the group *rh*, and even more rare *rrh*: *bero* "heat," *buru* "head," *gari* "wheat," *sare* "net," *xori* "bird," *xuri* "white," *zoro* "fool" (but Leiçarraga *erho* "crazy"), etc., never have aspiration, just like *berri* "new," *gerri* "belt," *xerri* "pig," *zorri* "flea," *zorrotz* "sharp," *arrats* "(the) nightfall," *arrau(l)tze* "egg," *gorri* "red," *larru* "skin," etc. Here also as usual, aspiration is more frequent in Souletin than in the other dialects: Souletin *á(r)hin* "lightly" (Leiçarraga *arin*), Souletin (Sauguis 67, Oihenart *Prov.* 501) *berho* "sown field" (Laburdin *berro*), *berrhetu* (Oihenart) "increased" (Laburdin *berretu*).[38]

Unlike our conclusion in 11.14, it is clear that in these groups the appearnce of *h* has changed the syllabic division: from *ma-na* we have moved to *man-ha*, etc. Perhaps the analogous action of the compounds has entered here: in *onhasun* (*unharzun*) from *on* (*hun*) or in *burhezur* from *buru*, the aspiration kept both members separate and this frequent model could attract to itself a certain mumber of words introduced in the language at different periods.

It is difficult to say up to what point *lh, rh*, etc., represent ancient groups or are continuations of an ancient voicing with secondary aspiration. We must recall the agreement of the spellings *lh* in Alava and the Rioja during the Middle Ages with the pronunciation *lh* of the northern dialects: *Elhor-, Olha-* in *CSMill.* 91: French Basque *elhorri, olha*, but later in the word *Angellu, Burgellu, Gaztellu* in *CSMill.* 91, French-Basque *Angelu*, the Basque name *Anglet, gaztelu* "castle," etc. There is only one example, in the name of a town, in which Spanish-Basque *g* seems to correspond to French-Basque *h* after *l*: *Elgorriaga* in Baztán, that should be equivalent to *El(h)orriaga*, from *elhorri*. In any case the dialect of Baztán is extremely close to Laburdin and had to have been more so in the past, when the valley belonged to the diocese of Bayonne.

Finally I must point out that *erhi* "finger" appears in compounds as *ert-* (*erkhain* [sic] "point of the finger," etc.), although this has little weight by reason of the generalization of *-t* in final position of the first member of a compound.

More Aspiration

"La aspiración," *Fonética histórica vasca.* 2nd ed. San Sebastián: Seminario de Filología Vasca "Julio de Urquijo," 1990, pp. 523–26.

11.1, d. The inscription from Lerga (Navarra), TAV, 1.12, demonstrates that *nh, rh* were already "groupes disjoints" or, in other words, heterosyllabic, in the Roman period: cf. NAR.HVN.GE.SI, A.BI.SVN. HA.RI, people's names. Some data about the separating interjection of syllables in Latin inscriptions from Vasconia and about the ancient merit of Basque *irakurri* "read" can be found in "La lectura en territorio vasco," *Zephyrus* 21–22 (1970–71), 281–287, where there is no exclusion of the possibility that the model for Iberian semisyllabic writing, also used in the Celtiberian zone, may have continued to operate in some way in the epigraphy of the first two centuries of our era.

With regard to note 3, it has already been pointed out in section 9.2 that Axular employed somewhat strange personal spellings: *cintqui eta fintqui, v(t)quitu, erho(t)queria, iltqui*. In part, this has to do with the transcription of a transitional sound (cf. Latin *sum-p-si, em-p-tum*, etc.) that Axular heard or thought he heard: the spelling *ailchatu* for "*altxatu*" (lift, raise) can serve as a term of comparison with -*il*-, which has every aspect of being the notation of a high lateral, that is, of [l']. But in *v(t)quitu, erho(t)queria*, cases in which such an explanation is excluded, it always has to do with unaspirated occlusives, and this can very well be due to a factor that is not casual. At any rate, there is at least one exceptional *ilkhi*, on p. 403: *Nahi eztuenac ilkhi dadin kheric, eztaguiela suric* "May he who does not want to create smoke, not make fire." See *FLV* 5 (1974), 107 onward, in my summary of L. Villasante, *Axular-en hiztegia*, Oinati 1973.

11.5 In the first edition (see, in particular, note 9) he did not keep duly in mind that the placement of the *T / Th* opposition in some Basque dialects (it could have been enough to dinstinguish morphemes, but in practice it hardly distinguishes them) has impeccable parallels in certain oppositions in well-known languages. In reality, in the very beginnings of the notion of phoneme, it is clearly established that it is something that *can* serve to differentiate signifiers; it does not necessarily *have to* distinguish them. The idea of functional performance (only that which serves a purpose is preserved in a language) influenced all of this, without taking into account the weight of inertia, about which Jean Séguy spoke of "historical servitude" (I don't know if he was inspired by A. de Vigny or by less literary models). As a show of regret, see "Distribución defectiva y evolución fonológica," in *Studia Hispanica in honorem R. Lapesa*, III, Madrid, 1975, 337–49.

Leiçarraga already had *merkhatu* "market" several times: *merkatu-etan,* with *k = kh,* Mt. 23, 7, etc. But the best example of opposition is that of *nota / notha* and derivatives: Salaberry has *nota* "note" and *notha* "lack, synonym of *nokhu,*" in Axular, p. 193, *notha* "stain," Haramburu, p. 333, *nothan* "in sin"; Axular *notatu* "noted" / *nothatu* "stained," cf. Haramburu, p. 134 bis, and following, *gure naturaleça nothatua* "our corrupted nature." It was already indicated in *FLV* 5 (1974), 186, note 7, that there is no need to go back to the pejorative value that *nota* had for *notha(tu), notare* in classical Latin (DELL, s.u.), and cf. for example, Plin. ep. II, 12, 4: *notatus a senatu in senatu sedere ipsisque illis, a quibus sit notatus, aequari . . .*): it is enough to refer to *REW* 5962, *FEW* 7, 196 onward. In Celtic languages the loan word seems to have had, more or less, the value of the Basque *nota, notatu*: J. Vendryes, *Lexique étymologique de l'irlandais ancien,* s.u. *not* "mark, sign."

11.6, 4. The text seems to imply, erroneously, that the number of discrepancies with regard to aspiration is rather small. I would add some other reasonably certain ones in which those that lack *h* are always the longer, more complex forms. The prefix *alba-* "if it is possible," from the so-called suppositional of the conditional, is without a doubt *ahal + ba- +* finite verb. Among the forms that contain the stem *ha(r)-* from the demonstrative of the third person, are counted the common *are* (see 7.1, a), the "genitive-ablative" used in comparative phrases such as *are gehiago* "even more," in *are . . . ere* "even, including," etc. In the introduction to J. de Urquijo, *Refranero vasco. Los Refranes y Sentencias de 1596,* republished by Editorial Auñamendi, San Sebastian, 1964, p. 14 onward, I demonstrated that the genitive with *-n* is documented as a complement of the comparative through the single example from *RS* 281: *Ator(r)en* [not *atorra!*] *baxen vr(r)ago narrua* "The leather closer than the shirt." But this *hapax* "single mention (Greek)" coincides entirely with the practice, the regular practice with domonstratives at least, from the Roncalese of Vidángoz, at the other end of the country: *beraren beino gasstuago* "more salted than his," etc. This *are,* in a broader sense, is present in the western *arean* "from there" (*arean,* sometimes replaced by *arik, etorriko da* "he must come from there") as well as "of it," in accordance with the Romance use in negative phrases: modern Bizkaian *arean ez dau* "he has none of it."

On the same subject, Laburdin *anartean* (*Man. Dev.* II, 94, etc., but *han artean* in Leiçarraga, *anhartian,* through 11.7, in *Onsa,* 23), Axular *anarteraiño,* written also *an arteraiño* "meanwhile, until then," from which undoubtedly comes the eastern *ararteko* "mediator" (western *bitarteko*), *arartekotasun* "mediation," etc. From *hala* "thus, in that way," an adverb corresponding to the same demonstrative, *alegia* "as if, etc." (+ *egia* "truth": *alegia egin* "to simulate," Belapeire, II, 26), Laburdin *ala Inkoa*, Souletin *ala Jinko*, formulas for oathtaking in the style of "thus God, as God is truth," etc.

From *hazi* "grown" and "seed" comes the general *azaro* "November, etc.," in Leiçarraga, Belapeire, etc.

11.9, 5, note. According to Rudolf P. G. de Rijk's personal indication, whose correction I cannot doubt, *er(h)o* continues to be general as an adjective: "crazy," western "silly." Its relationship with *erho* "to kill" (in *RS* 167 *ereçan* "I kill," from *ero* or **era (z)ezan*, 272 *erac*, imperative, in the series *iac, emac, erac* "wound him, give it to him, kill him," 89 *erayten*, verbal root, 227 *yre erallea* "(to) your killer") is very similar to that which links, for example, Italian *matto* (Latin *mattus*) with Spanish *matar*, etc. See Corominas, s.u.

11.10 For Souletin *hóki* "stool" and "normal state," cf. the French model *je ne suis pas dans mon assiette* (I am not in my seat), etc.

11.12, b, note. It is worth mentioning that the phrases that follow corresponded in form to old Irish *an-as maith la cách* "what each deems good," the old version *bat-bederak ohnesten duena*, with *on* "good," and current *maite duena* "that which each one loves." So there seems to be some syntagma in which *maite* was the equivalent of *on*. See *Sobre el pasado de la lengua vasca*, p. 145.

11.14 Although Azkue only gave *abari* "dinner" as being from the dialect of Salazar (in a manuscript addition it seems that Ulzama and Valcarlos are added), the form is already found in *FGNav.*: see *TAV* 2.2.13, p. 52 onward. Now it is confirmed by a note written in Pamplona at the beginning of the fifteenth century and published by F. Idoate, *FLV* I (1969), 287–90: & *jaunatiçula abarion* "eta Jaunak dizula abari on, and may God give you a good dinner."

11.15 From the old pronunciation in two syllables of *na(h)i* in Bizkaian evidenced in *RS* 336: *Galdu çe eguic aldia ta ydoro daye naya* "Do not waste time and you will find your desire." It is obvious that *na-i-a* is necessary in order to rhyme with *al-di-a*.

CHAPTER 7

About Basque Phonetics. The Distribution of Aspirated and Unaspirated Occlusives

"De fonética vasca. La distribución de las oclusivas aspiradas y no aspiradas," *Boletín de la Real Sociedad Vascongada de los Amigos del País* 7 (1951): 539–49. (Also in *Sobre historia de la lengua vasca* 1, San Sebastian: Seminario de Filología Vasca "Julio de Urquijo," 1988, pp. 212–19.

1. The preponderant opinion among Bascologists about the opposition between pure occlusives and aspirated occlusives, as it exists in some Basque dialects, could be summarized as follows: this opposition does not have etymological value in terms of diachronic linguistics, or from a descriptive point of view, it does not deal with a distinctive phonological opposition. This opinion, in its second aspect, was made clear in the well-known study by René Lafon on Basque aspiration: "It seems then that, in the French-Basque dialects, the unvoiced aspirated occlusives and the unvoiced unaspirated occlusives do not constitute phonemes, but rather phonetic variations. For each one of the voiced occlusives *b, d, g,* there is an opposing unvoiced phoneme that can occur as an unaspirated voiceless occlusive or as an aspirated voiceless occlusive, under conditions which one must try to determine for each variety and for the language of each author."[1]

The precise demonstration of this point of view would consist of determining the conditions in which the same phoneme can occur as a pure occlusive or as an aspirated occlusive. This article will attempt to serve that end. Since a direct study of the dialects that contain aspiration is unfortunately not possible for me, I have to limit my research to published materials. Basically, I have paid attention to the language of the authors of the sixteenth century, Dechepare and Liçarrague, to ensure homogeneity of the material, and to a modern variety, the dialect of eastern Low (Northern) Soule [referred to hereafter as SNO, based on the original Spanish "suletino nord-oriental," L.W.] as it has been described with all sorts of guarantees by Dr. Jean Larrasquet.[2]

2. There is a specific case that appears particularly adquate for fixating one of the conditions in which aspirated occlusives appear: the suffix *-tu* of the participle, whose Romance origin seems to be beyond doubt, presents itself at times, in some varieties, as the form *-thu (thü)*. Schuchardt, who incidentally was preoccupied with this question, thought perhaps that this variation could be determined by the preceding sound when he wrote: "There are some verbs that have *-thu* in the participle instead of *-tu*; thus *dei-thu* and, after final *r*, *sar-thu, sor-thu*, although the regular form is *r-tu: ager-tu, har-tu*, etc. The group *rth* is moreover very frequent in loan words, for example: *borthitz, verthute, zorthe*, along with *parte*, etc.; on the other hand, *urthe*, etc."[3]

It would not be difficult to demonstrate, with a great gathering of examples, how this point of departure is fruitless, but I prefer to show that by indirect means. The presence or absence of aspiration in the occlusives does not depend on the preceding sound, except in the well-known instance in which the preceding sound is a sibilant or hissing sound, in which case aspiration is always lacking (cf. *Rem.*, p. 57).[4]

It is enough to present a relatively large number of cases to encounter the norm of complementary distribution of both varieties. We have on the one hand, Dechepare *sarthu, sorthu, vathu* (cf. *gerthuz* "certainly"); Liçarrague *deithu, neurthu, onthu* (Ap. 14, 18), *sarthu, sorthu, çaurthu*; SNO *déithü, góithü* "vanquish," *górt(h)ü, greüthü* "to become progressively disgusted," *lánthü, léinthü* "to polish," *lothü* "to sleep," *minthü* (p. 201 *s.v. samin*), *sárthü*. On the other hand, Dechepare *chotiltu, loxatu, samurtu*; Liçarrague *aguertu*; SNO *agértü, agórtü, aizátü, ausártü, bardintü, be(r)ótü, edértü, ezagütü, gazitü*, etc. It is quite evident that the characteristic that is common to the first examples, fewer in number, is that all of them are bisyllabic, while in the second group, the list of which could increase indefinitely, the examples all have more than two syllables.

A similar case, with another participle suffix[5], is offered to us in Liçarrague *ilki [ilkhi]* (Dechepare *ialgui*), SNO *élkhi, jálkhi*, as opposed to Dechepare *eduqui*, Liçarrague *ebaqui, iguriqui*, SNO *ebáki, etxéki, idéki*.

This takes me into familiar territory. In this same magazine (VI, 1950, p. 457),[6] I formulated the law that regulates the presence or absence of *h* in the place of a previous intervocalic -*n*- in the following manner: "In disyllabic words, the dialects with aspiration—and particularly Souletin—always preserve the *h*; in trisyllabic words, it is preserved between the first and second syllables and lacking between the second and third." That essay could undoubtedly be modified to advantage by employing a more neutral terminology (without alluding to the possible loss of *h*) and eliminating the unnecessary restriction imposed by the word "trisyllabic." But conceived approximately in the following terms: "Aspiration, in the place of an ancient intervocalic -*n*-, is lacking at the beginning of the last syllable, except in bisyllabic words." I have not found any reason since then to question its validity.

Now we see that the same law can apply to the occlusives. And not only in the particular case that we have just considered, but also for the nouns and nominal forms of the verb in general.[7] I will limit myself to a few examples: Dechepare *vorondate*, Liçarrague *açauto, arropa, buruca, çapata, ezpata*, SNO *abéntü, erreka, erróta* "wheel," *ezpáta, mendékü*. This is truly the principal cause of the phenomenon observed by Lafon (*Rem.* 59) as to why aspiration has so little importance in derivational suffixes, apart from analogy.

In order to avoid possible confusion, I insist that this law, which is clearly restrictive, should be formulated in negative terms. Not every occlusive that is found in a position in which it could be aspirated is necessarily pronounced that way. Simply put, *in words that have more than two syllables, the initial occlusive of the last syllable is never aspirated.*[8]

3. Once this negative premise is in place, I will try to establish some positive determinations, valid at least in order of greater or lesser frequencies. In this specific sense I will utilize, for brevity's sake, the denominations "regular" or "normal" types and "irregular" or "abnormal" types. Before beginning this examination, one must remember that there exists in Basque a kind of "Grassmann's Law," that is, that two aspirations do not coexist in the same word (*Rem.*, pp. 56–57).[9] Thus are explained the examples *hartu* from Dechepare and Liçarrague or SNO *heltü*, as we saw Lafon point out.

Having no cause for dissimilation, it can be affirmed that interior unvoiced occlusives, except in the position cited earlier, normally occur as aspirants; and not only in intervocalic position, but also after *r, l,* or a nasal, in the cases in which they are not voiced after *l* or the nasal. For example:

> Dechepare *apphur, apphez epphe; bethe, bethi, dithi, othe, othoy, vathi; vrthe, leqhu, uqhen.*

> Liçarrague *appain, appur, eppel; çathi, muthil, othi; artha, bortha, çorthe; gako, laket; alki, golko, mulko; aurkán.*

> SNO *ápho, áphal, épher, láphitz* "marl, soil with clay and lime used as fertilizer," *lépho, óphil, ürpho; áthe* "pile," *éthen, gáthü* "cat," *ítho, móthel, xáthar; álthe, gáltho; ártho, áurthen, orthüts* (with stress on the *ü*); *mánthar* "woman's shirt"; *ákher, bákhotx, békhan, lákhats, ókher, zákhar; élkhi, mólkho; zánkho.*

And in words with more than two syllables:

> Dechepare *appayndu; bothere, gathibu, verthute; beqhatu* (and *beqhatore*), *iccassi, ioqhatu, yqharatu; barqhatu* (and *barqhamendu*).

> Liçarrague *appaindu, guppida; aithortu, atharbe, çathitu, deithore, ithurri; ekarri, ikaratu, ikeçu, ukaldi; bulkatu, galkatu; merkatari, urkatu.*

> SNO *aphi(r)íla, epháile, ephántxü, Laphúrdi; ürrüphéa,*[10] *emphá(r)ü, emphéltü; athértü, alhórra, mathéla; ba(r)anthálla* "February," *enthelegátü, lanthátü; akhüllü, makhíla, okhólü; inkhatz, txínkhor, ünkhüde.*

Moving on now to historical considerations, some specific reasons can be proposed to explain why this type has not been generalized; that is, why the aspirated pronunciation of the occlusives does not occur in all the locations in which it would theoretically be possible.

In Dechepare and Liçarrague *chipi, guti,* SNO *ttipi, txipi, güti,* one can justifiably think that a palatalized pronunciation (cf. Gipuzkoan *gutxi,* Bizkaian *gitxi*) has impeded aspiration. The fact that aspiration is also lacking in *aita* and *maite* would confirm Holmer's keen hypothesis (*BAP,* VI, 1950, p. 404) that sees the resolution of a *-tt-* in the group *-it-*.

It would seem that the occlusive of *jakin* "to know" is not aspirated everywhere either (*Rem.,* p. 57). Accepting the explanation that I have previously suggested, the personal forms (Dechepare and Liçarrague *daquit,* etc.), in which the lack of aspiration would be normal and which seem to have been used regularly at all times, would have extended this pronunciation to nominal forms. This theory, which could have some good support, is not lacking a certain arbitrariness (not infrequently in historical linguistics, the principal basis for a theory would rest on a subjective need to explain phenomena), since it would be necessary to accept that the intersection of analogical actions had created a confusing situation already at an early date.[11]

It is also natural that the type *-tu (-ki)*, the most frequent by far, has exercised an analogical action in the formation of other participles. Thus we find, for example, SNO *dóitü, jáuntü* or Liçarrague *iaiqui* (SNO *jáiki, jéiki*), *iauqui*.

Loan words constitute a third group, some of which are undoubtedly quite ancient, to which I can attest: Dechepare and Liçarrague *baque* (SNO *bake*, Dechepare *vaquetu*), Dechepare Liçarrague *neque* (SNO *nékez*),[12] Liçarrague *ceta* "silk" (SNO *zéta*), *gorputz, laco, lecoa, lucuru, mutu, trunco;* SNO *ánka, apáidü, daatü(r)ü, meta, nókü* (but Liçarrague *noku*), *oküpü* "pregnant." It is natural to think that the foreign elements that have been continually entering the language for centuries could not always be completely assimilated or that their accommodation was made in different ways. And if you prefer to think about the influence of systems rather than individual lexical elements, it seems no less natural that a phonological structure so different from Latin and the Romance dialects that surrounded and penetrated the language for centuries has, in this case as in others, resulted in us finding no more than tendencies that never fully developed or more or less abundant traces of systems. As is natural, there will be even more cases that will have to be classified and studied in detail.[13]

4. There remain to be studied the cases of conflict between various aspirations. Taking the question in the abstract, one thinks immediately of the cases in which aspiration of an interior occlusive has not been able to be produced because of initial aspiration or, inversely, of the loss of the initial aspiration because of an aspirated interior occlusive. But a review of the material suffices to convince us that the type *epher, ethen, akher* predominates in such a way that it must be considered normal, and that the exceptions, whose number is reduced, will have to be the object of a special study. I examine a few in the following.

In the first place, there is the type already studied of participles like *hartu,* SNO *héltü, húnthü, húrtü.* The last two are formed on *hun* and *hur,* and the first two, which correspond to the ancient foundation of the language, will have received the suffix at a not-too-ancient date.[14] Also, certain imitative words depart from the normal type, such as SNO *húpa* "hey!" and *hapataka* "galloping."

The SNO word *hátü* "means, richness" is a loan word: cf. Spanish *hato*, Portuguese *fato* (*REW* 3218). Also very probably a loan word is Dechepare *hautatu* (according to Azkue, Low Navarrese, and common Labourdin, with an extensive family).[15] In any case, it seems that the participle ending *-tatu* (and *-katu*) never or almost never receives aspiration (Liçarrague SNO *debetatu* [*-tü*], SNO *eskütatü, guitatü*; Dechepare Liçarrague *mendeca-*, SNO *antzakatu, bedekatü, bürükatü*).

Another abnormal case is Liçarrague *hunqui*, SNO *húnki*. The comparison with *ukitu, ikutu, ikuitu*, and the lack of voicing of the occlusive seems to indicate that the nasal is recent, perhaps the result of a foreign influence, as aspiration could also be.[16]

5. In words that begin with an unvoiced occlusive—loan words for the most part—sometimes it is aspirated and sometimes not. Once again, the conflict between internal tendencies and the influences of Romance phonology comes to mind. The examples of aspirations in Dechepare and Liçarrague are not abundant: Dechepare *phorogu (phorogatu), phundu, thornu* (which is perhaps an etymological spelling); Liçarrague *pherde, phorogatu, thumba, kardu, keinu, keichu*. It could be that the aspiration of initial occlusives has not been indicated consistently in the works of these authors, since there are abundant examples in SNO.

In ancient words, keeping in mind that this denomination is imprecise, aspirated pronunciation seems normal: Dechepare *qhen*, Liçarrague *thu, thustatu, karmindu, ke, ken*, SNO *phiztü*[17]; *théiü, thü, khe, khéntü, khiño* "bad taste," *khózü* "contagion," *khápar* "thorny plant."

Perhaps *quirax* in Dechepare may be a defective notation, keeping in mind Liçarrague *kirestu*, SNO *khá(r)ats* "bitter" (R. Lafon, *E.-J.* III [1949], pp. 150–51). Liçarrague *quide* "contemporary" could be explained by its use as a suffix:[18] cf. Liçarrague SNO *arte*.

Liçarrague *calte* "harm" constitutes a very interesting case. According to Azkue, *kalte* is known without variations in all the dialects except Souletin. This word which has been related to *galdu* (Gavel, *Phon. basque*, p. 375) presents in addition the anomaly of the *-lt-* group whose occlusive seems to have not been voiced anywhere.

6. When there are two unvoiced occlusives in the same word—both situated in a position in which aspirated pronunciation is theoretically possible—if one of them is aspirated, it is always the first one.[19] I myself have already formulated this rule (*BAP*, VI [1950], p. 446),[20] which is easily perceived, and probably others have done so before me. In SNO, for example, we have: *kháka, kháko, khalkatü* "to force feed," *khantü* "proximity," *khapar, khentü, kholko, khórpuz, khórte* "court of a king," *khúntü, khüto* "rapid, prompt"; *pharkátü, phartítü, phertíka, Phetí(r)i* "Peter," *phíka* "foot," *phíke, Phintakóste* (and *Phünta-*), *phíper, phüntü; théka, thípil, thipíña, thíti, thórpe*. Save the occasional exception (SNO *aphottoro*, Souletin [Azkue] *apholteka* "to vomit"), this means that when there are two unvoiced occlusives in the same word, if one is aspirated, it is always the initial one.

In SNO I have not found examples of aspirated occlusives in the interior of the word when the initial occlusive could not be aspirated, for example when it was followed by *r*.

The initial aspiration has negated the aspiration that would normally be found at the beginning of the last syllable in SNO *khíño* "bad taste" (Roncalese *kîo*, with nasalized *i*). But there are some cases of intervocalic aspiration in words that begin with an unvoiced unaspirated occlusive: *kehélla* "gate," *tahárna* "inn," *trahéll* "person with deformed limbs."

Thus we see that in words beginning with an unvoiced occlusive, which are generally loan words,[21] two types are clearly distinguished: one in which the occlusive is aspirated and the other in which it is pure, and in this latter case there is no other aspirated occlusive in the same word. A detailed examination would possibly show that words of first type belong, in general, to an older stratum than those of the second. But one must always take into account the interaction of both systems whose coexistence, with growing or diminishing vitality, has lasted for a long time. This does not include the type with an initial voiced occlusive, which has been considered normal for the oldest stratum, but whose effects are felt in isolation even in the most recent loan words.

7. To conclude these musings on the distribution of aspirated occlusives, I would like to emphasize that the principle of aspiration being conditioned by the number of syllables in the word is a rule that is generally applied. Although my study has been limited to occlusives, everything I have seen thus far strengthens my belief that aspiration, be it intervo-

calic, after a diphthong, or after *n (ñ), l(ll), r (rr)*, is always lacking at the beginning of the last syllable of words of more than two syllables.[22]

If I may, I would hazard the following provisional explanation. It seems natural to think that there is a connection between the presence or absence of aspiration and certain variations of stress or intonation, although I do not know if this connection is objectively necessary. Recalling the history of Welsh, where the *-h-* has only been preserved in the prevocalic position after the stress retreated one syllable (medieval Welsh *ehawc*, modern *eog* "salmon"; modern *eang* "wide," but *ehangder* "width"),[23] it is allowable to think that Basque aspiration has only been produced or preserved before the stress. One must admit in this case that bisyllabic words had a stress distinct from other words, in such a way that we would have *bahé, lihó, xahú* (and *aphál, athé, okhér*), but *aháte, diháru, aréa, arráin* (and *epháite, ethórri, ekhárri, ezpáta, ebáki*). The stress of these latter words is that found in Souletin, and the following forms would appear to confirm this point of view: SNO *a(r)akhói*, as already mentioned, and SNO *arrathú* (with a nasal *u*) "rat" (which on the other hand assumes an old form *-one*). But the stress of bisyllabic words, except in special cases, is also paroxytone (falls on the penultimate syllable) in Souletin, and there is not the least bit of direct evidence that the stress has existed anywhere that would posutlate for an older period on the basis of previous considerations.[24]

Here also would lie the explanation of aspiration that appears after *r (rr)* or *l* in some words and specifically in the initial position of the supposed stressed syllable—aspiration that was born within Basque itself to judge by the etymology, in some cases: SNO *bílho* "hair" (Liçarrague *bilo*), *gelhá(r)i*, Axular *solhas-* (SNO *soláz*: cf. Spanish *solaz*); SNO *á(r) he* "rake" (derivative *arhátü*), *sóho*; Souletin *béhez* (*Rem.*, p. 59), Oihenart *garhaitu* "to conquer" (Low Navarrese, Laburdin, Souletin, according to Azkue); SNO *aurhíde*, which has dissimilated the *h-* of *haur*. In the post-diphthong position, Souletin *góihen*.[25]

This undoubtedly has to do with a phenomenon of syllabification: the initial consonant of the stressed syllable was attracted to the preceding syllable. This phenomenon could be, and was, determined through compound words in which this syllabic break predominated. Compounds are so abundant in the language and the line between them and derivative words is so hard to trace. Suffice it to recall for *n*, Dechepare *anhiz, senhar, unharzun*, Liçarrague *anhitz* (SNO *hánitx*), *ginharreba*, *onherran, onhetsi, senhide, sinheste*, SNO *enhüde* (with stressed *ü*).

In the compounds there had to be a retroaction of the stress of the last element, as can be seen by the position of the aspiration in the last few examples, when the last element was bisyllabic. This stress was certainly the principal stress of the compound. On the other hand, when the first element was bisyllabic, it would lose its own stress and change position, moving from the second to the first syllable, if it was preserved with a secondary character. In this way we explain the fact that the *-i* (and probably the *-u*) of the bisyllabic elements was regularly lost when these became the first elements of the compound words (*bekain, betazal; satitsu*, SNO *bürhézür*); on the other hand, for the same reason, *-e* and *-o* changed into *-a*, if this phenomenon was phonetic, as I believe it was, although perhaps favored by some analogy. In words of more than two syllables, the last syllable was lost, that is, it lost its vowel, except in some cases where it would have left a labial occlusive as the ending of the first element. From here come the forms of the compounds such as *eliz-, euskal-; abel-, senit-; arat-, ugal-; itxas-, tolet-; berant-, eskont-*.[26]

CHAPTER 8

General Characteristics of Literature in the Basque Language

"Características generales de la literatura en lengua vasca," in *Euskal linguistika eta literatura: bide berriak*. Bilbao: Deustuko Unibertsitatea, 1981, pp. 259–78. (Also included in Luis Michelena, *Sobre historia de la lengua vasca* 2. San Sebastián: ASJU, 1988, pp. 680–93. A Spanish version, translated by Jorge Giménez Bech, can be found in *Koldo Mitxelena entre nosotros*. Irun: Alberdania, 2001, pp. 69–90.)

This is the title[1] that was offered to me here, in San Sebastian, to give as a lecture, and I present myself before you with something similar to that indicated by the title.[2] In any case, and before moving on to the subject, I would like to mention not what happened then but rather what is being related now so that perhaps some other person can be warned. So this is what happened to me. In the first place, if I am anything, I am a linguist, as everyone knows, and at most a linguist who has moved tangentially close to literature. I do not know what authority or permission to expound on literature may be conferred upon me by such a surperficial contact, even though it may be about literature in the Basque language.

Moreover, I have treated this topic already, and not recently but rather twenty years ago,[3] and during this interval I have not received, it seems, any special illumination either from on high or from any other place. From then to now, on the other hand, an enormous quantity of books about our literature have appeared, rich works loaded with facts. I do not believe, however, that those books offer anyone an all-embracing opinion, except for the one by Ibon Sarasola.[4] And what they are asking me for here are all-embracing opinions.

Therefore, there is nothing left for me but to renovate what has already been elaborated upon. And repeat what has already been said, since I have very little new to add.

Literature is not literature while the books and other papers are guarded and locked up on elegant shelves: said another way, until someone takes them in their hands and reads them. You could say, consequently, that it seems necessary, before anything, to broach the following question: What is *euskal literatura*, who creates it, and for whom?

Although we should do a better job of outlining this concept, there is something that has appeared previously with sufficient clarity, or so it seems to me at least. *Euskal literatura* can only be that which is created by Basque speakers for Basque speakers. That is, if any of the terms in this formula are not sufficiently clear, it is the term *literatura* and not the term *euskal*.

Consequently, any work written [in Euskera] by a Basque speaker—whether he became a speaker through family transmission or by later education—that falls within the domain of literature is *euskal literatura*. On the contrary, the inhabitants of Euskadi—and I consciously use this term, so as to avoid confusion with the first component of *Euskal herria*—to the extent that they write in a language other than Euskera, whatever it may be, cannot be *euskal idazle*. Even if they show themselves to be ardent Basquophiles,[5] the adjective that must be applied to them is the one that corresponds to the language they utilize in their works. In that sense, Silvain Pouvreau[6] was an *euskal idazle*. On the other hand, Pío Baroja and Jean de Sponde were not.[7] Therefore, *Zeruko Argia* and *Anaitasuna* had every right to proclaim in their publicity: "*Geu gara euskal prentsa.*"[8] And the rest can be *euskal prentsa* to the extent that they give room to Euskera, and in no other. There is a saying in a language that is well known to us, "Obras son amores, y no buenas razones" ("Works are loves, and not good reasons"), and those who affirm it have not strayed from the path.

The first problems are caused by the Castilian translation of the term. A few months ago, not too many, we had a long discussion about the form that the Spanish expression "escritor vasco" (Basque writer) should take in Euskera.[9] Poor me (and there were others who shared my opinion): I believed that, in order to merit the appellative, it was sufficient to be a writer on the one hand, and a son or daughter of Euskadi on the other, either by birth or by residence. Not too long ago, this latter condition was referred to by means of the term *euskotar*, even though currently, and for reasons that are not overly explained, that denomination has been banned among many Basquophiles.

However, is the mere fact of being from here sufficient, in spite of not knowing Euskera, or is it sufficient to speak Euskera in spite of not being from here? I have expressed my opinion already: whether from here or from there, the writer in question must write in Euskera, and if he does not write in Euskera, it's all the same whether he is from there or from here, in that respect.

Raúl [Guerra] Garrido, Kintana, and others, in the discussion we had about this topic[10] put forth something like this: "escritor vasco"[11] is not the Spanish equivalent of *euskal idazle*, nor is *euskal idazle* the Basque equivalent of "escritor vasco." It is painful to see our hard-working people in a continual doing and undoing, even in questions that others discern with manifest clarity now and for quite some time. Lizardi is not the most fogotten among those precursors, but all in all, no one has mentioned the lucid distinction they put forth (*Itz-lauz*, 1934, 146): "For that . . . within the Euskaltzale association, you writers in Euskera must form a specific group with your own Governing Commission: this group can call itself *Euskel-Idazle-Batza*, in Spanish the Federación de Escritores Euskéricos (Federation of Basque Writers)." Juan San Martin has been, as far as I know, the one who was most loyally attached to that Spanish denomination in his well-known book *Escritores Euskéricos*, Bilbao, 1968 (published ten years ago).

To tell the truth, I would prefer not to stick improper barbarisms into genuine Spanish. Even so, we must express the specificity of writers who write in the Basque language in Spanish (or in any other language different from Euskera). And if, for reasons inherent in Spanish, we do not accept the term "euskérico,"[12] then we would have to use "vascongado" and "literatura vascongada," as was proposed twenty years ago, since that was the adjective the surrounding Romance languages, and not just Spanish, genuinely used to designate our language. If we do not want to accept this term, and I quite fear that we will not accept it, being as stubborn as we are, our only recourse will be heavy, awkward phrases: "littérature d'expression basque" (literature of Basque expression), for example, or "literatura en lengua vasca" (literature in the Basque language), and other similar phrases.

Returning to our language, let us give to the prefixes *euskal*[13] and *euskaldun*[14] what each one deserves, at least to the extent that Karmelo

Etxegarai did when referring to the Basque speakers from the two banks of the Bidasoa:

> Or eta emen, ez da bat bera
> Euskaldun denen fedea?
> Ez da bat denok maitatzen degun
> Maitagarrizko legea?
> Ez da guztien izkuntz gozoa
> Euskera ezti maitea?
> Or eta emen, ez da esaten
> Euskeraz Aita Gurea?[15]

It is obvious that for Karmelo Etxegarai, as well as for all those who used this word at that time, *euskaldun* is one who knows Basque. The question we are presented with is how do we refer to those who do not know Basque but who are, one way or another, children of the Basque Country.

I do not believe there is any argument about this particular, at least; we all probably accept that *euskal idazle* is the writer who writes in Euskera and *euskal literatura* is the literature that is produced and expressed in Euskera. In any case, I am disposed to listen to the reasoning of anyone who can make an argument to the contrary, either at the end of this modest lecture or if you prefer, during the lecture itself.

We have defined this *euskal literatura* to which we refer by paying attention to the *euskal*, not the *literatura,* and from the literary point of view this definition is not a simple one, not only in the case of Basque literature, but in any literature.

There are works and types of works that everyone everwhere considers to be literature, in the same way that other works, including some in the histories of literature, are banned from that category. You may prove this very easily in the literature of any language. Is Descartes' *Discours de la Méthode* included in French literature? I would say yes, and I believe that the majority of the historians of literature also include it, in spite of the fact that the specific placement of this work is found outside the history of literature, and works of this type can be found in any literature and in any language. But there is a time for everything. For the moment we will not impose more limits (there will be time for that later), and we shall consider everything produced in Euskera, or at least the major part of it, to be *euskal literatura,* if there is no great objection, as well as much of what has been expressed orally in Euskera, in spite of the fact that it was not written down. I believe that we must deal with this subject at another time, but it is known that, in any language, what we know as oral literature exists alongside written literature, transmitted from mouth to mouth, and that for one reason or another, this oral literature acquires more weight in certain literatures than in others. Moreover, it acquires greater weight in some epochs than in others; for example, in the surrounding literatures or in those that we know best here, the presence of oral literature is usually much more evident in earlier times than later on. Of course, this evidence depends on the fruits of oral literature having been preserved in some form. On the contrary, and as the ancients used to say, *verba volant,* that is, words are carried away by the wind, and if they have not been preserved in some way, they are lost forever and no one will have any reason to worry about it.

Now that it is time to enter into the characteristics or specifics of literature in the Basque language, I do not know where we should begin. It seems that the negative aspects of this literature amply exceed the positive ones. I do not believe that such an affirmation constitutes a grave sin, especially if it is made in Euskera and among Basque speakers, since it is to our advantage to be conscious of it, instead of feeding excessive dreams and imaginings with regard to our patrimony. Of course, the first negative aspect our literature must deal with is the language itself, or rather, the size of the language. I understand that the preceding is not by any means an adequate sentence. We know that languages lack a body; therefore if they have no body, neither will they have measurements.

But be that as it may, we all speak of big and small languages, and when something like this is said, what is really being pointed out is whether we are dealing with a language that is used by many people or just by a few, whether the environment in which it is used is broad or reduced. Questions like these are the ones that we consider when we speak of the size of a language. Consequently, a language spoken by many millions of persons and spread over vast territories is a large language, and the one spoken in a reduced geographic region like the Basque Country and boasts only a scant number of speakers, in comparison to the others, is a small language. When the news came about the first atomic bombs—they still exist today, but it is no longer news, and people talk less about it—I believe I read something about uranium (and pardon me if I am mistaken), in order to complete its function (not uranium, I believe it was plutonium). It must possess a certain size, or "critical mass," and beneath that mass it produces no activity at all. I would affirm that something similar to "critical mass" exists with regard to a language, but its limit cannot be determined as precisely as with other materials. But a limit does exist. I want to say that a language that has fewer than so many speakers is small, and while it is small, and here lies the question, it needs help from other languages, but if it exceeds those limits, it is located among the larger languages and will not need the help of the others to such an extent. The language itself does not need anyone. The language itself, since it is a language, does not need anything from anybody. This can be expressed better in Spanish than in Euskera, given that in the Euskera we use, it is more difficult to play word games, unlike the language used by Hiribarren when, speaking about Euskera, he said "O *mihi ederrena, hasteric gabea!*"[16] Thus in Spanish one says "la lengua no tiene lengua" (the language has no tongue/language). That is, the language cannot talk to itself. The speakers who use the language are the ones who talk, and the language lacks hands with which to help itself, the reason why it doesn't need anyone, while those who do need help are those who know this language or speak it. Therefore, when we say language, we are referring to the speaker; not, in our case, to Euskera, but rather to the speaker of Euskera.

Owing to its size, Euskera has never had a broad extension, whether in territory, speakers, or literary works. Put another way, when we Basques move on to paper (you know that until the last century, almost up to now, man has had no other method but paper and ink or something similar for preserving, as we do with canned tomatoes, what he was saying or wanted to say), the evidence that has come down to us from past centuries is, for the most part, written evidence, collected on paper. And he who has found himself in need of using the papers from these eras knows all too well, and often learns it by means of a warning, that Euskera does not demonstrate great daring at the moment of passing onto paper, that Euskara does not look ahead, that Euskera is always left behind. In order to encounter one word in Euskera, one must read hundreds of words in documents written in some other language.

If we were lacking any other information, therefore, we could think that in the old days, in Gipuzkoa itself for example, everyone spoke Spanish. To judge by the evidence registered on paper, it seems that they were speaking Spanish. We know that such was not the case. We ourselves have been familiar with this situation and we know that it was then that Euskera did not show itself to be capable and valiant, to use Axular's words, and that this other language was the one that took the lead. As a result, no one will be surprised if we say that Basque literature arrived late on the scene in addition to being scant and poor, and we will examine this question later in detail.

In my judgment, there is something of greater gravity than what has been expressed so far. I have stated before, and I was not saying anything new given that everyone knows it, that the geographic region where Euskera was being used in the era we are familiar with, let's say in the last two thousand years, was truly tiny. Moreover, we have said that the population that lived in this place and used this language was not too numerous. But it is not only about this. A clear consequence can be inferred from my previous statements. Among us, and during the eras that we are familiar with, Euskera has never been our all-embracing vehicle of expression. There has always been another language at its side. Perhaps Euskera was the most beloved of the languages that were being used here in one way or another, perhaps it was the one most closely linked to feelings—the favorite one, or if you prefer, the language of the home—but when we left the home to dedicate ourselves to other tasks, we immediately began to use some other language, for this or that.

Often for unavoidable reasons, given that we were dealing with peoples who expressed themselves in other languages and who did not know Euskera, and we were less important; given that, in addition to knowing Euskera, we had learned some other language, we were, and still are, the ones who spoke to the others in that other langugae. Some things, and not exactly unimportant things, have always been expressed between us in languages different from Euskera.

I do not know if you have read the book of letters left to us by Ulibarri de Okondo, the blacksmith from Abando. It was published in facsimile form in Bizkaia, and to tell the truth, it is not easy reading, which is why I do not believe that you have sinned greatly if you have not read it. In any case, if you put forth a bit of effort on it, perhaps you will encounter one of the letters that this Ulibarri directed to father Zabala,[17] in which he was asking about translating the *fueros*, or laws, that are being talked about so much now. According to his words, each one possesses his laws, which are moreover specific to each place, and he states that the law of Bizkaia—leaving the rest to others—should be drawn up in Euskera and that someone should try to put them into this language. Father Zabala would certainly have more urgent tasks at hand and, in a very upset response, wanted nothing to do with Ulibarri or his project. He could not see why on earth the law of Bizkaia should be in Euskera. As far as I know, moreover, it is not now and has never been in Euskera. Therefore, the fact that our oldest and most esteemed laws have never been in Euskera demonstrates, as I have said before, that Euskera has not been the all-embracing mode of expression for Basque speakers, and that some other language at its side has always been necessary.

I have stated before that this occurred because our language is small, with the definition that we have given that term, but this is not all that is involved. Euskadi—and I repeat, Euskadi, to avoid *Euskal Herria*, and if someone has read or heard my things sometime, he knows that I always use *Euskal Herria*, and not Euskadi, but here, like it or not, Euskadi or some similar term must be used, and not *Euskal Herria*, if we want to avoid confusion—Euskadi, therefore, considered in its complete territorial extension, has never been completely and absolutely Basque-speaking during the epoch we are familiar with; that is, as I pointed out before, during the last two thousand years. I do not know what things were like beyond that two thousand years. It is certain that Basque was spoken in a fairly broad zone outside those boundaries, but Euskera was not the only language that was being used throughout that geographic spread. There was always another language alongside Euskera. Consequently, when we said that la Ribera of Navarra, Cascante for example, lost Basque and that we must re-Basquify it, we are not speaking the truth. According to what we know and in the time with which we are familiar, Euskera was not spoken in Cascante. This is the pure and naked truth, and approximately the same thing that happened in Cascante also happened in the Encartaciones of Bizkaia, in some zones of Alava, and in many other places. With all this, it is certain that Basque, or something like Basque, was spoken on both sides of the Pyrenees all the way to Arán. It is also certain, it seems, that Basque was spoken as far as the neighborhood of Burgos and to the south of the Ebro. But all in all *Euskal Herria,* or what has remained as Euskadi, has not been completely Basque-speaking during the last two thousand years.

In general, the non-Basque-speakers of these places could count on support that the Basque speakers in the same places did not have, and for that reason as I mentioned earlier—that is, that the weak always surrenders before the strong—we, the Basque speakers, have been the ones who have conceded in the face of those who were not Basque speakers, and not the contrary.

With attention to the sociological criteria that are employed today, in this differentiation among us—that is, in this separation between those who speak only Basque and those who speak only a language different from Basque—clearly we must make room for those who know both Basque and this other language. (In Euskera we call the person who does not know Basque *erdaldun*[18]; we call the person who knew a language other than Basque first *euskaldun berri*,[19] instead of *erdaldun*, and we call the person who knew Basque first *erdaldun berri*.[20]) Therefore, three groups existed. If we must give credit to Iztueta, for example—and his computations are not that old, dating from one hundred twenty-five years ago—in Gipuzkoa five out of every six people knew only Euskera. Since the language of administration and politics was Spanish, only one out of every six Gipuzkoans took part fully in political and administrative affairs. For such minorities, it would have been gratifying to find a good pretext like that one for marginalizing the others, and in my judgment it's just as well that such marginalization was never carried out to its full extent among us, in spite of what the documents would have us believe. In the *Juntas* (Assemblies) of Bizkaia, we hear incessant demands to the effect that the representatives in attendance must know Spanish, and to judge by the reiteration with which that precept is recorded, we must deduce that, in spite of the rules, the representatives being sent there continued to attend without knowing too much of it.

Let us move on now to another conflict. This one has also been mentioned before, but I believe that repetition does no harm. When we say Basque literature, the term evokes great confusion in us. If you take any history of Basque literature, I am referring to any of those two or three voluminous works now available to us, you will find in it the years and the works and all the other details. Basque literature, more so than any other literaure I know, appears to be mixed with things that in themselves have nothing to do with literature: for example, bibliography.

It is well known that things have changed a lot as a result of the new publishing procedures, but in the old days, especially up until Urquijo's era—since he was the one who opened new roads in this field, and who put so much information within the reach of everyone—bibliography constituted the principal motive for controversy in Basque literature. Urquijo himself began in that way, and you will always find titles like "Notas de bibliografía vasca" (Notes on Basque Bibliography) and others like it in his works. There you will find annotations such as "I found a Kapanaga in Bermeo; some captain from Bermeo possessed a copy of such a work, and I bought it from him" and so on and so on, or "There are three or four Leizarragas known at this time, and they are in such and such a place; I was just offered such a book for so many thousands of *duros*; this one and that one have been taken to America . . ."

Consequently, bibliography is not done by poor people—you already know that bibliography is a pastime reserved for wealthy people—and it is also, if one conducts oneself with alacrity, a way of earning a lot of money (it has been the source of innumerable conflicts and has been granted a large space in our books about Basque literature). Of course, linguistics is outside the realm of bibliography. I will not say that the majority are, but a lot of us who have manipulated the texts of Basque literature and occupied ourselves with them have been linguists. Are the *Dotrina* by Ochoa de Arin or the one by Kapanaga literature? I would doubt that very much. In another language, at least, they would not be considered literature, but it is clear, in our case, there are not many *Dotrinas* from the seventeenth century nor so much written evidence of the language that would allow us to set aside Kapanga's *Dotrina*. In Gipuzkoa of the eighteenth century, there was not that much written evidence from before Larramendi's time, and among the ones we have, Ochoa de Arin occupies a prominent place, for which reason he will always be mentioned, although because of the langue and for other specific reasons, he does not present excessive literary interest. At least until more books and documents appear than we are now aware of, both of these works will always be cited in a history of literature in the Basque language. Put another way, I believe that it is the abundance or lack of works on a certain theme that confers upon a work the right to be included in a history of literature or, contrarily, excludes it.

Another of the evident characteristics of literature in the Basque language is its tardiness, its permanent lateness: lateness both in its works as well as in its studies. This tardiness does not affect just the one part, but both parts.

There are very few texts in Euskera, and even so, there are many that no one knows about yet because they have not been published, or because we do not know where to find them if they have been published. To mention a recurring example, if there remains some copy of Sancho de Elso's *Dotrina*, published in Pamplona, we do not know where it is. They say now that it may possibly be found in the Madrid house of some Navarrese nobles. I don't know if that is true or not, but be that as it may, and given that there is no way to force whoever owns the book to show it publicly, if I'm not mistaken, the owner can keep it to himself if he so desires, until he decides to do otherwise.

As I said before, the books appear late. We can compare ourselves, more or less, to the the Lithuanians: our literature began in the sixteenth century, at the same time as Albanian literature. Some fragments existed before, just like in the two languages mentioned, but we cannot speak properly of literary works in Euskera until the sixteenth century.

I do not believe that we Basques have been especially gifted in the creation of new forms of literature, and with regard to classical forms, you know what era they belong to. *Peru Abarka* can be considered the first novel in Euskera, if you like. It is not completely and clearly a novel, but it can be taken for such; it dates from around 1800, and it remained unpublished until eighty years afterward. This is something to keep in mind. With regard to the theater, this genre is rather old in the Basque Country, but in addition to being old, it is very poorly known. The majority of us are only partially familiar with works such as the pastorales and similar creations, and we became so recently.

Consequently, I would say that this lateness constitutes an evident characteristic, both with regard to the works themselves as well as the studies about them, and what's more, those who have helped us in these studies, publications, and the rest have been people, especially linguists, who have not been overly interested in literature for literature's sake. The pieces pertaining to *Refranes y Sentencias*, a work located in Darmstadt, were published by a linguist, who did so because he was only interested in the idiomatic aspects of the work. Ochoa de Arin was discovered, in turn, by another linguist, as was Kapanaga. As a result, and as I have said, these materials, to the extent in which they have made possible historical studies about literature in Euskera, came about because of external influences and impulses, not from the environment of literature, but apart from it.

What was the first history of literature in the Basque language? At the end of a book about the history of something else—if I'm not mistaken, in the last part of the *Historia del Señorío de Vizcaya* by Labayru—I believe it was Father Arana who included some information on literature in the Basque language, but it cannot be said, and Father Arana himself did not believe it so either, that it constituted a history of literature in that language. The first one, it seems, was the one that Orixe did in Euskera. It is not my intention to completely discredit Orixe's work, but one can state for example that he makes no mention of theater, nor does he say anything about Barrutia. Another one appears in *Espasa*, the first edition, in the "España" volume, under the heading *Literatura Vasca* (Basque literature),[21] and this one was created, if I'm not mistaken, by Leizaola, but it is a very brief text, composed according to the measurements appropriate for an encyclopedia. The next one is Lafitte's, entitled *La littérature d'expression basque en Labourd, Basse-Navarre et Soule*, but it refers only to those territories and makes no mention of southern literature. The next one is the one I created, and after that came Villasante's, beyond which you will encounter quite a few.

As I said before, more attention has been paid to oral literature in Basque than in the surounding literatures. With all this, I must add that literature in the Basque language has not been only late, but also fragile. Put another way, it has not been durable, because as I pointed out earlier, the volatile word can only be fixated on paper, and the more times it is copied, the better. And if the work is in print and if the printed edition is long, so much the better. I don't know if you have stopped to think about how many works in Euskera have not come down to us, or if they have, in what pitiful condition they might be. The work *Refranes y Sentencias*, which I just mentioned, dates from 1596 and only one copy has come down to us, a copy that is not complete, without a doubt. Sancho de Elso's work, also from the sixteenth century, has not come down to us as far as we know. And there are a large number of other works that have not survived, or works that we only have one copy of. According to Oihenart, there were two editions of Etxepare in the beginning, the Burdeos edition that we are familiar with, and the one published in the city that Garibay mentions as *Erroan* [Rouen]. No trace of the latter edition remains except through the words of Oihenart, and with regard to the first well-known edition, we are left with one single copy in the Bibliothèque Nationale (National Library) of Paris. That copy could have been lost through some incident, and we would have been left without any work by Etxepare.

Oral literature, given that it did not use paper, is fragile in and of itself, and less durable than written literature. This is obvious. It is well known that oral pieces can also last, that they are passed down from century to century, preserved with some modifications, and they are much more durable than something created by an educated person of our time, who knows only books and paper. But with all that, this is changing and oral pieces are being lost. Perhaps someone may ask me how is it possible that oral literature from some countries has been profusely preserved, such as the oral literature of Ireland or Iceland or the Germanic peoples? Why? The explanation is simple. These pieces were compiled and written down in a very early period. In our case, on the contrary, the preoccupation with this matter did not arise until the last century. If I am not mistaken, the last *Hoja del Lunes* carried an article by Juan San

Martin, dedicated in the second part to commemorating Iztueta, and the author pointed out in this article that the word "folklore" was born around 1840. Of course, folklorists existed before the term came into being, and according to the article, Iztueta was one himself, at least in part. But Iztueta and others like him began working in the nineteenth century, and the nearly complete compilation (nearly because it can never be absolutely complete) was done in our century, especially by Azkue and Barandiaran.

How far back do the conflicts of Kixmi and the others go? Their story was told in *Jentilen azkena,* collected by Barandiarán. When was this story told for the first time? In the tenth century? A thousand years ago, consequently, and it is not easy for a piece to be preserved exactly as it was told after a thousand years, even in Ataun itself.

I believe that we are not sufficiently conscious of these changes. Ricardo Baroja, a writer in Spanish, has a work entitled *Pasan y se van* (They Come and Go), and there are too many things have have done exactly that, in literature in the Basque language. Take the medieval era, for example. What has come down to us from that time? I don't believe that more than a hundred *versos* have been preserved (and when I say *verso,* I am talking about a line of verse),[22] or at most two hundred, and even those that have come down to us have done so in a fragmented and isolated form. The same can be said with respect to the theater. We now know, thanks to Oihenart, that in the sixteenth century there existed pastorales and similar pieces also in Low Navarre, not only in Zuberoa, and Oihenart himself gives us one or another of the names of their authors as well as the name of one of the works, *Artzain gorria* (The red shepherd).[23] But we do not know anything but the name, nor do we know who that shepherd was.

With regard to what has occurred in this part of the country, you know that at a certain time the *Acto para la Nochebuena* (Play for Christmas) by Barrutia appeared in Mondragón, but today this piece is the only one that has come to light. I do not believe that it occurred to Barrutia to write his work out of thin air, without any influence but the light of heaven. It is evident that this work is the contemporary of many others, but we have completely lost all trace of them. With that I want to say that if literature in the Basque language is reduced, as is the Basque Country, its scant nature is for a reason and that reason does not reside in original and consubstantial poverty and lack, but rather in large measure in the gradual impoverishment and decrease registered century after century. It is necessary, even imperative, to mention some-thing else as well—the fragmentation of the Basque Country. If I have to say clearly what I really feel, I believe the moment has arrived to do so—forgive me if you think otherwise—I am not at all fond of the *fueros* (old Basque laws). Many of us appear to be Carlists now, to judge by the terrible foralist fervor that has suddenly been unleashed, and now I will tell you why I am not exessively in favor of the *fueros*. The *fueros* are not the cause of the dismembering of the Basque Country; on the contrary, the *fueros* were the result of the dismembering of the Basque Country. The tree of Gernika was not ours, but rather the Bizkaians', and it didn't even belong to all the Bizkaians. The Bizkaians of the Encartaciones had little to do with the tree of Gernika. And for a long time, neither did those of Duranguesado, who celebrated their assemblies in Gerediaga, where they had their holm oak or beech tree. To each his own.

This dismemberment plays a role in Basque literature as well. On this point we flutter around the most serious stupidity. Books in the Basque language have not been created for the entire Basque Country (and here "the entire Basque Country" means the territories where Euskera is spo-ken), but rather for a portion of it or for a single territory. And while things advance in one part, they move backwards in another. Certainly our writers in Euskera[24] knew those of the other region rather well. For example, if you read the recently published *Christau doctriñ berri-ecar-lea* by Ubillos,[25] you will find a fragment taken from Axular's book, not literally but with great fidelity, dealing with remorse. Consequently, Ubillos knew Axular well. Iztueta, in turn, knew writers from one part and the other[26] and took words and expressions from several of them. All in all, each one travels through his side, and that has caused enor-mous problems, especially in the peripheral areas like High Navarra,[27] for example.

On the other hand, these[28] were the authors who had the least rela-tionship with the others when it came to Euskera and the literature in that language. As proof, we need only to approach any writer from High Navarra—for example, Lizarraga from the eighteenth century. You will see clearly the scant relationship he maintains with the language that had already been cultivated in other locations. And it is not easy to find someone among the Navarrese who, like Lizarraga, knew and imitated the works of Larramendi and his followers.

At this point, we should recognize a good number of distinctions attached to different times and places. On the one hand, we find a truly long prehistory, as you know, but given that it is not possible to say too many things about that, it is better if I remain silent. Consequently, we will set aside that prehistoric period. Later, in the sixteenth century, there appeared some scattered books, beginning with the one by Etxepare, and in the seventeenth century there was a surprising flowering in Lapurdi (Labourd).

To tell the truth, I do not believe that this phenomenon in Lapurdi has been studied as much as it deserves. It is well known that religious books, written by clergymen, make up the major part of literature in Euskera, at least until recent times, and even now the majority of writers are, or have been, religious, although they may preach other types of religion. In any case, the hegemony of clergymen has still not ended, nor will it end easily. Be that as it may, it is well known that we have a great abundance of religious books. And this is due to one cause. The majority of the books appeared as a response to a need, and no one wants to write a book that is not going to have any readers. Here, the need was of a religious nature, and the Catholic Church was concerned about teaching doctrine and related themes, at least after approximately 1600, and given that it was concerned, it knew that it should use the vernacular language—that is, Euskera—in its teachings.

And on the margins we are left with nothing but *bertsos*[29] and entertainments. But if we consider the Labourdin seventeenth century, especially its most outstanding and well-known book, Axular's *Gero*, we will verify what the author tells us in the prologue, that the people who urged him to write the book were a group of friends who met with him, and after repeated negative responses and discussions, he finally gave in. And he added, "I am not writing this book for the educated people. And not for those who know nothing either."

More than one person has said, and continues to maintain, even in writing, that Axular created this book for his ecclesiastical colleagues, so that they might have at their disposal a great variety of themes for their sermons and preaching. But anyone who reads it without blinders on will immediately perceive that this book was not written for the clergy but rather for lay people, for people who lived in that century. To be an educated or semieducated person required at least one condition, knowing how to read with sufficient ease. When almost in the same time period, Etxeberri of Ziburu created his *Manual devotionezcoa*, he said that he had written his things in verse so that mariners would sing them—once they memorized them, of course—as you can read on page 4:

Giristiñoa, eman diat eskarazko bertsutan
Katholiko manuala neure asti ordutan,
Ikhusirik nola bainaiz iaiatzez eskalduna
Gure nazioa dela kopla maite duena.
Hartarakotz iakiara diat bertsuz ezarri,
Lasterrago ikhas eta maizago aiphagarri.
Lehenago nonbait urrun Greziako partetan
Herriko legeak eman ohi ituen kantetan.
Nola kantak maiz baitire mundukoen ahoan,
Hala kantez orhoiturik maiz zituzten gogoan.
Hekin bada kostuma onaz orhoiturik lerroka,
Manuala eman diat, den bezala koplaka.[30]

He purposely made use of lines and couplets.

Axular's book, on the other hand, was not intended to be memorized and sung, but to be read. On a certain occasion, we discovered that the first middle-class person in the Basque Country was Peru Abarka. I would say that the middle-class spirit appears in Axular much earlier, much more clearly, and to the extent that one could be middle-class in the seventeenth century, and his book circulated specifically among the middle classes. In that time period, Saint-Jean-de-Luz and Ziburu totalled jointly approximately the same population as Bilbao. We have in mind what happens now, and we never think about how things were in those days. As we are beginning to know today, the affair of *La Invencible* (The Invincible) and other conflicts of Felipe II caused the ruination of fishing, which in our zone was dedicated to whaling and cod, and those who continued as fishermen took themselves there [to Saint-Jean-de-Luz and Ziburu], this being the reason that fishing activity in those ports increased,[31] until later, when Louis XIV completed its destruction, as had already happened here. In order to know to whom Axular was directing himself, we need only refer to another author, for which we will take the book that gives us news of the first middle-class person in the Basque Country, in the judgment of some. Certainly, if anyone were the first middle-class person, that would not be Peru, but rather Mogel. The [first] book by Mogel, to tell the truth, was rather boring and plagued with errors: *Konfesio eta Komunioko Sakramentuen gainean erakasteak* (Teachings on the Sacraments of Communion and Confession), written in the Gipuzkoan dialect. And in it he said things such as: "In truth we can say that all of us priests, monks, and pastors of souls of the Basque Country have been sent or chosen to make known the new good that the soul can attain. Not to kings in their palaces, not to extolled noblemen, not to the Lords who ostentatiously show off gold and silver, not to vain men who consider themselves to be overflowing with Earthly knowledge . . . [Consequently, the wise man was excluded!] . . . but rather to workers, peasants, diggers, ironmongers, charcoal makers, spinners, weavers, tailors and other humble people who are forced to earn their bread by the sweat of their brow. We do not need to appear, like the Apostle Paul, in the main squares and academies of Athens to respond to all the questions of the ill-intentioned wise men; we must appear . . . [in the first edition, there follows an illegible word] . . . good and tender-hearted listeners, who will listen to us for the most part with open hearts and open mouths and always in silence. But what teaching or doctrine must be imparted to these people of scant enlightenment? . . . If we give the whole loaf with its crust to tiny weak babies, they will die of hunger, unable to eat it . . . Thus, with regard to knowledge, the majority of men and women, girls and boys of our Basque villages are like babies."

I reckon that this is sufficient to prove that Mogel in Eibar and Markina around 1800 and Axular in Sara of the seventeenth century did not write for the same type of people, but rather one wrote at one level and the other at a different level. The level determined who their readers would be, given that no one chooses his register in a vacuum without contemplating his readers as well.

With regard to the rest of the story, you more or less know it. Sarasola[32] has dealt with it and I believe someone else has also. In the 1800s, many changes were happening here as a result of the Basque festivals of Abbadie, of the San Sebastian magazine *Euskal-Erria*, of the end of the Second Carlist war, as well as the way in which it ended, et cetera. Later, around 1900, once again great changes happened, from the hands of Arana Goiri and Azkue (although they did not walk the same path, not even close, they somehow flowed toward the same end), as well as after the war. The continued inertia of the language is all too well known. At least from 1880 onward, the tendency was always the same: fewer and fewer Basque speakers. I want to say that their percentage was less, in spite of there being a greater number of speakers, given that the population here is greater. But the Basque-speaking community decreased, and as the oral use of the language declined, on the other hand, literature in Euskera increased, grew more and more daring and more widespread. That growth has not stopped, though it was marginalized during the war years. In this regard, we have not stopped advancing. It does not fall to me to say how far we will go, since in order to do that one must know the future.

At this point, I would like to tell you something else, and this is not the fruit of my reflection, but something I read in a well-known book, but I am convinced that it is appropriate to mention these things more frequently than has been done in the past. Father Donostia pointed out a while ago that the assemblies of our country (and I return again to the *fueros*) had no power whatsoever with regard to books and writings, since such power lay exclusively with the *corregidor* (governor appointed by the king). He said this with regard to Iztueta and Gipuzkoa. Later, Father Villasante brought to light a little book by Mogel,[33] in which Mogel explained to us that it had not been possible to publish that book, *Confesio eta comunioco,* and that he, at last, obtained special permission thanks to Lord Urquijo (that is, the marquess of Urquijo) to publish it in Euskera, but that such permission was granted him in a very exceptional manner, and he concluded as follows: "What a triumph for our persecuted language!"[34] This happened around 1800.

Since we should cite a Jesuit as well, let us mention Father Kardaberaz. You know that all of his works have been published in Euskera. I cannot state that they have seen the light in editions as reasonable as in the old days, but they have been published by Retana,[35] preceded by a presentation by the Jesuit Father Leon Lopetegi in which he explains to perfection the reason why Kardaberaz's *San Ignacioren bicitza*[36] did not appear in the eighteenth century, but rather in the last century, very probably on the initiative of Father Arana. Why did it not appear in the eighteenth century? The majority of books in Euskera were publsihed at that time in Pamplona. It seems that there were more printing facitlities there. Father Kardaberaz requested permission for this work a couple of years before the Jesuits were expelled from Spain, but in that era the Jesuits could not count on the favor of the authorities. Such was the case, but it is worth knowing the reasons or pretexts that were used to deny permission. They were the following: "The reflection of obstacles that the printing of the life of St. Ignatius in Basque could bring in his day is very consistent and the agreement taken by this Supreme Tribunal [unless I am mistaken, this was the Council of Navarra] to suspend the license to print that you inform me of by letter . . . in absence of the Viceroy [if he had been there, the matter would have been in his hands]. To this is added the political objection of it not being appropriate to print in another language other than Spanish, intelligible to the whole nation, and thus by general ruling they are denied for this Council [and this Council is the Council of the kingdom of Navarra; Aranda imposed a prohibition on the Council of Navarra] without my special notice, by archiving the original work of the life of St. Ignatius in Basque with the records of the case of its printing . . . making the printers of this kingdom understand that they may not allege ignorance, punishing any contradiction severely."[37] Our Consejo Real (Royal Council) met: "In Pamplona, in Council, on Monday the tenth of November of 1766 the very illustrious Lord Don José Contreras, regent of the Viceroy, his magistrates . . ." (and there follows a list of the all the others) "and in this state the Council finds itself prevented by letter from the first of the present month from the Excellent Lord Count of Aranda, president of Castilla, from permitting printings in any other language but Spanish, intelligible to the whole nation, and as a general rule similar licenses are denied to this Council without his special notice. Notice is taken."

There ended the whole conflict. The Council of Navarra regarded the instruction as good, by the mere fact that it was so ordered by the one who had the power to do so. [38]

CHAPTER 9

Foundations for a History of Basque Literature

"Euskal literaturaren kondairarako oinarriak," in *Euskal linguistika eta literatura: bide berriak*. Bilbao: Deustuko Unibertsitatea, 1981, pp. 279–92. (Also in Luis Michelena, *Sobre historia de la lengua vasca* 2, San Sebastián: Seminario de Filología Vasca "Julio de Urquijo," 1988, pp. 694–703. A Spanish version, translated by Jorge Giménez Bech, can be found in *Koldo Mitxelena entre nosotros*. Irun: Alberdania, 2001, pp. 91–106.)

Note: The notes included here are from the Alberdania edition.

Once again I present myself before you with a lecture with a terrible title. It isn't mine, but was proposed by others. I don't know why, but I have accepted the proposal. Perhaps because it is easier to say yes; more comfortable than saying no. In any case, I am not trying to evade my responsibility. In fact, the blame for the affirmative response lies with the one who takes it upon himself, and in no case on the one who makes the offer or request.

As I told you all on another occasion,[1] if I have at some time spoken about the history of Basque literature (that is, about the works produced in Euskera), I have not done so unless practically obliged to, at times when that field was not as cultivated as it is now. After everything, you will be able to tell me if I should continue to talk about it. Thus and as a result, I hope to say something that will prove useful. Useful, in the first place, for myself and afterward, perhaps, also for others. Because I do not believe, and I would prefer that my opinion were different, that in these last twenty years we have advanced as much as it seems.

Given that I am a linguist—and with regard to being a linguist, I am a successor to those beloved *Junggrammatiker*—I do not have too much to do with literature nor with the history of literature. However, I am also a philologist, according to the title that they gave me a while ago.

As you know, the rupture between the new linguists and the antiquated philologists occurred around one hundred years ago, but that break, whatever it was, did not open a deep pit for a long time. Certainly, whoever is not worried about the contemporary language, whoever does not see and hear for himself the circular reality, will need the evidence of the texts if he plans to identify the language of a specific period, even if that period is extremely recent, or if he plans to reach the depths of the language of a specific period through the language of that same epoch. And philology, beyond all else, is the science that must speak about the texts, or said another way, about the language (sentences, phrases, and longer periods) that has coagulated, converted into *érgon*. Precisely for that reason, and although I am not a philologist except *in partibus*, it does not strike me as arrogant, or at least not excessively so, to present myself before you as a philologist, in the way indicated by the refrain created and adorned by the ancient knowledge of our people (should I not say PEOPLE?): in the kingdom of the blind, the one-eyed man is king. I know that one-eyed men like myself proliferate among us, and I would like to fight hand to hand with them. It is possible, however, that there are also many who enjoy vision in both eyes, but since we do not know them very well because they do not make themselves public, we can in some way carry out this commitment with a certain tranquility, without fear of higher authorities.

When Sarasola published his *Euskal literaturaren historia*, one well-known commentator denigrated its precursors while exalting the work, being more Barthesian than Cartesian.[2] In fact, our critic asserted that those other works were not based on anything but philology and "semantic" criticism (I understood that he was referring to the only one that broached that theme) mixed with superficial brush strokes about the life of the author, instead of focusing on literary sociology. I have put back into Basque what had previously been translated into Spanish,[3] but I don't believe there is much difference between that text and my own.

Those who fly like eagles over the peaks of literary criticism do not need similar crutches that at most serve to place obstacles in their path. The same does not occur to those of us, on the contrary, who move on the broad plains at the foot of the mountain. Aided only by the power of our limbs, we must advance step by step. Some of us, moreover, will not reach the peak that others have distinguished, and perhaps even touched and stepped upon, and we will leave the exact measure of esthetic pleasure for better tasters to determine.

What's more, we think that even the best critics need solid foundations, and the foundations are usually in the lower part, and not on the roof. In the worst cases, no one, not even the most eminent researcher, will suffer any insult because of our humble peasant labor.

This humble but necessary work is, principally, that of the philologist. Philology, as you know, is a vast field, a confluence of quite different disciplines. It concerns the texts (and I will not, at the moment, deal with the oral ones), meaning that in this sense we can affirm that its realm is the *constitutio* and *interpretatio textus,* that is, the fixation and compherension of the text. Comprehension intended, clearly, to make them comprehensible to others.

In order to avoid having my point of departure situated halfway through my speech, we should above all attempt to answer the following questions: What is the author saying in a specific text? Or better, what was he saying in the original text? In fact, it is known that apart from the first text, the intervention of a good number of intermediaries is common, and these intermediaries who copy previous copies, never embelish or improve the text of another, but rather corrupt it, and even all too frequently they disfigure it completely.

According to what we read in Larramendi's *Corografía* (or rather, in the version published by Fita based on the manuscript of the *Corografía*), the *Credo* of Beriain affirms that Jesus was born *Virgina Mariaren bastatic.*[4] It is evident that, in place of *bastatic,* it should say *baitatic*[5] (*baytatic,* according to the spelling of the period). But not all the corrections needed by the deformed texts that appear everywhere are as simple as that example. In this case, moreover, we can go straight to Beriain himself, leaving the intermediaries aside, although such access is not exactly easy. And not even the intermediary himself, that is, Larramendi, went off the path, as Telletxea recently demonstrated for us.[6]

Let us take up, now, Barrutia's *Vulgata,* which we ultimately owe to Aresti. By means of a slight correction of what had been poorly transcribed, due to a change in spelling, we can arrive at a more faithful text in at least two passages, as I have managed to demonstrate in a recent issue of *Fontes Linguae Vasconum.*[7]

I have the first passage here:

> *Ostaturik ezpada Belengo errian*
> *Zeruko Jauna dago leku guztian*
> *Ordua etorri da esposo maitea*
> *Seinonek xaio beardau xokudi atea,*[8]

and given that right after this passage there appears the marginal note in Spanish "they knock at the door," it is evident that this passage WANTS TO SAY "*jo egizu atea*,"[9] or something similar. However, what it does say means nothing, except the insanity or drunkenness of the copier. On the other hand, it could perfectly well say something of this sort:

> *Seinonek xaio beardau xobidi atea*

given that on the seventeenth century paper the literal word was *xouidi*. Also this other fragment appears in a very disfigured form:

> *Ostatu eske gabilz ez arren beatu*
> *Zeuroen trabajua pagatuko xazu.*[10]

But what in the world could this blessed *beatu* be? It turns out to be as unknown as it is blessed. We can conclude, by examining its value, that it is not excessively obscure since undoubtedly what it wants to say is something like *ez, arren, ezetz esan*.[11] And given that in Euskera *ukatzea* and *ezetz esan*[12] are equivalents, I have reconstructed here without too much effort what Guerra disfigured by poorly reading *vcatu*: *Ostatu eske gabilz, ez arren ukatu.*

Therefore, the first thing we must know, before all else, is what is it that we are talking about, and to know that, as we just said, we need to know what the text says, or put another way, we must determine as closely as possible its original state. There are many literature texts in Euskera that are in need of this. Thus, in the *Manual* by Etxeberri of Ziburu there appears a small, extremely confusing fragment about whaling. Another one occurs in the dedication of the *Manual* or some other work by Etxeberri, in Latin couplets, which cannot be completely understood.

For a better example, look at the following pair of lines from *Manual devotionezcoa*, the Burdeos edition of 1669, p. 156, belonging to the prayer entitled "*Bale hill ondoco esquerrac*":[13]

> *Ecen çure baithan tturroñ batec etsajac*
> *Vrrutic ici deçan nahiz dela hangaja.*

In this case, we are not dealing only with a problem of words, which especially affects the term *hangaja*, which doesn't show up in any other part. The verse itself is poorly constructed. In the first line, a two-syllable word is lacking which could go between *ecen* and *çure baithan*. The mistake in the second line is easier to rectify. We need only read *vrrutitic* instead of *vrrutic*. As is so often true, we can lay the blame for this error on haplography.

I know that Manuel Lekuona and Justo Garate have attempted, each in turn, to correct these errors, but their attempts do not satisfy me, perhaps because I am an exceedingly difficult conformist. Clearly we would not find ourselves in the current frame of mind if we had been able to get familiar with another edition of the *Manual*, which has not happened, at least not in my case. The first one, from 1626,[14] was "examined" by Axular and Guillentena.

I have here as a colophon the lines by Eztebe Hirigoiti "*in laudem authoris*":

> *Nuper eras viridi redimitus tempora lauro,*
> *Sed Cedro laurus te veniente fugit.*
> *Nobilis est laurus, sed quantum sydera vincunt*
> *Terras, tam Cedro laurus et ipsa minor.*
> *Aequora qui sulcant debent tibi plurima, naues*
> *Quod tua fecit eis ingeniosa manus,*

Up to this point I understand the meaning correctly, I believe. However, I do not see what the ships could owe to Etxeberri and his able hand (or expert or skilled, as you prefer). Did he perhaps participate as a builder of boats in its fabrication? Or more than that, did he contribute in some way to the improvement of naval construction? But let's move on:

> *Quas furor ingentis Neptuni saevius, et quid*
> *In gremijs foueant terra, fretúmque simul.*
> *Non hominum liuor mordax abolebit: at ipsae*
> *Etcheuerri cum nomine semper erunt.*

Among other things (to which no one has responded in the twenty years since I asked the question), why must the ships carry the name of Etxeberri ("*ipsae*" referring to the ships, of course)? Because he was the owner, nothing more?

I have just alluded to the unattractive position in which Barrutia's text is found, which seems rather appropriately to hold a place beside the proverbs of the lord of Zalgize (and even next to the presentation that Oihenart wrote by hand in his collection of adages). Mogel's *Peru Abarka*, to make a long story short, remained underground, like a hidden river, for eighty years, until at last it was printed. Will there be some difference between the text that he wrote by hand and that which was composed in typeface? Perhaps not; surely not. But in these cases, it is preferable to examine what the manuscript says, in place of basing oneself on doubtful interpretations.

As we have seen, the work of philology is rather complicated, and always needs outside help. It has its rules, but in order to apply them, it needs an object on which to do so. And that object cannot be anything but a text, a written text of course. With regard to the evidence, the more abundant, ancient, and correct it is, the better, but it must be above all evidence. One must also know the language of the era and the place, that is clear, and some of the nonsensical things that we have read in the past and even today have stemmed precisely from a lack of knowledge of language and place. And given that the language is now *per definitionem* a written language, it is necessary to master contemporary rules of writing, from one end to the other, from before and after the time of the text in question. In fact, if we do not manage to interpret what each letter or group of letters in the writing can represent, our editions will never be correct. Neither are our modern editors free from sin in this regard.

It is also necessary to know the language itself, considering its lexicon and syntax as a whole. Should we doubt that[15] the 1596 book of proverbs (*Refranes y Sentencias*, Pamplona) was collected by its compiler and translator, and that he correctly understood the proverbs that he incorporated in it? At least, the example I put forth below, which I have dealth with on other occasions, does not seem well interpreted to me (*Refranes . . .*, 208):

> *Odol bearbaguea / agirtucoda eguia eurea*
> "Unnecessary blood / will discover its truth"

> (and 2 *bearbaguea* = 2 unnecessary, appears word for word).

It is certain, as we know, that *behar* means "necessary," for the majority of Basque speakers if not for all. For some of them it also means "work." However, is not as well known, and the compiler does not seem to know it (or if he knew it, he did not record it), that *behar* in some cases and precisely in the western zone can mean, in addition, "blame, fault." Thus both Landucci's dictionary and the old ballad *Milia de Lastur*, collected by Garibay, indicated this in the sixteenth century. And it seems that if we consider this *behar* as "blame" we obtain a better meaning than with "necessary." That is, that innocent blood will sooner or later make known its truth—that is, accuse the one who shed it, etc.—a belief widely held throughout the world, although in the majority of cases, it can turn out to be false, as false as it is comforting. This is the ancient pronouncement that Schiller collected in his poem "Die Kräniche des Ibykus," or closer to home, that we can read under the title "Itoxurak ziñaldari" in Kirikiño's *Abarrak*.

We have banished from our minds the initial question, the one we should always ask. "What did the author say in this text?" we asked. "What does he say word for word and letter for letter?" begged our initial questions, and from there, little by little, we have passed on to the following question: "What did he want to say?" And we have attempted to respond to this question, although superficially. Unfortunately, what is on the surface, and there lies the heart of the problem, is not always, nor perhaps commonly, what the infrastructure of the sentences would like to express. Said another way, the sentences do not possess any intrinsic desire, except for that confered upon them by the authors that shape and mold them.

But if by digging deeper into the subject matter, we ask why the text says what it says, it will not always be easy to find the answer. Let's open Aresti's work *Harrizko herri hau,* 1970, to page 126, and we find, among other new commandments or interdictions, the following:

> *Zortzigarrena:*
> *Ez ezakezue euskaldun haurrik ikastola: eskola ezakezue.*[16]

And from the grammatical point of view, it seems clean and clear to us. Affirmation and negation are equal with regard to form: *eskola ezakezue* would be *eikezue* in the Bizkaian dialect where it still persists, according to that *infinitiuum futuri,* as that form is called in Latin. As in the phrase from Plato that is frequently mentioned: *Cras petito* (future), *dabitur; nunc abi* (present). And similar forms existed, at least in the seventeenth century, more toward the east, such as for example in the works of Etxeberri of Ziburu.

We also know what *eskolatu* and ikastolatu[17] both mean, with their respective roots in *eskola* and *ikastola*. I can guess, moreover, what such verbs want to say, more or less, for a Basque speaker of 1978, to whom they speak. But we cannot know what Aresti intended to express, the Aresti of that time, by means of these verbs. A great deal of what we say and write ends up being fleeting, not lasting. And it is possible that these lines of Aresti's do not yet belong to the patrimony of eternal dates, *ktéma eis aeí,* for the reader whose memory of the value that those lines possessed at that time grows less and less every day.

Knowing something about the personality of the author and the life that has molded his personality does not constitute a pointless caprice of insubstantial research—at least, not always. I do not know how much of Guillén de Castro's work *Los mal casados de Valencia* can be explained by the misfortunes that the author says he suffered in his marriage. In any case, exploring that question will not do harm to anyone. *Condaira,* Iztueta's work, is easier to understand once we have access—thanks in the end to Elosegi y Garmendia—to relevant information about the life of the author from Zaldibia.

And Aresti, who lived so recently; Aresti whom we have known so much about; Aresti who spoke with such a booming voice, very often against one thing and another; Aresti has left us a multitude of obscure passages. I have mentioned one to you already, and it would not be difficult to find more keyless doors, more complicated than already mentioned, both in his poetry and in his prose.

Nor is the hunt for citations a useless task, since no one creates anything from nothing, but rather always needs guides and supports. In this field, some writers end up as skinflints, as in the case of Lizardi (at the margin of the renowned citation of Sully-Prudhomme), and Saussure, who only cited Whitney among his precursors. Others are more inclined to acknowledge precursors, such as Lauaxeta, especially the later Lauaxeta who also made use of the popular poem "Aita nuen saltzaile" that now appears, in its most ancient form, in the work of Oihenart. Among citations we must differentiate between, on the one hand, those that openly constitute *topica* and *loci communes,* studied so deeply and in such detail by Curtius, that may have been gathered, heard, or learned in any location, and those on the other hand that are true citations, strictly literal, whose sources one does not try to hide.

On a previous occasion I mentioned Ubillos to you. Ubillos owed a great debt to Axular when he spoke of the remorse of the sinner. I mentioned it aloud but I did not transcribe the passages:

Axular, *Gero,* 595:

> "Eta haur da gau eta egun, behin ere asse gabe, sossegatcera vtci gabe, alha çayen eta alhaco çayen harra: probechu gabeco vrriquia, dembora ioanez guerozco damua, dolua eta nigarra."

Ubillos, 156:

> "Hau dà, gau ta egun, beinere ase gabe, ta atsedeten utzi gabe, utsiq-uitzen arizaien, ta arico ere zaien arrá, probechu gabeco vrriquia, dem-bora joanez-guerozco damua ta negarra."

This is not a matter of one of those chance coincidences owed to dealing with the same theme that, without another meaning, can be produced among the words of two writers. Ubillos enjoyed outside help, and whoever analyzes his work in greater depth and with greater familiarity will surely find other sources of help that have not been cited here.

I have here another example from Ubillos, who it seems did not show any great inclination to make an effort if the work had already been done by someone else, no matter how poor or trivial it was. Let's see what he says (15): *Itoac utzi cituan, egui, aldapa, mendi, ta mundu guci arequin batean,*[18] following in Mendiburu's footsteps. See, by comparison, *Otoitz-gaiak,* by Mendiburu, published twenty-five years before, 3 (of eleven), 17: *ta, oriec ez, beste guciac itoac utzi cituen, egui, aldapa, mendi ta mundu guciarequin batean.* When all the cards are lined up, even though written by hand, these surprising discoveries are frequent.

John Steinbeck (and later E. Kazan when he took the work to the screen) used the title *East of Eden* with absolute tranquility, given that he was writing for communities that had been raised and educated in a Protestant atmosphere impregnated by the Bible. Also on other occasions I have found, in the literature of this origin, that same incidental phrase—more a wink and a nod than a citation (it suffices to point toward it with the hand so that my interlocutor knows which of these things I am referring to). But how many Basque speakers would recall without help that "well-known" passage from the Old Testament? *"Kain,"* says the Duvoisin translation, *"Jaunaren aitzinetik atheraturik ihesdun egon zen Edenetik iguzki-sortze alderako bazterretan."*[19] In the Vulgate, Genesis 4, 16: *"Egressusque Cain a facie Domini, habitauit profugus in terra ad orientalem plagam Eden."*

Citations (and the sources that are indicated by them) are surely the fruit of a specific environment. They are intelligible to those who live in that environment, but not, on the contrary, for the outsider. More precisely, many of those who belong to that environment can comprehend them, according to the thinking of the author; outside of that environment, only rarely will you come up against someone who recognizes them. In spite of not having read Chaucer, there are those who know

who the midwife of Bath was. Others will have heard something referring to the wedding of Camacho. And finally, many will guess the meaning of the nitpicking that Maisu Juan used to liquidate the excessive bill
at the inn.

In the final accounting, if the text has been correctly repaired and
clarified as far as possible, a complete interpretation will be pinpointed:
complete to the extent that our excessively poor interpretations can
achieve that level. And for that purpose we must analyze the work itself,
and the author as well, in a broader context: in the human environment
of his time period and location. In my previous lecture,[20] I matched up
Axular's piece *"Iracurtçailleari"* and the prologue of Mogel's sermons.
Then I spoke to you about rather well-known things. About how the
Navarrese author,[21] if we take his words literally, wrote his book "in
a place inhabited only by Basque speakers, and in good company," this
last referring to the friends who encouraged him to do it. That was where
he wrote the well-known phrase: "I do not create this little book for
scholars. And not for those who know nothing either." Mogel, on the
contrary, claims to address "workers, peasants, diggers, ironmongers,
charcoal makers, spinners, weavers, tailors and other humble people
who are forced to earn their living by the sweat of their brow . . . these
people of scant intelligence."

Etxeberri, in turn, does not mention the reader except on very rare
occasions, since his *Manual* is directed at very different people than
those mentioned by Axular: at least, he does not instruct his audience
to read what the books say, but rather to learn the content in one way
or another:

> *Hartaracotz nekha çaite, ikhasten Manuala*
> *Eta faltetaric guarda, hura obratçen duçula.*
> *Hartaracotz iaquiara diat versus eçarri,*
> *Lasterrago ikhas eta maizago aipha garri.*
> *Adisquidea, ikhasetçac othoi deuotionez,*
> *Nola nic baitarozquiat escaintçen gogo onez.*[22]

I have never been an expert in questions relative to publication and
the like. Perhaps that is the reason why the point I'm about to bring up
seems obscure to me. In the last few years, some controversy has arisen
around Tartas and his *Onsa hilceco bidia*. With regard to its appearance, however, that took place in 1666, with authorizations dated from
the interval 1657–65. I have never seen his other work, *Arima penitentaren occupatione devotaq*, although there is a handwritten copy that

can be found in the library of Urquijo. Quite some time ago, I found what follows on page 8 of the copy mentioned above: *"igaren vrthian [sic] eguindut, eta eçarri argira librutobat euskaraz . . ., gueroz aurthen Iincoaren aiutu sainduarequila baitan, eguindut, eta nahi camporat idoqui bertce pieçatobat, çoignen handitarçuna oro cerraturik baitago escubat paperen voluman, han icussico duçu hirur Princessa ederric, çoin baitira Orationia, Barura, eta Amoyna."*[23] In effect, it does deal with a "little book," since it consists only of 135 pages. Sorarrain's Catalog says it has 23–135.

What might be the work published "last year" then, if *Arima* dates from 1672?

Habent sua fata libelli, it used to be said at a certain time, like the "Poet," and also his readers, listeners, and whoever learns them bit by bit from memory. It was neither chance nor a sudden miracle that the nurtured group of educated authors in seventeenth-century Labourd and on the coasts of Saint-Jean-de-Luz and Ziburu (Soule), as well as in the interior territories of Sara, an area that occupied the role of *hinterland,* who cultivated literature in Basque in the form we are now familiar with, was composed of people who knew (for example) how to measure Latin verses without error, when a hundred years later Larramendi did not manage to create a single correct verse.

The naval industry, fishing on the high seas, and commerce of those places, a consequence of the decline suffered by those same activities on this side of the Pyrenees at the end of the sixteenth century,[24] had a great deal to do with the books we have in hand. Certainly, from what I know, it is not too common anywhere to have the Church explained by means of the mariner's arts of navigation, such as occurred in the *Manual* (I, 30 onward; on the duties of each, cf. II, 131 and following):

> *Eliça duc arbolabat içarrerañocoa,*
>
> . . .
>
> *Edo ezperen Eliça duc vntci berreguindua,*
> *Ifernuco vriz, eta haicez tormentatua:*
> *Hara huna ciabillac haice contraz luyetan,*
> *Eztuc ordean seculan galduco vhiñetan.*
> *Barkha hunen burgessa duc ene Aita eternoa*
> *Ni nauc guero buruçagui haren hurrenecoa.*
> *Spiritu Sacratua itsassoco pillotu,*
> *Ceñac tormentetan baitu bide onaz guidatu.*
> *Ama duc gure ondoan lehenbici parçuner.*

Apostoluac aguintari, laiecoac passaier.
Lagun Aphez eta fraide munduaz vkhatuac,
Eta ene gatic bici penosa hautatuac.
Soldaduac doctor, eta predicari iaquiñac,
Garaituaz doacela hirur etsai gordiñac.
Heretico thematsuac araüeco presuner,
Eliçama Sainduari ceñac baitçaizco aiher
Hunelaco Eliça duc gendez esquifatua,
Onac eta gaiztoac ere badic bere lekhua.
Bañan communqui Eliça guc aditcen duguna,
Guiristiño guztien duc Catholico bilduma.
Aphez gobernatçaileen eguia duc bilkhua,
Deitcen dugula Eliça batçuetan Saindua.
Parte principalenari guztiaren icena
Ematen çaiola ceren den señalatuena.[25]

I do not believe in any way that the economic expansion being experienced at that time could have forcibly rigged out the expansion of literature in Basque. This would be an excessively simple explanation because it happens another way with great frequency, among other reasons. Our Bilbao was not converted into an Athens between the years 1900 and 1922, by anyone's way of thinking. One thing had a great deal to do with the other, however. Money gave rise to leisure and free time, in such a way that the writers could write, and above all, so that what they wrote would find sufficiently educated readers—sufficiently educated and sufficiently abundant.

* * *

When I was preparing this lecture, it was suggested that I speak basically on another theme. I soon realized, however, that if I dealt with the preceding questions to the extent that I have, I would not have time for more topics. At least, not to treat them in the detail I would desire. I must expose what remains, then, with brevity, in spite of the fact that it may be the more urgent matter since the questions that remain are not tied to theme, to the marrow, but rather to form.

It is not easy, or rather, it is impossible, to limit the field of literature, at least if we are talking about limiting it with precision. When referring to literature in one language or another, one would include precisely the same thing that another would exclude. In ours, for example, owing to our scant thematic material, many, many things that we take into consideration would be excluded in other literatures, by virtue of the fact that those literatures are richer. The history of the language and literature, intimately linked in any place or time are certainly even more closely linked in our country than in our neighboring countries.

Be that as it may, it is the form, more than the power of the theme, that converts something into literary material. Jakobson's affirmation about "poeticity" is well known: its existence lies in the message itself, in the literality of the message. If we observe what has been said—that is, the text that we have mentioned so often—our first question will be not what has been said but rather how it was said. Better still, perhaps, that would be our last question as well, our first and our last.

When we say form, it seems that we refer only to the combination of sounds and the play of words, such as Jakobson's *I like Ike* which he elevated to heaven, or the *zinak eta minak, zintki eta finki*[26] of Axular and other such word play. But the nucleus of what is being expressed maintains a relationship with this: it belongs to our most ancient fragmented evidence such as *Oñetako lurrau jabilt ikara, gorputzeko lau aragiok*[27] and other remnants that have come down to us in poems from remote times. That *kléos áphthiton* "undying fame" of Homer's, from the point of view of form, is only likely to figure in a few determined locations of hexameter: since it's meter is (uu-uu). Nevertheless, other syntagmas as well were equally likely to experience "undying fame."

In continuation of Fernando Lázaro, I just spoke in an article in *Euskera* number 22 (1977), 721–33, about expendable language—that which we spend in our everyday conversation and leaves no echo— and enduring language, or put another way, about the language that springs from us with the intention of enduring, whether it lasts or not. And although the latter is not the only mission of literature, it must be included by literature in its goals, ineluctably (of course, as long as we are considering literature strictly in its artistic sense).

When referring to a closed form of language, surely poetry is the first thing that comes to mind. In fact, if something has been conceived in order to endure, that something is verse. With regard to ourselves, moreover, the better part of our literature, up until practically this very day, was created in this manner, and not in prose. And we must keep in mind that, if we were capable of commemorating the ancient legacy, we could see that it was more eminent and abundant than our prose.

All in all, if we were to affirm that we do not know to what we owe our laws of versification, it would not be a huge lie. We still do not know, at least I do not know, enough about meter, rhyme, pauses, and caesuras—especially if we leave modern poetry aside and delve into the more ancient variety.

The proverbs, those "ancient sayings" that we habitually use, form an original and motley body, both in content and in form. On the other hand, this part of oral literature has come down to us magnificently preserved, better than any other. I will not speak here about its form (its external and internal form, taking into consideration that *innere Form* of Humboldt's), because I would go on for far too long. I have just received "The grammar of the Basque proverb," presented last year by Terence H. Wilbur in the so-called Lacus Conference in Montreal. It is only a first approximation, but it constitutes for me a reason for rejoicing that others also desire to analyze the dimension of this special language.

If a demonstration is necessary of what I once called our ignorance (referring to my own), let me tell you about something that just happened to me: within a few weeks a brief article of mine will be published in *Fontes* in which I speak about, among other things, Aresti's meter. In *Maldan behera*, among the verses that Sarasola groups under the name "structure B," there are two distinct forms of thirteen-syllable lines: some must be measured as 7–6, and others as 6–7. The first type is clearly more frequent among us, and as a reminder we record some of them here. For example:

> *Baru baita, afarixka* / *egin dute etxean;*
> *Gero kontu-kontari* / *edo-ta musean*
> *Nor bere etxean edo* / *adiskidenean.*
> *Meza alaiera doaz* / *gauerdi danean.*[28]

And there are so very many others in addition to these—there are others whose first part is longer than the second, in 10–8 and similar measures. The thing is that, with regard to this question, I said the following: this form of verse has few precursors in Basque literature, if it has any. And when the article was already in press, I have here what I saw in volume 1 of Auñamendi's *Literatura*, page 362, the verses entitled "Euscaldúnac," written by Bonaparte in the manner of Ovid:

> *¡Neré anái lagún, maité zaituztedánok*
> *Teséoren fedéz lotú zatzaizkidánok!*
> *Obídiyok Tristéen librúban ziyóna*
> *Oráin zurí diyótsut, Euskalerrí oná.*[29]

And that 6-7 meter was not, of course, invented by the Prince [Bonaparte], but rather he learned it from a Basque speaker. I would have done better, therefore, to have set myself to studying instead of trying to teach others. That's how it goes.

CHAPTER 10

History of Basque Literature

Sixteenth and Seventeenth Centuries

Selections from *Historia de la literatura vasca*. Madrid: Minotauro, 1960, pp. 35–82.

Origins: Sixteenth Century

First Evidence

It is a notorious fact that Basque is a language with a poorly known past. In the Roman era, apart from a few place names that have been passed down to us by the classical authors, we have access to quite a few names of people and divinities that appear in Latin inscriptions in Aquitanian territory. Although rare, some are incontrovertible and it cannot be mere chance that at times they coincide exactly with Basque words. Thus, *Andere, Nescato,* a woman's name, *Cison, Sembe,* a man's name, are identical to Basque *and(e)re* "woman, lady," *neskato* "girl," *gizon* "man," *seme* "son." And if everything in Aquitainian onomastics is not so easily explained—clearly Gaulish names also figure into it—the coincidences are sufficient that we can affirm that in part of Aquitaine, in the era immediately preceding the Roman conquest and undoubtedly for a period of time afterward, they spoke dialects closely related to Basque.

These words are found not only in the mountainous region, from the valley of Arán (hydrographically and linguistically Gascon) toward the west, but also in the country of the Ausci. It is no surprise that the proofs are much less conclusive in Spanish territory, but before drawing hasty conclusions from the incomplete quality of our information, we must remember that only one inscription from the north slope of the Pyrenees was found in territory that was Basque-speaking in the last few centuries. In the end, it is highly likely that at the beginning of the Roman domination dialects of the Basque type, probably only slightly differentiated, were in use in a good part of the Basque Country and much farther east, in the foothills of the Pyrenees. Something similar must have occurred toward the west in the lands of the Varduli and Caristii, although some have argued about that.

Whatever the extension of these languages was at the beginning of the Roman influence, it shrank during the following centuries to the point where it was in imminent danger of disappearing, and the language was only saved by the decomposition of the empire that set in during the middle of the third century. The principal defense against Latin must have resided not in strength but rather in the very weakness of the country and its people. Without important cities (Pamplona, Alavese Iruña, and Lapurdum to the north were the principal urban centers, whose power of influence had to diminish after the third century because of the general process of Euralization), cultural decline made the temptation of Latin much less seductive, while the poverty of a good part of the territory did little to entice Rome to occupy and exploit it. The Basque langauge was profoundly affected by its early contact with Latin, but it managed to save itself. The spread of some nouns referring to persons through a good part of the Peninsula that had Vasconia at its center (calling to mind the elements *Aita* and *Annaya* magisterially studied by R. Menéndez Pidal) gives evidence of an expansive force that was no longer seen in following periods.

The dominion of Visigoths and Franks in Spain and France had little effect on the Romanization of Vasconia. With a rebellious and warlike spirit that contrasted notably with their tranquil acceptance of Roman domination, the Basques did not allow themselves to be conquered. Contained and repelled according to the chronicles, they returned again and again to spill over onto the plain, to the north and south. In those locations where stability and peacefulness reigned before, the inhabitants now appeared to have an excess of energy and a population seeking broader, richer lands.

When we return to sufficient documentation, the language occupies advanced positions on the southern border. Around the tenth century, Basque was spoken in rather extensive areas of the Upper Rioja and the province of Burgos.[1] The subsequent history of Basque, perhaps after a brief stationary period, was one of dark regression, poorly documented for centuries in the flattest and most exposed areas which were borderlands at the time. The decline was minimal or nonexistent on the northern border once that area was stabilized, though we're not sure when that happened. As for the rest of the border areas, decline was much more rapid, although the rate varied according to time and place.

After the year 1000, approximately, medieval documentation was not nearly as rare as is usually believed. Nevertheless, if it is precious to the language historian, by its very nature it has no literary value. In the medieval documents written in Latin, there are a huge number of nouns referring to person and place, glossed and translated at one time or another, designations of professions such as *unamaizter* and *buruzagui* that are called "lingua Navarrorum," according to evidence from the year 1167, etc. The terms that occur in the Fuero General of Navarra and the two Basque phrases from the "Glosas Emilianenses" (Glosses from the Emilian Manuscript) deserve separate mention. The "Glosas" was a brief list of words recorded in the twelfth century by a French pilgrim to Santiago de Compostela.

We can now add to our documentation a brief, partly damaged text that was hastily written on one of the last pages of a codex of the Library of the Cathedral of Pamplona, most likely before 1425. The legible part shows that it dealt with a magical prayer, a "little Our Father," as its beginning coincides in substance with that of some superstitious formulas collected in our time in Navarra and even in Gipuzkoa.[2]

The Old Ballads

The most ancient literary monuments of our language are the fragments of ballads referring to generally tragic events that occurred in the fifteenth and sixteenth centuries, ballads passed down to us by historians of the two following centuries such as Garibay, the Ibargüen-Cachopín chronicle, Zaldibia, Isasti, or Doctor Sáenz del Puerto, and Lazarraga whom we know by means of an eighteenth century writer, Floranes. Unfortunately, the fragments are meager as a rule and quite incomplete, and the copies in which they were found are sometimes very corrupted. All we can do is lament the fact, since corruption is inevitable. What is condemnable is that the readings that circulate contain gross errors, by sheer carelessness. For example, in one of the ballad fragments about the burning of Mondragón, we read:

> *Madalenaan ey dança*
> *viola trompeta bague,*

where *dança* "dance" is supposed to be related to the fatal dance performed by Presebal and Juanicote, without violas or trumpets, upon being mortally wounded in front of the Magdalena hermitage, when in reality the mansucript says *ey dauça*, that is, *ei dautza* "they say they lie."

In spite of everything, we can confirm that in Vasconia the epic genre, created in irregular verse, enjoyed great favor. Its language was well established and some stereotyped formulas were repeated in spite of the rarity of the texts, such as the one with slight variations that was put in the mouths of doña Sancha de Ozaeta and the fugitive don Pedro de Avendaño:

> *Oñetaco lur au jabilt ycara*
> *Lau araguioc verean verala*

which means, according to Garibay, "that the earth underfoot shook him and the flesh of his four quarters in the same way." Its rarity is all the more regrettable because, thanks to a poem preserved for us through oral tradition, we know that some of these compositions were far from wretched, from an aesthetic point of view.[3]

The atmosphere in which the ballads were born was that of the long and complicated rivalries motivated by *más valer,* or being better than the other group—rivalries between families and tribes that were united in the name of the Oñacinos and the Gamboínos, and in Navarra, with a more political tint, in the name of the Agramonteses and Beamonteses with their monotonous succession of battles, fires, pillaging, treasons, and assasinations.[4] We possess more or less coherent fragments of the Urréjola encounter in the second half of the fourteenth century, the defeat of Pedro de Avendaño by the followers of Aramayona in 1443, and the burning of Mondragón in 1448, with an Oñacina and Gamboína version, among others. The ballad of Sandailia refers to a previous state of affairs in which the men sticking to the ancient way of life tried to continue it in the face of the efforts of the Hermandad (Brotherhood) and the Corregidor (a governor appointed by the king).

We can formulate an idea of what some of the lost poems could have been by means of the Souletin ballad of Berterretch which has been passed down orally.[5] However, it is hard to believe that many attained its high quality. The account of the assassination of the young Berterretch in the first half of the fifteenth century is a model of dramatic quality and somber poetry. From its abrupt beginning so frequent in popular Basque lyric poetry (*Haltzak eztü bihotzik / ez gaztanberak ezürrik* "the alder tree has no heart, nor does cottage cheese have bone") that seems to have no connection to what follows,[6] to the final allusion to the great number of shirts that the dead man possessed, an allusion unexpected for the modern reader, the archaic nature of the ballad is evident in each of its strophes and stands out even more if we compare it to more recent compositions of novelesque character.[7] Heard from the mouth of a Souletin Basque with its somber melody and grave rhythm, it is an authentic echo of the past, miraculously preserved in the fragile memory of the people.

Other *eresiak* [oral verses sung in honor of individuals.—L.W.] composed on the occasion of weddings, funerals, etc., have a more familiar aspect. According to diverse evidence, they were composed by women and other women sometimes responded to them, giving rise to debates in canted verse similar to those of modern bertsolaris. This is what happened with the lamentations of doña Emilia de Lastur for her dead sister, which were answered by doña Sancha Hortiz, the sister of the widower. Also now the most complete and most beautiful example is the ballad of the tower of Alós, preserved orally and published for the first time in the last century.[8] Its authenticity cannot be in doubt because apart from the internal evidence at least one variation of it is known to exist.[9] What can be debated is its interpretation. One must not forget that the song is one thing, which must be studied in great detail, and the novelized version by Araquistain is another very different matter.

Although already collected by Zaldibia, the fragment of the ballad of Beotibar (the battle between the Gipuzkoans and the Navarrese happened in 1321) has a much more modern air, beginning with the meter. There is also very little of the medieval in the brief Gipuzkoan ballad by Juan de Lazcano, where the basic sentiment is loyalty to a state, not to a family or a tribe. But this ballad should be included among rhyming aphorisms which were often distichs or couplets in which an opinion is expressed about the life or character of some notable person. Examples include the one that refers to the death of Monsieur Chanfarrón in Irún; the one about the corregidor Gonzalo Moro (*Gonçalo Moro tati tati, gaxtoa gaxtigaetan daqui*); the one about restless Rodrigo de Villandrando (*Edrigu de Villandran, egun even eta viar an*); the epitaph of Martín Juanes de Labiero; and the refrain by Oihenart about the viscount of Baigorri (*Baigorrico Biscondea, beldurrac diacarquec ahalguea*). At other times the verse begins with the name of a town: *Villarreal de Urrechu, veti guerrea darraiçu; Bergara, ceñatu eta ygara.*

The Renaissance

In the last centuries of the Middle Ages, the maritime regions of Vasconia gave evidence of a more intense activity at a time when the Kingdom of Navarra, the ancient heart of the country, was losing its previous importance, having been politically obstructed and converted into a small kingdom with no exit to the sea. Gipuzkoan and Bizkaian intervention in Spanish affairs increased, and from 1492 on Basques were present in the recently discovered American countries. Laburdin fishermen and businessmen crossed the Atlantic untiringly. In the cultural order, naturally one can only speak of isolated personalities.

With the invention of printing and the new curiosity awakened by the rise of the vulgar languages, there were a certain number of references to Basque. A German pilgrim to Santiago, Arnald von Harff, included some Basque words and phrases in the account of his journey at the end of the fifteenth century, intended for other pilgrims so they might achieve the satisfaction of their more urgent necessities, one of which was not very holy, while passing through Vasconia.[10] The first printed phrase (*Bai, Fedea!*) appeared in the play *Tinelaria* by Torres Naharro (1513)[11] which was followed by the vocabulary included by L. Marineo Sículo in his *Cosas memorables de España* and the rather long but not very clear text that appeared in *Pantagruel* by Rabelais.[12]

Perucho's love song, contained in the *Tercera parte de la tragicomedia de Celestina* (1536) offers greater literary interest, revealing to us the existence of lyrical compositions alongside the narrative ones.[13] There is little doubt that some songs and *kopla zaarrak* (old couplets)—only written down much, much later—are at least as ancient as this example that we are aware of by chance alone, but they usually lack the historical evidence that allows us to date them. On the other hand, while the ballads of the tribal wars represent a genre that disappeared with the social circumstances from which they were born, lyric poetry appears to have remained faithful to the ancient type for a very long time.

The Ibargüen-Cachopín chronicle, written in the sixteenth century and remaining unpublished, contains two falsifications, in addition to various fragments in authentic verse. The fame of the supposed writings of Andramendi, which were drafted in Basque and dated 564 and 748, has hardly crossed the borders of our country, unlike the song of Lelo, which can almost be classified as world famous. Both ink and genius have been wasted on interpreting this alleged relic of the battles of the ancient Cantabrians, who are naturally identified as the Basques, or more exactly as the Bizkaians, under the leadership of Lecobidi, against Rome—without great result, in reality, since the ballad appears to be written in a jargon, undoubtedly to give it an archaic air, that deprives it of linguistic and literary interest. On the other hand, it does have interest as evidence of the myth of the unexpected and heroic resistence by the Basques against the power of Roman weapons, a resistance born, according to Guerra, during the reign of Charles V.

In 1562, possibly in Vitoria, the Italian N. Landucci, a native of Luca, compiled a vocabulary that is important for the history of the language. Landucci was also the author of two dictionaries, Spanish-French and Spanish-Italian, that are preserved in the National Library of Madrid. Although incomplete and defective in many aspects, his was the first extensive Basque vocabulary.[14]

Dechepare: The first book published in Basque was a short collection of poems entitled *Linguae Vasconum Primitiae* by Mosén Bernart Dechepare, the parish priest of Saint-Michel-le-Vieux in Low Navarre. It was printed in Burdeos in 1545. It has no more than fifty-two pages of text, including the dedication in prose.

We do not know much about Dechepare's life, and almost all that we do know comes from this work. On the title page he is called "Rectorem sancti michaelis veteris" and one of his compositions, the "Canto de Mosén Bernart Dechepare," talks about his imprisonment in Bearne, possibly in Pau,[15] which he attributes to the maquinations of his enemies before the king. Today we have reason to believe, thanks to some documents discovered by José María de Huarte,[16] that the reasons for his detention were political, for having supported the king of Castile in the disputes for the Kingdom of Navarra. The Souletin genealogist Jaurgain proposed that he was the brother of Juan, Lord of Echepare of Sarrasquette.

The volume contains religious poems that end with a "Warning to lovers," an invocation to the Virgin Mary, which is the link that joins this part to the part that contains profane poems whose only theme is worldly love, almost always described with crude realism. Thereafter follows the poem composed during his imprisonment and the book ends with two compositions in honor of the Basque language.

There has not been great unanimity among critics about the literary value of Dechepare's work. Without going as far as Schuchardt's categorical condemnation, Julio de Urquijo did not demonstrate great enthusiasm: "Everyone agrees," he wrote, "that Dechepare was not a great poet, even when beauty is not lacking in some of his verses."

Gil Reicher and René Lafon were the ones who fought the opinion that Urquijo considered dominant, and rightly so in my opinion. It would be a complete exaggeration to present Dechepare as an exceptional lyric poet, but he cannot be denied his preferential position among Basque poets. He always expresses himself with authenticity in the religious and in the profane, and his language is fluid, natural, and lively.

It was not quite fitting when Francisque-Michel and Vinson named him "the Basque Rabelais." The comparison is inappropriate not only because Dechepare was not a prose writer, but also because there is nothing in his work that would suggest a Renaissance man, save his enthusiasm for the invention of printing, which he hoped would put the Basque language above all the rest, if we take his words literally. In reality, he gives the impression of a medieval author above all.

The parallel with Juan Ruiz seems obvious. In addition to both being priests, one finds the same uninhibited mixture of the religious and the erotic in both. They were even both in prison, which no one has ever suggested should be taken metaphorically in the case of Dechepare. Keeping in mind the Basque author's smaller, yet much more interesting work, it is no exaggeration to say that, taken in isolation, his compositions are worthy of analogous passages in the archpriest's book.

Dechepare was above all a realist and did not pursue ideal beauty. His description of the relations between lovers, so rich and varied in its brevity, was simple and precise, and his dialogue was dramatic and slyly humorous.[17] The verse never tied him down.

Even though he may have composed the carnal verses at a different time in his life than the devotional verses, the fact is that he published them together, while he was a priest. We are dealing with a phenomenon that would be impossible among ecclesiastical authors of the following century and, even during the sixteenth century itself, for the protestant Leizarraga. We do not find a similar spirit in Basque literature except in some of the popular poetry. In reality, the relationship of Dechepare's work with popular poetry—in spirit, language, and versification—leaps to mind. Just as it made use of popular meters, so it employed the native tongue, the Low Navarrese of Cize. Effectively, an echo of his verses— or those of the common popular source—has come down to us through rhyming formulas preserved by the oral tradition in Navarra (Olazagutia, Aezcoa, Salazar).[18]

The enthusiasm that he felt for the language, expressed in his dedication, overflows in the final poems. Here he invites the Basque language to go out into the plaza and take part in the dance, to traverse the world: "Let all Basques lift up their heads because their language will be the flower of languages!" He was certain he would receive the gratitude of his compatriots for having been the first one, a son of Cize, to put their language in print.

The recognition he was hoping for only came very late. Either because of the extremely small print run or for other reasons we do not know—the great severity with which his erotic poems were later viewed could have played a part in that—his work did not spread far. One hardly finds it cited: for example, there is a lack of any reference to it in the dictionaries of Pouvreau and Larramendi. However, the Gipuzkoan Isasti was familiar with it. Around 1620 he transcribed one of the poems. And Oihenart also was familiar with it. He treated Dechepare with little appreciation without naming him.[19]

Leizarraga: The protestant Reformation had a rapid impact on Basque literature in the form of the translations of Joanes de Leizarraga.

Not much is known about his life. Born in Briscous, he must have been a Catholic priest before embracing the new ideas, which resulted in an imprisonment the memory of which, in his own words, "made my hair stand on end." The Synod of Bearne, celebrated in Pau in 1564 where he had taken refuge, conferred upon him the mission of translating the New Testament, the Calvinist catechism, and Calvinist prayers at the same time that it charged four other protestant ministers[20] with the revision and correction of his work. There are further indications that he was considered an expert in the language. He was ordained a minister in 1567 and sent to Labastide-Clairance, an area that was predominantly Gascon-speaking, and he died around 1600.

There is hardly a page of Leizarraga's extensive work that was not translation. The three books produced by his hand, of very different size, were magnificently printed in La Rochelle in 1571. They were the *Nuevo Testamento* "New Testament," the *Abc, o instrucción del cristiano con la forma de orar* "ABC, or instruction of the Christian in how to pray," and the *Calendario* "Calendar."

Leizarraga's translations were born of the desire of the queen of Navarra, Juana de Albret, to extend the Reformation throughout her Basque-speaking domain, Low Navarre, and through neighboring areas—Soule, closely tied to Bearne, and the countryside of Lapurdi— and they clearly demonstrated their intended ends. Above all, those goals had to do with healing the linguistic barrier that impeded the propagation of the new ideas in the Basque Country, or as Leizarraga expressed it in more polemic terms in his dedication to the queen, "to make war on Satan in your kingdom of Navarra." It was hoped that the reading of the translation would not be circumscribed to a single Basque province by his variety of language, but rather would extend to them all as far as possible.

The translator was openly conscious of the difficulties of his task. "The language in which I have written," he said, "is one of the most sterile and diverse, and totally unused, at least in translation . . . . Everyone knows what difference and diversity there is in Vasconia in the manner of speaking almost from one house to another." It was certainly not a simple task to build the prose of an uncultivated language through the translation of texts of an often-inappropriate character—texts which were owed the strictest fidelity—and to choose between different linguistic usages with the hope that the result of the selection would not automatically restrict the number of possible readers.

Taking everything into consideration, Leizarraga conquered these abundant obstacles with notable skill. If we did not have recourse to much evidence to the contrary, we could believe when reading him that he was writing in a language normalized by long years of literary practice. But in reality, according to Schuchardt, "it was Leizarraga himself who fixed the language in which he wrote."

It is possible that the cirumstances that explain the excessively literal character of his version [of the New Testament], often thrown in his face, have not been sufficiently taken into account. In the first place, he was a Calvinist who did not believe that the word of God should be the object of paraprhase and *ad sensum* translations, even though it would gain simplicity and naturalness by such means. For this reason, his translation of nonbiblical texts is much less besieged.[21] With regard to the lexicon, on the other hand, he was an unleashed practitioner of *culteranismo* who took pleasure in peppering his writings with terms (*fluvio* "river," etc.) taken from cultured languages. Thus he maintains, for example, the word *Sabbathoa* instead of Basque equivalents, because the evangelists used it in Greek in spite of its not being of that language. He says *(guiça) pescadore* "keeping more closely to the text" instead of *(guiça) arrançale*, although he recognizes that the usual term for "fisherman" is *arrançale*, and so on. Instead of a man of his own time, you could say that we have encountered one of those prose writers who in the previous century, in Spain as well as in France, dedicated themselves to taking Latin words into their hands whether it was necessary or not.

But while he may have been innovative with words, he was archaic with sounds and morphology. Schuchardt's opinion was right when he said Leizarraga's language was no less strange for a modern Basque from the same region than Luther's language for a German of today. It was the necessity of making his version accessible to the greatest number of Basques that carried him toward archaic usage, setting aside everything that was recent and differentiating, especially with regard to sounds.[22] On the other hand, the very character of the sacred texts made him employ a rigid, severe language, as different as possible from the daily language exchange. Although he wrote in a fundamentally Labourdin dialect, there is nothing written in that dialect that can compare in rigor, and this is not just a question of date. This occasionally causes the same impression of irreality and strangeness that the first Protestant versions of biblical texts in Spanish produced.

In fact it has to do with the version of a version, since basically for the source of his biblical texts he held to one of the French editions of the New Testament published in Geneva. All in all, according to R. Lafon, the Basque version departed on occasion from the French text in order to follow the Vulgate and even the original Greek.

Leizarraga's attempt did not have the consequences that it could have had for the fixation of literary Basque, consequences that the translation of the Bible has had in so many countries: it foundered with the failure of Protestant penetration into the country.[23] For as much as they must have made large print runs of his versions, which we know were well known by later authors (Pouvreau, a Catholic priest, made much use of the New Testament for his dictionary), their heterodoxical nature deprived them of any possible influence in later literature. With the rich blossoming of Catholic writers in the following century, the type of language established by him was replaced by another much less archaic, more popular, and accessible language, and one also more tied to local peculiarities: the Labourdin of Sara and Saint-Jean-de-Luz.

One rare Catholic catechism written in that century will be summarized in the following chapter. It most probably dates from before 1550, and is a formula for profession of the rule of the Third Order of

Saint Francis, written in a book printed in 1506 that must have been the property of the famous father Juan de Zumarraga.[24]

Collections of Proverbs

In the Spanish Basque Country two collections of proverbs or refrains were put together in the sixteenth century with a Spanish translation, more of linguistic than literary interest. The dialect of both was Biz-kaian, as was the dialect of the formula for profession that was just mentioned.

Historian Esteban de Garibay y Zamalloa, to whom we have already referred as the transmitter of some ancient ballads, was born in Mondragón in 1533 and was the author of *Compendio historial de las chrónicas y universal historia de todos los reinos de España* (Amberes, 1571) "Historical compendium of the chronicles and universal history of all the kingdoms of Spain." He indicated in his *Memorias* "Memories" that he had sent two collections of refrains in the Basque language to fellow Gipuzkoan Juan de Idiaquez from Felipe II's Council of State, at Idiaquez's request. It is assumed that one of them has been preserved in a codex (G 139) of the National Library of Madrid, a copy from the following century, and in a manuscript that has now disappeared (Cc. 79), contemporary with Garibay, that was found in that very library and was "given a gift" to Francisque-Michel by the erudite Benito Maestre. They did not see the light of day until the last century.

In 1596, the same year in which Betolaza's *Doctrina christiana* "Christian doctrine" appeared, mentioned in the next chapter, *Refranes y sentencias comunes en Bascuence, declarados en Romance* "Refrains and common sayings in Basque, declared in Romance" was published in Pamplona. There are 539 of them, and in part they do not appear to be of popular origin. The language used is extremely archaic.

This collection does not carry the name of an editor. J. de Urquijo suggested that this could be one of the collections mentioned by Garibay. Apart from the fact that its dialectal variety does not differ from that of the two manuscript collections, the attribution is founded on the fact that the number of proverbs it has in common with the manuscripts is summarily reduced, which makes it difficult to explain on the assumption that both compilations were independent. In this case it would mean that it was one of the two collections sent by the native of Mondragón to Idiaquez and published by the latter or by one of his heirs.

Seventeenth Century

Religious Instruction in the Diocese of Calahorra and Pamplona

If one event in modern history has had profound repercussions in Vasconia, it was the Council of Trent, the effects of which permanently altered
almost all aspects of life in the country. After that and as a consequence,
everything Basque came to be identified with Catholicism. Forgetting the
turbulence of a not-so-distant past, the country's civil order became a
model of peaceful and well-ordered villages, like that shown by the somewhat idealized image left to us by Father Larramendi from Gipuzkoa in
the middle of the eighteenth century. An ever-increasing restraint was
established as law in the area of customs, especially in matters related to
sex, and only traces remained of the old liberty and license in the most
popular forms of literary production. This was prolonged by the untir-
ing war waged against dancing by some missionaries of the following
century, with victories as spectacular as they were momentary.

Perhaps it was not at all by chance that the repression of witchcraft,
in Navarra as well as in Laburdi, reached its culmination in 1609 and
1610. However, it is not easy to say to what extent the practices that
were persecuted under the name of witchcraft represented attempts to
preserve an ancient state of affairs.[25]

Systematic measures were then taken so that priests would be in
charge of the religious instruction of the faithful in a regular and effective
manner, an activity that until those times was abandoned in many locations.[26] The bishops of Calahorra and Pamplona furthermore occupied
themselves with making sure that teaching the catechism and preaching
were both done in the vernacular language. Synodal constitutions and vis-
iting mandates established that all Christians must come to know Christian doctrine or at least its principal articles "in their own language." It
seems very strange to us today that this was not regularly done before
those dates, but we have proof of it in texts as explicit as the following
one by Echave: ". . . I want to explain to you, according to the Bishop of
Pamplona, who with divine agreement has ordered that the Hail Mary
be taught in these Provinces, along with all Christian doctrine, as it has
always been taught before, in Latin and Romance."[27] From the end of
the sixteenth century, on the other hand, there was abundant evidence,
provided that the parochial books were preserved, of the constant zeal
with which the ecclesiastical authorities stood watch, because the large

population in the country that did not know any other language but Basque was instructed in that language and no other.[28]

In addition to the new spirit born at Trent, the efforts of Juana of Albret to extend the Reformation in her domain and beyond by means of texts in Basque did not cease to have an influence on this situation. It worried Felipe II and helped him to convince the Pope to extend the limits of the diocese of Pamplona as far as the Bidasoa River and the Pyrenees in 1566. Neither must we forget the increasingly intense activity of the Jesuits in the country of their founder, especially in preaching.[29]

The first catechism in Basque that we know about, although no copy has been preserved, is the *Doctrina christiana* in Spanish and Basque by Sancho de Elso, printed in Pamplona in 1561, according to Nicolás Antonio.[30] Later, a provision dated from early 1608 by Antonio Venegas de Figueroa, bishop of Pamplona, assures that the doctrine "has been published in Basque and in the other languages that are used in this bishopric." This was confirmed by Echave. A few years later, the Gipuzkoan Isasti also spoke along the same lines: ". . . and the Bishop of Pamplona Don Antonio de Venegas ordered a catechism or letter of christian doctrine made in Basque, which is in print, and later others were written so that the children of Guipúzcoa and Vizcaya could learn the prayers and doctrine."[31]

With all of that, we have no direct knowledge of any Navarrese catechism after that of Elso until the bilingual *Doctrina christiana* (Pamplona, 1626) by the college-educated Juan de Beriayn, a priest and later abbot of Uterga from 1602 onward, to whom we also owe the *Tratado de cómo se debe oyr missa* (Pamplona, 1621) "Treatise on how to hear the Mass," also in Spanish and Basque, "the languages of this Bishopric of Pamplona." In all probability there were other Navarrese and Gipuzkoan doctrines, but none are yet known to us until the catechism of Ochoa de Arin for Gipuzkoa (*Doctrina christianaren explicacioa Villa Franca Guipuzcoaco onetan itceguitendan moduan*, "Eplanation of the Christian doctrine in the language of the Gipuzkoan people"), printed in San Sebastián in 1713, and the catechism of Eleizalde (Pamplona, 1735) for Navarra.

Thanks to S. de Insausti, the history of an aborted Gipuzkoan translation has recently come to light.[32] Martín Yáñez de Arrieta, a teacher from Azpeita, presented his version of Father Ripalda's primer to the general council meeting celebrated in that village in 1609, a version that was subject to the approval of the ecclesiastical authorities. Although approval was obtained, the Council of Villafranca in the following year "decreed and mandated that there was no room for Martín Yáñez de Arrieta's request." His request was simply that the Province pay the 200 ducats demanded by the printer. This demonstration of a barbarous lack of comprehension of all spiritual necessity by the Gipuzkoan council deserves to be mentioned along with the attitude of the states of Low Navarre and the *Biltzar* (Council) of Lapurdi regarding the projects of P. Bidegaray and Etcheberri, respectively. Even so, the Gipuzkoan authorities come off badly in the comparison since the states of Low Navarre were proposing plans for innovative and audacious education up to a certain point, while the village of Arrieta only wanted to tend to the Gipuzkoan religious formation of the most elementary character.

With regard to the Bizkaian dialect, the limits of which coincided approximately with the bishopric of Calahorra, the synodical constitutions of Calahorra from the year 1602 contained a disposition in which the bishop don Pedro Manso ordained that primers of the Christian doctrine be printed every year from that time on in Romance and Basque, "which we have begun to do in our time."[33] In fact, we are familiar with a *Doctrina christiana en romance y basquençe* (Bilbao, 1656), translated by Doctor Betolaza by mandate of this prelate.

In spite of that disposition, and perhaps owing to the disappearance of copies of other editions, one must wait almost sixty years to find the *Exposición breue de la Doctrina christiana* (Bilbao, 1656), with the Castilian text of Ripalda's catechism and the translation of university graduate Ochoa de Capanaga. It is true that there is also another Bizkaian doctrine that should be placed in this century, although its date and place of printing are unknown. It begins with the words *"Viva Jesús"* (Jesus lives) and is entirely in Basque, except for the first lines. Near the end of the century, in 1691, we have news of another Bizkaian doctrine—that of Nicolás de Zubía, printed in San Sebastián.

Micoleta

It goes without saying that these catechisms lack any literary value, no matter how valuable they are for the historian of the language.[34] While talented and knowledgable people in the French-Basque Country developed an important literary movement in the seventeenth century, even if limited to the religious field, it seems surprising that on this side of the Pyrenees we find only translators of catechisms who appear to have met with many difficulties in their task, in spite of resorting to loans and literal translations at every turn. Already at that time the greatest familiarity with the written use of the language was manifested by the French Basques, a familiarity that has endured down to modern times.

Meanwhile it is worth mentioning that in 1653 a clergyman from Bilbao, Doctor Rafael Micoleta, wrote *Modo breve de aprender la lengua vizcayna,* a manuscript unpublished until the last century, preserved in the British Museum. It contains some unenlightened grammatical observations, a rather extensive vocabulary, some brief notes on versification with examples, and a few bilingual dialogues. The latter are certainly not original, but no one has indicated their source as yet. Although written in a language impregnated with Romanisms, they are animated and constitute at any rate the only example of nonreligious prose written in the seventeenth century in Spanish territory, with the exception of the refrains collected by the Gipuzkoan Isasti. Full of archaisms and recent innovations, and picturesquely described by an author at the end of the eighteenth century as a type of neither Basque nor Romance tertium quid, the remnants of the Basque dialect of Bilbao have been affectionately collected by Arriaga and Unamuno, and thus have a monument of notable antiquity.

Verse

The study of Basque versification is not very advanced, and for that reason it would be rash to move beyond general indications about its character. Leaving aside the most ancient ballads of irregular meter, later versification is normally based on the number of syllables and on the rhyme, as with the *mester de clerecía* [a medieval school of poetry written by clerics and educated men.—L.W.]. The rhyme is assonant—or more accurately, assonant and consonantal rhymes may alternate—and although generally richer rhymes are sought, it is considered sufficient that the vowels of the last syllables coincide. Alliteration, a type of initial rhyme, is practically nonexistent, contrary to what has been occasionally suggested, even in the most ancient poetry. Stress appears to have played no role in the examples that have come down to us, even in the dialects like Souletin which today has a stress similar in intensity to that of Castilian,[35] and differences in quantity of vowels has also played no role.[36]

In popular usage, verse is intimately linked to song, but even though writers are free of this shackle, they have preferred to tie themselves to song meters instead of more closely imitating the versification of neighboring languages.

According to Micoleta, during the seventeenth century in Bizkaia two types of verse were known, both with assonant rhyme: those that he proposed to call "bascuences" (in the manner of "romances") and those that were sung "by the sound made by *las vacas* (cows)." To judge by his examples, and if we discount a certain imprecision in measurement, the second category corresponded to what today we call *zorcico mayor* [sic], with lines of four verses (10-8-10-8), in which even lines rhyme. In the first category, with the same rhyme, the odd lines have seven syllables and the even lines have six or five, meaning they were not too different from the current *zorcico menor* [sic] (7-6-7-6). The former is the measure of a very cultured elegy published in Lima in the following century for the death of the queen María Amalia of Sagonia,[37] and the second pattern approximates that of the song about the quarrel between the heart and the eyes of an enamored man written on the last page of a book printed in 1609 from the parochial Archive of Elorrio (Vizkaia), discovered not long ago by Jaime de Querexeta.[38]

Micoleta suggests on the other hand that some modern writers have written *décimas* [a verse of ten eight-syllable lines, abbaaccddc, also called *espinela*.—L.W.], *liras* [a verse of five lines, two endecasyllabic and three heptasyllabic, with consonantal rhyme aBabB.—L.W.], and sonnets following the Castilian in form, "but it is a work of little enlightenment because of the few who understand this meter in Basque." Moreover, according to his evidence, there was a very vulgar genre: "Leaving aside the Lelori Lelori couplets that girls used to sing on festival days, that do not belong in the most serious Basque poetry." It seems clear that this *lelo*, used as a label with the value of "song, chorus" was nothing more than a "monstruo" (used by Dechepare) in the sixteenth and seventeenth centuries "to give consonance of understanding for the lines and metric units that follow," according to the explanation in Ibargüen-Cachopín's chronicle.

At least since Dechepare, the purest verse is that in which the lines that rhyme have one syllable less (sometimes two less) than the free lines, or rather if you prefer, lines divided by a caesura into two hemistiches of which the second is shorter than the first. In the end, it would be better to speak of distichs (couplets) than of quartets because, since only a few cultivated poets have practiced enjambment, what normally constitutes a unit of meaning, a phrase separated by a pause, is the unit $n+(n-1)$ or $(n-2)$. There is a certain correlation between metric and linguistic elements (phrase, part of a phrase, group of words) with some possibilities for variation within the established metric pattern. For example, in an eight-syllable line or part of a line, rhythmic groups (groups of words) of 4+4 syllables, 5+3 syllables, or 3+5 syllables can alternate.

The verse most used in the sixteenth and seventeenth centuries is of the type 8-7 / 8-7, such as:

> *Aha-sabaiari lehen*
> *datchecala mihia,*
> *ecen guc çu gogotic utz*
> *gueure iaiat-herria,*

a translation of Psalm 136, 6, in which the monorhymed stanza can have more or fewer lines, although it generally has two or four. A good part of Dechepare's work is composed in this verse and, in the following century, it was used by Etcheberri to whom we owe the line cited above, as well as by Harizmendi and d'Argaignaratz. On this side of the border, the short poem from 1619 in honor of Our Lady of Roncesvalles[39] and before that the song of the battle of Beotibar, transmitted by Zaldibia and Garibay, followed this model.

With regard to its origin, the suspicion naturally arises that it was an imitation of the Castilian romance with acute rhymes, as mentioned by C. de Echegaray.[40] In the same way the lines of the *zorcico menor* [sic] "little eight" would be none other than Alexandrine lines, also with acute rhymes. But one might also think, as does G. Herelle[41] among others, that the model lies in the meters of the Latin hymns of an early period, and perhaps this is closer to the truth. As Lafon tells us, the fifteen-syllable line with a caesura after the eighth syllable already appeared in the well-known song of the soldiers of Aureliano (*Tantum vini habet nemo, / quantum fudit sanguinis*) or in Christian hymns such as that of the final judgment, attributed to St. Ambrose (*Apparebit repentina / dies magna Domini*).

In opposition to traditional versification, first place goes to Oihenart, the enemy of "masculine" verses, who tried to follow foreign models more closely at the same time as he remained faithful to his native Souletin dialect, when he asked that the last word of each line be taken as a word with penultimate stress, the type of words that predominate in Souletin. Gasteluzar also followed this path of penultimate rhymes or isosyllabic lines. Both in Spain and in France, the Jesuits are the players most known for this cultured manner of writing that did not prevail over popular rhythms. Other examples of the same type of versification include the version of the eight-line verse "*Yo ¿para qué nací?*" "Why was I born?" by the college-educated Suescun, collected by Isasti;[42] the funeral eulogy for Felipe IV, very much of the period; the work of the Navarrese historian father Francisco de Alesón;[43] and in the following century the attempts by Father Larramendi.

In the prize-winning poems of the Pamplona competitions of 1609 and 1610, organized by the bishop Venegas de Figueroa, lines were measured like Castilian octosyllabic lines, but it was left to the poet's discretion whether his final words were to be grave or acute, a procedure also followed later by the Navarrese Joaquín Lizarraga, which gives them a strange air. The compositions of 1609 are fresh and pleasing, within the common places that were inevitable on such occasions.

By means of the scant fragments of popular poetry that have survived from this period, we can infer that songs of erotic theme enjoyed great popularity.[44] The enchantments of the beloved and the suffering of the unfortunate lover were treated in a galant and conceptual manner similar to what we find in the Castilian poetry of that time. One of the effects of the Counter-Reformation was the passing over, if not the disappearance, of this genre in favor of moral and religious themes, of humor and satire with a great predilection for dry description and precise detail.

The still unpublished satirical lines discovered recently[45] in a lawsuit initiated in Tolosa (Gipuzkoa) in 1619, copied from posters put up by some clergy against a notable person from the village, have not added much to our knowledge. The dark allusions—evidently with evil intent—that fill them will make necessary a long labor of interpretation and their rhythm is very irregular.

Religious Literature from the Country of Lapurdi

In the face of scant and disconnected previous activity, in the seventeenth century there appeared here unexpectedly a circle of authors who worked in close relationship with each other. The names of some were repeated in the approvals or tributes in verse or prose that prefaced the books of the others.[46] It was a movement of clergymen who counted among their readers and supporters a certain number of educated lay people. The goal that they pursued was above all religious education and edification, in agreement with the already current idea that both the people and the bourgeoisie should be given spiritual nourishment in their native language. In reality, unlike the Spanish authors of catechisms, they all addressed rather cultured people who were accustomed to reading: "I do not write this little book," said Axular in the prologue, "for those who are highly educated, but neither for those who have no instruction." Moreover, to judge by the several editions achieved by some of his works, that public was not meager in number.

They wrote in a language that had a much more modern, more middle-class aspect than that of Dechepare and especially that of Leizarraga. It was everyday language (the Labourdin of Sara and Saint-Jean-de-Luz), elevated effortlessly to a literary language. Some of the authors possessed a magnificent humanist education and all of them had received at least an initiation into the fine arts. It is not strange, then, that they did not experience any purist concerns in either their lexicon or their syntax, nor did they flee with horror from that which might slip into their Basque writings from their readings. Nevertheless, they never at any time reached the Latinizing excesses of Leizarraga.

One notable peculiarity was the proportion of works in verse. Given the material, it seems out of proportion to us today. Etcheberri, who apart from his *Noelac* composed two extensive prayer books in verse, gave the Basque affection for verse as the reason,[47] an affection mentioned also by Oihenart, and his example was followed by Harizmendi, d'Argaignaratz, and Gasteluzar. In fact, it was not a cultured innovation, because in catechisms and even in prayer books of the period we repeatedly find rhymed versions of the commandments.

The great majority of the works were translations and arrangements/rule books. Father Estebe Materre[48] headed the list. He was a Franciscan, not Basque, who composed a *Doctrina christiana* (1617), approved by Axular, which was reprinted in 1623 and again in 1693 with additions from the abbot Duronea. We owe Father Juan de Haramburu for the work entitled *Debocino escuarra, mirailla eta oracinoteguia* ("Manual of devotion, mirror and prayer book"), published in 1635 and two or three more times within the century,[49] the contents of which he says he took from other books of devotion and added his own material. The priest P. d'Argaignaratz wrote *Avisu eta exhortacione protebetchosac bekhatorearentçat* (1641) in prose and a rather mediocre *Devoten bre+vearioa* (1665) in verse, which Vinson suggests was an imitation of or was translated from a French book of hours for ladies. Of higher quality is the *Oficio de la Virgen* (1659), versified in even meter by C. Harizmendi, from Sara.

One interesting figure is Silvain Pouvreau, who was born in the diocese of Bourges. With his gift for languages and his skill with a quill

pen he was secretary for the famous Jansenist leader Duvergier de Hauranne, the abbot of Saint-Cyran, "Basque by origin and temperament"
according to Daranatz y Dubarat,[50] but Pouvreau was not won over by
his ideas. He began to learn Basque in the abbot's house. Ordained a
priest in Paris, he was presented to Bishop Fouquet of Bayonne by M.
Vincent, later Saint Vincent de Paul. The bishop gave him the parish of
Bidart in the Basque Country. In Paris he published the Basque versions
of *L'Instruction du Crestien* by the Cardinal Duke of Richelieu (under
the title *Guiristinoaren Dotrina*, 1656), the *Introduction à la vie dévote*
by San Francisco de Sales (as *Philotea*, 1664) and the *Combattimento
espirituale* by Father Lorenzo Scupoli (as *Gudu espirituala*, 1665). In the
National Library of Paris, apart from other manuscripts, two copies of
a magnificent French-Basque dictionary[51] are preserved. Unfortunately,
it was never published although it's certain that lexicographers after
Humboldt made heavy use of it. In order to compose that dictionary,
Pouvreau carefully studied the printed works of various Basque authors
(Leizarraga, Axular, Harizmendi, and Etcheberri, but not Dechepare)
and counted Oihenart among his informants.

He also left a translation of the *Imitación de Cristo* in manuscript
form. The first printed version of that work was that of Arambillaga
(*Jesu Christoren Imitacionea*, Bayonne, 1684), who was a native of
Ahetze. His work only comprised the third and fourth books of that
work since he never fulfilled his intention to publish the rest.

Etcheberri

Joanes Etcheberri, doctor of theology and a native of Ciboure (different
from the second Etcheberri, from Sara, doctor of medicine) was one of
the most important authors of that century, as much for the quantity
as for the quality of his work which was composed almost entirely in
verse. He had studied in a Jesuit school and in an enthusiastic tribute he
declared that he owed all he knew to that school.

In 1627 he published his *Manual devotionezcoa* (2nd ed., 1669) in
Burdeos, the first part of which explained the things that every Christian should know and the second contained a very detailed collection of
prayers for different moments of life. *Noelac* must have been published
for the first time in 1630 or 1631 and had several printings. It consisted
not only of *villancicos*, but also poems on the life and passion of our Lord,
the hours, and canticles and hymns in honor of various saints, especially
Saint Ignatius of Loyola and Saint Frances Xavier, "both Basques by

language." In 1636 *Eliçara erabiltceco liburua* appeared, approved by Axular, the same as the first one. It was reprinted in 1665 and 1666.

In spite of how many forced rhythms there are in his work (especially in the translations, but also in the freer compositions, the order and disposition of which were imposed upon him by didactic necessity), in spite of its length and the inevitable repetitions, Etcheberri emerges as a first-class writer if not always as a great poet. His language, with a certain inclination to hyperbaton [the inversion of the normal order of words.—L.W.], is easy and fluid and his frequent fresh and natural images spring effortlessly from his pen. His well-assimilated erudition is only used moderately when the opportunity arises, never to astonish the reader. His gifts for clear and precise exposition are extraordinary and one might lament that he did not write in prose, in spite of the authentic poetic values that abound in his work. Nevertheless, his style always maintained a decorous level. For the modern reader perhaps the most suggestive would be the greatness of certain passages dedicated to the *Novísimos* (Newest) and the detailed information he provides about the life of his time and in particular about the lives of men of the sea. Etcheberri, like the village of his birth, looked out more on the Atlantic than on the dry land that lay behind it.[52]

Axular

Pedro de Axular has been generally considered to be the prince of writers in the Basque langauge, or more exactly, the best of the prose writers. Born in Urdax, in High Navarra, in the second half of the sixteenth century, there is reason to believe, as indicated first by M. de Lecuona, that he studied in Salamanca. He received his minor orders and subdeaconry in Pamplona (1595) and his deaconry in Lérida in the following year. For reasons unknown to us, he moved to France and in the same year, and in 1596 he was ordained a priest in Tarbes. The old parish priest of Sara left his position for Axular, but not without another aspirant for the position filing a complaint alleging that Axular was born in High Navarra *"que l'Espagnol occupe aujourd'hui"* "occupied today by the Spaniard." But Axular went to Paris and undoubtedly made a good case for the rights of Henry IV as the legitimate sovereign of all of Navarra,[53] because after 1609 there is agreement that he was confirmed in his office.

When his only book *Guero* (1643) was published, *"de non procrastinanda paenitentia,"* he was recognized for his knowledge and talent:

"viro magni nominis in nostra Cantabria, ac celebri nuper Rectore de Sara," Salvat de Dissaneche said of him in the dedication. It is not surprising then that in the literary circle referred to by the author in his prologue, when discussing the appropriateness of writing a book on this theme in Basque, everyone indicated Axular as the suitable person for that task. *Guero* gives evidence to the certainty of their choice, in spite of the fact that the author only wrote the first of the two parts that he had planned to write.

In the words of Saroïhandy, this is "one of the rare books of devotion in use in the Basque Country that is not a translation." Overall, some doubts have arisen about its originality and Father Luis de Granada has been pointed out as a source. It is certain that Axular knew Granada and also certain that in two passages, and probably in others, he followed him closely. Nevertheless, we should not give too much weight to the accuracy of this theory, at least until more detailed studies are carried out. Within what pertains to human originality in general, it is evident that one cannot expect a great deal of originality in the doctrine of an ascetic Catholic book. Neither can one expect all of the copious citations of sacred scripture, the Holy Fathers, and the classic authors contained in Axular's book to be first hand, naturally.

As far as possible, *Guero* is personal in content and in form. It is an ascetic book, with nothing mystical or speculative about it. With a very Basque preoccupation, its attention centers excusively on conduct. It is directed not at those who are advanced on the road of virtue, but rather at the common sinner, although not precisely at men of weak faith, because at every moment it is tacitly assumed that the truth of the dogma is outside the realm of doubt. The reasoning is always clear and direct, the ad hominem arguments are selected and presented with rare skill, and the language is of a frankness not found in any other Basque books of piety.

With regard to style, there is no need to paraphrase again the numerous tributes that have been paid to this work. The style of expression is consistent and has a slight tendency toward eloquence. It is always precise and used to underline the force of the reasoning. In Axular there are no traces of excess, and yes, there is a certain similarity to the style of Father Luis de Granada, although Axular is more somber. His admirable versions of Latin texts, as Basque as they are exact, have always been celebrated with good reason.[54]

The Writers from Soule (Zuberoa)

The viscounty of Soule has always had a very unique physignomy within Vasconia. In the sixteenth and seventeenth centuries, figures such as Esponde—noted for their capability and erudition—emerged from its noble families in which Protestantism was more firmly rooted than in the other Basque regions.

Arnaldo Oihenart from Mauléon (1592–1667) today appears isolated among the Basque authors of his century. He was a layman who almost always wrote about profane themes, and his name was well known outside the country.

He studied law in Burdeos and held public office, first as a town councillor in his native village and later as a member of the Parliament of Navarra in Saint-Palais, where he went to live by reason of his marriage to Juana de Erdoy, who was from a noble family. Apart from a writing that had more to do with a legal indictment than with history,[55] his fame is based on his *Notitia utriusque Vasconiae tum Ibericae tum Aquitanicae* (Paris, 1638), a work that is every bit as good as the best work produced by the learning of his century. One must remember, however, that within Vasconia at that time, the broad, critical historical work of the Navarrese Father Moret was also written.

One of the best collections of Basque proverbs, printed in Paris in 1657 with a French translation, is owed to Oihenart. Along with its supplement, *Atsotizen vrrhenquina* contained 706 proverbs. Some of them were probably not popular proverbs, but rather composed or altered by the author.

At the same time, his verses were published: *O[ihenar]ten gastaroa neurthizetan*. He proceeded with the express purpose of avoiding the popular varieties and producing cultured poetry by means of his meters,[56] his "concepts," and his allusions. His language was also different from that of other authors of his time because of his more purist nature, which was manifested especially in the systematic and generally well-conceived use that he made of the possibilities of the language by his formation of words.

His Basque production had hardly any influence: it would be more exact to say that his ideas of all types were not well received in the country. Oihenart was a well-educated intellectual, cold and critical, an uncommon type of person who was not very appreciated by us. His linguistic opinions that today seem generally correct to us, at least in their orientation, were rejected by Basque grammarians of the following century,[57] and some of his opinions were considered disrespectful. He was considered too impartial and too fond of exacting proof to be a good patriot. It is a shame that his original work in Basque was in verse, because Oihenart was not a poet, but rather an extraordinarily skilled versifier, and he had a great knowledge of the language. Even when an authentic feeling moved him, as in the elegy on the death of his wife added to the verses of his youth, he did not manage to transform it and sublimate it.

We know that he had a precursor, because of a beautiful sonnet that he dedicated to his memory, the Souletine Huguonot Bertrand de Sauguis, whom he believed was the consummate poet. This man's poetry has unfortunately been lost, and we have only preserved his collection of 205 proverbs, preceded by a vocabulary, which he sent to Oihenart. The first Basque proverbs published in France, by the way, were those by a compiler named Voltoire in *L'interpret ou traduction du François, Espagnol & Basque* (around 1620), translated rather than collected from a popular source.

Another small collection of adages was left by the Souletine Jacques de Béla (1568–1667) in his long-winded manuscript *Tablettes*. He was a member of a noble family who gave proof of his fondness for witing at different times. Jacques expressed his passion for books in this couplet:

> *Virgo flores, fur aurum, mare navita, Bela*
> *Libros, sic ultro singula quisque capit.*[58]

He liked writing at least as much as reading and we know that among very different treatises (one on mnemonics, in which he was an expert) he composed a dictionary and a compendium of Basque grammar, the location of which is unfortunately unknown.

Jacques's father, Gérard de Béla, was Catholic but took the religion of his wife. Jacques was Protestant, although with very tolerant criteria to judge by his writings. One of Jacques's sons (protestant like his father, although with very tolerant criteria to judge by his writings; he later converted to Catholicism) was Athanase de Bélapeyre, the Catholic priest of Chéraute, famous for his altercations with the bishop and author of *Catechima [sic] laburra* (1696, in two parts) in the Souletin dialect.

Although born in Mauléon, Oihenart did not use Souletin in his writings, even though he could not or would not keep certain peculiarities of that dialect from slipping into his Navarrese-Labourdin dialect. The first to use it in an extensive work, mixed however with Low Navarrese, was Juan de Tartas from Chéraute, born around 1610, and parish priest of Aroue. His two books were *Onsa hilceco bidia* (How to Die Well) and *Arima penitentaren occupatione devotaq* (Devotions of the Penitent Soul), published in Orthez in 1666 and 1672, respectively. Compared with Axular, the learning displayed by Tartas seems extravagant and prideful, and at every moment his love for the extravagant, the exaggerated, and the tremendous is patently evident, in the manner of Father Nieremberg from *Diferencia entre lo temporal y lo eterno*.

Gasteluzar

At the end of the century, father Bernard Gasteluzar, a Jesuit, published his *Eguia Catholicac* ("Catholic truths") in Pau in 1686. He was a refined and delicate poet, as well as an expert innovator in the area of meter, who walked the same path as Oihenart, perhaps without knowing it. His verses, in spite of his popular and didactic goal, were cultured by reason of his varied versification and mythological dressing, although as a Jesuit he only introduced mythology in order to tear it down. Thus in the first lines of the book:

> *Urrun adi Parnasseco*
> *Musa çahar profanoa*
> *Eta çu çato ceruco*
> *Musa berri divinoa.*

("Go away, old profane Parnassian Muse, and come hither new, divine Muse of the heavens.")

Two technical books were published in this century. One was intitled *Ixasoco Nabigacionecoa* (1677), translated and augmented by Piarres d'Etcheverry, called Dorre, from *Les voyages aventureux du capitaine Martin de Hoyarsabal, habitant de Çubiburu* (1633), of great interest for its detailed description of the routes to Newfoundland frequented by Basque fishermen.[59] The other was a treatise on veterinary medicine (1692?), attributed to Mongongo Dessança.

Orthography

"Ortografía." in *Euskera* (Bilbao) 13 (1968): 203–19.

I. Foundations: How We Seek Unification

1. We believe that it is absolutely necessary, a matter of life or death, to put Basque on the path of unification. If one is teaching our children and young people in Basque and if Basque is to survive, we must use it for teaching—it is indispensable that we teach them in a unified manner. The unification that we need is in written Basque, at least for the first few steps. And within written Basque, we need unification in teaching, more than in "beautiful" literature created for the pleasure of the reader.

2. Of course, it would be better if each Basque speaker knew all the dialects: those from this side of the border and those from the other side, the old forms and the modern forms. It is obvious, however, that one cannot request such a thing except of a Bascologist. If one is a Basque speaker, it is all he can do to understand the other dialects in which he is not fluent. He is usually not capable of speaking or writing another dialect.

3. If we are ever united, our language will lose something more than trivialities. It will lose the abundant versatility that is so pleasant to the eyes and ears. Nevertheless, since Basque has a dangerous pallor at the moment, we prefer a living Euskera over any surface beauty of the language.

4. Euskaltzaindia would not want to hurt anyone in this matter, but it cannot move toward unification without hurting someone sooner or

later. However, Euskaltzaindia does not have any right or power, neither its own nor that of others, to complete the unification. It would like to appear as a guide, a pathfinder, in the situation we are in, to the extent that it is able.

5. These are the goals that it would like to achieve by means of resolutions:

    a. First of all, that the dialects not be too distant from each other

    b. Later, to the extent that it is possible, it would like the dialects to move closer to each other

6. For now at least, Euskaltzaindia is not the one who should choose which dialect will be used for the foundation of unification. However, it seems that the central dialects are more appropriate for the needs of writing in Basque than the peripheral dialects (since Bilbao is not a Basque-speaking area). At any rate, we will all find ourselves in need of compromise, more or less, if we want to achieve our goal.

7. Before delving into the problems that lie deep in the marrow, we must first achieve unity on the surface, because it is easier and even more necessary to heal those wounds. It is true that a language is a system, and that the pieces or parts of that system are not anything when separated from the system. But it is necessary to mention, if we're going to the heart of the matter, that Basque is no longer a single system but rather a dual system, and that we must come to an agreement on the appearance of that dual system, if we are to unify the marrow at a later date.

8. We will outline the requests presented to Euskaltzaindia in the following manner, from the easiest to the hardest: (a) a writing system or orthography; (b) the forms of old Basque words; (c) the usage of new words and the adaptation that is taken from others; (d) morphology— noun (pronoun) and verb, and; (e) syntax.

In some cases, there is nothing we can do for now, because no one has done the studies needed in order to accomplish them. In other cases, however, even if the creation of unity among the dialects is difficult, we need unification at least within each dialect itself, and that is in our hands.

II. Orthography

I am taking as my foundation the decisions made at the meeting held in Bayonne in 1964, by slowly touching on most of the points involved.

1. We should use these letters at least: *a, b, d, e, f, g, h, i, j, k, l, m, n, ñ, o, p, r, s, t, u, x, z;* and for writing names and foreign words, *c, qu, v, w* and *y* in addition.

F of course is well accepted and not just in words taken from foreign tongues (*fede, faltsu,* etc.), but also in others. It seems more correct to write *afari, alfer, Nafarroa,* than any other spellings.

2. The diagramatics (two like or unlike letters joined to express a single sound) that must often be used in Basque are these: *rr,* to express the hard *r* that some write as *ŕ; dd* (if we do not keep *y* for that, since we have removed some of the others) *tt,* and *ll,* like *ñ,* all "wet" sounds, to express palatals when needed; *ts, tx* and *tz,* as in the old days, the characteristic of the harsh side of *s, x,* and *z.*

3. The writing system of a living language that is used in oral and written forms cannot be built on the suitability of one letter or sound at a time. Carried too far, this can result in using the phonological or phonetic transcriptions employed in linguistic works. But it is not appropriate to move toward an oral language on the one hand and a reading language on the other. Furthermore, in addition to phonetics and phonology, morphophonology must be taken into account: German *Tod* can be written *Todes,* and Russian *rog* can be written *roga,* whether those intervocalic and final *b*s and *g*s are cut differently.

4. Neutralization must quickly be taken into account: perhaps two separate phonemes that are not always and everywhere distinguishable. For example, in Spanish *r* and *ŕ* are distinguishable at the beginning of a syllable within a word and after a vowel exclusively, and at no other time (*rosa, arte, honra, pagar,* etc.).

Similar situations are often seen in Basque:

a. In nasals, at the end of a syllable, either within the word or at the end. However, often a single letter is used, *n,* according to custom: *ganbara, indana, antxu, zango,* and so on.

b. Likewise *r* (*argi, erdi, prestu* and, except in Errongari, *ur, hur,* and so on). Here, *r* has only been used within a word. But at the end, a so-called morphophonological distinction could be required: *paper-a, zer-a,* but writing *ederr* and *izarr* since they are *ederr-a, izarr-a.* Having few words that end with a soft *r,* because most are otherwise, it seems more economical and more pleasing to the eyes to use a single *r* in those as well. I would not change anything if it had been done differently up to now, but since *hamarrak* and *hamar* have been used in writing almost totally, it seems better to me to leave things as they are.

c. After some sounds the distinction between *p/b, t/d* and *k/g* is also habitually destroyed, especially after *(t)s, (t)x* and *(t)z: (hitzak) hizpidea (ekarri), harist(o)i, lokarri,* etc. In my opinion there is no hard law because *bereizgarri, ikusgarri,* and similar constructions are widespread. In the end, one can say by way of advice that it would be better in doubtful cases to keep that rule in mind; Aizkorri in Gipuzkoan for example, is better than Aitzgorri. In other words, we do not have to be caretakers of the etymology in those cases, except on the side of phonological rules that have taken root in past centuries.

d. Sibilants are like that as well, as *Aizkorri / Aitzgorri* have shown us. First of all, today most Basque dialects, perhaps all of them, do not distinguish between *tz/z* and the like at the end of a syllable, if that syllable is not at the end of the word (*apaiz/apez,* but more often *arrats, zorrotz,* and so on): in those cases, writing *z, s, x* alone is better, in the way we have always done (*hotz* but *hoztu, huts* but *hustu,* and so on). However, at the beginning of a syllable, after *n, l,* and *r,* now *ts, tx,* and *tz* are chosen most of the time (*entzun, altzo, altxatu, hartz, saltsa, suntsitu*); after *r,* nevertheless, I do not believe that that rule is rigorously applied in all areas.

e. Still on the topic of sibilants, there is an obvious distinction among dialects. In all of them, I believe (if one removes a few unusual words and their like), we only use *z* and *s* at the beginning of a word. But we can use either *tx* or *x* according to the strength of the word (*tximist, txori,* but *xamur, xuxen*); a few others, however, use only *x.* If someone needs to bend in another direction, perhaps it would be more efficient if we compromise in this matter.

5. Those who do not know how to distinguish between z/s *(tz/ts)* must learn the honest distinction from others, in writing at least. The most severe break occurs in Bizkaia and thereabouts, with forms and words that are not used except for there. In those cases, the truth must be found in Bizkaia itself, that is to say, in the old Bizkaian writers who used to distinguish those sounds so beautifully: consequently, *deutsat, deust, deutsut,* but *deustazu, zoru,* etc.

6. Also in the dispute regarding *h*, by following the current direction, the Bayonne decisions can be taken as a foundation. Along that path, I see levels of necessity, beginning with the following.

   a. We need to use *h* between two like vowels, when otherwise they remain too far from each other,* as in *ahari (adari* and so on) and *ari, mahai(n),* and *mai, zuhur (zugur),* and *zur,* etc.—of course, between two like vowels, *when it is needed and only then*: consequently, for example, *semeei, gazteen,* without *h,* etc.

   b. Next, between two vowels, whatever they may be: *aho, ahur (eskukoa), behar, behor, bahe, bahi, lehoi(n), ohe,* etc. Here also only when it is necessary, of course, and in places where it is needed: *nahiz* "whether" but *naiz* "I am," *ahur* but *haur* "child" and so on. Some people will not want to read the *h,* but that shows us at least how many syllables the word should have.

   c. If we go to unification, let us never use *g* and similar letters between vowels *(r, d,* etc.) in cases such as the following: *ehun* "100," not *egun,* and even if we do not write *leihor (zeihar,* etc.), at least let's use *lehor,* but never *legor.* And even less so *legun* instead of the *leun* of dialects that possess the *h.*

   d. On the other hand, we need *h* at the beginning of the word: *hats, hede, hitz, hots, hotz, huts,* and so on. For that purpose we need a short orthographic dictionary, with the spelling of the doubtful words in it. And that *h* should not be taken into account alphabetically; otherwise our regional people would not know how to find the words.

   e. No *h* will be written after consonants that are completely enclosed in the word *(aphez, athe, ekharri,* and so on). According to what

---

* Editor's note: Although the original text indicated "too far from each other," it is obvious that the meaning was the opposite: "too close to each other."

was decided in Bayonne, neither should it appear after other consonants: *erho, belhar, unhatu,* and the like.

f. Likewise, neither should it appear after a diphthong: it is *aien, auen, oian,* not *aihen, auhen, oihan.* In Bayonne, they decided it should work that way in the declension of nouns as well: for example *edozein gaietan,* like *edozein ibarr-e-tan,* not the model of *edozein mendi-tan.* On the one hand, it is true that this has not always been the ancient pattern because it has always been *Bizkaian,* but *Bizkaitik, Bizkaira,* and so on, and furthermore, the suffix *-(r)ik* does not work that way. Among ourselves, and in all the regions in the past as it seems, *ez da, ez, etsairik* and similar words have been written; however, those from other regions write *etsayik,* like after a consonant, keeping the letter *y* for that purpose.

On the one hand, it is true that this has not always been the ancient pattern because it has always been

We must keep one thing in mind about the *h* of that case: all Basques do not divide the syllables the same way. In those cases, some divide them *er-ho, ai-hen,* etc., and others *e-ro, a-ien,* and so on.

7. If it were decided not to write any *h* after diphthongs or after the consonants *l, r, n,* we must keep in mind compound words (*oinhatz, onhartu*). On the one hand, it would not be good to write *hartu* but *onartu,* and on the other hand, neither would it be good to write *onhartu* but not *unhatu.*

This difficulty with compound words appeared to us above (4, b) with the hard *-r* at the end of words that we mentioned then: *itur aldean,* or perhaps the preferred *itur-aldean,* but we should write *iturraldean,* and the same with *gor,* but *gorraire, gorreria,* and so on.

8. One can say this about the so-called wet sounds: They are found in very few places if we continue along the path we have been on. With regard to the best unification, I suggest the following.

a. Let us write *iñ* and *ill* instead of *ñ* and *ll,* at least if they are not some of those expressive words (like the ones that carry the suffix *-ño*): *baiña, baiño, oillo,* etc., not *baña, baño,* and *ollo.* In addition at the end of words, we should always use *-in, -il; gain, zail.*

b. But writing only *il* and *in* would be better since often in their dialect, because of that *i,* the following *l* and *n* are wet. Among

Gipuzkoans for example, customarily they have read *ibilli, baiña, gaiñetik, laiñ* (or *baña, gañetik, lañ*), and *miñondo* for what is written as *ibili, baina, gainetik, laino, min-ondo*.

9. Of course, like always, we must write *j* for now: *jakin, jende, jo*, etc. Likewise, *birjiña, ebanjelio*, etc. However, it seems that one can also use it instead of *dd* after a consonant, like they do in other regions: *onjo = onddo*.

10. When the ancient sound is *x* (an ancient one in all of the Basque Country and in many regions today), if we are moving toward unification, *x* must be tied to us: *axola*, not *ajola*, etc.

11. With regard to punctuation, we could often do as those around us do, setting aside special characteristics (such as apostrophes). On one subject (the placement of question marks and exclamation points) we are in need of a decision, and I would use *?* and *!* at the end of the sentence, as they do in French and the other languages of Europe.

12. The so-called apostrophe (') is better kept to express a sound or letter that has been "swallowed"; *t'erdiak* and so forth. In other cases, a hyphen (-) seems more fitting as a distinction.

13. When faced with proper nouns: *Axular-ek* and *Orio-n* are better than *Axular'ek* and *Orio'n*. However, it seems that this distinction is not always necessary. Often we do not know—at least I do not—where divisions are needed: some would have us write *Paris-en*, others *Parise-n*. And in the case of place names with a definite article, where do we make the division? *Iruine-an* or *Iruinea-n, Bizkai-an* or *Bizkaia-n*? Next, in well-known proper nouns division is not necessary (*Axularrek, Orion, Parisen, Bizkaian*, etc., being permitted); but if the writer thinks it appropriate, he can make separations when he knows it will make the word easier for the reader, especially in foreign names: *Scott-ek, Piaget-ek, Calmette-k, Bremen-en*.

14. If the noun carries an attached suffix, most of the time separation seems unattractive: *Jaungoikoak* or *Jainkoak, Euskal-herrian, Euskal-herritik*, etc., not *Jainkoa-k* or *Jainko-ak*, etc., as is seen so many times.

15. The serious problems lie in dealing with parts of words and between words. I will mention a few as examples, so that we may touch on the subject:

a. Here is the most clear-cut case. Especially in citations (as in grammatical citations), but also in other places, in the ones where we only mention the necessary word or name it (*"Homo" est dissyllabus,* etc.), we need something to completely link and separate the pieces: "*luze*-ri -*tu* atzizkia eransten bazaio," "*x*-en ordez *x'*+ *a* ipintzen badugu," "*Euskera*-tik hartu dugu artikulu hau," and so on. In those cases, as with proper nouns, but on this occasion without direction, - (a hyphen) can be used, for either separation or for linking different elements.

b. Should we write the affirmative and conditional *ba (bai, ba da / baldin bada)* two different ways, in the manner of Spanish *solo* and *sólo*? That sort of distinction will perhaps make the reader's job easier; by increasing the writer's labor. Since that *ba* does not change the following sound, the easiest thing could be always writing it together: *bai, badator* and *baldin badator.*

c. What do we do with *ez* and *bait*? Here I do not clearly see the reasoning of those at Bayonne. Since both of them force the same change on the following sound (*eztu: baitu, etzuen: baitzuen, eluke: bailuke, enizuke: bainizuke,* etc.), it seems that we should use them both the same way: both joined or both independent.

d. Using them independently clearly has two bad sides. On the one hand, the symmetry is not complete because some writers from Bidasoa from the eighteenth century on, and also those who did not acquire Basque at home or as children (beginning from Gipuzkoan Beterri and heading west), are used to writing *bai du* and the like. On the other hand, and even worse, some take the separation of *ez du, ez zuen* etc. (pronouncing them as two separate words!) to be more elegant. And by writing them independently, keeping in mind the power of the written word, I fear that such a way of speaking will become more prominent among us.

e. But by writing them together, several doubts could arise: *eluke, enuke* is not written everywhere and every time, *baikabiltza* could seem harsh to more than one person, and so on. With regard to writing the language, I believe it would be better to place the two words *ez* and *bait* independently, by explaining that *bai* is also permissible next to *bait*.

f. Do we need to distinguish the compound words that we just mentioned, or not? As happens too often in English, we can see among ourselves some words not so far from each other, *elkar-rizketa, elkar-izketa* and perhaps, *elkar izketa; hitzegin, hitz-egin* and *hitz egin; dirugose, diru-gose* and *diru gose.* There do not seem to be any rigorous rules in place here (and very similarly in matters of punctuation). At the most we have something like this: (1) when the creation of the word is distant, it is better not to divide the pieces (*amuarrai[n],* etc., *otordu* or *oturuntza, galbide,* etc.); (2) in cases where those pieces need to appear separate, it is better to write them independently: *hitz egin,* now that they say *hitzik ez du egin; on egin* because they say *ez dio onik egin,* etc.

g. Some suffixes that go with the verb at the end of the sentence give us problems. Some people write *Jainkoak agindu duenez gero(z),* and others write *duen ezkero(z):* the former is older, of course, and the one that is tied more closely to the meaning, but if we accept it, we will also have to write *atzoz gero(z),* not *atzo ezkero(z).*

h. Another one is *-t (-da)* from the Bizkaian region and Goierri: *aserretuta etorri da,* on the one hand, and *ez du egin, ez daki-ta,* on the other. That first one has an older and more widespread counterpart, of course (*haserreturik*), and even when using it, we often write it in one word as always. The second one (*ez daki, eta ez du egin. Ez daki (e)ta, ez du egin. Ez du egin, ez daki (e)ta*), can be written separately as well, if you like.

III. About the Forms of Words: Old Basque Words

1. "*Euskal hitza*" does not refer here to some decision made at some time by Euskaltzaindia, but rather to the word that we Basques have been using for some time, independently of its origin.

2. Only antiquity gives a word authenticity. Worrying about the final source is appropriate for an etymological dictionary, not for a language that is used either orally or in written form. Language is a way of speaking and a means of expression, not the teaching method of the give and take of history and prehistory.

3. If there is unity among us in this matter—that is, if there is language all Basques or the vast majority of us will use—then that is what we must accept, and nothing else.

4. When there is no unity, we have habitually had two different types of differences: either: (1) the words from one side or the other have no resemblance to each other (*ahaide* and *askazi, ate* and *borta, belar, boronde, bekoki* and *kopeta, etorri* and *jin, irten* and *jalgi, dai(ke), dezake* and *diro*, etc.); or (2) they have the same root, they are related to each other, but sound changes have separated them (*barri / berri, bertze / beste, erran / esan, hertsi / itxi, heuragi / ugari / jori, irten / urten, itxi (etxi) / utzi*). There is a rule that applies to the second of these: *arrazoi(n), arrazio* and *arrazu*, for example, are not the only ones where that difference in the ending (*-oi(n) / -io / -u*) occurs, because it appears in the same manner in several other words (*arratoi(n) / arratio / arratu*, etc.).

5. In the first case above (in number 4) (and not so easily in the others: look at *ugari / jori* in our regional writings), it would be worthwhile to separate the words according to expression, sense, and meaning, limited only by our desire. We can use *aurkitu*, for example, when we discover or find a paper that we had lost, and *eriden* (or *idoro*) when we invent or discover an unknown law of physics. But wanting it is not enough, because it is also necessary that it be possible. The truth is, these kinds of restrictions are a daily occurrence in the artificial, partial languages that are set by agreement and usage of the moment—that is, the languages of knowledge and technical fields—but they are not frequent occurrences in living, natural languages. Even in those specialized fields, schools need to transplant the terms and reinforce them.

6. Euskaltzaindia cannot disdain any Basque word, neither from here nor there, neither old nor newer. It prefers the ones that have survived over the ones that have grown old; the ones that are used most and are most widespread. Euskaltzaindia is always looking at the richness more than at the purity.

7. Now that we are writing in Basque, that wider distribution is what the words have had and do have *in Basque literature and in Basque reading matter*. Still now according to some people the words they have as favorites but are hidden away in a corner, the ones that are not used

(*adei, dedu, jeben* and counterparts of those), are not proper in Basque literature (that is, they cannot compete with what is spread in Basque writing).

8. Even if the clear path is not seen too often, some opinions can be taken as a foundation, when words are just transformations of each other:

a. Some changes—all too frequent—must simply be set aside and not used in Basque writing: *biar, bier,* for "behar," *biño* for "baino," *abitu* for "abiatu," *zun* for "zuen, zuan" *ero, eo, o* for "edo," *ixen* for "izan," *abua* for "ahoa," *uetu* for "ohatu," etc. Those kinds of dialectal forms for the most part can be taken in the special meaning they have in their original region: from *itzal* comes *itzel* "big, enormous" like Spanish *juerga* (= *huelga* by formation) or French *rescapé*.

b. The abbreviations that too often have been taken as more authentic are disdained, because each region makes them in their own way: the old *legez,* which was alive outside of Bizkaia and is still understood, has become *lez* (and the diminutive *letxe*), to the detriment of those who are not Bizkaian because they do not see the *lege* that was seen there before. The same thing happens with many Zuberoan *-r-*s and in all regions more or less with intervocalic *b, d, g,* and *r* (*nipe, nik e,* from *nik (b)ere,* etc.).

c. The changes that the dialects, i.e. Basque itself, have made are accepted, even if the method has not been completely the same: *arima,* therefore is the only one that has appeared for a long time, not *anima.*

d. Among the newer and older forms, when it is obvious which is which, dominance is given to the older ones. Sometimes the old ones are too old (*azeari,* for example), and at other times antiquity and origin appear to be enemies, as in the special Basque form (*probetxu / progotxu / protxu*).

e. In several words this type of change is often found at the beginning of the word, mostly in those of Spanish origin but also in others: *b-, d-, g- / p-, t-, k-:* within the word, after *l* and *n.* In my opinion they are preferred because that has been at times the flow of Basque, *bake, barkatu, bekatu, bike, daratulu (-uru), dolare, dorre, gapirio, gerezi, gapelu,* and so on, on the side of counterparts having *p-, t-, k-;* in the same way, *aldare, denbora, jende, -mendu* are better than *altara, denpora, jente, -mentu.* That is true, of course, when the latter are not widespread. We cannot begin writing *baradizu* or *dipula* again.

f. The series of variations (they may be longer or shorter, but they are always series) should be examined one by one and at length. As yet, most of the time, we do not have any foundation for making many decisions. There are collections and categories in some books (in my own *Fonetica histórica vasca,* for example, even if I created it for something else). In that way, *honek/hunek, bertze/ beste* (perhaps *uso,* could be the one chosen to the detriment of *urzo*), etc., and especially, one ancient *-n-* has created abundant changes of appearance: *ardao, ardo, arno,* etc., *liho/liñu,* etc., *-ai(n); -ae, -ai, -ain; -oi(n), -io, -u; -ino(e), -io, -ione, (n)ehor/ inor,* and some others.

g. Special forms of the excluded dialects have a few rights compared to the others: the dispute belonging to *(errazoe), arrazoi, arra- zoin, arrazio,* and *arrazu* can be simplified by removing Zuberoan *arrazu* (also *arrazio* from a period in Navarrese history) because it does not have a widespread presence often in Basque reading matter. Consequently, it seems that those excluded dialects must bow down to the central dialects on some occasions, such as in these words: *barri, ultze, ukuzi, bühür (bior), sento (sonto), uzen,* etc./*berri, i(l)tze, ikuzi, utzi, bihur, sendo izen,* etc.

h. When the excluded dialects are in agreement, once again, they have more power than the central dialects: *burdina,* for example, is better than Gipuzkoan *burni(a).*

9. Be that as it may, when one of the distinguishing sounds is lost in some regions (*z/s* in Sartaldea, *r/rr* in Zuberoa, *a/e,* after *i* and *u,* here and there, etc.), the writers from there should not also exclude in writing what they do not distinguish orally.

10. A serious problem appears in words from foreign languages, more often than in others. This occurs for two reasons, of course: because we often have pairs of words from the same source (or even three words) (*arima/anima, goilare/kutxare, kanpae/kanpana, zeinu/sinu,* etc.), and because to some, since they are foreign, it makes no difference whether they use one word or the other, and because they do not often appear in dictionaries either.

11. But those words are just as Basque as others and we need them just as much as the others. In fact, their form must also be well chosen, not haphazardly, in every detail: do they have a distinct final -*a* or not, is the ending -*o* or -*u* (*artikulu, minutu,* but *katoliko, soldadu/ -o*), should they be written with *s* or *z* (*zopa,* not *sopa, zaku,* not *saku* or *sako,* etc.)?

12. We have need of one little orthographical dictionary, at least, but it is mandatory that it also contain short explanations of the meanings of words, so that we may know what it is about. Of course, those who have in mind the dialects that are being written now are not in total agreement, and since our foundation is written Basque, the dictionary must be built on the vocabulary of some chosen authors.

13. Let us always remember that the dialects are more and more frequently being distinguished by borders, especially from the side of vocabulary. For example, even if Laburdin is closer to Gipuzkoan for a linguist than it is to Bizkaian, in speaking we are much more likely to be Giputz-Bizkaians than Giputz-Laburdins because those of us from the south side live in one foreign-language environment and those from the north in another.

IV. New Words

1. A living language is always in need of new words: it creates them from within itself at times, and at other times it takes them from other sources. Two paths are permitted and needed and who will organize beforehand the measure and limitations of each? What Euskaltzaindia said on a certain occasion was valuable only for this problem: there is no need to create any new words to express truly old Basque words with the intention of excluding them just because they were originally borrowed from a foreign language.

2. When creating Basque words and when speaking about whoever creates them, we must always keep in mind the structure of our language, because we have always had an easiness about that, by means of joining words together, especially. That source of originality must inevitably continue if the language is going to survive.

3. In making new compounds and by choosing them from among old words, we are always working two strengths: on the one hand, the old models and on the other hand the so-called analogy—*luze* offers *luza-tu*, *luza-ro, luza-mendu* and so on by following the ancient patron: analogy, however, seems always to require "luze," given that its companions always go hand in hand. Without carrying it to excess, in my opinion, we should do whatever possible to maintain the first tendency, because what we see today seems to indicate the opposite path.

4. As we are "receivers" in questions of culture—indebted to others, as a result—it seems reasonable that we appear as receivers and as indebted in questions of dictionary. If we consider it as we do matters of knowledge, we do not need to translate the words that have been created in another language. But being as we are, we often perceive that need. Basque does have copious word origins, but there also exists an obvious lack of such when compared to the neighboring languages. We don't have any prefixes (once we remove *des-* and a few like it) that are as powerful as Latin *ad-, ab-, co(n)-, de-, dis-, ex-,* and others. That lack can have more than one remedy, but much thought must be given to how it plays out without delay.

5. In the past we took words from other languages, and there is no option but to do the same in the future. However, there are two opinions among us about the appearance of those words: some people would like to maintain the original appearance as far as possible, in the French manner, and other people prefer changing and simplifying the appearance, in the Spanish manner.

6. To tell the truth, if we were thinking of highly educated people, I would take the former path, but that is not happening. I would increasingly lean toward simplicity, or at least toward a compromise (middle of the road), but excluding *y, kh, th (psykhologia,* etc.) and those kinds of spellings.

7. Of course, those letters must be maintained in proper names at least (*c, qu,* and the like). The transcription of nouns from other languages (those that do not employ the same letters) must be decided today or tomorrow, but that is not our most urgent task. We must first of all decide, and teach, the form of Basque names themselves.

8. Concerning words and names, it does not seem like a good idea to me to restrict what those from the other side are doing: writing *Mozku, zozializta,* and things like that. In these cases, the spoken form (French form) is imposed to the detriment of the written form and unification.

9. I would mention as reasonable the keeping of *v* in new words from Spanish and leaving unchanged the majority of consonants or not make it a rigorous rule: *vektore*; and in words with a final *-logia,* and the like, I would keep the *g,* letting each one pronounce it in his own way: *jeolojia,* etc., could be better for the ears, but not for the eyes. And the eyes receive the written language before the ears do.

V. Morphology

1. When we say morphology here, it is meant to express the bare form, not the value of the form.

2. In our grammar, the morphology section is separated into two categories: the declension of nouns on the one hand and the conjugation of verbs on the other.

3. About the noun, the distinction they held so dear in their decisions in Bayonne we should also maintain and enforce since it belongs to both sides and was meant to last forever: that the noun has one usage when it is definite and another very different one when it is indefinite. Because that is what the new writers forgot, especially in Gipuzkoa: *zenbait gizon, edozein lekutan, bi mendiren erdian, zein ikaslek, ez du begik ikusi,* and so on certainly.

4. To that end, it is inevitably necessary to know if the *-a* carried at the end of a word is its own or is affixed. And even if there are doubts, they should appear one by one in the appropriate form in a Basque dictionary.

5. The decisions they made in Bayonne about the noun seem fine to me, at least taken as a whole. In my opinion, the most dubious are these: *mendietatik* in the plural, not to mention *-tarik;* in living things, internal *-gan-* would need *baitan* (written independently) next to it (*-gandik,*

baitarik, and so on), both being permitted. Of course, in Bizkaian, *gaz* is totally permissible, instead of the *-rekin* of other regions.

6. In my opinion, we should attempt to save the so-called instrumental case. Thus, moving outside the form, one should explain that *ezpataz jo,* for example, is more clear than *ezpatarekin jo;* similarly, and even more so, the same can be said for *ezpataz jo* and *ezpataz (=ezpataren gainean) mintzatu,* among those for whom that case is alive and well.

7. We must remember and keep in mind that we still have serious problems with pronouns, whether or not the declension of the noun is rather clear. I will mention the demonstratives (*hau, hori, hura* and their derivatives), reminders of the confusion that we have in this matter.

8. Let's go on to the verb. For now, to tell the truth, it does not seem to me that unification is within reach. Even in the mere matter of form, there are too many sides from one to the next: in coming together, many would have to abandon their verb forms, surrender, and bend to the will of another. But I do not say that we must give up. We have much preparatory work that must be achieved beforehand.

   a. Complete paradigms for each dialect (or for the ones I mentioned earlier). We do have them, piecemeal at least, but we must examine them slowly and in great detail.

   b. In those paradigms, let the forms worth choosing always be the ones that exclude the least number of the other dialectal forms: *ditu(z)* not *dauz, gaitu(z)* not *gauz,* on the Bizkaian side, etc. The rare Gipuzkoan use of second person familiar (*natxegok,* etc.) should be completely excluded, of course.

   c. It is not easy to choose between the old and the new, but the old form that has been used in Basque literature for a very long time always deserves close examination. Even giving the new forms their due, we should denounce the recent ugly neologisms (such as our *zetoztene*).

   d. Neither is the verb system the same in all areas, although it is similar. But in these matters we are feeling our way in the dark, as soon as we leave one's own dialect. Attempting to perpetuate some distinctions could be pointless, perhaps, but even so that may not always be the right thing to do. Now that we have beautifully distinguished between *on da* and *on litzake,* for example, why not keep the distinctions between *egin dezake* and *egin lezake (dai(ke) / lei(ke), diro / liro),* my slightly corrupted brothers?

e. When we are using the verb, we find "nominal elements" like *sar, sartu,* and *sartzen* more and more necessary, in addition to verbal elements. The first two are used in places where they are distinguished from each other and that usage survived in old Bizkaian, even though it was not inevitable: *sar bedi, sar diteke, sar dedin, iraul beza, iraul dezake, iraul dezan,* but *sartu da, sartu behar du,* and so on. That is the path of unification, in my opinion, but let those who do not want unification also learn, at least, when they should remove the *-tu* and *-i* endings and when they should leave them where they are. Otherwise, we are heading for confusion, not unification.

9. If we had come to an agreement on other points, no great harm would have come as yet from using more than one form of auxiliary verb. It can be proven that those auxiliary verbs are isomorphs in each dialect, and are also necessary from one dialect to another. We could demonstrate to a computer the manner of passing from *diot* to *nion* quite well, without any great mystery, and likewise show how we got from *deutsat* to *neutsan* and from *diot* to *deutsat.*

VI. Syntax

1. Disputes about stylistics and syntax may enter this head of mine: the value of grammatical forms and the way of using them, word order, sentences, etc. In these things more than any others, it is necessary to stand on simple foundations, without taking any steps forward.

2. It is obvious that we are not speaking Basque—at least, not pure Basque—if we are not using it as we should, whether we are using the forms permitted by unification or not. However, being a living language it cannot and will not always endure in total agreement. Euskaltzaindia's obligation is to conscientiously maintain the old laws, of course, and not surrender unless absolutely necessary. It has superb Basque authors as a model and a healthy foundation, even if time more or less changes opinions about them.

3. There is more than one level in Basque writing. We have had cultivated poetic speech for a very long time and now we also have those who
create it for us. We have more than one path in that category and no one
is forbidden from heading down those new roads. Likewise I would say,
even if there are not as many, where dialog is concerned, it appears more
closely tied to oral speech: theater and novels show us what they are and
what they can be.

4. As most Basque speakers, even if they are not the best, speak and
write like M. Jourdain, and we are used to expressing our opinions,
right or wrong, without discussion, we would like to examine the
essence, the condition, and the mistakes of common Basque prose cultivated "in grammaticalness," but without sticking to the path of simple
"grammaticalness."

5. If you will permit me to mention two different natives of Errenteria,
one might somehow say that Xenpelar knew Basque a lot better than
I do. Xenpelar's way of speaking is so proper, it has no value for me.
Put another way, the prose of western languages is skillful and learned
walking on several paths, next to Latin, of course, without mentioning
anything higher. In the same way, even if not to such a degree, we find
our language.

6. Those excursions have made the language faster, more complex, more
flexible. We Basques do not have any separate culture, except for folk
culture: we are of this century, we live in this area of culture. Therefore,
we have been unable to be independent with regard to language. That
independence was perhaps achieved in the eighth, thirteenth, and sixteenth centuries, but not now, and even less so in the future. We carry on
our foreheads the mark of Latin and the languages from the east. Let's
admit it, let's accept it, and let's move on.

7. Modern prose does not belong to one language or another, but is
rather international—what B. L. Whorf called "standard average European." Neither do most of the Basque writers behave in any other way.
We cannot exclude or disdain the cultivation of the language that we
owe to them, even if we are not always the winners in those encounters.

8. What we consider the "Basque smell" or the "Basque taint" is fine, of course, when we are dealing with Basque subject matter, when we want to make the reader aware of the mountainous atmosphere of the Basque Country. But apart from that, it seems that prose as it needs to be must be the equivalent of clean water: without aroma, color, or flavor. If the Basque taint flows, it flows from within, not from any decorative surface.

9. Word order and selected rules are not chains to bind the writer, but rather tools that will increase his strength by making more evident the hidden power of his words. The writer's duty is easy to explain and hard to carry out: by subjugating himself to the language, he can conquer the language, he can turn the bonds and difficulties of the language's rules into aid and sustenance, like the air beneath the bird's wing.

CHAPTER 12

From Arantzazu to Bergara

"Arantzazutik Bergarara," *Euskera* (Bilbao) 24, 2 (1978): 467–77.

(Bergara, September 4, 1978)

Good afternoon, everyone.

Somehow after ten years I am appearing before you, not voluntarily, but rather because Euskaltzaindia has assigned me to do so. After ten years! And they call that fast, even though that period was long and laborious. Long and laborious on the one hand—on the other hand, it seems that the years have slipped through our hands in an instant.

I do not come proud and boastfully by any means because of what was done ten years ago at Arantzazu. Even less so, then, with current and future humility and modesty. I don't know if what happened there was good or bad, but it was not a troublesome and thunderous assembly, like someone said who speaks with another person's voice.

In my opinion, it did not rise too much above what our inner anger and the gravity of the current confusion requires. Furthermore, we would need those who are fond of peace in the forefront, not in a distant corner, when they have the opportunity to turn into peacekeepers.

Father Villasante has spoken with his usual expertise about the unbreakable ties that Euskaltzaindia has had with the efforts to unify Basque. Those ties arose in the very beginning because those responsible for Basque culture at the time requested that it be so, and later—after years and years—because they could not turn a deaf ear to the noisy or silent call for the need for unification evident among us in any subject, even in that of language.

Nor will I come to speak to you all about the results of Arant-zazu. Tomorrow they will explain those results to us, as we know, or at least a few of those results that they can measure. Those measures may be despicable as well, but if the disdain will have weight, new and better measurements must be done.

And in passing, I would like to add a simple explanation to some-one else's calculation. One thing should be well known, but unfor-tunately and shamefully it is not: that linguists have always been the most rabid enemies of the unification of Basque (and other languages). Not, I might add, just enemies of the attempts to unify here and there, but also of any paths toward unification on principle. That is not sur-prising: most of them prefer, or perhaps it is better to say they used to prefer, wild plants over those cultivated by any hand.

Furthermore, we can look at other people's language with a colder eye than our own. Menendez Pidal would never say about his language what he said in 1921 about ours (and our Basque promoters also men-tioned this speech now and then, strengthening their opinions!): "Let life and death forge themselves providentially in the arcane opera-tion of nature." That is, let death take away what it has marked with blood, without anyone getting their hands dirty.

Apart from this, foreign linguists have a clear-cut reason for not taking part in our matters. For that reason they will walk in the back, not in the front, here or there, bending to the will of others perhaps rather suspiciously. Be that as it may, here is what William H. Jacob-sen Jr. says in the book the Nevadans published in honor of Jon Bilbao, about the Basque forms he uses in his work: "Forms unspecified as to dialect are taken from Villasante, 1972 [*La declinación del vasco liter-ario común*], a reliable and convenient guide to a conservative variety of Basque," using *haran* as an example, instead of Villasante's *ibar*. And Jacobsen being the first, as far as I know, is not the only one.

I return once again to the subject. When I recall Arantzazu and what happened afterward, I am filled with happiness, not sorrow. If I were to say that I have not experienced any kind of sorrow, I would not be lying. Euskaltzaindia made the decision it had to make without direction, one that was not made because of thousands of reasons or excuses (shame, fear of what others would say, the desire to maintain a façade of peace in a place where there was no peace . . .). They made the best decision they could, one that was owed to the Basque Country

for a long time, even if it would hurt all Basques: they set out deliberately and energetically on the path to unification, without leaving
things for later.

This path to unity, however, can have many crossroads. Therefore, I don't know whether we chose the best branch of the road, or
whether the choice was made in the best way. Euskaltzaindia was not
offered a choice anyway, at the time of choosing left or right. If it were
offered, it would have been a few years later.

Unlike ten years ago, it seems that we are at the doorway of some
kind of autonomy. With or without that, Euskara will have some kind
of official status, even if it is of the lowest level, if you will. Then what
happened a long time ago with the *Boletín oficial del País Vasco* must
not happen again (and in truth we know that it has not happened).
Not knowing how, the translation of that text appeared in Gipuzkoan.
I do not say that someone did it poorly. What was done poorly was
something else: according to what I have learned, the government did
not make that decision. Officialdom entered through the back door (in
the *Boletín,* at least), and a push was given to that style of Basque.

It is all well and good that *bertsolaris* respond in an immediate
manner, almost without thinking. But I would wager that they would
inevitably do it this way, even if they did not wish to. Choices relating
to language, then, especially the paths that the authorities are choosing about languages, are not ones that should be made extempore or
impromptu, if the need does not compel it. They must be well thought
out beforehand. And if they are thought out ten years in advance, all
the better. All of this does not shame or dishonor the one who was
able to speak before the critical moment arrived, the one who spoke
earlier, in addition to having thought about it. If anything, it is the
other one who is at fault.

Before continuing, I must make a small note regarding my speech.
I did not come here either to start a war or to explain the plans made
by the session. Certainly I will speak in a lively manner, as I am accustomed to doing, but always on the side of something, not too often
against this or that, according to what happens here among us.

Some say the Arantzazu path (I will call it that for short) had a
bad side; some say that it created anger, and even did serious harm. In
a word, we who started the movement either created unity or we created
a bitter dualism in its place.

I will not deny the strength of that truth. Yes, perhaps, I would deny that the name "dualism" is appropriate for our situation. It's not really a type of dualism, as I called it before, but rather a pluralism. The only abnormality of the point of view is what originally was plurality turned into dualism. If being against the Arantzazu path is enough of a foundation for coming together, then, yes, there are two groups and no more. If we examine the large number who are against it, once again, we will soon see that they are not in agreement among themselves: They are not one, therefore, but many.

Harshness has usually been important in this matter among us, unlike among others (for example, in Catalunya). I will not deny that either, and I myself perhaps am very often harsh, harsher than I need to be. If that is so, forgive me. But that is only telling half the truth. I at least knew what I was starting when I set out with that miserly obligation. It was obvious, whether striking here or there, that a mess would result. The troubles have not been as violent as I thought and feared they would be beforehand. Perhaps I am one of those optimists who always sees the future through rose-colored glasses.

Whether in the homeland or abroad, the one who sets out in search of unification will never derive any benefit from it. He immediately will create bitter and painful separation. The most well-known example of this is what happened with the two popes.

The first two were not enough, and they found themselves with three popes after rescinding the appointments of the first two and choosing a third.

Something similar has happened in most of the places where people desire to give birth to and implement a standard language. Also those who are working for us in Catalunyan (or better, in Catalan) would need to give us some straight and detailed news.

And let us not forget that it is one thing to propose a "unified" language, another thing to spread that "unity," and yet another and final thing to obtain official status by means of the law in a country or region.

In losing, the dialects may be affected, and what's more one will inevitably receive more damage than the others. Yes, that is the way it is, at least from one point of view. But I do not believe that anyone is the enemy of dialects and even less that anyone is seeking the end to dialects.

I would accept their opinions now, even without knowing what they will say or who will speak about it.

On the other hand, dialects are no one's "mother tongue," as Villa-sante has recently shown so beautifully. Somehow, the dialects them-selves are unified by use and custom, when used not as common and everyday language, but in a more elaborate way—not merely, even if it seems the contrary, for elaborate writings and erudite homilies. Xen-pelar was from Errenteria and from the Oiartzun side of Errenteria: in his compositions he used *det, zan,* and *zebillen* instead of the *dut, zen* and *zabillen* used among his friends. Lardizabal from Zaldibia does like-wise when he writes *duen, duten* and *zuen, zuten* instead of writing his household and regional *duan, duen* and *zuan, zuen.* Are the *goiherritar-rak* less valid than the *beterritarrak*? Being less in number, are they per-haps weaker? In those matters, measurements of that type have no merit even if some think otherwise.

In these last ten, fifteen, or twenty years, Basque has become more daring and skillful, but it has also become more clumsy and awkward. The flower of beauty has gone. I recently read something like that. It has lost the authenticity, the tenderness, the sweet aroma of our land. I myself would agree. In any case, however beauty is measured, more than one will perceive beauty in Frege's *Die Grundlagen der Arithmetik* or Faulkner's *The Sound and the Fury.* Of course, not anything like that which can be found in *Garoa.*

Back to our earlier topic. We need a unified Basque (this model or some other) and we need it soon, if we do not want the only language of the offspring of those who used to speak Basque to be a unified foreign language: and unfortunately it would not be just one foreign language, but we would have at least two. Moreover, if Basque is to survive, it must lose also that sweet aroma of the land. How will our land not lose it, in so many places, if what springs from it is not some other stench? Society has also changed on us, how it has changed, and Basque cannot endure as it is if it wants to be that sweet society's language in the future.

At one time, children who would be Basque-speaking learned their Basque in a Basque environment, at home and around the home. But we saw that Basque society's pillars were coming down one by one, and the Basque language was on the path to ruin if it did not obtain some help. And forced by the need, we began trying to teach our children Basque in a Spanish environment, especially by means of the *ikastola.* Amatiño showed us that long ago. Meanwhile, if the school has been the household's enemy—our opinion can be expressed in this way—let us change the school in the future into the counterweight of the Spanish-speaking household, or at least the half-Spanish household.

More and more commonly, Basque speakers are not "spun from the mother's thread, raised from the mother's breast" as Lizardi said (*Itzlauz*, 1934, 85). Basque speakers get there more and more by means of the baby bottle; they are bottle-fed. The ones who are otherwise must give thanks to God. And the ones who know Basque by means of the *ikastola*, primers, and magazines, let them keep their Basque [language] families in their hearts. And the Basque that exists for them will not be the equal of the one that we learned and used in the past.

Someone, taking Gavel as a helper, gave this response to Euskaltzaindia: it [meaning the standardization model] plays out like Spanish. In fact, they say the French Academy never orders anyone to do anything. Cultivated people master the manner of speaking used by the majority and they accept that, without using any force or violence, by needing to correct those who are wrong in their thinking.

But the ones on this side, because they see themselves as rule-givers, do not stop changing this and that to one thing or another. And they say it is obvious that Euskaltzaindia has taken this wrong path blindly, without having in mind the most direct way there.

By way of responding, I will not begin saying that anyone has lied, that the happy custom of courtesy among us has been tilted. I must confess, however, that what I have brought up is not, in my opinion, the truth or even close to the truth, if it deals with Euskaltzaindia's behavior with regard to unification, and that's what it deals with. It is said at Arantzazu, and it has been repeated a hundred times, that no one was planning anything. They gave in to a tendency that appeared in and was strongly provided by Basque literature, *an inclination or direction that we had before us at the time.*

And since trends are a mere flowing and inclination, we attempted to define that trend and make it precise, without going too far.

This is not just gossip—this can be proven, and easily too. Let those who think differently read Aresti's long poem "Maldan behera" from 1959; it does not seem boring to me, but if it seems that way to someone else, with effort he will grasp some of the prize of knowledge without the work. There, as Ibon Sarasola said recently (and Joan San Martin also earlier, it seems, in a passage that I do not have at hand), there it is right there, the complete unified Basque or unification of Arantzazu, period and comma, and the aftermath of Arantzazu, verb and all. What Aresti used there was exactly what Euskaltzaindia accepted later, even though Aresti was against it. And as you can see, there you have the story from nine years before the meeting at Arantzazu.

It has been told again and again how we arrived at that model. But now the Gipuzkoan model of Azkue that we have mentioned over and over, in order to not search further, is of course Gipuzkoan, and lowland Gipuzkoan at heart. Orixe had more talent for enriching the language than for unifying it. At heart, somehow, although tinted on the surface, the childhood habit he brought to the east was always Navarrese. And he pushed Lizardi to the east, especially that Lizardi who left us too soon. The source that *that* Lizardi—in Orixe's shadow—showed us from the very beginning, on the other hand, was not far from the border of Lapurdi. Those of us who began working on Basque after the war, whether older or younger, were for the most part joined together by some unbreakable bonds. Sooner or later we began to realize that if Basque possessed a richness unlike any we believed, much of it would be found in the unknown old authors who were often avoided and quite disdained. Furthermore, being old was not too much of a requirement; it was enough to be from the turn of the last century to be considered old.

Reading the old documents, before long we noticed something that could have been the path to unification, and likewise an opinion. We realized that our old dream of a unified language was more behind us than ahead of us; and if it was not precisely unification, it was at least the seeds and buds of unification.

It seemed clear to us, for example, that words like the *lên* and *zâr* that Azkue and Lizardi used to use, from time to time at least, were nothing more than entry and exit paths for something that could have felt even more terrible to somebody else.

We obviously had a need for unification, and we perceived that the fervent desire for unification was widespread among the people. If the lack of the people's unification brought difference, destruction, disruption, annihilation, and shredding to the language (written and spoken), then unification of the language would be a sign of, and the result of, the unification of us Basques.

We found ourselves in need of unification ten years ago, and there was not a lot of choice. At least the problem that the French call *embarras du choix* did not worry us.

Only one path was offered to us, and behind that single path the strength and impetus of one solid group was clearly perceived. Of course, we did not know how far it could go, but in such matters, and not just in the *pelota* (handball) court, one must wager on the future. But whose side should we wager on—on the side of those who said yes to something, or on the side of those who responded against it?

And what about Azkue's Gipuzkoan model? Was there no candidate there?

I do not think so, and I am telling you the truth. I have always viewed Azkue's plan with great respect. As far as I know, he did not get too specific theoretically, but he wrote a few things in that beautiful style of Basque, things that showed us the main points sufficiently. Let us allow, however, that he left an explanation as detailed and fine as necessary.

Unfortunately, he never had any dynamic strength. The Gipuzkoan model was Azkue himself: Azkue's knowledge, Azkue's name and reputation, and a few students and followers. But in addition to being scarce, his followers were not loyal enough, or if you like, not obedient enough. I would say otherwise. There is not a lot written in complete Gipuzkoan by Azkue's own hand. Yes, of course, he wrote some things that are like Gipuzkoan, and some other dialects when he made additions. But the texts will bear witness that he continues to write in his own way, manner, and style.

Right now there are those who ask for Euskaltzaindia's help on the side of the Gipuzkoan model, while at the same time they need *o(i)lloak, ba(i)ñak, egiñak* and *abillak*. I have in my hands his 1932 *Prontuario fácil para el estudio de la lengua vasca popular* "Easy Rulebook for the Study of the Popular Basque Language" (on the one hand, easy! and on the other, popular Basque language!), and the creator of the *easy* handbook for learning the people's Basque writes, of course, *oilo* and *bainan* and *egina*, always, not just now and then, but next to *bella* for 'bera' (his/her/its) and *ttantto*. What are we doing, then? Why aren't they saying about Azkue the same garbage that they are saying so often about others?

Because the Gipuzkoan that has been and is used the most, this Gipuzkoan model that has almost been forgotten until now, also has its own well-known parents. I will not speak of the fate of unification or the so-called *Batua*, because it is enough just to mention it. I must mention in passing that the work of setting boundaries in unification has not stopped and that now we have the verb also to be discussed (an objective that I considered impossible, almost unthinkably impossible, at Arantzazu). Everyone knows how many books, weeklies, and dailies have been written in that kind of Basque. There are also abundant texts, books for studying and for teaching, and dictionaries, because the educational field has by no means stopped in the last few years.

Now I would like to point out a few things. Let me explain my opinions as clearly as possible. We are all in favor of Basque—that is the primary thing—or at least we should be. We are on the side of the Basque language, and not, first and foremost, against other Basque speakers. A person has a total right to defend his interests, but not by doing so to belittle the main interests of the language.

We know that any attempt at unification will do damage to some dialects, and not because we want to do damage, but rather because there is no other solution. In Azkue's model, it was the Gipuzkoan dialect that benefitted most, as indicated by its name.

We must make the effort, therefore, to minimize what is removed and to calm the resentments created by such removals. It always happens with many available opinions. The majority are reasonable from one point of view, and not so much from another point of view. Must it be so difficult for each one to try to state his case?

Opinions and beliefs about our overall situation vary greatly, at least that's what I hear. Nevertheless, everyone must confess, like it or not, that the current atmosphere is better for Euskara, so much better than at the time of the Arantzazu meeting ten years ago. That seems so pleasing to me, because our language needs an atmosphere of peace and tranquility if it needs anything. In fact if it had to endure a new oppression similar to the last one, it would not survive.

It seems that we will have language matters in our own hands to a certain extent.

That extent will be limited, certainly, but I am not worried about those who want to deny us, who will not give it to us, but rather about those of us who are capable of taking matters into our own hands. In that situation, it will be seen more clearly than the sun what we are and are not capable of. Euskara will need the help of the political powers that be and the unions, especially any help offered in a generous manner: sensible help, help that knows where the language is going and why. And if the one who must give the help is a Spanish speaker, or a Basque speaker who knows only the Basque of the household, it seems to me that we have the right to request something: they must know what the problem is and what it is based on. It doesn't seem too much to ask. Indeed, it seems absolutely necessary, after reading and hearing a few things (I will leave it at "things") that are going around.

It is said that Euskaltzaindia is not trustworthy, in the opinion of some; it does not provide a sufficient level, it is said, in either wisdom or in action. It would not surprise me at all if something like this were to happen: if *euskaltzales* like myself are implicated, because in the end the Academy is made up of academics. Let us accept that this is the way it is. If this is the case, it would correspond to what is expected. Euskaltzaindia is the reflection of our people, even if it is not the cleanest of mirrors, and Euskaltzaindia's level is all of us, and at any level, it is the reflection of what we have at hand. So let's all try to raise our level and in that way perhaps we will also raise the level of Euskaltzaindia, as well.

To tell the truth, even though it may sound arrogant, I believe that Euskaltzaindia deserves a little more confidence from native Basque speakers and native Spanish speakers as well. We are not overly intelligent, but we saw the negative side of some of the decisions we have made, and we have not read too much, but we did have news of some of the texts that they have shown us. We are not overly familiar with what has happened in various foreign countries with regard to unification, but we have learned some things out of necessity. For example, Serbo-Croation (the main language in Yugoslavia, if not legally then de facto) had a mess with the *h*, and as it happens in such matters, the most conservative dialects maintained the *h*. They write it even still in Greece (by means of the so-called *spiritus asper*), even though it was completely lost by Homer's time around two thousand years ago, and in so many dialects.

There are not too many of us, we are not overly dressed with knowledge, but our language comes to us in serious condition, although it is in no danger of dying. If we all come together, each with his own opinion, to examine the language that we say we love, the weak can strengthen the weak. And the weak ones strengthening each other can serve to bolster the stronger ones. Especially if we adopt as our own the desire of the creators of Eusko-Ikaskuntza: "The little one will conquer the big one with wisdom and knowledge."

CHAPTER 13

Standardization of the Written Form of a Language: The Basque Case

"La normalización de la forma escrita de una lengua: el caso vasco," published without notes in *Revista de Occidente*, nos. 10–11 (Special Supplement 2: *El bilingüismo: problemática y realidad*) (1982): 55–75. (Also in Luis Michelena, *Lengua e historia*. Madrid: Paraninfo, 1985, pp. 213–28.)

1. What I intend to do here is lay before you, with its background and consequences, the ongoing attempt to arrive at a standardized and, where desirable, unified model of the Basque language, a model designed above all for written use. I understand very well that this is something that will interest some of you more than others, and also, from another point of view, that it involves facts and circumstances with which some of you are all too familiar. But despite these things, I believe that the question must be of some interest to many, or even most, of those gathered here. If not for other reasons which each of us can imagine without effort, at least because in a field such as ours there are not many occasions in which we have proceeded ahead with an operation, or at least a serious operation—indeed, there surely are those who will say that we are operating *in anima uili*.

Let me stress that I intend this to be, as far as humanly possible, an annotated exposition of facts and events in a process, not a speech by the Ministry of Justice or Defense. In any case, it is only fair that we should shoulder the burden of informing people about the process before expecting them to know things to which they have had no access.

2. There is no need to point out that the Basque language, or *euskara* to give it its proper name, is and was conflictive. Its very longevity, its survival down to the present day, presupposes conflict—and let's not forget how surprising this phenomenon has been, since according to all reasonable expectations, it should have fallen into disuse at the very least over a millennium and a half ago, before Rome's imperial administration became seriously disabled by repeated attacks of hemiplegia. I will quote just one such recent forecast, made by an expert (if ever there was an expert entitled to make such forecasts), since it was formulated by Wilhelm von Humboldt over 150 years ago. His opinion was that by 1900, the only remnant of Basque to be found would be whatever had been set down in writing.

Another matter of conflict, although one that took longer to manifest itself openly, is the question of the *status* that should be accorded the language within Basque society itself, even if we disregard (something more easily done in theory than in practice) the general Spanish-French context in which it survives and which varies from time to time. It is well known that until now Basque has not been the only, or perhaps even the main, vehicle of expression of that society, even in periods when the Basque regions enjoyed broad autonomy. And when I say "until now," I do not mean to exclude the present from this consideration.

3. I needn't remind you that here we are treading on ground that has little to do with immanent linguistics, with the consideration of languages as nonspatial, nontemporal systems whose tenacious or insecure hold in certain human communities is irrelevant. Going to the other extreme, we could ask whether aspects touching on the realm of form can play a role in concrete social problems involving interests and passions, such as the one that I am going to discuss.

And the answer is yes. I believe that purely linguistic factors can have a lot to do with the support and decline of languages. Thus, while many are keen on emphasizing phenomena of affinity as important to the life of languages, instead of paying due attention to family relationships, it is nevertheless evident—and Basque alone would suffice as proof—that family relationships can be a valuable support, just as their nonexistence, or genetic isolation, can be a serious problem. It would be difficult to overestimate what Basque has received from its neighbors; in fact, even the effect of the latter on the former is visible, in the opinion of many, who usually point to the domains of Spanish and Gascon. But loan words of whatever kind cannot dispel the isolation that accompanies Basque, an isolation that makes learning the language a somewhat long, arduous task for people whose mother tongue is a Romance or even Indo-European language. In the case of any two other languages within the Iberian Peninsula or southern France, it would surely be easier to become bilingual.

This weakness is compounded by the fact that, on top of not having genetic relationships, Basque has also been a small language in two senses. For as far back as we can see, to the beginnings of our era, more or less, it has not (or no longer?) occupied a large territory, and the territory that it did occupy could not have been densely populated, according to all indications. What is more, Basque seems always to have been subordinate to other tongues. Take for instance the overwhelming predominance of written works in Latin and Romance, a predominance that lasted for centuries and from which people have often drawn totally mistaken conclusions about which language was spoken most. One of the oldest manifestations of this subordination might even be seen in the well-known abundance, underscored by Gómez-Moreno and others, of non-Latin Indo-European personal names in Alava, found along the Roman road Iter xxxiv and also along the Navarra-Alava border, from Gastiain southward, a finding that contrasts with the lack of Basque (or at least Basque-like) proper names, which in the anthroponymy have only recently been discovered in the eastern region of Navarra (which was considerably Romanized, by the way) and even in Aragon.

4. Since we have touched on the matter, I am going to go further and make some observations on the peculiar characteristics of the use of writing in the Basque domain. We all know how hard it was for the Romance languages, when severing their Latin apron strings, to become individualized and autonomous in written form, if only to leave such modest records as the Oath of Strasbourg, the Emilian Glosses, or *l'Indovinello Veronese* (the Veronese Riddle). There must have been a situation of diglossia between, on the one hand, language forms that were nonwritten almost by definition[1] and that were becoming increasingly differentiated from one region to another in the Romance-speaking world, and, on the other, a written Latin that was reasonably uniform in script and that could largely neutralize, or mask if you will, differences in pronunciation.

"Diglossia" is a term that justifiably enjoys widespread use, and which has certainly been the rage around here in recent years. Of course, like any other word, it can be given whatever content people wish, as long as it does not create confusion. Having said this, I think that the meaning that Ferguson attributed to it in his seminal article of 1959 is worth being preserved, using this term or some other—that is, the levels concerned are not just any two varieties of language, nor are they even varieties linked by some genetic relationship. They are two facets of something which—and this, while difficult to define, is easy to understand for anyone who has experienced the phenomenon—is "felt" to be one and the same language, under different accidents. One of the illustrations put forward by Ferguson and, I believe, the most important one, is the case of Arabic, whose "high" form is called *literal*, in unmistakable allusion to the single written standard that is often able to unite what pronunciation divides, from Morocco to Iraq. However, no matter how fragile the idea of distance between two varieties (mutual intelligibility is largely subjective and can change between a first encounter and after longer contact, and no generally accepted system seems to have been arrived at for quantifying differences), it nevertheless constitutes a reality that helps to explain why, for example, written Romance first took off on its own in northern Gallia rather than in Italy.

Returning now to our subject, in historical times Basque never actually diversified to the point of speciation.[2] Despite the incursions that historical sources attribute to the Vascones in the general direction of Zaragoza throughout the seventh century, and to the north as early as the end of the sixth, they did not leave any permanent linguistic sediment. As for Aquitania, written records fail to clarify what role Basque-speaking people played in such movements and what role can be attributed to Gallo-Romans. In any case, it turns out that the equivalence of Vasconia, Wasconia, Guasconia, or vascones = gascons, whose etymological soundness is readily apparent,[3] not only does not coincide with their respective linguistic domains, but does not correspond even to an equal distribution. While the Vascones (if understood as *euskaldunak*, or people who speak *euskara*) are confined to the narrow limits of what is historically the French Basque Country (and those limits have not changed a dot for as long as we have had sufficient knowledge of that region), the Gascons, who spoke a Romance language no matter how influenced by Basque we wish to imagine it, came out as the indisputable masters of nearly all of what used to be Aquitaine as a result of the well-known tripartite division undertaken by Caesar.

To the southwest, on the other hand, in lands where the chronicles do not tell of tumultuous movements, the Basque language expanded into both the Rioja highlands and into areas of Burgos, in Montes de Oca and La Bureba. As I have noted elsewhere,[4] we are probably not fully entitled to claim, as I have just done, that this was an extension of the Basque domain. This is, however, the most natural hypothesis, as well as being the one that is most commonly accepted. At any rate, in my opinion, that linguistic frontier has little to do with the campaigns of Sancho Garcés I in the Rioja region during the first quarter of the tenth century. The Navarrese could hardly have exported a variety of the language that they didn't use themselves. More comprehensible would be to admit the permeability of the Roman *limes* or border, marked by the cities of Veleia and Pompaelo.[5] That movement, which could very well have been peaceful in large part, could have occurred at least as far back as the sixth century of our era, and perhaps even earlier. It is one of the many secrets guarded by the long, drawn out transition linking the late Dark Ages to the early Middle Ages.

5. While one of the forms of Latin—its highest level—continued almost unaltered (and I am speaking here of words as they are written), the language spoken in everyday use changed and became differentiated from region to region, everywhere distancing itself from standard written Latin. In any event, the continuity of written Latin is much greater in seventh century Visigoth Spain than in the Merovingian Gallia of the sixth century; or, to give names, it is greater in Ildefonso of Toledo than in Gregory of Tours, although a text such as the Mozarabic Chronicle of 754 perhaps allows us to glimpse what underlay the classical surface. In order for the gaps between the levels of Latin to be perceived as they actually were—that is, as unbridgeable—suffice it to say that following the accident of the Carolingian Reform, French remained completely individualized, although still in a permanent osmotic relation with Latin.

When the separation occurred with all its consequences, Latin and Romance did not, and could not, remain on an equal footing. Instead, following the previous (theoretically) unitary phase, there was a stratification which could be represented thus:

Latin

Latin

Romance

where, because Latin is supraordinated, it seems to have the most important functions. This is only the case, however, if we take into account just the written language together with certain special kinds of speech: solemn oratory, academic explanations, language for relations between speakers of different mother tongues, etc.[6]

What happened among us, in the Kingdom of Navarra, was quite different. In certain communities, there were two competing languages that could never, even in people's wildest dreams, be considered as varieties or registers of a single language; besides, one of them had a monopoly on almost all writing done in connection with official affairs, beginning with government and, one could even say, urban life *per se*, while the other was the general vehicle of speech in a society that was still largely organized according to lineages. But with the advent of Romance as an independent entity, which, apart from the clearly Mozarabic vestiges found at least in the vicinity of Tudela, developed to the south and east of present-day Navarra, there appeared a new stratification with a third level:

Latin	*Latin*
Basque	*Romance (Navarrese)*
	Basque

Latin, which had reined practically alone in all matters put down in writing, found itself competing in this with Romance. In the Kingdom of Navarra, this happened no later than in the Kingdom of Castile. Latin still served for "higher" uses, but in everything else it started losing ground to Romance. In speech, it is clear that Latin continued to be a valid international language, backed above all by the apparatus of the Catholic Church.[7]

Obviously, from the time of the Roman Empire, Basque remained intact as long as the society which it served—a society based on lineages—was not destroyed. The language was that society's instrument of communication, and a highly useful instrument indeed, to judge by the tenaciousness with which its users held onto it. Something must have remained of this lineage-organized or tribal society (even though it was almost always overshadowed and hidden by more modern realities and appearances) in the Kingdom of Navarra beyond the ninth century, and in later political entities such as the Seignory of Vizcaya. After all, many vestiges of the old social order were clearly kept alive for a long time, since at least some traces of it have been handed down to our time.

In any case, Basque continued being the vehicle—essentially for speech—of that old way of life, particularly in what Julio Caro Baroja called, appropriating the term from Pliny, the *saltus Vasconum*, or northern mountainous region. In modern times, it failed to take permanent root outside the country, especially in America south of the mouth of the Saint Lawrence River[8] but it did continue to be widely used especially among first-generation Basque emigrants, from Fray Juan de Zumarraga to Sor Juana Inés de la Cruz, for the two of whom it formed a highly appreciated bond.

6. By the tenth to eleventh centuries, when information on Basque begins to be considerable, albeit insufficient,[9] we find the language diversified into different dialects which have continued to become more distant from each other ever since. Some authors, following a line of reasoning that we could call Kretschmerian,[*] have insisted on seeing Vizcayan as contrasting with all the other Basque dialects. These include Lacombe, Gorostiaga, and, in extreme form, Uhlenbeck.[10] It is also true that convergence factors have brought closer (or, to be more precise, have not further distanced) the different Basque dialects, at least in favorable cases such as common innovations in the handling of voiced (understood as *sonorant*) phonemes, or the handling of the endings of first members in word composition or derivation processes. But the Vizcayan of the sixteenth century was much closer to the Lapurdian of that time than the two dialects are today. Moreover, there is no sustainable reason for interpolating, rather than inverting the direction of the process in a prehistoric period when, in any case, we should be looking much further back than the first or second century of our era.

Are Vizcayan and the other dialects so different from each other? The answer depends on point of view—of the one who is asking, the one who is answering, or of both. I am reminded of what Tovar, *El euskera y sus parientes* (Madrid, 1959) p. 174, says about Vizcayan: "It is a very distinct dialect, but not actually independent. It forms part of the com-

---

[*] Ed. Note: Ernst Kretschmer (1888–1964), a German psychiatrist, author and professor at Marburg and Tübingen, established the idea of constitutional body types based on two essential types of temperament.

mon Basque heritage; it is a treasure chest of linguistic heirlooms, like all the other dialects, but it does not allow us, using the reconstruction based on it, to go back very far." In other words, for a comparativist, there is only one witness, albeit one that gives different testimonies that slightly contradict each other. And the point of view of the comparativist—or of the reconstructor, if we can call him that—while partial and limited, is nevertheless legitimate within its own domain. This is confirmed by Hans Vogt, *BSL* 51 (1955), 260, who has not generally tended towards historicism:

> *L'unité primitive des parlers basques ne fait aucun doute. La structure phonétique et morphologique est sensiblement la même partout, et derrière la mass énorme d'emprunts, surtout romans* [which in large measure constitute innovations that are common to all varieties of Basque], *on entrevoit un vocabulaire basque assez homogène. Le basque commun—l'origine commune des parlers actuels—ne doit être très différent de ce que ces parlers sont de nos jours.*

7. But (let us hasten to recognize) the position taken by the language comparativist or historian represents only one of several possible points of view, and perhaps not the most important one. Forgetting for the moment the distance that separates near or distant varieties and the difficulties they pose for intercommunication, etc., we are going to present a distinction introduced by Louis-Lucien Bonaparte throughout his work on dialectology and later used by Arturo Campion, a distinction that no one working on these issues has ever tried to refute.

According to the Prince (who, no doubt because of his horror of general issues, qualifies but does not define or specify his qualifications), Basque dialects, varieties, and speech forms should first be subjected to classification before moving on to any other consideration: there are, on the one hand, literary dialects (Vizcayan, Guipuzcoan, Lapurdian, and Souletin, according to Campión who, although from Navarra, did not include in his list any of the Navarrese dialects from either side of the border) and, on the other, nonliterary dialects. This would seem to prefigure the official custom of Soviet linguistics (or official Soviet custom, period), which characterizes such and such a language as *bespís'mennyj jazyk*—that is, as unwritten.

Bonaparte had a perfect understanding of how Basque literature had evolved and how this had led to the situation that existed in his time.

But here it is true that to a large extent he had to make decisions, rather than remaining in the role of an objective, preferenceless observer, as he probably should have. To give a simplified example, there were in his time two Vizcayan and two Guipuzcoan literary dialects which we could call (after the people who used them) Moguel-Añibarro and Lardizabal-Aguirre, each with a territorial base not necessarily coinciding—particularly in the case of Lardizabal—with the place where the writer grew up. The prince and his collaborators, acting as legislators on standards, gave to Moguel and Lardizabal a precedence that has weighed on Basque letters ever since.

There were, therefore, dialectal standards, standard varieties with dialectal overtones, that were imposed on writers whenever they wanted to rise a little above the level of everyday speech. This could happen simply if they wanted to write within a sphere not strictly confined to family or friends (and even so), or also when a *bersolari*[*] abandoned prose to speak in verse and song. This is something that apparently escapes the comprehension of today's all-out defenders of what they call *amaren hizkuntza*, which could be translated as "mother tongue" were it not for the fact that its advocates take it in the literal sense of "speech that the child learns from his mother's lips." It doesn't occur to them that the dialects designated as literary by Bonaparte represent standardized, and therefore uniform, language varieties—standardized and uniform perhaps more in intention than in reality, but this is not as important as it might seem. In questions of this kind, what matters most of all is the desire to lay down general guidelines.

8. As has been explained, Basque took a long time in becoming a written language. In the field of prose, the motivation was first and foremost religious, as occurred with so many European and non-European languages: Protestant with Leizarraga and Juana de Albret, Catholic after Trent. Special mention should be made, because for the first time it went further than the individual essay, of the "Lapurdian school" headed by Pedro de Axular, which was founded and flourished in the seventeenth century, in the area of Saint-Jean-de-Luz–Ciboure and Sara.[11] These

---

[*] Ed. Note: Poet who sings improvised verse in public. For more details, see Gorka Aulestia, 1995. *Improvisational Poetry from the Basque Country*. Foreword by William Douglass; trans. by Lisa Corcostegui and Linda White. ISBN: 0-87417-201-2., and Jose Mallea (in press). *Basque Poetry in the American West: Bertsolariak*. University of Nevada Press.

works, although almost always religious in nature, were written (the ones in prose, at least) for a secular public containing many who knew how to read and who enjoyed exercising this knowledge. This public, made up mostly of town and city dwellers, undoubtedly existed thanks to the prosperity created by cod and whale fishing in what was known as Terranova (Ternua), centered in the Saint Lawrence estuary, and the trade (mostly with Bilbao and San Sebastián) that this generated. To a certain extent, this religious prose can be said to have served as a model, but a model that became increasingly distant and less operative (for example, it influenced Larramendi and Guipuzcoan and Navarrese authors of his day), so that by the time Etcheberri the doctor decided to have it implemented as the official standard, the goal though feasible a hundred years earlier could no longer be accomplished.[12]

Etcheberri was furthermore one of the earliest, if not actually the first, person to try to have Basque become the vehicle of education. To be more precise, he wrote in Basque so that the language could become the means for studying Latin, which students needed to master in order to go on to higher education.[13] Later there were others, such as Iturriaga in the last century, who worked for the same ends, but until very recently, Basque served only as an indispensable aid for students who still knew very little Romance (we needn't recall that the art of writing correctly in Castilian was, for two centuries at least, our house specialty). However, religious education was, more and more systematically, conducted in the language of the country [Basque], and while not the direct objective of this policy, it did enable many or all to gain a certain familiarity, in writing or in speech, with different forms of the language that were supposedly higher than the Basque used in common, everyday interactions.

In more recent times (taking 1877 as a representative year in this regard), there was an increase in written output in that language, accompanied by an inevitable, but for a long time modest, secularization. This resulted in greater breadth and variety of the genres cultivated and more ambitious works, producing in the best cases not disdainable achievements. However, it would be erroneous to suppose that there was parallel progress on the issue of standardizing the written language. Quite the contrary: since the arrival of something new rendered whatever had gone before as old-fashioned, respect for the old standards (which were becoming less and less familiar, as well as less and less current) declined to the point[14] that there was no longer a standard in effect outside of each community or group. Nicolás de Ormaechea, "Orixe," who spearheaded the most active minority, was in fact a master of the language, an archaist and innovator, greatly enamored of local color and at the same time introducer of influences from the most diverse places in space and in time, but also an anarchist who modeled language according to his personal taste. He always defended the author's freedom to break all rules, except, curiously enough, as regards the order of words in a sentence.

In the French Basque Country, the area where the once classical Lapurdian had naturally remained most permanent, a break with the past occurred, particularly as of the Liberation. Considerations of demography and also of territorial extension contributed to the fact that in order to serve a larger public, the small area of Lapurdi, whose culture had become more diluted because of tourism, was marginalized on behalf of a Navarrese, or Lapurdian Navarrese, the new written Koiné, which gradually displaced the previous one. The main codifier of this triumphant trend was Pierre Lafitte with his excellent *Grammaire basque (Navarro-labourdin littéraire)*, re-edited several times since 1961.

9. At the I Congreso de Estudios Vascos (First Basque Studies Congress) (Oñate, 1918), steps were taken to create an Academy of the Basque Language, whose most urgent task would be to set clear guidelines on the problem of unifying the language,[15] a problem that was addressed amply and without reservations in a talk delivered by Luis de Eleizalde, who became one of the academy's founding members. In line with expectations, once the newly created academy had completed its membership, it proceeded to call for preliminary reports, etc., in order to have arguments on which to base necessary decisions. But decisions were not forthcoming, except on details of lesser importance, and reasons exist to account for this inhibition. Not everyone was in favor of adopting rule-setting resolutions; instead many, perhaps even the majority, seemed to think that the best and, of course, most convenient thing would be to let nature take its course. Moreover, the criteria by virtue of which one variety of Basque could or should be preferred and others ignored were not at all clear in the minds of those concerned, even though Eleizalde had already listed the ones that should be taken into account—albeit without evaluating them comparatively. Furthermore, as a general principle, no region or dialect could ever, in the opinion of its people, relinquish its rightful place more or less at the top, and besides, the border on the Bidasoa River marked a limit that could not be trespassed. That is, everybody preferred to live in accordance with routines (none of which were very

traditional, by the way), without taking into consideration the practices of others, which almost always merited an unfavorable opinion.

A specific project did exist, however, which was amply exemplified, although never set down systematically so that it could be taught and made known. This was the dialect known as *gipuzkera osotua* or "Completed" Guipuzcoan (completed, naturally, with the help of items taken from other varieties of Basque) and championed by Azkue, president, until his death, of the academy. To study this dialect, one should not read the theoretical and asystematic *Guipuzkera osotua*, 1934, but Azkue's *Prontuario fácil para el estudio de la lengua vasca popular* (Bilbao, 1917; 2nd ed., Bilbao, 1932), or the novel, complete with translation, entitled *Ardi galdua* (Bilbao, 1918).

I will describe or comment on Azkue's plan only in passing. Apart from controversial features which are always inevitable in a personal work, and more so when the subject is such a thorny one, Azkue's project seems today to be, in principle, a quite reasonable attempt that offered, at the very least, a basis for discussion. The fact that it was hardly discussed at all was because the support that should have been forthcoming—support which, in the first instance, should have been political, more than social—could not be found anywhere. Azkue, the man who presided over the academy with such a firm hand, failed to put pressure on the institution or even on individuals, no doubt for fear of creating an irreparable schism within. Perhaps he had the hope that one day his idea would find a more favorable climate, but if that was the case, he was sadly mistaken.

10. It is not necessary, I believe, to talk about the post-Civil War years in Spain, or the additional effects of the occupation of France and what came afterwards. When Basque began again to emerge, first in America and later among us (earlier on one side of the border than on the other), many apparently immovable things had changed. The new writers, most of whom were the youngest of the old generation, were followers of trends in vogue immediately preceding the war. Naturally, however, particularly following such a brutal convulsion, they also contributed innovations. New, increasingly manifest trends that were highly critical of events and ideas of the past curiously ushered in a strong traditionalist current that harked back to far-off times in matters of vocabulary, grammar, and even style.

Azkue's model, as noted above, failed to prosper among writers, except for a few details forming part of the (quasi) Guipuzcoan that many of them used, but which, of course, was not the only dialect employed in writing. And what was not found in the immediate past, which among the "new" writers was looked on with disapproval (occasionally merited and also satisfying, since there is nothing better than to have a scapegoat on which to blame all past, present, and even future errors), was sought elsewhere: in northern authors (there were none around here worth reading) from the sixteenth to seventeenth centuries. What in America is or was called *el grito* "rallying cry" was sounded by Federico Krutwig in Bilbao and also, although a "lone navigator," by the Souletin Jon Mirande from Paris. Both men had, although not in the same sense, very broad, linguistic knowledge that was exceptional for nonspecialists, and particularly so for nonspecialists among us.

The term "classical Lapurdian" is used with approval by all those who follow this current, but the same unanimity is not true regarding the meaning of the term. In Krutwig's opinion, it was generally the language of Leizarraga (1571), which even then was deliberately archaic-sounding, except insofar as vocabulary was concerned. Krutwig followed Leizarraga in this, except that in addition, as more of a *culterano* than *cultista* [*culterano* = follower of a sixteenth century literary movement; cultista = learned], he wanted loan words to have the original form that they had in their source, generally the classical languages, and not the Latinized version which the Calvinist translator [Leizarraga] always preferred. By contrast, Father Villasante thought that the common language had to be faithful to its label (and Mirande probably shared this opinion), which takes us back only as far as Axular and the seventeenth century in Lapurdi, to a type of language that is much more accessible to readers of today. These were not, however, the only trends present in the general drive for renewal. Under the same banner, there were even extremely populist attempts to use in writing a kind of *dimotiki* [standardized form of Demotic Greek], a style close to urban speech with all the "impurities" that the scrupulous would find in it—a trend that is not at all dead at the present moment. But today the climate is not really conducive to analysis and criticism.

The movement has had a rich history, bearing in mind the favorable and adverse reactions that it aroused. Positions were taken by individuals and groups of people, some of whom belonged to this cultural field and also some who did not, but who spoke for certain states of opinion. Finally, in 1968, a half century after being founded primarily for this objective, the Academy of the Basque Language considered that the moment had finally arrived to publish its criteria. To this end it organized public meetings in Aránzazu, where a number of papers and communiqués were delivered and discussed. At the end of the meetings, the academy itself adopted a set of resolutions which, though quite moderate in their literal wording, nevertheless opened up a well-marked path as far as fundamentals were concerned.

A basic question was the setting of criteria that would make it possible to choose between variants of what, not only for historical reasons, is considered the same word—e.g. *eihar, ihar, igar, iar, ear, exar,* forms which, even at the beginning, did not all have equal weight for "dry, stiff, rigid." In any case, it may be instructive to note that spelling conventions, which are so decisive because they determine the visual aspect of the language—since, as the academy stressed, it was the written language above all that was at issue—took the lion's share, both then and in the fierce discussions that ensued. What was arrived at there is a kind of Navarrese-Guipuzcoan (from Beterri, the area closest to San Sebastián), with Lapurdian-sounding touches, including—and this was more than just a touch—the partly obligatory use of the letter *h.* This point, as if there were no others that were equally or more debatable, and certainly more important, became, as I believe everyone knows, the *shibboleth* of the reform.

In short, we arrived at a writing system which, with a few small modifications introduced over the past ten years, could be deemed somewhat archaic. It is not, however, a historical script except insofar as it turns out that way in the end. More than anything, it tends, without too much violence, to meld into the uniformity of writing the diversity of speech. And this was exactly the path followed by Azkue in his "Completed Guipuzcoan," a circumstance which the adversaries of our so-called *Batua* overlook in silence, either knowingly or out of ignorance. To speak like Schane, therefore, we could say that there is an inventory of segments and their distribution, but that the rules still have to be written.

11. To be fair, we should say that the Basque proposed by Azkue represents a more western, more Guipuzcoan variety, although always from Beterri. The simple fact that he did not allow the letter *h* shows that this is so. Nevertheless, what time and constant work have added to the outline sketched at Aránzazu is fast closing this gap.

Noun morphology, in contrast to that of verbs, posed no real difficulties, and indeed conformity had been reached prior to the Aránzazu
meetings on the points of dispute. But on the matter of verbs, and particularly the auxiliary verb, which is so essential to the functioning of the
language, only one option appeared possible: selection and exclusions.
There was no other way to achieve agreement among those present.

And that is what was finally done. Following long discussions within
a commission, the assembly finally adopted a Navarrese-Guipuzcoan
auxiliary verb which is (or was), in part, also used in common Basque.
In other words, what is specific to the eastern system, particularly to
Lapurdian, was disregarded, along with, especially, what is characteristic of the western dialect, better known as Vizcayan.

Undeniably, and this is the most painful aspect of the initiative,
the latter dialect came out of these transactions as the greatest loser.
Although it is not as individualized as some have claimed, Vizcayan is
marginal, and the only factor that could have neutralized this eccentric
situation (that is, a Basque-speaking Bilbao) did not exist. The Basque-
speaking roots of Bilbao, which are not so remote, are undeniable. But
the Bilbao of industrial expansion and economic boom is no longer
euskaldun to a sufficient extent. And it is not a question of making fun of
that *tertium quid* spoken by the people of Bilbao and which the Vizcayan
Juan Antonio Moguel characterized in 1800 with this expression: *Ené,
ara toroa plazaan manzania jaaten.*

12. Sometimes, and usually always, appearances can be deceiving, but
I feel fairly safe in saying that the (often quite furious) battles that took
place after the declaration of Aránzazu are now mostly a thing of the
past. Since the issue is a language form designed primarily for writing,
people's eyes decide; and from what one sees (and even from a lot of
what one hears), the new standard has clearly prevailed, with no possible competitors, in the most vigorous part of the country. Even so, *a
posteriori* we might want to ask about the reasons for this choice and for
the apparent success of *Batua.*

    a. The desire for renewal, the drive which, without exaggeration,
       could be called revolutionary, is explained by the breakup of the
       old bases of life in the Basque-speaking community, and even
       in a good part of the Basque community without distinction of
       language. To simplify, let us just say that the traditional Basque
       household and farming in general went into a decline which,

judging by what we see today, seems irreversible. So, with the disappearance of these Basque refuges, new ones had to be found if the language was to survive. To this must be added the fact that, almost overnight, the foundations of the Catholic community were seriously damaged, not the least because of the mass defection of the clergy (aspirants and members) that ensued following an unwise proliferation of erstwhile vocations. Old-style Catholicism was, among us as elsewhere, a preserver of linguistic values. The rejection of Latin, moreover, occurred at a time and in circumstances that could hardly favor Basque.

b. Whereas transmission of the language had formerly occurred within the natural setting of the home and the local community, with all the drawbacks that this could entail, the new changes in social bases meant that the *locus* of transmission had to be transferred to the Basque schools known as *ikastolas* and to schools in general for children and students of all ages. Among the new generations, which have mostly learned or perfected Basque in this way, there is no longer that respect for tradition where one goes overboard in cherishing the trifles characteristic of the group in which one was born and brought up.

c. The Basque speakers known as *euskaldun berriak*, or persons who have learned Basque as (at least) a second language, are playing an increasingly important role in Basque society, and very especially in the fields where the language is most used. Far from considering themselves inferior in this area to native speakers, they consider themselves superior, if I may put it that way, because in contrast to the latter, they have what is usually called a grammatical knowledge of the language and also the custom of expressing themselves in Basque on subjects far removed from everyday affairs, comparable in principle to the proficiency of people educated in another language, whereas many *euskaldun zaharrak*, or native Basque speakers, are (almost) illiterate in their language.

d. In well-informed circles at any rate, even before the Spanish Civil War, there was the conviction that the literature prior to the purist renewal was more worthy of imitation than condemnation, as far as language and style were concerned. This conviction soon began to predominate, causing more than one, as noted above, to consider Axular as the master par excellence of Basque prose.

Curiously enough, this movement, which could only be based on a better knowledge of our classics, was helped in good measure by, for example, Manuel de Lecuona with his publication of *Gero*, and Father Justo Mocoroa, who in 1935 considered the Navarrese author [Axular] to be a paradigm of deep-rooted, functional language.

e. The growing tendency to avoid localisms and provincialisms, to try to understand and use Basque as a symbol of unity, free as far as possible of regional idiosyncrasies, made many people feel that something that was called, or could be taken as, e.g., Guipuzcoan, could not be adopted as a standard for the language. By contrast, Lapurdian, the quality of whose literature made it recommendable, was paradoxically favored precisely because it was weak and did not inspire fear in those who sought hegemony. Even the controversial letter *h* became what someone called a touch of distinction, besides being seen as a symbol of an ancient common core.

f. But the decisive reason, as is almost always the case, was utilitarian. With the spread of education in Basque (precisely during the years that were least propitious) and the increase in Basque publications, etc., people couldn't help but see that a normalized, reasonably unified standard was not only advisable, but essential. Now that Basque is being used as a vehicle at other levels of education and is present in government agencies and dealings with the public, *Batua* has become official *de facto*, a situation which would now be very hard to reverse.

13. Having said all this, I do not wish to leave anyone with the impression that the new standard (which now is no longer so new) is practically stabilized. On the contrary, and even at the level of written Basque to which I have confined myself here, there is still much to be done. Indeed, a choice will have to be made among rival currents, which in fact are more divergent than contrary. Dialect knowledge must have a place in education, if only to make transitions possible, with more emphasis in some regions than in others. As for literature per se—to be on the safe side, ever since Aránzazu we have referred to [a standard for] written, not literary Basque—this might be where a certain rigidity is noted and has yet to be overcome, at least in some genres.

Unification, understood in the broad sense, is, in my opinion, a necessary condition for survival of the language in today's world, but neither I nor anyone else feels that it is sufficient. The life of a small, exceedingly isolated language which, on top of everything else, is spoken by a population which partly knows it and partly does not, poses delicate problems. Nothing can be achieved without enthusiasm and effort, but nothing can replace prudence and precaution. In theory, and perhaps also in reality, the key would seem to be to find a *locus*, a niche or spot into which it could fit. Failing to limit ambitions would almost certainly be counterproductive. And we should add in conclusion that there is no reason why a member of any other language community should feel any sort of threat. To speak of danger in the circumstances in which we find ourselves sounds simply like a very poor joke.

CHAPTER 14

Common Language and Basque Dialects

"Lengua común y dialectos vascos," in *Palabras y textos*. Bilbao: Universidad del País Vasco/Euskal Herriko Unibertsitatea, 1987, pp. 35–58. (Originally from *ASJU* 15 (1981): 291–313.)

1. These considerations will not deal at all with the space that Basque dialects can or should occupy from today on, forced to compete with a normalized form of the language, under rather unequal conditions. Such a situation, in which the advantages and disadvantages do not lie in the same part, is not so new among us as it might seem at first glance, since local and regional variations have had to compete for centuries with the so-called literary dialects of the Basque language, dialects that, on the other hand, neither appeared nor had validity all at the same time. The determination "literary" is correct as long as we understand it as a synonym for "written," as Bonaparte used it, since it deals with fixed standard forms, or those that wanted to be fixed, for written usage. Also, "literary" is undoubtedly correct for certain oral uses, but for those that have a character that is more derived than primitive in relation to the written language.

These considerations will not be prospective, then, but rather retrospective. They will not deal with the present and future of the varieties of Basque language, but rather with its past, in an attempt to approximate its origin, in the sense of linguistic history, or better still, just plain history. In fact, it is at this point where one has fallen or frequently falls into error because of the mirage that makes us accept as an absolute principle that which is no more than a point or segment of the continuity of the narration that, only for subjective reasons born in general of the radical limitation of our knowledge, we are accustomed to considering distinguished by its special importance. For this I refer to Jean Haudry, "Une illusion de la reconstruction," *Bulletin de la Societé Linguistique de Paris* 74 (1979), 175–89.

In every process that develops over time, be it physical or social, a situation is no more than the continuation and development of the previous situation: also here *omnis cellula e cellula*, according to Virchow, or in other words, every state of language proceeds from a previous state. If we take a situation (a state of language) as the initial one, this only happens for reasons of convenience and comfort, if not for sad necessity, since the tale will always have to begin—if not *ab ouo*, then at least from a state of things that has been chosen in order to make a fixed point in the ocean of universal transformation. In the case of the Basque dialects, the last horizon is determined by the available documentation. It is not necessary to underline that this documentation by nature is variable, since new data may appear or since one may learn to utilize other data that have not yet been taken into account. In any case, this final horizon is unexpectedly nearby in comparison with so many other languages or language families, in which it is possible to go back much farther. But there are always barriers—near or far, stable or fluid—that cut short our efforts to go farther into the past.

2. I cannot deny the speculative character of what follows. I have never felt enthusiasm for penetrating territories as blindingly bright as they are slippery with pure possibilities, but perhaps it is also fitting in this case, as in others, to make an exception to the rule. This, moreover, in our case is certainly a profitable expedient, as I have learned over long years of professional activity. If someone, qualified or no, expresses an opinion either among us or about us, no matter how crazy it may seem, regarding genetic relatives of the Basque language (which is nothing more than another way of referring to its point of departure, or in a certain sense of the word, its origin), such an opinion will be unfailingly collected—with approval if it supports in some way the ideas of the transcriber, but in any case collected—by prehistorians and historians of antiquity. Quite the contrary, the Pyrrhonian posture that I have always attempted to maintain does not seem to awaken interest. No one bothers to collect reasons from someone who declares himself an agnostic or nonbeliever.

I am convinced that this practice is irrational and that, furthermore, it goes against the spirit of the era, against the vice of believing that which is unknown and may perhaps continue to be unknown to the end of time as if it were a demonstrated truth. It goes against affirming and negating emphatically what one does not know, the incredulous, which limits one to pointing out the insufficiency or the fallacy of the reasoning of the dogmatics.

I must add that I remain firm in my disbelief in the face of my most vivid desires and my deepest inclinations. I think simply that no one has proven any genetic relationship of our language with any other so far: I caution, in case it is necessary, that I am speaking of the genetic relationship in the sense of Indo-European linguistics, Uralic, Hamito-Semitic (Afro-Asiatic, Lisramic, or whatever), etc. I fear, on the other hand, and here I'm dealing with the affective coloration of my belief, that there is little hope that this situation will change in the near future.

3. We all know, both outsiders and insiders, given that we are dealing with widespread news, that the Basque language is not unitary. "Unitary" does not mean exactly that it is not "one"—assuming that preaching this about a language might have some meaning. It means that it has not had a variety that, being the standard, would serve as a point of reference for certain uses of the language. Much to the contrary, it has been and it is divided into dialects and different ways of speaking, some literary and others not, according to the terminology of Prince Bonaparte.

This in itself is not extraordinary, since there has never existed a unitary language in this world. All those we are familiar with have geographic dialects, some can have caste variations, and in all of them there are differences of register or level, to say nothing of the differences that can be noted between the states of the same language separated by decades or centuries. What is unique in our case could be described as a conjunction of two circumstances. The motley diversification, first of all, that is evident in a country of such reduced area, as Leiçarraga wrote, *batbederac daqui heuscal herrian quasi etche batetic bercera-ere minçatzeco maneràn cer differentiá eta diuersitatea den* ("everyone knows in the Basque Country what diversity and difference there is in manner of speaking from one house to another"). And in the second place, the fact is that a normalized or standard language, whatever you want to call it, did not exist, with respect to which the dialectal diversity could have been defined.

Thus, as Coseriu says—and what is moreover evident—while "language" is an absolute term that is self-defined (the Basque language, or Turkish language, etc.) without referring to anything exterior to the language itself, "dialect" is always relative to something. "Language" is a "noun" or functions as one: something is a noun or it isn't, and at most, within a framework such as the theory of *fuzzy sets*, it can be more or less a noun. But "subject" is nothing but the reference to another thing, to a transcendent framework: it is always "subject of." In the ineffable French phrase, *Paul bat Pierre* ("Paul hits Peter"), always at the disposal of people with little imgination, Paul is a subject and a proper name, but although it continues to be a proper name in *Pierre bat Paul* (Peter hits Paul), it is no longer the subject but rather the object.

Now then, "dialect," like "subject" and unlike "language," is always by necessity a "dialect of" with an inevitable reference to another term that the majority of us consider dyadic, in addition to asymetric, but possibly transitive. And "dialect of" can only be "dialect of a language."

This requires a somewhat more attentive consideration. There are Italian dialects just as there are Basque dialects, but there is also an Italian language invested with authority alongside and on top of them, although it seems more than doubtful that the Italian dialects are, in the historical sense of the word, varieties of that supradialectal Italian of a more or less Tuscan base. On the other hand, if one begins by establishing that Sardinian, or more precisely the Sardinian dialects, occupy a position *a se*, close but distinct from Italian, without large concessions to the arbitrariness of conventionalism, one can ill decide where the dialects begin and where they end, dialects that in a strict sense must be called Italian.

According to all evidence, our case is analogous to that of Greek prior to the Hellenist era, more so than the Italian case, and this is not merely a desire to seek out a high-toned relationship: there is Dorian and Dorian dialects, with *Doris mitior* and *seuerior*, there is Arcadian-Cypriot, Ionic-Attican, whatever you want, but there did not exist a Greek language par excellence that assumed and eliminated these particularities, surrounding us in a superior synthesis. And it's not that there was a lack of rules of usage for writing, including literary purposes, before Alexander. There was an epic dialect, Homeric by its model, which was already a conflation of elements of quite diverse origin. In the choruses of the Attican tragedy they did not use the same Greek as in the *stichomythia*, and so on. And as is well known, such varieties associated with literary genres continued to live along with the *koiné*. This "common dialect" had its own dialectal base, since it was not going to spring full grown from someone's head, like Athena, with weapons and everything. The traditional dialects existed alongside it, more and more indistinct and apart from the light of writing, until the *koiné* supplanted them almost entirely. With regard to its origin and current situation, we could say as much about common Italian and the Italian dialects, although these have not disappeared (not yet, some would say) in the presence of common Italian.

Neither have rules been lacking in our case, no matter how much less illustrious it is than the Greek, but rather there has been an abundance of them. None of them has succeeded in imposing itself in totality over the majority of the country, although each and every one has extended itself outside the limits that would have been considered natural. Also, in classical Greece more than a few isolated remnants of western *koiné* were found, which did not have the luck of the *koiné*. And following with a Hellenic parallel, the literary advantage in the Greek style of our dialectal diversity, such as Orixe proposed at the beginning of his career, does not seem possible, or at least things did not go that way in the end. On the contrary—and to my understanding we are lucky that there exists an outline of common language for written usage as the first step toward normalization in certain usages of the spoken language, and that is what has come down to us today. What is being built on this foundation will serve as a point of reference for the multiplicity of dialects and varieties, the knowledge of which (and not free invention) will have to nourish the common language in its development and education. The suggestion of lifting a new country above its traditional roots (*azal orizta, muin beti-rakoa,* in Lizardi's words) will not succumb by impotence in the face of cruel battles between interior and exterior enemies.

4. I cannot begin to discuss here how divergent the distinct Basque dialects are. I will say only that a scientific consideration of this and other similar problems demands some operative procedure for quantifying linguistic distances, and I will refer to the proposal of our friend who died before his time, Jean Séguy, to whom M. J. Azurmendi makes reference in *Euskal linguistika eta literatura: bide berriak,* University of Deusto, 1981, especially pages 233 and following.

Lacking some manner of measurement, one must refer to estimations of order of magnitude, at a rough guess. Thus it is possible that those differences seem very large to the ordinary speaker who is only initiated in the Basque of his local or regional circle, but for a comparativist, and this is the point of view we must adopt here, the divergences are desperately small.

In accordance with the classical opinon defended in this exposition, the dialects of any language proceed from the differentiation of a common language. This, according to all evidence, was not unitary nor could it be, but the margin for variation within it was less than that shown among the dialects that formed later, in such a way that they were acquiring autonomy. This manner of looking at things, by the way, is the one adopted by those in the know when they speak with spontaneity and without fear of incurring heresy in their own eyes and in the eyes of others.

However, through opposition to the premises and results (none completely satisfactory) of classical comparative and historical linguistics, there has arisen the propensity to defend paradoxes that, to me at least, seem more specious than useful. Suffice it to record the article in which Trubeckoj tried to define the Indo-European family by means of structural characteristics, attempting to reduce what is no more than genetic classification to typological classification, although this relationship usually carries with it *et pour cause* typological consequences. Another type of reductionism (Ernst Lewy and his followers, V. Pisani of *Geolinguistica e indeuropeo,* etc.) tends to dissolve the genetic relationship (that is, the bare relationship) into affinity, conditioned by neighbor and contact relations.

Within the same order of ideas, anyone could think, and has at one time or another, that the dialects of ancient Greek tended to be more and more divergent, after a relatively unitary prehistoric past, which does not mean ignoring the importance played by acts of convergence, always inevitable among close varieties and moreso when these varieties are contiguous. But we need only record the *Einleitung in die Geschichte der griechischen Sprache,* 1898, with which P. Kretschmer won undying glory at the cost of replacing the points of view that seem obvious and peacefully following events through other more elaborate points of view, or as we say now, more sophisticated ones. The tendency to value the undeniable importance of the convergence phenomena has been very general in post-Marrist Soviet linguistics, and it manifests with evidence immediately following the thaw brought on by the Stalin-Chikobava intervention.

5. With regard to our dialects, I have always agreed in principle with the opinion expressed by Hans Vogt, who has nothing of the extreme comparativist in him, in *BSL* 51 (1955), 260: *"L'unité primitive des parlers*

basque ne fait aucun doute. La structure phonétique et morphologique est sensiblement la même partout, et derrière la masse énorme d'emprunts, surout romans, on entrevoit un vocabulaire basque assez homogène. Le Basque commun—l'origine commune des parlers actuels—ne doit pas être très différent de ce que ces parlers sont de nos jours." Or in other words, to summarize in light of what follows, in Vogt's judgment the Basque dialects even in our days are little differentiated, and the coincidence in their underlying structures (phonolgy, morphology, vocabulary) are owed to the fact that they originate in common from a proto-Basque, the most important characteristics of which we can almost count on our fingers.

A very different point of view is the one expressed by Georges Lacombe in the 2nd edition of *Les langues du monde*, p. 260, an opinion that coincides with the one expressed on various occasions by Juan Gorostiaga. Both men begin with the idea that fundamentally, contrary to appearances, there are no more than two Basque dialects: Bizkaian or the western dialect, on the one hand, and the rest of the varieties on the other, to which the first is uniformly opposed. *"Nous justifierion ce classement,"* says Lacomb, *"par la considération suivante: on passe par gradations insensibles d'un dialecte à l'autre parmi ceux qui consituent ce groupe, tandis que le saut est assez brusque quand on passe du guipuzcoan au biscayen. Ce dernier se distingue en effect, dans toute une partie de sa conjugaison, par l'emploi d'auxiliaires qui lui sont propres, il offre des particularités typiques dans maints détails de grammaire en plus grand nombre que les autres dialectes, et enfin son vocabulaire a souvent des mots non compris de autres Basques."* ("We would justify this classification with the following consideration: one passes through meaningless gradations from one dialect to another among those that constitute this group, whereas the leap is rather brusque when one passes from Gipuzkoan to Bizkaian. The latter is distinguished in fact, in part of its conjugation, by the use of auxiliary verbs unique to it, it offers typical particularities in many details of grammar more than the other dialects, and in the end its vocabulary often has words not contained in other Basque dialects.")

This discrepancy with the traditional opinion reached the point of exasperation in a work by C. C. Uhlenbeck (*EJ* 1, 1947, 544) who, in the last part of his life, seemed determined to demonstrate his repentance for sins of neogrammar committed in his youth and into his maturity. As Tovar says in *El euskera y sus parientes*, Madrid, 1959, 146 (chapter 15, *"El vizcaíno entre los dialectos vascos"*), "He ended up affirming that differentiated languages, that undoubtedly occupied the most extensive territories, had been reduced to one zone and there it had been possible to produce a reconciliation or fusion between languages that were very different before; thus we would have an explanation of the variety of known Basque dialects, and especially of the peculiar characteristics of Bizkaian."

We have evidence that in determined and very special cirumstances, something that can be called more fusion than reconciliation of languages has happened, but what has been born of this process is a tertium quid, which is neither of the two component languages (let's leave it at two, for simplicity's sake). I am speaking, as you might guess, of pidgins, of Creole languages, etc. And here taki-taki, for example, is not English + X + Y + . . ., but rather it is taki-taki pure and simple. But, be that as it may, there is not in our case any linguistic or extralinguistic reason that advises the adoption of a (shall we say) hypothesis of hybridization, and there are many very powerful reasons that argue against it.

6. Although I cannot extend myself here as far as I should in properly linguistic considerations, I think it worthwhile to summarize briefly some of the reasons I have alluded to (already presented in part by Tovar) which do not at all accredit the bipartition defended by Gorostiaga, Lacombe, and Uhlenbeck.

  a. The reasons in support are, I believe, irreparably subjective—that is to say, impressionistic. Never is it specified for whom Bizkaian is so different. I would concede, then, that for me, born in the old lesser archpriestdom of Gipuzkoa within the diocese of Pamplona, with a language that is not really Gipuzkoan but rather High Navarrese (in other words, of an eastern language before western), to whom the speech of Goizueta or Saint-Jean-de-Luz is rather familiar, I would have a first run-in with the marked differentiation of Bizkaian. But I, at that time, say 1935–37, did not have the least idea about spoken Souletin nor could I guess the surprise that many aspects of the moribund Roncalese would hold for me when I would encounter it years later.

  b. Without leaving impressionism, it is certain that the Gipuzkoan-Bizkaian border presents itself abruptly for he who goes, for example, from Brinkola to Oñate, as we used to do, crossing some mountains along the way. "Abrupt" has meaning here if we compare the isoglosses collected in a linguistic atlas with the level lines represented on a map: the closer the lines are to each other, the greater the effort needed to overcome the difference comparable to the effort required by the linguistic leap necessary for mutual comprehension. But this border, which coincides with the front of the war as it was stabilized in October of 1936, has never been explored—as far as I know—in detail, point by point. Thus, in relation to the "distance" between Brinkola and Oñate, what is the distance that separates Eibar from Elgoibar or Ondarroa from Motrico? Before advancing theories, it would be necessary to dedicate some time to the humble, penurious, but indispensable task of observing the facts. Given that the considerations are quantitative, we would also have to see if there isn't a way to quantify our observations.

c. We are faced with the well-known circumstance, on the other hand, that several of the so-called Bizkaian facts, so-called because it is presumed that they are exclusive to this variety of Basque, also cover broad areas that are linguistically Gipuzkoan. For example, the type of nominative singular exemplified by *arrebea*, from *arreba* + -*a,* and its prolongations (*arrebearen, arrebeari,* etc.); the modal use of the auxiliary *egin* instead of -*eza*, in imperatives such as *eman eizu, emaizu,* instead of *eman ezazu (emantzazu),* etc.; the transitive use of *erten* (Bizkaian *urten dau*); the same lexeme *erten, irten, urten* that, at least when it means "leave," is exclusively western and reaches all the way to San Sebastian, and if I'm not wrong, to Pasajes de San Juan. On the other hand, the eastern *kin* "with" penetrates broadly into territory that is dialectally and administratively Bizkaian.

d. In almost all the explanations that have been made in the last 100 or 200 years about Basque dialectal boundaries, the greater part of Alavese territory has been left out even in the preceding one, except for a nominal mention. The exceptions consist of Aramayona, Villarreal plus Urbina, etc., Cigoitia, Barambio, Llodio, points or zones that are always marginal in proximity to Bizkaia. Larramendi's evidence about "what happens in Alava, that it shares in all of them [the other dialects], more or less syncopated and varied" (*Arte*, p. 12); Landucci's vocabulary, wielded against him by Mayans; the verses of Gamiz, a native of Sabando and neighbor of Pamplona; plus current and historical place names, and residual terms collected by Gerardo López de Guereñu: all of this allows us to affirm that the language preserved some differences that generated the temptation to place them on the ancient border between eastern Varduli (plus the Vascones) and western Caristii. In any case, whether this is true or not, it does not seem that the same abrupt leap was made to the south that we estimate was made to the north between Gipuzkoan and Bizkaian. Furthermore, and above all, the language that reflects the lexicon of Landucci was something that could not be confused in any way with the Bizkaian dialect, although it shared western characteristics. One cannot, then, discount the testimony of southern Basque (Alavese, Riojano, Burgalese) whose evidence, though scant, covers almost a thousand years.

7. Bizkaian is just a Basque dialect. It is one among various branches, to use the familiar arboreal image, not one among two. As Tovar says (*El euskera . . .*, p. 174): "We are dealing with a well characterized dialect, but definitely not independent. It forms part of the common patrimony of the Basque; it is a treasure of linguistic antiquities as are all the other dialects, but it does not permit us to go back much farther, with a reconstruction based on it." The characteristic elements of its personality, I might add, are owed in large measure to its condition as a marginal dialect. Now then, we must keep in mind that, in addition to being repositories of antiquities, the lateral areas, unlike the central ones, are also nurseries of innovations fostered in the warmth of bordering languages.

This opinion can be defended from various points of view that I merely point out here, and I leave the proofs for a more opportune occasion. Nevertheless, before beginning my enumeration, it might be useful to indicate one aspect of the question that has more to do with *chronology* than with *geography*. For many years, perhaps since the end of the last century, the deliberate undertaking to confuse Bizkaian with what I call hyper-Bizkaian has wrought havoc. This hyper-Bizkaian has been formed by applying one rule: something is Bizkaian by language if, and only if, it appears here and is lacking in other varieties of the language (continuing to suppose, however, that Bizkaian is a dialect). If it does not reach this extreme but always desirable perfection, something is Bizkaian to the extent that it has fewer partners or, in other words, to the extent that it is not common Basque.

It is enough to consult the available documentation to arrive unhesitatingly at the conclusion that the differences between Bizkaian and more eastern dialects have increased unceasingly since the fifteenth and sixteenth centuries. Consequently, I see no reason not to extrapolate or suggest that these differences were less marked in the tenth century.

In accordance with the universally accepted conventions in historical linguistics and in comparisons, one cannot take into consideration facts whose modern character becomes evident merely by consulting the texts for establishing ancient interdialectal relations. Neither in the sixteenth nor the seventeenth centuries, (nor, I believe, in the eighteenth) do we witness the Bizkaian *gintzazan* "we are," but rather only *ginean* or variations that agree with *ginan, ginen* from the other dialects. We do not find *dauz* "has them," but rather *ditu* or, later, *dituz*; not *ebazan* "had them" (although yes, without variation, *eban* "had it," as opposed to *zuen*, etc., from the more eastern zones), but rather *zituzan; eustan* "had it to me" and other forms with zero index of third person are not, contrary to what many authors suppose, unique forms that exist in Bizkaian (although the ones of older attestation are), given that the continuations of *zeustan*, etc., with *z-*, are used in broad Bizkaian zones from Eibar to Bermeo. We must not forget that forms of the preterite of that class have been documented from the earliest texts, such as *zidin* or *zizan*. The Schuchardtian myth of the original nature of the lack of a prefix (tied to the strange idea that *egoan* "was" was in some way not explained "the same" as *egon* "to be, been") can have glottogonic foundations ("zero" has to be previous to "something"), but lacks textual reasons to support it.

I arrive now at my list:

a. There is no more than one lone nominal declension. The only exclusive western particularity (since *-rean* "of, from" is an archaicism, traces of which are also discovered in other parts) is the comitative suffix *-gaz* which, as I already said, does not reign only in Bizkaian. Landucci, on the other hand, has no more than *-kin*. That which is exclusive to Bizkaian is not, in any case, the ending *-z* which is the common form of the instrumental, but rather the element *-ga-*, which never functions as a clear postposition: *lagun-a-gaz*, plural *lagunakaz* (from **lagun-ak-gaz*), but never *lagunaren / lagunen + gaz*, as there is *lagunaren / lagunen ga(i)tik* "because of the friend / of the friends." On the other hand, this fact has a counterpart in the dative plural where only the extreme east has *-ér*, as opposed to *-ai / -ei* in the west and central areas, variations of one prototype.

b. Neither does the pronominal flexion differ much, and the divergence is reduced to the stems, without affecting the endings. As
in the other dialects, there appears in the first and second person
demonstratives the duality of proper stem / oblique stem: *au* /
onek, ori / *orrek*, etc., as in old Labourdin *haur* / *hunek, hori*
/ *horrek*, etc. While the other dialects distinguish the singular
proper stem of the third person demonstrative (*hura*, probably
hur-a) from the oblique stem *har-*, Bizkaian has uniformly *a(r)-*:
singular *a, ak, ari*, etc., old plural *aek, aen*, etc. It is curious that
there is an anomaly here, undoutbedly the result of an innovation in Roncalese and Souletin, at the other end of the country:
singular absolute case *hura*, plural *hurak*, today *húa, húak*, in
Souletin.

With all this, there is a correspondence that can qualify
as perfect in the usage of the three demonstratives as articles,
according to what can be studied in the most ancient usages and
in archaic practices, so much so that these have been documented
in marginal and marginalized dialects such as the southern High
Navarrese of Egüés or Tierra Estella. We have, in fact, singular
first person *-au*, Bizkaian and southern High Navarrese, Labourdin, etc., *-or*, from **-aur*; second person common *-ori*; third person *-a*, which has supplanted the others, except in residual traces.
In the plural, the duality of proximate *-ok* / nonproximate *-ak*
predominates from the earliest evidence, since it practically reigns
supreme in those early texts. To the extent that the inflexion of
the articles gives evidence of the inflexion of the demonstratives,
which at first do not consist of anything more than enclitic variations, that inflexion speaks in favor of *bitematismo* (dual stems)
in the singular of *"éste"* and *"ése"* (Spanish "this" and "that")
which is how a common characteristic has been seen. But also, at
the same time, it speaks in favor of the single-stemmed character
of the plurals, formed on the proper case and not on the oblique
stem. In fact, the general *-ok*, from which follow the other cases,
can only proceed from variations strictly related to *hauk* and
horiek, absolute plural. Beyond any reasonable doubt is the
fact that the plural *-ok*, exclusive in two different and seemingly
opposite meanings ("us" but not "you [familiar]"; "you [famil-
iar, plural]" but not "I"), continues at the same time to the plurals of the demonstratives of the two first persons. With regard
to the presence and function of the three articles in old Bizkaian,

just like in the High Navarrese of Elcano in the second half of the eighteenth century, we need only examine the letter of 1537, written or dictated from Mexico by Father Juan de Zumárraga, published and discussed in *Euskera* 36 (1981), 5–14.

c. It is true that, in the persons, there appear disagreements as spectacular as western *neu, eu,* etc., which to the Gipuzkoan is what every Bizkaian is obliged to say when he says *ni, i,* etc. I do not know how right or wrong we are, but it is evident that the divergence is superficial, lacking in meaningful historical depth. It is enough to remember that from ergatives like *neurk* (cf. *zuhaurk*), etc., well documented outside the Bizkaian area, it is a very short distance to Bizkaian ergative *neuk, zeuk,* etc. The distance, in addition to being scant, is easy to salvage if one remembers that the Bizkaian ergative of the interrogative *nor* "who" is *nok,* in the same way that in the third person ergative demonstrative *ak* corresponds in that dialect to the oblique stem *ar-* of the dative *ari,* etc. One can guess then the phonological rule by which the soft *r,* very rare at the end of a word within the historical period of the language, was lost after the vowel and before the occlusive. The exclusively western opposition of plural *nortzuk* to singular *nor,* etc., is not much older than the Castilian innovation that today opposes *quiénes* to *quién* ("who," plural and singular) according to their number, although the model of pluralization (*batzu* "some" from *bat* "one" plus *-zu,* from which come *batzuk, batzuek, batzuak*) is not recent.

d. There is no end to the coincidences in the verb, and the more ancient the texts, the greater the number of them. The system of tenses and modes is the same, give or take a point. The distribution of simple and compound tenses is very similar. The differentiation of the various auxiliaries is identical. The allocutive forms of the familiar "you" are general and so is the temporal-modal usage of *-te* (and *-ke*), in such a way that old Bizkaian *axate* "you (fam.) will be" superimposes exactly in form and meaning on Leiçarrague *aizate;* the Bizkaian imperative of the future also occurs in Labourdin of the seventeenth century, and so on successively. All in all, it is here where the most attention-grabbing differences stand out, especially in the auxiliary verbs.

Even in this limited domain, nevertheless, things are not so shocking if all the forms are aligned, from west to east. Thus, if we compare the series *deust / dit / deraut* (from which we have *draut, daut, dereit, deit)* "he has it to me," it quickly becomes apparent that the high Navarrese-Gipuzkoan auxiliary (which is in evidence more or less throughout the country in forms with a third-person recipient of the type *dio, diot)* is not formally more distant from Bizkaian than from its eastern neighbor. In a similar way, when we compare the Bizkaian potential *dai(ke)* (and what can be said of the potential also holds true for the subjunctive and the imperative) to the central *dezake,* as if dealing with an insurmountable contrast, at least three things are forgotten. The form *ordi diro* "it can make him drunk" is as different from *dai(ke)* as it is from *dezake.* The first thing is that there is still an eastern *diro* (only potential!), already seen in Dechepare. The second thing is that the auxiliary *-eza* was current in Bizkaian areas in the not-too-distant past. See *RS* 429: *Ydiac eta veyac yl ezauz ta loben baten biriac yndauz* "Kill oxen and cows and give me a light goring with horns," with *ezauz* from *ezazuz,* like *yndauz* from *indazuz,* by dissimilation. And lastly, *-(g)i* for *-eza* also has been known and is known in an extensive Gipuzkoan zone. Everything is reduced to different choices, variables down through time, elements of a common foundation.

e. In the formation of words there are many elements that are common to the entire Basque-speaking region, even without mentioning the procedures for their formation. Thus in place names the presence of the language seems to be coextensive with the area of utilization of suffixes such as *-aga, -(k)eta,* and *-zu.* Also, what they had in common was more abundant in past centuries. As a suffix, *-bait* is general, but as a connective prefixed to verb forms everyone accepts it today as eastern: you could almost say that it is one of the characteristics that separates Gipuzkoan from High Navarrese. Nevertheless, this is not what happened in the sixteenth century, at least in formulas fixed in meaning, as Azkue points out, *Morf.* § 529. See *RS* 20 *Celan baysta ojala alacoa mendela* "As the cloth is, so shall the edge be" or *RS* 35, *Celangoa baysta amea alangoa oyda alabea* "As the mother is, so shall the daughter be."

f. I do not believe that the distribution of the lexicon has the value that some give it as a criterion of dialectal demarcation (suffice it to refer to Porzig or Solta in their known works). I expounded on this point of view, along with others, in "La fragmentación dialectal: conocimientos y conjeturas," *REL* 6 (1976), 309–24.

Make of this what you will, the fact is that—returning to our sheep—if Bizkaian *jazo* "to happen" sounds strange to those of us who are accustomed to *gertatu* (or to *suertatu,* in any case), does our first encounter with the eastern *agitu* feel more familiar? Faced with *etsai* "enemy," we have *arerio* to the west, but also *izterbegi* to the east.

8. Even in the phonological, a field that I know better than any other, there is little in Bizkaian or, more generally speaking, in western Basque that goes beyond the banal processes, in the style of *barri* for *berri* or *baltz* for *beltz*. Only the correspondence *u-: i-* in aspirated or nonaspirated initial position of a word, which I will deal with below, could perhaps relate to something reasonably remote in time, even though it seems unclear to us. Nevertheless, the lines of phonological diversification have always been the first and last that we make use of when dealing with demarcating dialectal domains, because of their ease of manipulation but also because of their singular utility when it comes to fixing relative chronologies.

Combined with what I said previously, this corroborates the rejection of the hypothesis that sees Bizkaian as an adjacent branch, though sprouted from the common trunk, a branch that in union with the whole of "Basque" dialects (that is, Basque dialects without Bizkaian), would give a basis for the reconstruction of a Bizkaian dialect, comparable in the field of reconstructions to the Indo-Hittite of Sturdtevant. Or in a field that is easier to understand, there does not seem to be any reason to see in Bizkaian something that is related with the other Basque dialects in the manner in which Tsaconian is related to modern Greek dialects.

Although it may be politically satisfactory to some of us, this result will not be satisfactory for comparative reconstruction, since it deprives us of the possibility of elevating ourselves to a higher level since, as Tovar points out, it deprives us of the possibility of elevating ourselves to a higher level, to which an MCM is within a reticular structure.

9. The above would have greater value if the evolution of the Basque dialects had taken place in unconnected spaces, after their geographic separation, something that did not happen in reality. In that event, the aphorism collected by Etcheberri of Sara, which originated with the great Tertulian, if I'm not wrong, as so many complete and somewhat sophisticated sentences do, would have had a more direct application to

our problems: *Quod apud multos unum inuenitur, non est erratum, sed traditum.*

But as things have unfolded among us, the coincidences are far from originating in a common heritage, and this is more than mere suspicion. Quite the contrary, we know by internal and external indices of the language that to a great extent the coincidences are the consequence of innovations *shared by all the dialects,* Bizkaian included. If we consider the compact distribution of the place names in *-aga* already mentioned (supra, §§ 6, 7, e) that extend from *Liginaga,* French *Laguinge,* in Soule (Zuberoa) to *Lizarraga,* undoubtedly as well to *Fresneda,* in lands around San Miguel de Pedroso (eleventh century), and which cover the entire territory surrounding the modern Basque Country (at least) in which Basque was spoken in the High Middle Ages, one must suspect that their abundance and compact distribution indicate relatively recent dates.

To illustrate the innovations in the phonological treatment of the *sonorants* (which I called *sonantes* "voiced phonemes" in their day, knowing full well the impropriety), for example Basque *an(h)oa,* Latin *annona, goru,* Latin *colus, zela,* Latin *sella;* the "voicing" of these initial consonants, occlusives above all, that is produced by the confluence of two Latin series (outside of loan words we can only conjecture), thus in *bago, bake, daraturu, dorre, gatilu, gaztelu;* the treatment of final sounds of the first part in composition and derivation, as is deduced from the comparison, for example, of *ardan-, har(r)-, organ-, ata, besa- / ardao, harri, orga, ate, beso,* and I'll stop here with a list that could go on *ad libitum.* All of this, which is common Basque except for tiny details, does not have to be in addition, by necessity, proto-Basque. If we abstain from conjecture, we will have to limit ourselves to testifying that, although Lafon has adduced some uncertain examples of the latter case for the ancient era, the processes were completed at the height of the tenth century, which is as far back as our documentation reaches, except in the case of the *sonorants,* the evolution of which is still in progress. Here, moreover, we know that in Aquitaine they were still intact.

It would be easier still to extend the relationship if we leave phonology and enter into a different order of things. It is generally believed that the determinate article, or the system of articles, mentioned above, § 7, b, was born at the same time as the Roman article and the articles of other western languages (Germanic, Celtic), and the same can be said for the indeterminate *bat / batzu.* This parallel holds for the analytical forms of the verb, what we call the periphrastic forms, in the past as well as the future: *etorri da, egin du, est venu, is gekommen* (old form *es venido*) / *ha hecho, a fait, hat gemacht; joanen, joango da,* literally "is of go," *eginen, egingo du* "has of do." From there arises the somewhat paradoxical contrast of a language in which there is no choice but to use only compound forms with the majority of the verbs and at times with all of them, along with synthetic personal forms of extreme complexity (whose number has been decreasing during the short hstory of the language). Forms like *aizate* "you (fam.) will be" (in addition to "you (fam.) can be," "perhaps you (fam.) are," "you (fam.) are or will be at any moment," etc.), *date* "he will be," etc., were already in retreat faced with *izanen / izango da,* etc., in the early documents, and today there are no more than traces left whose value is above all evidential.

The nominal plural, which appears always with the determiner, and cannot appear without it as an *overt category,* will not be, almost by definition, more ancient than the generalization of the determiner. I am speaking of the system that historical Basque has for expressing the difference in number, which does not mean that this did not have any expression previously. It is not silly in principle to think that pluralization as we know it, which is common Basque in every detail, is something that has only come on the scene relatively late and established itself in the language. As Matteo Bartoli would say, it would have to do with an *innovazione di età romanza,* rather than *romana.* And this extrapolation has meaning to the very broad extent that Latin and Romance are the most solid means of affixing the stakes of our linguistic history.

At any rate, there is also an internal reasoning that advocates for a not-so-remote date. In Bizkaian, as we know, in nominal stems ending in *-a,* a certain phenomenon of accommodation (dissimilatory) takes place when the determinate article follows that vowel: from *domeka* "Sunday" we have *domekea* "the Sunday," ergative *domekeak,* etc. But curiously enough, this only happens in the singular with the exception of the locative *domekaan,* from which we get *domekan,* but never ***-ean.* In this way, while we get *domekeak* from ergative singular *domeka + -a + -k,* nothing more than *domekaak,* and by contraction *domekak,* comes out of absolute and ergative plural *domeka + -ak* (if you like from **-ag*). From the descriptive point of view, other explanations will not only fit but be necessary. But they do not invalidate, nor can they make concurrent, the historical explanations that the plural, like the locative singular, was formed in Basque in a rather late era, when the law that changed *-a +* *-a* to *-ea,* etc., was not yet operational. As Greenberg recently reminded us, there are no forms more solid than those that have historical reality, since these have existed, not only in the deep or superficial layers of the consciousness of the speakers, but also in the intersubjective surface of their daily discourse.

10. I believe that it is reasonable to suppose, in agreement with what I have already explained, that there existed something at some moment, even if we can't put a date to it, that we can correctly call proto-Basque (not *proto-Basque), that was not a simple *vue de l'esprit* nor a mirage of reconstruction, like Kurylowicz used to say, but rather the unifying source within what is possible with regard to historical Basque dialects.

It seems necessary to indicate here, however briefly, what the normal processes are, normal by virtue of being immensely majoritarian, which according to our historical (and personal) experience follow dialectal diversification on the one hand, and the replacement of languages on the other. A language, any language, always tends toward diversification, but the variations that may result as a consequence of the process can very well not achieve sufficient autonomy (although the process is fomented with all the extralinguistic aparatus, as in the case of Moldavian) in order to constitute a language *a se* (in and of itself). Now there are historical consequences in which one variety, by more violent or more spontaneous means, is converted we might say into the authorized representative of the language, in a word, into just the language. This however does not usually happen because the diverse ingredients mix together in equal doses or at least in a similar order of magnitude. On the contrary, what usually occurs is that one variety displaces, marginalizes, or supplants the others. That is what happened with Greek *koiné* in which Attican removed its most bothersome horns (the *tarátto:* type, the *neó:s* declension, etc.) in order to continue with the suppression of peculiarities that, like the optative, were Ionic and even just Greek, in addition to being Attican. In old Italy, avoiding more modern cases, Latin did not exchange isoglosses with Oscan, Umbrian, etc., as Pisani seems to think. It eliminated them, it erased them from the face of the earth like it had erased Etruscan, although it left traces for those of us who have access to exceptionally high-quality documentation, such as *rufus* (cf. Latin *ruber*), *bos*, etc., to stay on the beaten path.

If I postulate, then, an earlier state of Basque which I will call *euskaro* (I try to avoid bothersome confusion with proto-Basque or ancient Basque that could have a different definition) as a unifying basis for historical Basque varieties that we have known down through history, I do so only under the assumption that it was treated like a *koiné,* a common language that drew together and united a dispersion and diversity that had been much greater. Then (and why not?) this common language split into varieties each more divergent than the last, which were prevented from constituting different languages by the continuation of material contact between the various dialectal zones and the phenomena of convergence that inveitably followed such contact. And how great a role was played as well by exigencies of space and the number of speakers?

11. Can one attempt to date the historical Basque dialects with documentation? As an *ante quem* term, one can say with confidence that a phoneme /h/, aspiration, did not exist until the tenth century in High Navarra, at least in the zones from which we gather the available documentation. It is even more doubtful, to my understanding, that this affirmation was valid for the whole area, especially for Atlantic Navarra and for El Baztán. We know, in fact, that on the border there remained a small island of preserved aspiration in the time of Bonaparte.

It is clear, and was proven by Luchaire, that it existed all along the Labourdin coast. It is difficult to make a pronouncement with regard to Gipuzkoa and Bizkaia, but its frequent presence in Alavese Basque was a certainty even into the fourteenth century. I take as an example from Menéndez Pidal, *Documentos lingüísticos de España* I, number 142: *Harriaga,* twice, *Harana* (in the same document *Ffaro* is written for Haro), but *Adurça, Ylarraça, Alaua* (1291, Vitoria): *Hasquarçaha* in 1325, *Hascarzaha* in 1025, the initial letter of which could not have been capricious, etc.

To judge by the spellings, aspiration could occur before the vowel, after the vowel or a pause, but also, as happened in the modern era, after the *sonorant* (voicing), in *groupes disjoints,* that is, heterosyllabic groups, such as *lh (Olha-, -olha), rh,* etc. This was current in Aquitainian place names, and in the inscription of Lerga, also from the Roman epoch, syllabification was assured by the insertion of aspiration. In High Navarra aspiration was known, and there are examples of it (*-nh-* in Sofuentes) in the modern province of Zaragoza. The conclusion we are left with is that the (non-Indo-European) language of the Basques coincided in this respect with that of the Aquitainians. Aspiration was lost in Navarra through Pamplona, Estella, or Aoiz during the long documental hiatus that ran from the second century to the tenth, if we allow ourselves to mark these approximate milestones.

Already through the tenth and eleventh centuries there were manifestations of contrasts (cf. above § 8), western *baltz, barri*/eastern *beltz, berri,* with an insignificant divergence, if it had not gained importance thanks to the lack of usable material. Of greater importance is the western opposition *(h)uri* eastern *(h)iri* "village," the reason for which is unclear, to my understanding. In the zone that was later of Gipuzkoan dialect, there was only *iri,* it seems, but *huri-* covered Alava, clear to its eastern border and even beyond, so that its area comprised Arana, for example, and Val de Lana in Navarra. The boundaries indicated by Menéndez Pidal in works that later appeared together in the book *En torno a la lengua vasca* (Buenos Aires: Austral,1962), pp. 73 on, demanded some retouching within the zone itself, certainly a Basque-speaking area.

Although *Ili-, Ilun- (-ilon-)* was documented around one thousand years before *huri-, -(h)uri,* I am inclined to give priority to these latter forms with the idea that the vowel change from posterior to anterior was simpler, and it was better supported by parallels than the contrary. In any case, the isogloss, an indicator of dialectal diversity, was already established by the year 1000. It was possibly established before that date, but this is conjecture, not fact.

In ancient place names there were signs of polymorhism, such as the alternation *t / h* in *Tals-co- / Hals-co-,* etc. I suggested once that Aquitainian *Ombe- (-co, -xo)* might be the correlation of *Vm.me-,* with an indication of a syllabic border, that reasonably is nothing other than Basque *ume* "child, infant," cf. *Umea,* a medieval nickname frequent in Navarra. But even if this were so, we would only have an easily interpolated indication of a stage in the reduction of /nb/, that is, [mb], to /m/, assured for example by the correspondence Aquitainian *Sembe-:* common Basque *seme* "son."

12. If a type of common language had to exist as a root for the known dialects and if that common language was not too far distant from us, as measurements go in historical linguistics—and this is what Vogt roundly affirmed, as we have seen, and what seems to be the unformulated thinking of many others—we would have to ask ourselves then how it came to be. In fact, such a thing could not have happened by itself, since languages do not unify *motu proprio,* but rather are unified by someone or something, by men operating within certain historical conditions.

Jan Safarewicz, *Linguistic Studies* (La Haya-Paris, 1974) p. 122, puts forth with particular clarity that a language, to the extent that it is common, is united with the organization of a society, an organization that permits an efficient and long-lasting exchange between more or less compact or disperse groups. And he adds, when speaking of a common Italic, something I also believe in although this belief does not appear to be in fashion, representing in any case a much more hypothetical entity that our common Basque: "According to this point of view the hypothesis of the existence of a common Primitive Italic language must take into consideration the existence—at some prehistoric period—of a social organisation which was able to bring about the creation of a uniform language. Of course we have no concrete data that might confirm the hypothesis, although there are not indications denying it explicitly, either. The reasoning in this case must be limited to inference from the linguistic facts alone."

Ab esse ad posse ualet conclusio is, as far as I know, generally accepted in whatever current variation of modal logic, but the inference of the possiblity to the reality is not considered undoubtedly valid, because Safarewicz's reasoning, which I must make my own, continues to resemble that famous *Docuit, potuit, ergo fecit* that the visible approbation of a heavenly Lady helped Doctor Subtilis, as they tell it.

A certain type of probable reasoning, nevertheless, does not lack verosimilitude, or in any case, is far from being absurd. Given that postulating a relatively recent common Basque seems less than necessary in the order of reality and not merely a theoretical requirement of methods of comparative reconstruction, we have to think about the causes that led to it. Do not forget that a common language suggests a sacrifice by extinction of the dialects in favor of one of their number. On the other hand, as linguistic unification is usually the result of (and a factor of) social cohesion, it is quite appropriate to think that a process of sociopolitical concentration preceded and accompanied the dialectal leveling. At any rate, here as elsewhere, anyone can see that the chain of reasoning will be no stronger than its weakest link.

13. Admitting this for the moment, although only as a "mathematical hypothesis" as they used to say in Copernican disputes, the question that comes immediately to mind is that of the moment or epoch in which such a process could be situated with some certainty.

The upper Paleolithic, in which some have seen the beginnings of a genetically differentiated population, is situated, by all evidence, at an astronomical distance. If we were able to make use of methods for going back in time at least ten millennia, we would not have the reason we now have for complaining about the instruments that we avail ourselves of. The periods prior to the "Pyrenaic pastoral community" of the neoe-neolithic mentioned by Bosch-Gimpera or Pericot, not to mention those closer to home, are inaccessibly distant.

The Roman epoch does not seem totally impenetrable to us, how-ever long a period it may cover. With regard to the language, as with the previous pre-Latin Indo-Europeanization, it is certain that linguistic Romanization (Latinization) in the Basque-speaking zones caused a drastic reduction in the Basque-speaking area that must have received population from outlying zones, especially in periods of violence and insecurity, along with the inevitable *brassage* of speakers of very diverse dialects and varieties. Here we allude to a process that could have lasted until the middle of the second century in the shortest chronology and probably longer according to more likely estimates. We should under-line that, with remissions and intermissions, the general sense of the evo-lution had to be the same: a reduction of territory, and for that reason, some concentration of population whose origins had to be diverse.

We are not insisting on the influence that Latin exercised, not just directly with regard to supplanting indigenous languages but also indi-rectly with regard to the indelible stamp it left on us, a stamp that the Basque language has preserved down to modern times. It is also clear that outside the area connected to the *saltus Vasconum*, there must have been isolated pockets that survived for a while, some quite late. It is obvious, in any case, that the *"dialecte mixte basco-roman"* that could have lasted until the tenth and eleventh centuries in Pallars and Alta Rib-agorza (cf. J. Coromines, *Estudis de toponímia catalana* I, Barcelona, 1965, pp. 106 on especially), or other Basque or Bascoidal dialects dis-tant from the preserving center, had little to do with the supposed com-mon language we are talking about.

14. It is to be expected that in the zone outlined by the large character-istics we are calling nuclear (the zone, partly neighboring the Pyrennees, partly the division between Hispania and Gaul, and the Atlantic slope of the later Basque Country), the old tribal organization was undoubtedly maintained, an organization that had clear economic attractions in con-

trast with the urban-estate-based Roman order. On the other hand, it seems obvious that no one tried to impose the latter, along with the language that served as its vehicle, in any systematic way. Although there were more than enough means to do it, there was a lack of interest. And the tribal society was reinforced once the imperial administration began to function poorly, one would say at a fairly early date, and this must have allowed thieves and rebels in general to maintain and extend their activity.

In the same way that the language received the imprint of Latin, the traditional organization that we just mentioned must have been modified as well, even without imposition, by the influence of the Roman model, the superiority of which was obvious, no matter how heavy the burden it imposed on its unprivileged subjects. As J. Maluquer de Motes said so well, *II Symposium de Prehistoria Peninsular. Problemas de la prehistoria y de la etnología vasca* (Pamplona, 1966) p. 126: "Roman influence had been very light, perhaps null, in broad zones, both in the socio-economic as well as the spiritual aspects. But Roman action could have contributed indirectly, and perhaps by the very fact of its administrative structure, to the awakening of a certain sense of unity, and in any case, of security, that would grow stronger during the turbulent stage of Visigothic domination, a sense that should not be underestimated, given that in it we possibly find the basis of the later appearance of the Navarrese monarchy." One could say in a way that Maluquer, whose concerns were very different from those that inspired these lines, has given the best possible defense of the point of view that I have tried to express.

For what followed, I now cite A. Barbero y M. Vigil, *BRAH* 156 (1965), 333: "The chaos that was produced on the Peninsula because of the barbarian invasions facilitated and effected the consolidation of the independence of the Cantabrians and the Vascones. The old rebellion against the Romans was transformed by the new historical conditions into a situation of political independence in the face of the Visigoths and the Franks. Thus, during the reign of Leovigildo the Cantabrians were governing themselves through their own assemblies and they as well as the Vascones had leaders in later epochs whom the Franks called *duces*. Also, when the wars against their neighbors went badly, they transformed themselves into their tributaries without losing their political personality. The social organization in which these peoples would live was evidently not the same that they had when the Romans conquered them, since Roman dominion would have destroyed it in part and in part it would have been transformed by assimilated material progress."

The fifth century and a good part of the sixth had to be times of, if not liberation, then at least extreme fluctuation of external dependencies for these places, in such a way that when the pressures of the Franks and of the kingdom of Toledo were felt at the end of that century, there was enough power and organization to oppose a resistance that in the end was victorious. (We must remember the dates of 581 with the campaign of Leovigildo and 587 when a particularly sensational expedition through the plains of what was to become Gascony took place.) All of this meant adaption to the new conditions. Thus possibly the importance of relationship ties diminished and the hierarquization of society with its consequent inequality increased (the more open the zone and the more "progressive" the social structure, the greater the increase, certainly). What must have grown was the exchange, the tendency toward greater unity and centralization, with inevitable and more or less immediate consequences for the language, unfavorable for dialectal fragmentation and isolation and favorable for the establishment of common forms of the language, capable of leaping local and regional barriers.

Very different dates are given for the introduction and settling in of Christianity (the early ones and the later ones are possibly equally valid for different parts of the country), but it contributed to the consolidation of the new order, the culmination of which we can place with the establishment of the kingdom of Navarra, our great political realization. Neither would I forget the seigneury of Bizkaia (and Durango), although of lesser importance, that presented characteristics of extreme archaicism in many aspects, although with a very modernized façade. This insertion into the Asturian-Leonese sphere that some think is obvious is by no means clear to me. It's not that I want to rewrite *Bizkaya por su independencia* or believe that the battle of Arrigorriaga was fought in 888 with the death of the Leonese leader, but I can't help wondering if in our modern rejection of the myths (which is at bottom and even on the surface, no more than substituting others that sound better at the moment for them) we are not passing over ourselves. The Arrigorriaga matter was already in evidence in the first half of the fourteenth century, an infrequent occurrence among us, and may contain, as so many legends do, some grain of stylized and exaggerated truth.

At any rate, it does not seem risky to think that Bizkaia was the Basque region that had and retained the strongest personality and that it was more resistant to the influences that arrived from Pamplona or other centers situated outside its territory. Added to its lateral character, we could find in this an explanation of the strong personality of the Bizkaian dialect that everyone recognizes, myself first among them, as long as we are not trying to convert autonomy into independence.

CHAPTER 15

Basque Vocabulary (Essay about an Interpretation of the Basque Language)

"Vocabulario vasco (Ensayo de una interpretación de la lengua vasca)," in *Lengua e historia*. Madrid: Paraninfo, 1985, pp. 329–33. (Previously published in *Boletín de la Real Sociedad Vascongada de Amigos del País* 16 (1960): 384–87.)

I have before me two thick and handsome volumes in which Monsignor Griera proposes an interpretation of the Basque language, a definitive one in his judgment. The book's reputation—an uncommon reputation in this type of work whose interest is usually limited to a narrow erudite circle—had reached me before the book did, through commentaries that appeared in the daily press. Only those of us who know Monsignor Griera can appreciate how bothersome this publicity must have been for his modesty.

The effect expected from this book has been compared with that of a bomb, to use the customary excess of newspaper language. However, in spite of the time that has passed since its appearance, it does not seem that its presumed destructive results have manifested anywhere, not even in this rather abstract and fantasmical world of ideas and theories. The amiable smile that it has provoked in the eminent Romance specialist Gerhard Rohlfs (*Scienza nuova ou décadence linguistique? Lettre persane*, Tübingen, 1960), for example, could not have been produced by comtemplating a catastrophe. If we are dealing with a bomb, to use an antiquated metaphor, it must be loaded with wet powder.

In reality, it is more like a sea serpent than a bomb. As Bishop Pontoppidan of Bergen, Monsignor Griera has not lost faith in these animals, as frightening as they are poorly identified. Thus, it is not strange to hear an echo among the journalists that is usually demonstrated by sincere or interested believers in the existence of any monster, be it maritime or terrestrial, especially when other news is at low tide.

Monsignor Griera has a specific serpent that he pursues through seven seas. In his eyes, as we know, the Basque language, which in general is considered isolated or only distantly related to languages also distant, is nothing more than a Romance dialect, a modern form of Latin. One could go so far as to say that, purifying his reasoning a bit, in its oldest depths Basque is nothing more than a Catalan dialect, although he did not elucidate whether it was eastern or western Catalan.

The first appearance of the serpent dates from several years before our war, or if you prefer, it was then when the first bombs exploded, since during that period the explosive was distributed in articles and reports of a more fickle variety, instead of being concentrated in two massive volumes. See for example *"Els noms vascos dels mesos de l'any," ZRPh* 47 (1928), p. 102 onward. It is not easy today to judge its effect because mention of it, if it existed, was rare in books or magazines, and the daily press was not even aware of its existence.

The serpent, which meanwhile did not raise its head, reappeared in 1958, preceded by a journalistic fanfare, in a report delivered at the Oslo Congress and published in the *Proceedings of the Eighth International Congress of Linguists*, 1958, pp. 614–16. There was no lack of Romance specialists or Basque specialists there, all capable of judging the value of such a surprising thesis: however, according to the acts, no one discussed it, perhaps because of the resistence that inertia always puts up in the face of great discoveries. I am not surprised, because I must confess that I myself have the distinct feeling that I am doing something I should not.

All this suffices to demonstrate that the extensive "Vocabulario vasco," published in 1960, contains nothing new that would scandalize anyone who is somewhat current on these matters. I also suspect that its fate will not be very different from that of the essays that have preceded it. The author is weighed down with a rare fatality, the causes of which are worth meditating on in detail. His ideas at first glance are collected avidly by journalists and silenced by specialists, exactly the opposite of what usually happens with the works of their colleagues. Whether this silence, and that echo, is justified is another question.

Certain evident deficiencies speak out againt the book from the first moment. In it, there is neither material culture nor traditions nor history, in contrast to what was promised us in the introduction. There are only words, words taken from a unique source—Azkue's *Diccionario*—copied with a wealth of misprints, words whose meanings have been arbitrarily summarized. The most surprising thing is that Monsignor Griera, the leader of linguistic geography in Spain, does not take care to point out the dialectal distribution of the words. Because his affirmation that Azkue "does not place words in locations" (p. VII) is not certain: the diffusion of words is always indicated and at times with great detail, although naturally not without mistakes and some imprecision.

One cannot help but think on the other hand, that the author has proposed an overly ambitious undertaking in many ways. He wants to explain through Latin, mixed in a shocking manner with the Romance languages, the entire Basque lexicon and even its grammar, and explain them without leaving any residue behind, when no one, save some incorrigible optimist, has attempted thus far to propose Indo-European etymologies for all the words in Greek and Latin or to find the antecedents of all Spanish and Catalan vocabulary through Latin. It will surprise no one, then, that Monsignor Griera has accomplished the authentic deed of finding good etymologies for words that properly speaking never existed: *aitor, arnari, lausku* "cross-eyed," *sorbo* "horn," etc. Azkue, although competent to the highest degree, was not infallible.

The disposition of the book in its enormity has not seemed advisable except to paper manufactuers and printers of whom there are too many with too little work. Evidently it could have been sufficient to explain the simple words and derived suffixes, but instead he has undertaken the task of clarifying the entire lexicon word by word, including derived words, compounds, and dialectal variations. From here spring errors, the inevitable children of the prodigal son: distinct origin is attributed to forms scarcely different that the word itself or to different appearances of the same element. Thus the reader is left free to think that Basque *seme* "son" comes from *semen*, from *homo*, and even from *simius*, or that *al(h)aba* "daughter" (written *alaaba*—I don't know why) came from *ama*, from *amata*, and even from *pava*.

An example pulled from an innumerable number of others like it will suffice to judge the quality of many of the proposed etymologies. Already commented upon was the one that laid the origin of Basque *(h)erri* in the Latin *populus*. It is true that *(h)erri* in its oldest and most extended uses meant "land, country," completely different from "group of citizens" ("town, group of persons" is casually said as *populu* in some

Basque areas), but we are not going to stop at this picky point: the difference in meanings is no greater than that between *nor?* "who?" and *nullus* "not any," that only has its parallel in the well-known episode of Ulysses with the Cyclops. Neither will I emphasize the rarity of the supposed phonetic changes, since they are not impossible and I remind the reader of the inevitable Armenian examples. The bad thing about these changes lies in what has been decided *ad hoc,* in order to explain that specific word, which is not an obstacle to introducing other different changes to explain other words. To get involved in a dispute with Monsignor Griera in the game of etymologies is like confronting an adversary in chess who has the disconcerting habit of moving bishops like knights whenever he likes or letting his castles replace his king in order to avoid the inevitable checkmate. The game is surprising at first in its novelty, but one loses all interest after a few moves.

It has already been pointed out that one of the etymologies is picturesque for semantic reasons. None moreso than that of *al(h)aba*: "The woman is an *andera* female goat (sic): the man a *gizon* bison: the daughter can very well be a *turkey hen*." Why not, if the son can be a simian? It is upsetting to see our ancestors as a Franciscan communion of the animal kingdom, although the Basque home seen by Griera calls to mind more the passengers of Noah's ark (the bottom floor) than the Holy Family, but those who are fond of jokes can look to these passages for easy jibes not lacking in humor. When seeking a precursor for this style of etymology, no greater parallel can be offered than our great Larramendi. Of course, Larramendi committed the sin of not taking his own stupendous and extravagant occurrences seriously.

We must mention one last objection, the most serious of all, although the author has not taken notice of the possibility. We accept as demonstrated the affiliation between Latin and Basque, although not without abusing our tolerance. If *eipe* procedes from *lei* (from *leisa*) plus *pede* or alternately from *atrium*, if *gau* "night" (translated "day" on p. VIII undoubtedly to simplify things) can come both from *nocte* and from *diurnu*, one thinks that with such potent methods it is possible to prove that Basque is the twin brother of Chukchi or Potawatomi. What has not been considered is that, if Basque is a modern form of Latin, it is also evidence for the reconstruction of the latter, evidence as authoritative (remember the case of the Indo-European languages of Anatolia) as any of the Romance languages, large or small.

What kind of Latin is showing us its evidence! I disregard the obvious misprints and even the bunglings that wind their way like unasterisked ants through the pages: in the family of *pasco* we find *pascaceu, pascalotu, pascanu, pascatu, pastariu,* and *pasterata*; at least **pascatatione* (*askatasun* "freedom") is not deprived of that adornment. A Latin in which "fern" is designated as *filice-terra* or "buttock" as *merda-mamma,* a Latin that juxtaposes *novella* with *novellus* or admits combinations in the style of *spera-care, per-en-ad, genitus-lacte-bal* or *vercia-troncho-el* (!!!) is something that cannot be called Latin, not even with the most exhorbitant poetic license: *aegri somnia* was what Horace called nightmares of this genre.

In summary, Monsignor Griera has not explained Basque except at the price of converting Latin into a jargon of lunatics. The price is too high and few will decide to pay it. Liberties can be taken with the Basque language, it is almost customary: to the point that one can create a Basque etymological dictionary without knowing the language. Not so with Latin, even though only because Cicero and Saint Augustine wrote in it and because it is well known. At least it is supposed that Romance specialists know it by definition, if the Basque specialists may not.

Some words from the prologue (p. VI onward) undoubtedly explain many of the mentioned peculiarities: "In order to find an interpretation of the Basque language, I have ignored all the studies and research done on this language; also I have omitted all the grammatical treatises, structured in different ways. Like the young David, equipped only with my Romance baggage, knowing the Pyrennean culture and language to which dominion the Basque tongue belongs, I have taken it upon myself to seek out the origins of this language."

No matter how worthy of praise this declaration of individualism may be, the result is not recommendable. It makes much of the fact that research has ceased to be a work in which one may surpass the labor of his colleagues; it also makes much of the fact that the sling does not figure among the most efficient weapons. An eminent Catalan, Juan Corominas, has recently carried a gigantic work to its end, but great care has been taken to close one's ears to the opinions of others.

Many of us will agree that the work I am summarizing, save for a few correct suggestions, is no more than a venial sin (no lighter in any case than *El enigma del vascuence ante las lenguas indoeuropeas* by F. Castro Guisasola), which is better forgotten and which in no way tarnishes Monsignor Griera's merits in the field of Romance dialectology.

After all is said and done, fortune did not accompany Newton either as interpreter of the Holy Scriptures. The sin is particularly excusable for Basques, born as it was of affection toward our language and our things in general.

Abbreviations for journals and books used in Mitxelena's text:

Journals:

ASJU – Anuario del Seminario de Filologia Vasca "Julio de Urquijo" (published by the Diputación Foral de Gipuzkoa)

BAP – Boletín de la Real Sociedad Vascongada de Amigos del País (new abbreviation)

BRAH – Boletín de la Real Academia de Historia

BRSVAP – Boletín de la Real Sociedad Vascongada de Amigos del País (older abbreviation)

BSL – Bulletin de la Société de Linguistique de Paris

EJ – Eusko-jakintza

FLV – Fontes linguae vasconum

GH – Gure herria

NTS – Norsk Tidsskrift for Sprogvidenskap (Norwegian Journal of Linguistics)

PV – Príncipe de Viana

RFE – Revista de filología románica (Madrid: Universidad Complutense)

RIEV – Revista internacional de estudios vascos

Books:

CIL – Corpus Inscriptionum Latinarum (A compendium of Latin inscriptions from antiquity)

CSMill – La Reja de San Millán (1025) (List of toponyms of Alava of the eleventh century)

DES – Dictionnaire étymologique de la langue latine (Ernout & Meillet)

DRAE – Diccionario de la Real Academia de España

ELH – Enciclopedia lingüística hispánica (Manuel Alvar Lopez, ed.; Madrid: Consejo Superior de Investigaciones Científicas, 1960–67)

Hom. Martinet – Homenaje a Martinet (Universidad de La Laguna, 1958)

Hom. Urq. – Homenaje a la memoria de D. Julio Urquijo e Ybarra (Bilbao: Junta de Cultura de Vizcaya, 1973)

Lafon, *Syst. – Le système du verbe basque au XVIe siècle, vol. II* (Bordeaux: Ed. Delmas, 1943)

Man Dev – Manual Devotionezkoa (Joanes Etxeberri de Ciboure (1669); Donostia: Hordago, 1978)

Oihenart *Poes. – Les proverbes basques, recueillis par le Sr. D'Oihenart; plus les poésies basques du meme auteur* (1657). Basque edition: *Euskal atsotitzak eta neurtitzak* (Bilbao: Euskaltzaindia, 2003)

Oihenart *Prov. –* Same as Oihenart *Poes.: Les proverbs basques . . .*

Onsa – Onsa hilceco bidia (Juan de Tartas (1666); Bilbao: Deustuko Unibertsitatea, 1995).

Prim – Primitiae Linguae Vasconum by H. Schuchardt (Halle: Niemeyer, 1923)

REW – Romanisches Etymologisches Wörterbuch by Wilhelm Meyer-Lübke (Heidelberg: C. Winter, 1935)

ZRPh – Zeitschrift für romanische Philologie (Halle, 1877)

Notes

AN INTRODUCTION BY PELLO SALABURU: **Mitxelena's Life and Legacy**

1. To those of us who worked or studied with him using Basque as our vehicle of expression, the name of our esteemed professor will always be Koldo Mitxelena, as generally used here. However, his written works were signed Koldo Mitxelena or Luis Michelena, depending on the language of publication.

2. The term "Basque Country" ("Euskal Herria," in Basque) is ambiguous. On the one hand, it designates a sociolinguistic community with no precise geographical borders but mostly found in a small territory straddling the Atlantic Pyrenees in Spain and France. More recently, however, the term has also come to designate a political community that is larger than the speech community, and which has never enjoyed official recognition of any kind. This "Basque Country" is made up of two of Spain's autonomous regions (Euskadi and Navarra), plus a region in France. As envisaged by Basque nationalists, this ideal political community would comprise seven provinces, four in Spain and three in France. In Spain these would be the three historic Basque provinces (Alava, Bizkaia, and Gipuzkoa, which together make up the Basque Autonomous Community, known in Basque as *Euskadi*), plus Navarra, which is an autonomous community in its own right. The three provinces in France lack official recognition, but are known to Basques as Lower Navarra, Lapurdi, and Zuberoa. This state of affairs has given rise to the slogan *zazpiak bat* (literally, "the 7 [are] 1", with versions such as *laurak bat* ("the 4 [are] 1") and others. As noted, Euskadi is the Basque name for the autonomous community formed by the three Basque provinces in Spain. However, its translation in Spanish is the "Autonomous Community of the Basque Country," or simply "Basque Country." However, to most Basque speakers, "Euskadi" is a term of recent creation and is more restrictive than "Basque Country," since it is a political denomination and is mostly used as the equivalent of an autonomous community—i.e., a political division of a country. As can be seen, the situation is quite complex and the term "Basque Country" rather imprecise, causing frequent confusion over proper use of the term.

3. Childhood information taken from Martin Ugalde 1987 ("Koldo Mitxelena," in *Koldo Mitxelena, gizona eta hizkuntza, Egan*, special edition, May–Dec. 1987, pp. 27–33).

4. The Spanish government used to issue a document known as a "Penal Certificate," certifying that the bearer had a record of exemplary conduct and had not been tried for any criminal offense. Obviously, Koldo Mitxelena was unable to obtain such a document.

5. There are numerous editions of this work. Here we refer to the revised and expanded edition of 1977: Luis Michelena, *Fonética histórica vasca* (revised and expanded second edition) (Series: Publicaciones del Seminario Julio de Urquijo) (San Sebastián: Diputación Foral de Gipuzkoa, 1977).

6. I would like to pay homage here to a man of great integrity, whom I had the honor to meet when I defended my Ph.D. thesis, which he had come to examine as a member of my dissertation committee.

7. Until very recent years, high school and university teachers in Spain have had to belong to a corps of "functionaries," having the status of civil servants. Under that system, positions were awarded on the basis of public examinations open to candidates meeting certain requirements. During the time in question, presentation of a clean penal record was an essential requisite for attaining a teaching post.

8. Altuna, professor at the University of Deusto and member of Euskaltzaindia, was one of our most influential Basque philologists. Sarasola, also a member of Euskaltzaindia and professor at the University of the Basque Country (UBC), is without doubt the most prominent Basque lexicographer ever.

9. André Martinet, a renowned French linguist, enjoyed a special friendship with Mitxelena and an excellent relationship with the UBC. At the time, Martinet was a leading authority in Europe, where the intellectual environment was quite different from that in the USA. Noam Chomsky was already a leading influence on the other side of the Atlantic, and his book *Aspects of the Theory of Syntax* (MIT Press, 1965) was contributing decisively to the trend towards generative grammar. André Martinet did not agree with Chomsky's theories, and in fact I recall hearing him say, at a dinner around 1984, that he still had in his house the original copy of *Syntactic Structures* that Chomsky himself supposedly sent him for publication in Europe, which Martinet did not agree to or support. Curiously enough, Mitxelena contributed to the spread of generative grammar in Spain and opened the doors so that his students could study it, although he always remained critical of this school. Today, generative grammar is thriving at the UBC School of Philology, which he helped to set up.

10. For an excellent history of the UBC, see Santiago de Pablo and Coro Rubio, *Historia de la UPV/EHU 1980–2005* (Leioa: UPV/EHU, 2006).

11. José L. Melena (ed), *Symbolae Lvdovico Mitxelena Septvagenario Oblatae* (UPV/EHU, Instituto de Ciencias de la Antigüedad, 1985). Tribute on the occasion of Mitxelena's retirement.

12. *Languages and Protolanguages* (Bilbao: UPV/EHU, 1997).

13. Mosen Bernart Dechepare, *Linguae Vasconum Primitiae* (Bordeaux, 1545). A facsimile edition exists with a translation of the complete text into several languages, published by the UBC in 1995.

14. For example, that of Luis Villasante, published in 1961: Luis Villasante, *Historia de la literatura vasca* (Bilbao: Sendo, 1961). Rather than a critical analysis, however, this volume is more a catalogue of authors and texts.

15. (1843–1916). After having studied in India, Vinson published several works on different aspects of Basque. Of these, the best known is his 1891 volume entitled *Bibliographie de la langue basque,* which for many years was a fundamental resource for scholars interested in Basque.

16. Luis Michelena, *Historia de la literatura vasca* (Madrid: Minotauro, 1960), p. 20.

17. (1889–1991). Basque ethnographer and anthropologist. A selection of his work is included in volume 3 of this collection.

18. L. Michelena, *Historia de la literatura vasca*, 1960, p. 13.

19. See, in this same collection, Juan Madariaga Orbea, *Anthology of Apologists and Detractors of the Basque Language* (Reno: Center for Basque Studies, University of Nevada, Reno, 2006).

20. Foreign linguists have always been interested in studying Basque, a rarity in Europe since it is a language with no known relatives. One such linguist was Louis Lucien Bonaparte (1813–1891), who made important contributions to the study of Basque dialects.

21. We will use various equivalent names to refer to this institution: Royal Academy of the Basque Language, Euskaltzaindia, or simply the Academy.

22. Koldo Mitxelena, "Ortografía," in *Euskera* (Bilbao: Euskaltzaindia) 13 (1968): 203–19.

23. By convention, peninsular Basques are those who live on the Spanish side of the border, while continental Basques are those who live on the French side.

24. Etxenike (or Echenique, in non-Basque spelling), professor of physics at the UBC, is today one of our most-cited and widely known researchers—and definitely the one who has achieved most awards, both at home (the Euskadi Research Award, the Prince of Asturias Award, etc.) and abroad (Max Planck, Dupont, etc.).

25. *Languages and Protolanguages* (UPV/EHU, 1997).

26. Koldo Mitxelena, "The Ancient Basque Consonants" (1957) and "The Latin and Romance Element in Basque" (1974), published in Joseba A. Lakarra and R. L. Trask (ed.), *Towards a History of the Basque Language* (Amsterdam: John Benjamins Publishing Company, 1995).

27. Koldo Mitxelena, *La lengua vasca* (Durango: Leopoldo Zugaza, 1977).

28. As editor of this anthology, I of course bear full responsibility for the final choice of its contents. However, I owe profuse thanks to my friend and colleague, Joseba Lakarra, professor of Basque philology at the UBC, for his helpful suggestions during the entire process.

29. Koldo Mitxelena, "Los vascos y su nombre," *RIEV* 29, 1 (1984): 9–29. (Also included in Luis Michelena, *Sobre historia de la lengua vasca* 2 (San Sebastián: ASJU, 1988), pp. 538–54).

30. Koldo Mitxelena, "Romanización y lengua vasca," in *FLV* (Pamplona) 16: 189–198. (Also included in Luis Michelena, *Sobre historia de la lengua vasca* 1 (San Sebastián: ASJU, 1988), pp. 156–65).

31. Koldo Mitxelena, *Textos arcaicos vascos* (Madrid: Minotauro, 1964). We have used the 1990 UBC edition.

32. Koldo Mitxelena, *Sobre el pasado de la lengua vasca* (San Sebastián: Editorial Auñamendi, 1964.) (Also included in L. Michelena, *Sobre historia de la lengua vasca* 1, pp. 1–74).

33. Luis Michelena, *Fonética histórica vasca* (revised and enlarged second edition) (San Sebastián: ASJU, 1977).

34. Luis Michelena, "De fonética vasca. La distribución de las oclusivas aspiradas y no aspiradas," *BAP* 7: 571–82. (Also included in L. Michelena, *Sobre historia de la lengua vasca* 1, pp. 213–219)

35. Koldo Mitxelena, "Euskal literaturaren bereizgarri orokorrak," in A. Tovar (ed.), *Euskal linguistika eta literatura: bide berriak* (Bilbao: Deustuko Unibertsitateko Argitarazioak, 1981), pp. 259–78. (Also included in L. Michelena, *Sobre historia de la lengua vasca* 2, pp. 681–93. A magnificent version in Spanish, translated by Jorge Giménez Bech, can be found in *Koldo Mitxelena entre nosotros* (Irun: Alberdania, 2001), pp. 69–90.)

36. Koldo Mitxelena, "Euskal literaturaren kondairarako oinarriak," in *Euskal linguistika eta literatura: bide berriak* (Bilbao: Deustuko Unibertsitateko Argitarazioak, 1981), pp. 279–92 (Also included in L. Michelena, *Sobre historia de la lengua vasca* 2, pp. 694–703.)

37. L. Michelena, *Historia de la literatura vasca*, pp. 35–82.

38. Koldo Mitxelena, "Ortografía," 203–19.

39. Koldo Mitxelena, "Arantzazutik Bergarara," *Euskera* 23 (1978) (2nd edition): 467–77. (Also included in L. Michelena, *Sobre historia de la lengua vasca* 2, pp. 984–90).

40. Koldo Mitxelena, "La normalización de la forma escrita de una lengua: el caso vasco," in *Revista de Occidente* (Madrid) nos. 10–11, suppl. 2 (1982): 55–75.

41. Koldo Mitxelena, "Lengua común y dialectos vascos," in *ASJU* 15 (1981): 291–313.

42. Koldo Mitxelena, "Vocabulario vasco (Ensayo de una interpretación de la lengua vasca)" *BRSVAP* 16 (1960): 384–87.

CHAPTER 1: **The Basque Language**

1. Written Basque was standardized in 1968 (see below in this volume) and called for the use of the letter *h* on the Spanish side of the border as well as in the French Basque Country. Mitxelena refers to this new "fashion" with characteristic irony, heightened in this case by the fact that he was the one to propose its use.

2. As Mitxelena suggests in the following discussion, *erdera* refers, according to some authors, to *erdi-era*, where *erdi* means "half," and *-era* is a suffix used in naming certain languages: e.g. *indoeuropera* "Indo-European," *bulgariera* "Bulgarian." Thus, all other languages would, for a Basque speaker, be merely "half languages."

3. Pronounced /awski/ in Latin, singular Auscus.

4. The etymology of *ummesahar* is obscure, but is perhaps related to *ume* "child" as an evolved form of **onbe/*unbe*.

5. The dialect spoken in Soule, the eastern-most area of the Basque Country, located on the French side of the border.

6. Similar to "the pot calling the kettle black."

7. Mitxelena is referring to the two protagonists of the Basque novel *Peru Abarka*, written by Juan Antonio Mogel at the beginning of the nineteenth century.

8. Two regions belonging to the province of Navarra.

9. As Mitxelena mentioned earlier, in Basque, all other languages are "half languages." Accordingly, a person who speaks only a language other than Basque is an *erdaldun* (*erdara+dun*), just as one who speaks Basque (and possibly some other language as well) is an *euskaldun* (*euskara+dun*). The term *erdaldun huts* emphasizes, through the adjective, that the person concerned speaks only Spanish or French, but not *euskera* in the Basque Country. The terms *arrotz* "alien" and *atzerritar* "stranger/ foreigner" refer to people from outside the country.

10. A major problem in Basque, dealt with at length in the chapter "Basques and Their Name," is the fact that while there is a name for a person who does not speak Basque (*erdaldun*) and a name for a person who does (*euskaldun*), there is no term in Basque for a native of the Basque Country to stand in opposition to the word for foreigner (*arrotz*)—hence the X.

11. Schools where all subjects are taught in Basque from kindergarten through twelfth grade.

12. The speech of Lapurdi, in the eastern part of the French Basque Country, whose maximum exponent was Axular.

13. The written Guipuzcoan standard that Azkue proposed as the standard for all of Basque.

14. Mitxelena is referring to the conjunction *eta* "and," which is identical to the acronym ETA, the name of the persistent Basque terrorist group.

CHAPTER 2: **Basques and Their Name**

1. See the recent Antonio Tovar, "Vascos, vascones, euskera," *FLV* 49 (1987): 5–9, and earlier his "On the words *vascones y euskera*" *Aingeru Irigarayri Omenaldia*, (San Sebastián: Eusko Ikaskuntza, 1985), pp. 245–55.

CHAPTER 3 **contains no notes.**

CHAPTER 4: **History and Prehistory of the Language**

1. Cf. U. Weinreich, "A Retrogradate Sound Shift in the Guise of a Survival," in *Miscelánea homenaje a André Martinet* 2 ([La Laguna, Canarias]: Universidad de La Laguna, 1958), pp. 221–67.

2. Ramón Menéndez Pidal, *Manual de gramática histórica española* (Madrid: Espasa-Calpe, 1941), p. 307ff.; Frederich Hanssen, *Gramática histórica de la lengua castellana* (Buenos Aires: El Ateneo, 1945), p. 105ff.

3. Among linguists it is common to write that the Roncalese *untxi* "rabbit" is related in one way or another to the Latin *cuniculus* (cf. DELL, no vol.), although the details of the relationship are not very clear, without observing that another variation of the Basque word exists, *enchea* in Araquistáin (Gipuzkoan or Alavese-Navarrese?), whose pronunciation is probably less altered that that of *untxi*.

4. Abundant information about that which follows can be found in two books with the same title: *Historia de la literatura vasca,* recently published by Father Luis Villasante (Bilbao, 1961) and by this author (Madrid, 1960 [2nd ed. San Sebastián, 1988]).

5. For the boundaries of the language, see Julio Caro Baroja, *Materiales para una historia de la lengua vasca en su relación con la latina* (Salamanca: Universidad de Salamanca, 1945), p. 7ff., and the works of various authors collected by B. Estornés Lasa in *Geografía histórica de la lengua vasca,* two volumes (Zarauz: Editorial Icharopena, 1960–61).

6. His works have just appeared in the book *El vascuence en La Rioja y Burgos* (San Sebastián: 1962).

7. See notes 1 and 2.

8. Nicolaas Gerard H. Deen, *Glossaria duo Vasco-Islandica* (Amsterdam: H. J. Paris, 1937).

9. See Julio Caro Baroja, *Los vascos* (Madrid: Minotauro, 1958), p. 466ff and the note.

10. *Egan* 1960, p. 229.

11. José M. Lacarra, *Vasconia medieval, historia y filología* (San Sebastián: ASJU, 1957), summarizes the sources, published and unpublished.

12. It is number 91 of the edition by Father L. Serrano, *Cartulario de San Millán de la Cogolla* (Madrid, 1930).

13. A. Marcos Pous, "Una nueva estela funeraria hispanorromana procedente de Lerga (Navarra)," *PV* 21 (1960): 319–33.

14. *Materiales,* between pp. 36 and 37.

15. Cf. Michael I. Rostovtzeff, *Historia social y económica del Imperio Romano* (2nd edition) (Madrid: Espasa-Calpe, 1962), p. 104ff.

16. "Los pueblos del norte de la Península Ibérica," Madrid, 1943, p. 103 and following. In this work we find the most acute and detailed study of Romanization of those peoples.

17. See J. Maluquer de Motes, "Contribución de la arqueología al conocimiento de la formación del pueblo vasco," *Zumárraga* 4 (1955): 57–67.

18. "Sur une couche préromane dans la toponymie de Gascogne et de l'Espagne du Nord," *RFE* 36 (1952), 209–56.

19. Ana M. Echaide studies the distribution of the names in -*oz* in her as yet unpublished report to the Third International Congress of Pyreneean Studies (Gerona, 1958).

20. Antonio Tovar, *El euskera y sus parientes,* p. 88ff.

21. See especially the acts of the Sixth International Congress of Onomastic Sciences, Munich, 1960, p. 105ff.

CHAPTER 5: **Relatives of the Basque Language**

1. Emile Benveniste, "La classification des langues," *Conférences de l'Institut de Linguistique de l'Université de Paris* 11 (1952–53): 33–50.

2. "A Quanititative Approach to the Morphological Typology of Languages," *International Journal of American Linguistics* 26 (1960), 178–94.

3. Cf. Alfred North Whitehead, *La ciencia y el mundo moderno* (Spanish translation of *Science and the Modern World*) (Buenos Aires: Losada, 1949), p. 44ff.

4. "Gab es Nominalklassen in allen kaukasischen Sprachen?" *Corolla linguistica. Festschrift F. Sommer* (Wiesbaden, 1955), 26–33.

5. "Parenté linguistique." *Lingua* 3 (1952): 2–16.

6. Cf. *DES* II, p. 404ff.

7. *DES* I, p. 74 and 482.

8. P. 26: "das Bestehen lautgesetzliche Wortgleichungen."

9. The Hittite forms, in simplified spelling, are taken from J. Friedrich, *Hethitisches Elementarbuch* (Heidelberg, 1960).

10. Cf. C. C. Uhlenbeck, "Basque et ouralo-altaïque," *RIEV* 6 (1912): 412–14.

11. Antonio Tovar, *ELH,* p. 5–26. The points of view summarized here are developed in "Comentarios en torno a la lengua ibérica," *Zephyrus* 12 (1961): 5–23.

12. That is, those who are not specialists in questions of language. See for example D. Fletcher Valls, *Problemas de la lengua ibérica* (Valencia, 1960), pp. 40ff.

13. Included in it, for example, Nubian. Schuchardt's most important work in this area is "Baskisch-hamitische Wortvergleichungen," *RIEV* 7 (1913): 289–339.

14. See Marcel Cohen, "Langues chamito-sémitiques," *Les langues du monde* (Paris, 1924), p. 82–181.

15. "El vasco y el camítico," *RIEV* 25 (1934): 240–44.

16. Cf. nevertheless, G. Deeters, "Der Name der kaukasischen Iberer," *Mné·me·s khárin. Gedankenschrift P. Kretschmer* (Vienna, 1956), 85–88.

17. See, above all, *Baskisch-kaukasische Etymologien, Heidelberg, 1949,* and "L'euskaro-caucasique," *Hom. Urq.* 3, 207–32. Many of the comparative works of Bouda and Lafon have appeared in *EJ* and in the *BAP.*

18. "Les origines de la langue basque," *Conférences de l'Institut de Linguistique de l'Université de Paris* 10 (1950–51): 59–81. "Concordances morphologiques entre le basque et les langues caucasiques," *Word* 7 (1951): 227–44, and 8 (1952): 80–94. *Etudes basques et caucasiques* (Salamanca, 1952). "Le géorgien et le basque sont-ils des langues parentes?" *Bedi Karthlisa,* Nos. 26–27, November 1957.

19. Adolf Dirr, *Einführung in das Studium der kaukasischen Sprachen* (Leipzig: Verlag der Asia Major, 1928). G. Dumézil, "Langues caucasiennes," *Les langues du monde,* 228–54. Karl Bouda, *Introducción a la lingüística caucásica* (Salamanca, 1952).

20. Suffice it to mention the debate carried on by different specialists in the Voprosy jazykoznanija in Moscow, 1954–56, about internal and external relationships of the Caucasian languages.

21. Emile Benveniste, "Langues asianiques et méditerranéennes," *Les langues du monde*, 184–225. Cf. also René Lafon, "Le basque dans la nouvelle édition des Langues du Monde (1952)," *BAP* 9 (1953): 229–34.

22. See his "Bericht über sprachliche und volkskundliche Forschungen im Hunzatal," *Anthropos* 55 (1960): 657–64, with bibliography.

23. There is a useful comparative lexicon, more useful for the material gathered than for the analyses, by A. Čikobava, *Dictionnaire comparé txhane-mégrélien-géorgien* (Tiflis, 1938) (in Georgian, with summaries in French and in Russian), where Svanic correlates are also cited when they exist.

24. *Das Kharthwelische Verbum* (Leipzig, 1930), p. 2.

25. See K. H. Schmidt, *Studien zur Rekonstrucktion des Lautstandes der südkaukasischen Grundsprache* (Wiesbaden, 1962), which we have not been able to make use of here.

26. H. Vogt, "Structure phonémique du géorgien," *NTS* 18 (1951): 5–90.

27. Marr himself saw this, "Le terme basque udagara 'loutre'," *Recueil Japhétique* 1 (1922): 7.

28. "Contribution à la grammaire historique des langues khartvéliennes," *Archiv Orientálni* 23 (1955): 77–89.

29. See the lists of words included by K. Bergsland and H. Vogt, "On the Validity of Glottochronology," *Current Anthropology* 3 (1962), 115–53.

30. Cf. H. Vogt, "Alternances vocaliques en géorgien," *NTS* 11 (1939), 118–35.

31. "Etudes comparatives sur le caucasique du nord-est," *NTS* 7:178ff and 9:115ff.

32. The most important is "Nordkaukasische Wortgleichungen," *Wiener Zeitschrift für die Kunde des Morgenlandes* 37 (1930), 76–92.

33. "La position linguistique des langues caucasiennes," *Studia linguistica* 4 (1950): 94–107.

34. Cf. the Russian preterite, of nominal origin, whose four forms are distinguished according to gender and number, singular masculine *pisal* "he wrote, you wrote," feminine *pisala*, neuter *pisalo*, plural (for the three genders) *pisali*.

35. Article cited in note 4, "Gab es Nominalklassen. . ."

36. Cf. H. Vogt, "La parenté des langues caucasiques. Un aperçu général," *NTS* 12 (1942): 242–57.

37. Cf. *Problema jazyka kak predmeta jazykoznanija*, Moscow, 1959. For the caucasian languges, "O dvux osnovnux voprosax izučenija iberijsko-kavkazskix jazykov," *Voprosy jazykoznanija*, 6 (1955): 66–92. "Iberijsko-kavkazskoe jazykoznanie, ego obščelingvističeskie ustanovki i osnovnye dostiženija," *Izvestija Akademii nauk SSSR*, otdelenie literatury i jazyka, 17 (1958): 113–29. "Die ibero-kaukasischen Gebirgssprachen und der heutige Stand ihrer Erforschung in Georgien," *Acta Orientalia Hungarica* 9 (1959): 109–61.

38. Compare among ourselves Campión's incomprehension of the neogrammatical methods as they appear for example in *Euskariana* (10th series), *Orígenes del pueblo euskaldún* 3rd part, p. 106ff.

39. "Le basque et les langues caucasiques," *BSL* 51 (1955): 121–47.

40. Cf. *Problema èrgativnoj konstrukcii v iberijsko-kavkazskix jazykax* (in Georgian, with a summary in Russian) Vol. I (Tiflis, 1948) and Vol. II (Tiflis, 1961). For Basque, see furthermore A. Martinet, "La construction ergative et les structures élémentaires de l'énoncé," *Journal de psychologie normale et pathologique* 55 (1958): 377–92, and "Le sujet comme fonction linguistique et l'analyse syntaxique du basque," *BSL* 57 (1962): 73–82, in response to the critical observations of Lafon, *BSL* 55 (1960): 186–21.

41. See Vogt's summary of Bouda's *Baskisch-kaukasische Etymologien*, NTS 17 (1950): 537–49.

42. *Hom. Urq.* II, p. 229ff.

43. There is no reason to hide the fact that other authors arrive at more optimistic conclusions than those expressed here. Also Tovar, *La lengua vasca*, p. 25ff.

44. *BSL* 26 (1925), 273. [Citation originally in French.]

45. "El método léxico-estadístico y su aplicación al vascuence," *BAP* 17 (1961): 249–81.

46. C. D. Chrétien, "The Mathematical Model of Glottochronology," *Language* 38 (1962): 11–37. What Chrétien disputes—certainly with good reasons—is not the mathematical model as is natural, but its applicability to the problems of dating in diachronic linguistics.

CHAPTER 6: **The Ancient Consonant System**

1. "Las antiguas consonantes vascas," *Hom. Martinet* I, 118 passim.

2. *Economía*, 885ff.

3. In *janegazu(e)* "eat it," etc. the interpretation of -g- in the place of a sibilant depends on the way we understand the appearance of *h, g, r* between vowels, that the majority of authors have generally considered "epenthetic" (the insertion of an unetymological letter into a word). Here on the contrary a greater entity is attributed to them: In the reconstruction they have at minimum the value of marking the ancient syllabic limits, at least most of the time. On the other hand, the supposition that -g- in this example continues an ancient voiced aspiration, the residue of a sibilant, is not at all impossible.

4. *Le basque souletin nord-oriental*, 31. See also *RIEV* 23 (1932): 168ff.

5. For everything having to do with aspiration a fundamental text is Rene Lafon, "Remarques sur l'aspiration en basque," *Mélanges Gavel* (Toulouse, 1948), 55ff.

6. Groups like *nth, lth* are rare, except in Souletin, for the reason indicated in 12.6 and 18.9.

7. Luchaire, *Orígenes*, 27ff; *Etudes*, 207.

8. Menéndez Pidal, *Orígenes*, § 41$_6$ a, p. 215. The names of La Reja can now be compared with those of an original document from the middle of the thirteenth century, published and annotated by A. Ubieto Arteta: "Un mapa de la diócesis de Calahorra en 1257," *Revista de Archivos, Bibliotecas y Museos* 60 (1954): 275ff.

9. The names of towns without references came from *CSMill*, 91.

10. If Basque *olha* is effectively a part of *Barolha*, which is far from certain, we would have a Romance evolution from Basque *lh* analogous to that of Latin *lj*, *c'l*, etc. (modern *Baroja*), while in *Olhabarri* (modern *Ollabarre*) there would be a coincidence with Latin *ll*.

11. Cf. the passage from Menéndez Pidal cited in note 5: "The *h* was able to disappear in writing: . . . we do not know if this depended on having different grades of intensity, ending with not being pronounced at all, or if it was not written because it was not considered a true "letter" but rather only an accessorial modification." See also, for this whole question, Jungemann, 378 onward.

12. Also distinct would be *merkátü* "reduced in price," derived from *mérke* "inexpensive," and *merkhátü* "market." The recent contribution of Rene Lafon, *Hom. Martinet* II, 77ff., is important. In the Souletin of Larrau, there are hardly any cases (p. 91 on) in which the oppositions *t* / *th* and *k* / *kh* constitute the only distinction, and those that are cited are rather artificial: it seems that there are none for the opposition *p* / *ph*. We have then the interesting theoretical characteristic that unites all the necessary conditions for differentiating signifiers, only it seems that it does not distinguish any.

13. Examples of parasitic *h* are found in many languages, if not in all that possess this phoneme: Spanish *henchir*, *hinojo* "knee," French *haut*, German *heischen* (old High German *eiscōn*), Attican Greek *he-méra*, etc. But the Basque examples turn out to be comparatively more numerous. This does not mean, however, that some of the explanations that are usually offered in other languages do not apply in our case. Thus *harroka* could be *arroka* x *harri* "stone," *hezkabia* could owe its beginning to a cross with *hatz* "itch, mange," etc.

14. The explanation proposed for Greek *heúo* "I burn," Welsh *haiarn* "iron" could be valid for example for *(h)ezur* < **ehazur* < **enazur* (see 5.8, note 16).

15. In Dechapare *(h)eure*, Etcheberri of Ciboure normally *heure*. The protoBasque form should have been **hi-haur-e*, or **hi-hor-e* literally "from this, that, you (fam.)." In Dechepare "you (fam.) yourself" is *hiaur*, ergative *hiaurc*, *ihaurc*, *ihaurorrec*.

16. If *or(h)oitu* "remembered" originated with **ko-*, a possibility pointed out in 4.12, note 16, the secondary interior aspiration could have been the cause of the loss of the initial aspiration.

17. Cf. Ioh. [sic, biblical] 17, 26: *niri on eritzi draután onheriztea* "dilectio quam dilexisti me." The same difference between *on eritzi* and *onherizte*, where the aspiration is the mark of a true compound, is found by comparing Lc. 6, 26, *onherranen çaituztenean* "cum benedixerint uobis" with 1 Cor. 4, 12, *vngui erraiten dugu* "benedicimus."

18. Cf. old Logudorese *maistru de aschia* "carpenter" (*DES* I, 133 a), Catalan *mestre (de cases)* "bricklayer," etc. We must add *aieru* "signal, mention" (Axular 265, etc.) which later authors translated as "conjecture" (Schuchardt, *ZRPh* 11 (1887): 476), in the last term from Latin **pagella* (*REW* 6144) by mediation of Gascon: cf. Aezcoan dialect *pazeilu* "tailor's measurement, metric tape without divisions." The spelling *ageru* (*Manual* II, 100) reveals it as a loan word, where it probably means "doubt."

19. French-Basque *ahetz* "binding of wines," Latin *faex*, undoubtedly owes its strange appearance to Gascon *héts*, *ahéts* "sediment" (Rohlfs, 185, p. 48). The clearest

exception would be *ahutz* "cheek," if it comes from Latin *fauces*: cf. *autzak* "chubby cheeks" in Añibarro, who gives *pautza* as the Bizkaian equivalent.

20. In *CSMill.* there are, among others, *Hagurahin, Harhaia, Hereinzguhin, Bahaheztu,* modern *Maeztu.* It once also carried *h* after the sibilant: *Malizhaeza.*

21. Michel Lejeune, *Traité de phonétique grecque* (Paris, 1955), 77.

22. In Leiçarraga's Souletin vocabulary *cathiña* "chain" must have been a mistake, since modern Souletin has *khatiña.*

23. Some derivative suffixes, dealt with in the following §§, be they old free forms or not, carry aspiration, especially in Souletin.

24. The same thing happens with other demonstratives used as articles: Dechepare *Ez batori ahalduquet ezetare vercia* "I will not be able to have either one," Leiçarraga *guiçon gazteorrec* "that young man" (Mt. 19, 22), Axular *haur guztior* "all this [sic]," etc.

25. Remember that an imperative can start the phrase without any prefix, which does not normally occur with other finite forms. Compare the initial from Leiçarraga *abila* "you (fam.) go" / *habil* "go (imperative)" *(haitsa* "go down").

26. The principal exception is Leiçarraga *erekhar,* Souletin *e(r)ákhar* "to have something brought," where the simple *ekhar* will have influenced it. Perhaps *erho* "to kill," a two-syllable word, is a causative (from *jo* "to hit, wound" or from *eho* "to grind").

27. Lafon, *Système* I, 473ff. and 491ff. The adverbial determinants, originally nouns, such as *ahal, ohi, othe,* however, have not lost their aspiration.

28. One of the exceptions is, as will be noted, the loan word *hautatu,* mentioned in 11.6, where *h-* is secondary.

29. Lhande suggests that Leiçarraga *hertu,* Souletin *hértü* "diminished, reduced" is derived from *erdi* "half."

30. The nasal must be secondary, otherwise it would rarely happen that *nk* not be voiced as *ng* in any place.

31. See my article "La distribución de las oclusivas aspiradas y no aspiradas," *BAP* 7 (1951): 539ff. In it, one peculiarity of Leiçarraga's language was not recorded, because I did not notice it. He noted aspiration in designative participles between the second and third syllables in cases such as *eyarthu* (Mt. 6, 6: 13, 6, but Mc. 9, 18 *eyhartu,* cf. Oihenart *Poes.* 51 *eihartu,* Onsa 101 and 104 *ayhartu*), *garaithu* (Ioh. 16, 33, 1 Tim. 1, 14, but Ap. 3, 21; 13, 11 *garaitu,* cf. Sauguis 1, Oihenart *Prov.* 267, verbal stem *garhait,* etc.). But it deals with a peculiarity that is not confirmed by any other oral or written text, based on what I could find, and disregarding the inconsistencies observed in Leiçarraga's own work.

32. Aspiration is more frequent in Souletin: *phárti* "get underway," Leiçarraga *parti; pháusü* "calm," Leiçarraga *pausu; khúntü* "account," Leiçarraga *kontu; khandé(r)a* "candle," Leiçarraga *kandela,* etc.

33. See *Via Domitia* 4 (1957): 20.

34. According to Nils M. Holmer, *BAP* 6 (1950): 404, in the common forms *aita* "father" and *maite* "beloved" the *it* could be the result of old *t'* (see above, 10.3 b): cf. perhaps for the first, Aquitanian *Attacconi* dative, *Attacconis* genitive, *CIL* 13: 265.

35. In case someone wishes to go back that far, I note that in pre-Latin Basque terms that have been considered of Indo-European origin, one can compare the initial sounds of Basque *argi* "light, clear," Hittite *harki-* "white, clear," Basque *arrano* "eagle," Hittite *hara(n)-* "eagle." With regard to Basque *hartz* "bear," we are not sure that Hittite *hartagga-* has that meaning (J. Friedrich, *Hethitisches Wörterbuch* (Heidelberg, 1952), no volume).

36. For the possibility that g and r are really continuations of old *h*, cf. Grammont, *Traité de Phonétique*, 206: "Au point d'articulation du g l'*h* sonore est un phonème que le latin ne possède pas non plus: mais rien ne ressemble à un g comme un r post-palatal (cf. dans certains parlers allemands les confusions perpétuelles entre *wagen* et *waren*). Il se produit donc en latin une confusion auditive entre ces deux phonèmes, puis un remplacement articulatoire du premier par le second; ensuite l'*r* ordinaire du latin, qui est alvéolaire, se substitue à cet r postpalatal." (At the point of articulation of g the voiced *h* is a phoneme that Latin no longer possesses: but nothing resembles a g like a postpalatal r (cf. in certain German dialects the perpetual confusion between *wagen* and *waren*). Thus in Latin there is produced an auditory confusion between these two phonemes, hence an articulatory replacement of the first by the second; consequently, the ordinary Latin r, which is alveolar, is substituted for that postpalatal r.) The letter that represents a voiced velar fricative in the original has been reproduced here by g.

37. More examples in my article "De fonética vasca. La aspiración intervocálica," *BAP* 6 (1950), 443 onward. Consequently *nahi* is written for *na(h)i* in an extensive manuscript, strange for several reasons, that is found among the papers of the Bonaparte collection in the General Archive of Navarra, entitled "Doctrina para la Instrucción de la Familia de Casa en Vascuenze."

38. As a reminder, some facts studied elsewhere relative to the groups *rh* and *rrh* are summarized here: r can be secondary and originates from (Latin) *l*: sorho. In Souletin the distinction between *rh* and *rrh* had to be maintained in some way, given that their modern reflections are kept quite distinct: *h* and *rh* respectively. Aspiration then does not seem to behave like a consonant since the opposition r / R is neutralized before a consonant. Finally, before *rh* there is Souletin *u* from old **u*: Gèze *burhaso* "ancestor," *burhau* "basphemy," *gurhi* "butter." In compounds, nevertheless, *bürhézür*, where the simple *bü'rü* has had an influence, like *ür'he*, *ürháts*, etc.

CHAPTER 7: About Basque Phonetics

1. René Lafon "Remarques sur l'aspiration en basque" (*Mélanges Gavel*, 1948), p. 60. The references to this article will be abbreviated from now on as *Rem*.

2. *Le basque de la Basse-Soule orientale*, a linguistic collection published by the Société de Linguistique de Paris, XLVI, Paris, 1939.

To indicate aspirated occlusives, Dechepare uses *pph*, *th* and *qh* (sometimes *cc*); Liçarrague *pp* (*ph-*), *k* (while *qu* and *c* (*c* before *a*, *o*, and *u*),denote the unaspirated unvoiced occlusive) and *th*. Dechepare's notation is clearly defective, in the sense that aspiration is not always indicated: *vortizqui* along with *vorthizqui*, *gertuz* along with *gerthuz*, *icussi* along with *iqhussi*, etc.

I have kept in mind naturally the dictionaries of Azkue and Lhande, but I only use them in a very restricted manner, indicating them as the point of origin in each case.

Their inestimable lexical richness makes them very difficult to use in a work like this one, given the heterogeneity of their sources and the frequent impossibility of controlling their data.

For the Basque dialectal varieties and some publications I utilize the same abbreviations I used in a previous article in this *BAP* ("De fonética vasca. La aspiración intervocálica," 6 (1950): 443–59).

3. *Prim* (Halle, 1923) § 156, p. 30. In this sense Lafon understood that it referred expressly to this passage of Schuchardt: "Dans les dialects basque-francais, il devient *th* après *r* ou après diphtongue: Liçarrague a *deithu* 'appelé,' *sarthu* 'entré,' *sorthu* 'né,' *neurthu* 'mesuré'; toutefois *agertu* 'apparu' a gardé son *t*, ansi que *hartu* 'pris,' ce dernier à cause de son *h*- initial. Le *th* apparaît aussi dans *bathu* 'uni, rencontré,' de *bat* 'un'." *Le système du verbe basque au XVIe siècle* 2, p. 13. (In the French Basque dialects, it becomes *th* after *r* or after a diphthong: Liçarrague has *deithu* "called," *sarthu* "entered," *sorthu* "born," *neurthu* "measured"; *agertu* "appeared" has always kept its *t*, as well as *hartu* "taken," the latter because of its initial *h*-. The *th* also appears in *bathu* "united, found," from *bat* "one.")

4. In Larrasquet (p. 204) I find, however, *suskhandera [ssüszkhândéa]* "lizard," given as common Souletin.

5. Lafon, *Syst.*, II, p. 14.

6. See the article cited in note 2.

7. The personal forms of the verb require special study, since the phonetic conditions to which they are submitted are not the same as those of the nouns, as in other cases. From here arises the difference between Dechepare *iqhussi*, Liçarrague *ikussi* and Dechepare *dacussat*, etc., Liçarrague *badacussat*, etc., as Schuchardt saw: "it is the effect of a difference in stress." (*Primitiae Linguae Vasconum*, § 106, p. 26). Aspiration is in general less frequent in the personal forms. As an example of vacillation, referencing Larrasquet (p. 19), I will cite the difference between *balekio, balekie, balekit,* etc., from the Tardets area and *balekhyó, balekhyé, balékhit* from SNO.

8. Naturally I do not exclude the possibility of special cases. One must also deal with errors, principally printing errors, that can appear in the texts. Thus, for example, Liçarrague *eyarthu* (Mt. 13, 6; in the index of Lc 6 there is *escu eyarrha* clearly impossible), cf. Liçarrague *eyhar* and *eyhartu* (Mc. 9, 18) (*eihartu* also in Oihenart, *Poesías*, p. 51); *garaithu* (Ap. 13, 11), cf. *garaitu, garaita* (Ap. 3, 21) and Oihenart *garhaizea* (*Prov.* 550), *garhaita* "advantage" (Prov. 629). The *barathü* that we read in Etchahun's poems, published by Lhande and Larrasquet (Euskaltzaleen-Biltzarra, 1946, p. 65); if I may venture a conjecture with my imperfect knowledge of Souletin, it must be through *baratü* (cf., SNO *baátü* "to remain, to stop"). In Azkue I find a Low Navarrese *anetha* "fennel."

The principal exceptions are compounds such as SNO *a(r)akhói* "carnivore," where one must keep in mind the position of the stress, and Souletin (Azkue) *artolha* "shepherds' hut on the mountain," based on the simple *olha*. Cf. SNO *sarjálkhi* "entrance and exit."

9. Except, it seems, in some compounds: Dechepare *hilhoça*, Liçarrague *hilebethe*. But I would need to know to what point this has to do with etymological spellings and even if it has to do with true compounds.

10. Larrasquet (p. 21) corrects the *ürrüphe* "flat land" given by Lhande with *ürrüphéa* "extended plain." In view of Souletin (Azkue) *ürrupeira* (sic) "flat lands belonging to various owners without separations by walls," we are probably dealing with a representation from Latin *ripa* (Meyer-Lübke, *REW* 7328): cf. Spanish *ribera*, Provençal *ribieira*.

11. Apart from the already mentioned *ikhusi: dakusat*, we have Liçarrague *ethorri* (participle), *dathor, dathorren, dathorrela, niathorrec, athor, bethor,* but *datocen gatocen, banatorque (baniatorquec), badatorque, çatozte* (imperative), where it seems aspiration is lacking in the plural forms and in the forms possessing the suffix -*ke* (Dechepare *nator, nyatorqueçu*), and Liçarrague *ekarri* (particple), but *decarque, dacarqueitela, dacazquet, çacarquela, çacarqueitela* (although also *daccarraçuen, daccarqueçue,* but none with *k*), Dechepare *dacarrela, dacartela, dacacela*. In the imperative forms such as Dechepare *eqhardaçu*, Liçarrague *ekardaçue* we are surely dealing with a recent agglutination.

Also interesting is the fact that at times aspiration that exists in the simple forms is lacking in the nominal forms of the causative: Liçarrague *eracutsi, iracatsi*, SNO *e(r) akatsi, i(r)akutsi*. Cf. also Liçarrague *iracurri*, SNO *i(r)akur*. Liçarrague has on the other hand *erekarri* (SNO *e(r)ákhar* "to make someone carry"), with aspiration even in the finite forms (*ezterakarran [sic]*).

Without a doubt, Dechepare's *vaduqheçu* is very rare.

12. There are various cases in which infinite forms of denominative verbs present aspiration that is lacking in the noun: Liçarrague *nekatu* [sic] along with *neque*, SNO *maithátü* along with *máite*.

13. The SNO word *óker* (and *ópets*) "burp" is very interesting. It seems to be distinguished from *ókher* "twisted" by a lack of aspiration. There exists a variation *poker* that occurs in Oihenart (*Prov.* 496) and is in addition High Navarrese (Baztán), Low Navarrese, and common Laburdin, according to Azkue.

14. Liçarrague (Ap. 18, 7) translates the Greek *pénthos* as *vrthueria*. His first element is probably the participle *urthu* (Liçarrague *vr*, SNO *hur*). I am not familiar with the etymology of SNO *hértü* "to diminish in volume or quantity."

15. Karl Bouda (*EJ* 4 (1950): 326, n18) derives it from Latin *optatum*. But given the lack of Romance representations of *optare*, it would perhaps be preferable to think *aptare* (and *aptus*) with a pronunciation of the -*pt*- group analogous to that of certain Galician learned words. This pronunciation is evidenced for *adaptus* through Provençal *azaut* "handsome, capable" (cf. Catalan *asalt*), *azautar* "to be pleased with something" (*REW* 146).

The Latin word *adaptum,* specifically with sibilation of the apical consonant as in Provençal, could be also, better than *fascis*, the origin of Liçarrague *açauto* "handful," High Navarrese, Gipuzkoan, Laburdin, Bizkaian *azao*, Bizkaian *azau* "sheaf" (SNO *azáu*, with unvoiced *z*, "sheaf (of wheat)"; derivative *azautü*): cf. Spanish *atado*.

A non-etymological aspiration before *au-* is seen in *hauzu, haizu* "permitted, allowed," Souletin (Azkue) *haizü izan* "to dare," from Latin *ausus* (*REW* 809).

16. René Lafon (*RIEV* 25 (1934): 54–55) thinks that the preservation of *u* before *nk* is normal in Souletin. The preservation of *u* would be in this case a proof of the relative antiquity of the nasal. In any case, we lack the examples necessary for a conclusive demonstration.

17. Although H. Schuchardt (*Primitiae Linguae Vasconum* § 135) and Karl Bouda (*Das transitive und intransitive Verbum im Baskischen*, p. 64) seem to doubt that *bizi* and *p(h)iztu* (cf. *biztu*) are etymologically related, I do not believe they have good reason.

18. Complete data for *(k)ide* in René Lafon, *EJ* 3 (1949): 146–49.

19. Larrasquet (p. 22) expressly rejects the existence of Souletin *parthítü* "to divide," pointed out by Lhande, by correcting it with *phartítü* "to divide, to depart."

The form *cathina* given as Souletin by Liçarrague could also be a mistake. In SNO it is *khatiña*.

One must wonder if *f-* could also be the cause of dissimilation: cf. Liçarrague *fico, ficotze* (SNO *phiko*). I am not familiar with any case of coexistence, but the examples of *f* are rare. This could explain the lack of aspiration in Axular *faun* (from the same origin that High Navarrese, Gipuzkoan *bao* "empty" for which Bouda found a correspondence in Circassian): cf. *bahe, xahu,* etc. But we also find in Axular *plaundu* "to demolish, to raze" (p. 32) and, according to Oihenart, *deblauqui* or *debloqui* was used in Sara and Ascain (*RIEV* 4 (1910): 220).

20. Article cited in note 2.

21. Bouda presents a truly satisfactory equation, satisfactory at least if the period of the Basque-Caucasian linguistic community was a recent matter, between the Georgian *t'it'vél-i* "naked, bald" (Meckelein gives only "naked") Mingrelian *t'ut'eli* and Souletin *thípil* "deloused" (Chaho) "clearing (in a wood)," "mere, naked, clearly," *thipíltü* "to pluck." In addition there is the variation *bip(h)il* (High Navarrese, Low Navarrese, Laburdin) that in a Laburdin variety has the meaning "valient, resolved," *bip(h)ildu* "to pluck" and "to rob." But Latin possibly offers a simpler explanation in *depilare,* an etymology that I believe has been proposed somewhere.

22. This limitation cannot extend to a medieval document such as the so-called "Reja" of San Millán where the letter h, whatever its phonetic value happened to be, appeared in this position (*Hagurahin,* with double h, *Hereinzguhin*) as well as once after a sibilant (*Malizhaeza*).

23. H. Pedersen, *Vergleichende Grammatik der keltischen Sprachen* 1, p. 290, § 195.

24. Notice that the prosthetic vowels, the ones added at the beginning of the word (*errota, arropa, arroka*; cf. also *ezpata*) must always be kept in mind like any other syllable.

25. Aspiration is more frequent after *l*, although there are cases of vacillation such as Dechepare Liçarrague *alaba,* SNO *alhába* and even some words in which there is never aspiration, to the point that it was almost the rule in relatively ancient words. There are, on the contrary, several words in which aspiration is always lacking after r: *bero, buru,* etc. But even though these conditions can serve to support the presumption that *lh* and *rh* (Liçarrague distinguishes between *rrh* and *rh*) do not have etymological value, it would be premature to generalize this thesis without a detailed examination of all the material.

26. This is the explanation for SNO *orgambide, organhága* (*orgánta* is not completely clear to me) that Larrasquet explains, erroneously in my opinion, by *orgaren bide,* etc. Because SNO *orgá* (with nasal *a*) "cart" assumes a form **orgán-* (plus a

vowel), keeping in mind its irregular stress and the nasalization of the final vowel. The loss of the last vowel in the compounds is previous to the appearance of the intervocalic *-n-*, as indicated by the forms (especially the Bizkaian ones) *ardan-, aren-, arran-, borin-, burdin-, don-, garan-, kanpan-, pazin-, sen-, tupin-,* etc.

One should make the same observation with regard to SNO *bigá* (with nasal *a*) "heifer of eighteen to twenty months of age": cf. Bizkaian *bigae* and the etxended *bigantxa*.

CHAPTER 8: General Characteristics of Literature in the Basque Language

1. The original title was "Euskal literaturaren bereizgarri orokorrak," where the expression *euskal literatura* "Basque literature," according to K. M.'s explanation, could only be applied to literature written in the Basque language. Also, according to criteria put forth later by the author, the same occurred with expressions such as *euskal idazle* "Basque writer," *Euskal Herria* "the Basque Country," *euskal kultura* "Basque culture" and *euskal prentsa* "the Basque press," for example. Nevertheless, even among Basque speakers, a certain confusion can arise from time to time, because the term *euskal* is often used in reference to the Basque territory, in addition to the language. In the present article *euskal literatura* will be translated as "literature in the Basque language" or "literature in Euskera" and *euskal idazle* by "writer in the Basque language" or "writer in Euskera." Nevertheless, when the comprehension of the text requires it, the expressions *euskal idazle, Euskal Herria, euskal kultura,* and *euskal prentsa* will be preserved.

2. This lecture was dictated by K. M. at the University of Deusto (San Sebastian campus) during the school year 1977/78. The current text was transcribed by others and later became part of the book *Euskal linguistika eta literatura: bide berriak* (Basque Linguistics and Literature: New Paths).

3. *Historia de la Literatura Vasca* (Madrid: Minotauro, 1960).

4. *Euskal Literaturaren historia* (San Sebastian: Lur, 1971); *Historia social de la literatura vasca* (Madrid: Akal, 1976).

5. In the sense of "lovers of the Basque language."

6. Writer in the Basque language born in Bourges (seventeenth century).

7. Writer in the French language born in Mauleon (sixteenth century).

8. "We are the Basque press." J. G. B.'s translation into Spanish: "The press in the Basque language is us." [L.W.]

9. In Spanish in the original.

10. The discussion is collected in the book *Narrativa vasca actual. Antología y polémica* (Madrid: Zero zyx, 1979).

11. In Spanish in the original.

12. "Eusquérico," according to the *DRAE* (Dictionary of the Royal Academy of Spain). The words in quotation marks in the current paragraphs come from the original in the same form and language in which they are transcribed here.

13. See note 1.

14. Collected in the *DRAE* under the form "euscalduna" with the double meaning of "person who speaks Basque" and "Basque." K. M. uses it here in the first sense, which is the only meaning that the term fits in Euskera.

15. There and here, is not the faith of the Basques one faith? / Is not the venerable law we all love one law? / Is not everyone's sweet language the beloved and affable Euskera? / There and here, is not the Our Father said in Euskera?

16. "Oh, most beautiful language, with no beginning!"

17. The letter alluded to is found on pages 46–50 of the facsimile edition. Julio Urquijo published it previously in the article "¿Historia o novela? El herrador vascó-filo Juan Pablo Ulibarri," *Euskalerriaren Alde* 5 (1915): 225–31. (Note by Blanca Urgell.)

18. A term composed from the Basque word *erdara* or *erdera,* which designates, in its first meaning, any language different from Basque (although, in its current usage, it tends to identify with the language closest to the one using it, generally Spanish or French). *Erdaldun,* therefore, should be translated as "speaker or knower of a language different from Euskera," given that K. M. always has in mind both the neighborhood of Spanish as well as French, which invalidates here such restrictive equivalents as "Spanish speaker" and "French speaker." Nevertheless, K. M. himself, a few lines further on, utilizes the term *erdara* to refer to Spanish as the language of Gipuzkoan politics and administration.

19. Literally, "new Basque speaker." It refers to someone who has acquired Euskera after his maternal language.

20. Parallel to *euskaldun berri,* but referring to one who has acquired a language different from Euskera.

21. In Spanish in the original.

22. K. M. specifies the term "verso" (line) here in order to avoid having the Basque speaker interpret it as "estrofa" (strophe, verse), which is the commonly held meaning of the Basque word "bertso."

23. The red/ruddy shepherd.

24. K. M. seems to refer here to the writers of the peninsular Basque provinces [the provinces in Spain] when he says "our writers."

25. He is referring to the facsimile edition put out by the publisher Hordago in 1978.

26. K. M. appears to refer here to the Basque authors from one and the other parts of the Pyrenees.

27. Peninsular Navarra, in contrast with Low Navarre, a territory of the continental Basque Country [in France].

28. K. M. refers to the authors in Euskera from the territory to which he just alluded with the name of High Navarra, which corresponds to the modern territory of the Comunidad Foral de Navarra (Foral Community of Navarra).

29. Generically, pieces of popular poetry, commonly oral and extemporaneous, although they also circulated on written fliers (*bertsopaperak*).

30. Christian, I have given to you in Basque verses / The Catholic manual in my spare time, / Seeing, as I am Basque by birth, / That our nation has a love for couplets. / For that reason I have deliberately put it into verse for you / So that you may learn it sooner and recite it more often. / As before in distant Greece / They used to give the laws of the people in Song. / Since songs frequently rise to the lips of the people of the world, / In this way, by memorizing the songs, they will often come to mind. / Using that good custom line by line, / I have given you the Manual couplet by couplet.

31. K. M. refers here to the fishing fleet of the peninsular Basque coast.

32. *Historia social de la literatura vasca* (Madrid: Akal, 1976), p. 135. (Note by B. Urgell.)

33. "Texto de dos impresos sumamente raros de Juan Antonio de Moguel," *BAP* 20 (1964): 61–73. K. M. refers here to "Prospecto de una obra bascongada intitulada *Confesio ta comunioco sacramentuen gañean eracasteac*" [Teachings on the sacraments of confession and communion]. (Except for brackets, note by B. Urgell.)

34. In Spanish in the original.

35. *Obras Completas Euskéricas,* 2 volumes (Bilbao: La Gran Enciclopedia Vasca, 1973).

36. *Vida de San Ignacio.*

37. The brackets are by K. M.

38. With a view to the later publication of the current lecture, K. M. added a text "*Eranskin gisa*" (By way of attachment), in which he broaches diverse philological questions referring mostly to Ubillos. He initiated it through a parallel transcription of a text by Axular and another one, very similar, by Ubillos. Said parallel transcription has been collected, within the present book, in the text of the lecture "Bases para una historia de la literatura vasca."

CHAPTER 9: **Foundations for a History of Basque Literature**

1. See note 2 of the preceding text: "Características generales de la literatura en lengua vasca."

2. He refers to Luis Haranburu Altuna and, more concretely, to the criticism he made (Anaitasuna 217, August 30, 1971) about Ibon Sarasola's work *Euskal literaturaren historia* (History of Basque Literature). (Note by B. Urgell.)

3. In the article "Descubrimiento y redescubrimiento en textos vascos" (*FLV* 8 (1971): 149–68). (Note by B. Urgell.)

4. "From the saddle of the Virgin Mary" (*basta*: saddle, harness).

5. According to that correction, the text affirmed that Jesus was born "of the Virgin Mary."

6. See the edition of *Corografía de Guipúzcoa* published by Telletxea (San Sebastian: Sociedad Guipuzcoana de Ediciones y Publicaciones, 1969). (Note by B. Urgell.)

7. "*Xokudi* y otros en Barrutia," in "Miscelánea Filológica Vasca II" (*FLV* 30 (1978): 398ff. (Note by B. Urgell.)

8. If there is no inn in the town of Bethlehem / The Lord of Heaven is everywhere / The hour has arrived, beloved spouse / This child is about to be born, knock on the door (once the correction indicated by K. M. is incorporated).

9. "Knock on the door."

10. We are looking for an inn, do not deny us, please / Your effort will be rewarded (once K. M.'s correction is incorporated)

11. "Please do not deny us [shelter]."

12. "Deny."

13. "Act of gratitude after killing the whale."

14. The second edition dates from 1669, and is the only one we know.

15. *Refranes y Sentencias.*

16. "Do not ikastolacize your children: school them."

17. "To school" and "to ikastolacize" respectively. [L.W.: One must understand the differences in the educational systems and philosophies of the 1970s in the Basque Country in order to grasp the nuances of Aresti's usage.]

18. "He drowned them, along with all the hillsides, slopes, mountains and that whole world." (The fragment from Mendiburu that follows in the same paragraph is slightly different at the beginning: "and except for those, he drowned all the rest . . .")

19. "Cain left the presence of the Lord and lived in the Lost Land, east of Eden" (Genesis 4, 16).

20. See the previous lecture: "General characteristics of literature in the Basque language."

21. Axular.

22. To that end make an effort to learn the Manual / And by working in agreement with it, keep yourself from sin. / To that end I have put it in verse for you / in such a way that you will learn them sooner and recite them often. / I beg you, friend, to learn them with devotion / since I offer them to you with all good intentions.

23. "Last year I wrote and published a little book in Basque . . ., after that, this year, with the sainted help of the Lord, I have made, and want to bring to light another little piece whose greatness is enclosed in a fistful of papers, in it you will see three beautiful Princesses, which are Prayer, Fasting, and Alms."

24. For more details on the origin (because of Felipe II) of the decline that Bizkaia and Gipuzkoa suffered, see Selma Huxley Barkham, "Guipuzcoan Shipping in 1571 with Particular Reference to the Decline of the Transatlantic Fishing Industry," in *Anglo-American Contributions to Basque Studies: Essays in Honor of Jon Bilbao* (Reno, 1977), 73–81. (Author's note.)

25. The Church is a tree that reaches the stars, / . . . / Or put another way, the Church is a ship restored, / Tormented by the rains and winds of hell: / Windward against the wind from here to there, / Nevertheless, it will never shipwreck on the swell of the wave. / . . . / The burgess of this ship is my eternal Father / I am that captain's second. / The Holy Spirit is the pilot / Who guides us with great skill through the storms. / The Mother, at our side, is the first crew member. / The Apostles govern, the lay people are passengers. / The priests and friars are companions who have denied the world, / And

on my behalf they have chosen a life of pain. / The preaching wise men and doctors are soldiers, / Who vanquish the three angry enemies. / Recalcitrant heretics are prisoners according to the rules, / Since they hate the Holy Mother Church / Thus the Church is manned by the peoples, / The good and the bad all have their place. / But the Church as we commonly understand it / Is a Catholic congregation of all Christians. / The truth of the governing priests is the meeting place, / which in some Churches we call Holy. / Giving the name of the whole to the principal part / Since it is the most visible.

26. "Oaths and sufferings, legally and strictly."

27. The earth trembles beneath my feet, like the quarters of my flesh. (Translation by Jon Juaristi in *Flor de baladas vascas.*)

28. Being a fast day, a frugal dinner / they prepare at home; // Afterward they tell stories / or play mus // each one in his home / or in the home of some friends // They head for the happy mass / when it strikes midnight.

29. My brothers, my friends and those I love / Tied to me by the faith of Teseo / What Ovid said in the book of Sadness / I say to you now, good Basque country.

CHAPTER 10: **History of Basque Literature**

1. R. Menéndez Pidal, *Orígenes del español*, 460ff. and map.

2. D. J. Gifford and M. Molho, "Un antiguo texto en vascuence," *Príncipe de Viana* 18 (1957): 241–43; D. J. Gifford and L. Michelena, "Notas sobre un antiguo texto vasco (Biblioteca de la Catedral de Pamplona, codicile 7, folio 142 verso)," ibid., 19 (1958): 167–70.

3. According to Julio Caro Baroja, *Los Vascos*, 514, "a juzgar por las que nos quedan . . . era tan buena como la contemporánea de cualquier otra parte de España, si es que no la avantajaba en ciertas cualidades líricas" (to judge by the ones that remain . . . it was as good as the contemporary from any part of Spain, even if it did not enjoy certain lyric qualities).

4. See "Linajes y bandos," in Julio Caro Baroja, *Vasconiana (De Historia y Etnología)* (Madrid, 1957), p. 17ff. and lastly Ignacio Arocena, *Oñacinos y gamboínos. Introducción al estudio de la guerra de bandos* (Pamplona, 1959).

5. It seems to have been published for the first time by Salaberry in 1870.

6. See Odón de Apraiz, "Euskal-olertiyaren berezikai bat. Izadiyari deya maitasunezko olerki-asikeran," in *Homenaje a C. Echegaray* (San Sebastián, 1928), 601–09. It has to do with the "supplementary image," that is, the introductory image that is in counterpoint to the final "focal image," in this case *enian uste erraiten ziela / aitunen semek gezürrik* "I did not believe that noblemen told lies." Cf. Thomas A. Sebeok, "Sound and Meaning in a Cheremis Folksong Text," in *For Roman Jakobson* (The Hague: Mouton, 1956): 430–39.

7. As an example, "Aphal, aphal büria" ("Goizian goizik"), the protagonist of which is Gabrielle de Lohitéguy, who kept the dead body of her husband by her side for seven years. He was poisoned by a sprig of flowers on the very day of their wedding, a theme well known in other literatures. See P. J. A. de Donostia, *BRSVAP* 10 (1954): 333ff.

8. By Juan V. Araquistain in 1866.

9. The one about the tower of Aldaz in Lequeitio, collected by Azkue, *Euskaler-riaren Yakintza* 2:34–35 and 4:169–70. Its beginning (*Aldaztorreak ateak ditu letuez / ango plater-pitxeruak zidarrez*) is a clear parallel to the introduction of the ballad of Sandailia.

10. H. Gavel, "Un pélerin de Saint-Jacques au Pays basque à la fin du XVe siècle," in *GH* 2 (1922).

11. Father A. de Legarda, "Primera fase vasca impresa conocida en Torres Naharro, 1513," in *BRSVAP* 7 (1951): 41–48. See also in the same: "Primicias del vascuence impreso en el marqués de Santillana" (on the refrain "Sardina que el gato lleva . . ."), ibid., 15 (1959): 237–45.

12. Julio de Urquijo, "¿Cuál es el primer texto vasco impreso conocido? Observaciones sobre los pasajes en vascuence de Marineo Sículo y otros autores del siglo XVI," in *RIEV* 4 (1910): 573–86.

13. Julio de Urquijo, "La Tercera Celestina y el canto de Lelo," in *RIEV* 4 (1910): 573–86.

14. *Dictionarium Linguae Contabricae* [sic] *(1562)* (San Sebastián, 1958), M. Agud and L. Michelena, eds. Cf. Annamaria Gallina, *Contributi alla storia della lessicografia italo-spagnola dei secoli XVI e XVII* (Florencia, 1959), chapter 8.

15. René Lafon, *BRSVAP* 8 (1952): 172ff., and 178ff.

16. Julio de Urquijo, *RIEV* 24 (1933): 664ff.

17. Songs in dialogue are frequent in popular Basque poetry. G. Herelle, *Canico et Belchitine*, 122, note 3, indicates that 23 of the 75 songs published by Francisque-Michel are of this type.

18. R. Lafon, "Dechepareana. A propos de prières populaires recueillies par le P. Donostia," in *BRSVAP* 15 (1959), and L. Michelena, "Tradición escrita y tradición oral," ibid., 16 (1960).

19. He cites two of his verses as an example of the "intolerable vice" indulged in by "the ordinary couplet poets" of writing verses with acute rhymes (*Noticia*, p. 61).

20. At least two were Souletin. Jean d'Etcheverry, called de La Rive, "autrement le Petit Basque," was Labourdin from Saint-Jean-de-Luz, according to Teodoro de Beza. See Raymond Ritter, "Jeanne d'Albret et la Réforme chez les Basques," in *EJ* 5 (1951) and 6 (1952).

21. R. Lafon, *Système* I, 57.

22. In his foreword "Heuscalduney" he says: "For this reason, with respect to the language, without departing from the true meaning, we have insisted as far as possible on being comprehensible to everyone, and we have not completely followed the speech of any specific location."

23. On this question, in addition to the article cited in note 20, one may consult the book by V. Dubarat: *Documents et bibliographie sur la Réforme en Béarn et au Pays basque*, I (Pau, 1900). Cf. A. Destrée, *La Basse Navarre et ses institutions de 1620 à la Révolution* (Zaragoza, s. a., thesis read in 1954 at the University of Paris), p. 23 and following, with bibliography.

24. Father Ignacio Omaechevarría, "El vascuence de fray Juan de Zumárraga," *BRSVAP* 4 (1948): 293–314. There are some sentences from the sixteenth century in procedural acts published by A. Irigaray: "El euskera en Zufia," *RIEV* 24 (1933): 34–36, and "El eskuara en Artajona," *Yakintza* (1934): 128–30 (Tolosa, 1557). In the margin of a 1516 document from the General Archive of Simancas Father Modesto Sarasola found the following sentence (refrain?): *Galdua, çure arpeyco narrua.*

25. A. Irigaray points out correctly that it can only be taken as a manifestation of nonconformity, no less eloquent for being silent, that Axular makes no mention of witchcraft in his extensive ascetic book, even though he lived so close to the centers of witchcraft, both by virtue of the place of his birth and his place of residence. Add to that the fact that Eecheburri [sic], in 1636, does not dedicate more than these words to witchcraft in a long examination of conscience: "If I believe in dreams, magicians, witches, writings and other diabolical arts." Isasti's credulity can be compared to the circumspection of these Labourdin authors. See Julio Caro Baroja, "Cuatro relaciones sobre la hechicería vasca," *Anuario de Eusko-Folklore* 13 (1933): 87–145, and Azkue, *Euskalerriaren Yakintza* 1:391ff. There is a very brief and very valuable Basque text referring to the preaching of the Franciscans for the purpose of converting those initiated in these practices in Father Juan de Luzuriaga's *Paranympho celeste* (Mexico, 1686 and San Sebastian, 1690), an older version of which was published by father I. Omaechevarría, *BRSVAP* 12 (1956): 191–95.

26. See I. Zumalde, *Historia de Oñate* (San Sebastian, 1957), p. 460ff.

27. *Discursos*, folio 58 recto.

28. See for example Julio Caro Baroja, *La vida rural in Vera del Bidasoa* (Madrid, 1944), 219, the note.

29. J. Malaxechevarría, *La Compañía de Jesús por la instrucción del pueblo vasco en los siglos XVII y XVIII* (San Sebastian, 1926).

30. Isasti, around 1620, said that it was written "100 years ago" and calls Elso "Navarrese among Basques," that is, from Ultrapuertos.

31. *Compendio historial*, 164 and following.

32. "El primer catecismo en euskera guipuzcoano (?)," in *BRSVAP* 14 (1958): 78–83.

33. J. de Urquijo, "Cosas de antaño. Las Sinodales de Calahorra (1602 y 1700)," in *RIEV* 14 (1923): 335–52.

34. This hypothesis will not seem surprising in light of the the precarious condition in which other catechisms have come down to us. We have already seen that Elso's was lost without a trace and it appears that only one copy of the doctrine of Betolaza has been preserved, and another of Beriayn's, the property of Angel Irigaray. The "Viva Jesús" is known from a copy made by Vinson from a physical volume whose current whereabouts are unknown. The snippets we are familiar with from Zubía come from the *Vida del apóstol Santiago* (Mexico, 1699) by José de Lezamiz.

35. In the Souletin canticle "Hox aingurieki" (in *Noelen lilia*, Pau, 1821, p. 4 onward), to cite an example, *sendotcen* rhymes with *beitcen*, and are pronounced *sendótzen* and *beitzén*. Oihenart himself, upon presenting his translation of the first verse of "Lauda, Sion, Salvatorem" in order to prove that trochees and dactyls are

natural in Basque verse, converts *Láuda dúcem et pastórem* into *árzain éta aizin[d]
aría* (*Noticia de las dos Vasconias*, 61), when in Souletin it would be in reality *artzáñ
éta aitzindaría.*

36. In words such as *zaar* "old," Bizkaian dialects (Marquina, etc.) have twinned or
double vowels rather than long vowels. In any case, they do not appear to be taken into
account in the line. For Moguel (*Peru Abarca*, 1881, p. 61ff.), *soñoco zaarac cacuan* or
jo neban beeco videra has eight syllables the same as *Maisu Juan Barberuba.*

37. G. Lohmann Villena, "Poesías vascas en Lima en el siglo XVIII," in *BRSVAP* 12
(1956): 417–22.

38. See *Euzko-Gogoa* 9 (1958): 703.

39. J.-B. Daranatz, "Une poésie de 1619," *RIEV* 6 (1912): 197–99.

40. "Orígenes de nuestra música popular y sus relaciones con la métrica," in *RIEV*
13 (1919), 1–27.

41. *Canico et Beltchitine*, XII on and p. 109 onward.

42. *Compendio historial*, 171.

43. Pamplona, 1665. Reprinted in Paris, by Burgaud des Marets: *Elogio fúnebre al
rey nuestro señor Felipe IV el grande, en vascuence* (1865).

44. Like the four lines (7-5-7-6) included by Lope de Vega in *Los ramilletes de
Madrid* (Gerardo Diego, cited by Urquijo, *RIEV* 15 (1924): 642). Sister Juana Inés de
la Cruz, of Basque descent, included snippets of profane poetry in a villancico. See J.
Manterola, *Cancionero vasco* III, 261–63, and René Lafon, "Phrases et expressions
basques dans un villancico de Sor Juana Inés de la Cruz," in *Bulletin hispanique* 56
(1954): 178–80.

45. By don José Goñi Gaztambide.

46. See Julio de Urquijo, *Obras vascongadas del doctor labortano Joannes
d'Etcheberri*, L. s., and Father L. Villasante, *Euskera* II (1957): 56.

47. "He escrito, oh cristiano, en versos vascos este manual católico en mis horas de
ocio porque veo, siendo vasco como soy, que nuestra nación es muy amigo de coplas.
Por eso lo he compuesto en verso con plena conciencia, a fin de que pueda ser apren-
dido con más facilidad y mencionado más a menudo. Así en otro tiempo, en las lejanas
comarcas de Grecia, se solín cantar las leyes de la ciudad." (Oh, Christian, I have written this Catholic manual in Basque verse in my leisure time because, being Basque as
I am, I see that our nation is very fond of couplets. For that reason I have composed
it in verse with full awareness, so that it can be learned more easily and mentioned
more often. Thus in another time, in the distant regions of Greece, they used to sing
the laws of the city.)

48. Larramendi (*Diccionario trilingüe*, 1745, prologue, p. XXXV) says that he had
been the guardian of the convent of Avela (?) [sic]. According to Lafitte, his *Hor-
loge spirituelle* had already been published in French in Paris. Materre affirms that he
learned the Basque language in Sara.

49. J. Vinson, *Revue de Linguistique et de Philologie comparée* 48 (1915): 87ff.

50. See José de Arteche, *Saint-Cyran: de caracteriología vasca* (Zarauz: Icharopena,
1958).

51. It often includes the Castilian translation since Pouvreau knew this language, Latin and even Hebrew very well. In his dictionary there are also many Castilian proverbs, along with the Basque and French ones.

52. He must have been very closely tied to navigation, since Hirigoity in the couplets he dedicated to him, wrote: "Aequora qui sulcant debent tibi plurima, naues / Quod tua fecit eis ingeniosa manus."

53. The Navarrese found in the dispute an excellent opportunity to enjoy both citizenships. See the title of the work by M. de Vizcay, cited by M. Herrero García in *RIEV* 18 (1927): 555, n2: *Derecho de naturaleza que los naturales de la merindad de San Juan del Pie del Puerto tienen en los reinos de la corona de Castilla* (Zaragoza, 1621).

54. *Guero*, like Etcheberri's *Eliçara*, was dedicated to Bertrand de Echauz, archbishop of Tours. Perhaps Beltran de Echaus whose 1584 letter in Basque to his brother has been preserved should be identified with him. See J. Vinson in *Revue de linguistique et de philologie comparée* 17 (1884): 215–22, and *Notice bibliographique sur le folk-lore basque* (Paris, 1884), pp. 58–64. With regard to Axular's language we should note, since this detail is not always kept in mind, that in his native village Urdax, Labourdin is spoken even though it is located in Navarra.

55. *Déclaration historique de l'injuste usurpation et rétention de la Navarre par les Espagnols* (Paris, 1625).

56. One of which, certainly used with great skill, is from the song by Juan Lobeira "Leonoreta, fin roseta," that had Latin antecedents.

57. Thus, for example, his correct analysis of -*a* in many Basque names as the determinate article: Larramendi, however, accepted it, with his natural good sense. Concerning the opinions of Moret, Oihenart, and other Basque authors on Basque-Iberianism, see Julio Caro Baroja, *Emerita* 10 (1942): 236ff.

58. When mentioning his favorite authors (French, Spanish, Bearnese, and Gascons) he cites among the Basques Etcheberri and Verin. Nevertheless, according to his publisher, Michel Verin was not of Basque origin and only wrote in Latin.

59. Evidence of the contacts by our mariners with Iceland remains in some vocabularies from that century, preserved in Copenhagen, which offer, in addition to many Basque words, curious examples of the picturesque pidgin language to which Icelanders and Basques resorted to in their mutual relations: N. G. H. Deen, *Glossaria duo vasco-islandica* (Amsterdam, 1937). For the writings born of the turbulent conduct of some Basques in that country see *Spánverjavigin 1615 sőnn frásaga eftir Jón Gudmundsson laerda og víkinga rímur* (Copenhagen, 1950), edited by Jónas Kristjánsson.

CHAPTER 11 does not contain notes.

CHAPTER 12 does not contain notes.

CHAPTER 13: **Standardization of the Written Form of a Language: The Basque Case**

1. I think this is close to the ideas that Ernst Pulgram has defended in books and articles for thirty years now. For references, I suggest his still recent "The Accent in Spoken Latin (Proto-Romance)," in *Festschrift K. Baldinger* 2 (Tübingen, 1979), 139ff.

2. The term is employed without the slightest sense of shame, for here such a feeling would be wrong because there are no grounds for it. First, words like *organismus, organisch, etc.*, have had a long and illustrious history, and we must read in them simply the meaning that the many authors who used them felt they were conveying, not what they seem to mean to us. Secondly, many years ago R. D. Stevick, "The biological model and historical linguistics," *Language* 39 (1963): 159–69, showed (there was no need for demonstration) that the *analogon* of a language is not a live organism, or member of a species, but the species itself.

3. They say that Montaigne called himself *Gallus*, specified as Basque.

4. "Onomástica y población en el antiguo reino de Navarra: la documentación de San Millán," *XI Semana de Estudios Medievales (Estella, 1974)* (Pamplona, 1976), 51–71.

5. Olite, a city which like the other two existed in the Roman period but may have been expanded by Suintila, must have been, sooner or later, one of the outposts of Basque speakers spreading along the Cidacos, towards the Ribera, although they do not appear to have implanted the language there. The city's Basque name was *Erriberri*, according to historians of the sixteenth and seventeenth centuries, and *Erriberri*, far from being the equivalent of *Villanueva* ("Newtown," which in Navarra is *Iriberri*), means "Terranova." Therefore, it would be something like what in Spain has been called, in different locations, *Extremadura*, or what in Russian is *Ukraine*.

6. Rodrigo Ximénez de Rada used vernacular languages as a kind of embellishment, in addition to Romance languages, in the 4th Council of Letrán (1215).

7. It would be good to know the root of the miraculous vehicle for preaching that enabled Saint Vincent Ferrer to make himself understood in widely diverse places. According to Garibay, he had preached in Mondragón, Guipúzcoa, during the lives of his mother's great-grandparents. According to his mother, "Thanks to the institution and doctrine of the Saint, we have these two lines of his in the language of this land: *Fray vicentec esala, Fedea cina liçala.* In Castilian, they mean that Fray Vicente said that faith is an oath." But we suppose that the historian's mother is responsible for this translation of what the saint said.

8. When Axular, 1643, p. 17, says that this language, in addition to being spoken in Upper and Lower Navarra, in Soule, Labort, Vizcaya, Alava, and Guipúzcoa, was also spoken in many other places (*eta berice anhitz leccutan*), he is plainly not thinking of neighboring districts but of nuclei of Basque emigrants, first in Castile, Andalusia, etc., and then in the New World.

9. Sufficient knowledge, comparable to a certain extent to the knowledge which for Latin facilitated the work of Plato (but in our case we are dealing with a language that is much more differentiated spatially) doesn't appear until 1545–1571.

10. Having repented of his Neogrammatical past, he did not free himself of his partisan passions—a defect often found in converts. See *Lingua* I (1948), 59, where he expresses his general point of view: ". . . plus on remonte dans le passé, plus les unités ethniques et linguistiques se trouvent être petites. Avec Franz Boas nous croyons que toutes les unités linguistiques importantes ne se sont formées que para 'acculturation' assimilante."

11. Axular, who ended up as the parish priest of Sara, had graduated in theology from the University of Salamanca (1595: see Itziar Michelena, *Fontes linguae vasconum* 9 (1977): 57ff.), and was born in Urdax, a town in Navarra whose speech is Lapurdian, according to Bonaparte.

12. The prosperity of the coast and of the Lapurdian *hinterland* ended, or declined seriously, not only due to the Treaty of Utrecht, but also because of the earlier policy of Louis XIV, who requisitioned boats and men just as Felipe II had done a century earlier in the ports of Guipúzcoa and Vizcaya.

13. Etcheberri, who usually exhibits a great deal of erudition, ranging from Tertulian to "Ockham's Razor," seems quite "Spanish" in background, in addition to being much more Scholastic than Hippocratic.

14. The high or low point, as the reader prefers, could be placed at 1936 and the long years of clandestine existence following the civil war.

15. I say "unification" because that is the term that people have used for very different aspects or ways of understanding the problem, which is generally to achieve a standardized, and as far as possible common, variety of Basque for written use at least. Here we take into account its reference, not its possible meanings.

CHAPTER 14: **Notes appear in the text.**

CHAPTER 15 **contains no notes.**

Selected Bibliography

Selected Works by Koldo Mitxelena

Mitxelena wrote hundreds of articles and book reviews in the journals and publications of his epoch. Many of these articles have been reprinted, grouped more or less by subject, in several books over the years. (His writings in the Basque language alone take up nine volumes, in one of the publication series.) Despite the fact that some of these articles are among those most consulted by specialists, and therefore should be included, for this bibliography we have felt it more appropriate to limit our list to books. Readers interested in consulting the full list of his publications may consult the Regional Library of Bizkaia website at http://biblioteca-foral.bizkaia.net/search*eng/ for further information.

Apellidos Vascos. San Sebastián: Biblioteca Vascongada de Amigos del País, 1953.

Historia de la literatura vasca. Madrid: Minotauro, 1960.

Fonética histórica vasca. San Sebastián: Diputación Foral de Gipuzkoa, 1961.

Lenguas y protolenguas. Salamanca: [Talleres Gráficos Cervantes], 1963.

Sobre el pasado de la lengua vasca. San Sebastián: Auñamendi, 1964.

Textos arcaicos vascos. Madrid: Minotauro, 1964.

Estudio sobre las fuentes del diccionario de Azkue. Bilbao: Centro de Estudios Históricos de Vizcaya, Real Sociedad Vascongada de los Amigos del País, 1970.

Mitxelenaren idazlan hautatuak. Bilbao: Mensajero, 1972.

Zenbait hitzaldi. Bilbao: Mensajero, 1972.

Fonética histórica vasca. Revised and expanded 2nd edition. San Sebastián: Diputación de Gipuzkoa, 1977. 3rd edition, expanded and with corrections, 1990.

La lengua vasca. Durango: Leopoldo Zugaza, 1977.

Lengua e historia. Madrid: Paraninfo, 1985.

Diccionario general vasco/Orotariko Euskal Hiztegia. 16 volumes. Bilbao: Real Academia de la Lengua Vasca/Euskaltzaindia; Desclée de Brouwer; Mensajero, 1987–2005.

Palabras y textos. Bilbao: Universidad del País Vasco, 1987.

Euskal idazlan guztiak. 9 volumes. Zarautz: Euskal Editoreen Elkartea, 1988.

Sobre historia de la lengua vasca (I y II). San Sebastian: ASJU, 1988.

Koldo Mitxelena entre nosotros. Translated by Jorge Giménez Bech. Irun: Alberdania, 2001.

Koldo Mitxelena gure artean. Irun: Alberdania, 2001.

Selected Works in English by Koldo Mitxelena

"A Note on Labourdin Accentuation." *Anuario del Seminario de Filología Vasca "Julio de Urquijo"* VI (1972): 110–20.

The Basque Language. Translated by Gloria Castresana Waid. Madrid: Beramar; [Bilbao]: Basque American Foundation, 1987.

"The Ancient Basque Consonants." In *Towards a History of the Basque Language*, edited by José Ignacio Hualde, Joseba A. Lakarra, and R.L. Trask, 101–35. Amsterdam: J. Benjamins, 1995.

Languages and Protolanguages. Translated by John Tynan and Charo Pascual Pérez. Bilbao: Universidad del País Vasco, 1997.

Selected Works about Koldo Mitxelena

Aulestia, Gorka. "Luis Michelena: A Basque of International Fame." *Basque Studies Program Newsletter* 41 (April 1990): 3–6.

Haritschelhar, Jean, Endrike Knörr, and Martín de Ugalde, *Koldo Mitxelena (1915–1987)*. [Vitoria-Gasteiz]: Eusko Jaurlaritza, Hizkuntz Politikarako Saila; San Sebastián: Danona, 1989.

Ibarzábal, Eugenio. *Koldo Mitxelena*. San Sebastián: Erein, 1977.

K. Mitxelena, Gizona eta Hizkuntza. Special supplement, *Egan. Boletín de la Real Sociedad Bascongada de los Amigos del País.* 2nd series, 40 (May–December 1987).

Lakarra, Joseba A., ed. *Memoriae L. Mitxelena Magistri Sacrum.* Annex of the *Anuario del Seminario de Filología Vasca "Julio de Urquijo".* San Sebastián: Diputación Foral de Guipúzcoa, 1991.

Index

dialects and common language
and, 306
lost, of Basque language, 155–56
morphemes and, 137–39
proving, 136–37
size of Basque language and,
284–85
using prehistory to prove,
154–55
Giese, Wilhelm, 87–88
Gipuzkoan model, 279, 280–81,
294
Glorious Uprising, 73
glottochronology, 155
Goiri, Arana, 86, 92, 103, 105
Gómez-Moreno, Manuel, 37, 69,
140, 285
Gorostiaga, Juan, 37
grammar
complication of, 58–59
ergative constructions, 59–60
morphology and, 267–69
preverbs, 77–78
syntax, 269–71
verb conjugation, 60–62
verb suffixes, 261
Granada, Luis de, 249
Grassmann's Law, 168, 183–84
Greenberg, J. H., 135
Griera, Monsignor, 327–32
Guero, 248–49
Guevara, Ladrón de, 103
Guipúzcoa, 72
Guipuzcoan
Bonaparte's classification and,
79–80
history of use of, 67
liturgical Basque and, 82
use of *vizcaíno* and, 97

H
/h/. *See* aspiration

Hamitic-Semitic languages, 139,
141–42
Hamito-Semitic hypothesis, 70
Haramburu, Juan de, 246
Harff, Arnald von, 232
Haritschelhar, Jean, 26
Harizmendi, C., 246
Hauranne, Duvergier de, 247
Herelle, G., 244
Herri Batasuna, 12
heuskara, 46
Hirigoiti, Eztebe, 215
Historia de la literatura vasca,
29–30
historical novels, 121–24
history of language
Basque dialects and, 133–34
Basque literature and, 128
beginning of Basque language
and, 130–31
Caucasian languages and,
150–52
distinctions in, 125
prehistory and, 126, 129–30
proving kinship of Basque and
Caucasian languages and,
154–55
reconstruction of, 126–28
Romanization and, 131–32
Hortiz, Sancha, 231
Huarte, José María de, 233
Humboldt, Wilhelm von, 37, 50,
116, 284

I
Ibargüen-Cachopín chronicle,
232–33
Iberian
genetic relationship to Basque,
140–41
Hamitic-Semitic languages and,
141–42